ALSO BY PAUL SCHNEIDER

Brutal Journey

The Adirondacks

The Enduring Shore

Bonnie and Clyde

OLD MAN RIVER

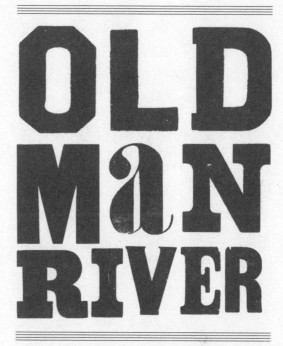

OLD MAN RIVER

THE MISSISSIPPI RIVER IN NORTH AMERICAN HISTORY

PAUL SCHNEIDER

A JOHN MACRAE BOOK

HENRY HOLT AND COMPANY   NEW YORK

Henry Holt and Company, LLC
Publishers since 1866
175 Fifth Avenue
New York, New York 10010
www.henryholt.com

Henry Holt® and ® are registered trademarks of
Henry Holt and Company, LLC.

Library of Congress Cataloging-in-Publication Data

Schneider, Paul.
  Old Man River : the Mississippi River in North American history /
Paul Schneider.—First edition.
    pages cm
Includes bibliographical references and index.
ISBN 978-0-8050-9136-6
1. Mississippi River—History.   2. River life—Mississippi River—History.
3. Mississippi River Valley—History.   4. North America—History.   I. Title.
  F351.S345 2013
  977—dc23   2012049786

Henry Holt books are available for special promotions and
premiums. For details contact: Director, Special Markets.

First Edition 2013

Designed by Kelly Too

Printed in the United States of America
3 5 7 9 10 8 6 4

He is blessed over all mortals who loses no moment of the passing life in remembering the past.

—HENRY DAVID THOREAU

One cannot see too many summer sunrises on the Mississippi.

—MARK TWAIN

CONTENTS

BOOK THREE: RIVER OF FORTUNE

The Spanish Exit, the French Arrive, the Iroquois Take Action

BOOK FOUR: RIVER OF EMPIRES

The English Enter, the French Exit, the Iroquois Negotiate, and the Americans Take Over

BOOK FIVE: LIFE ON THE MISSISSIPPI

Flatboats and Keelboats, Steamboats and Showboats, Songsters and Soul Drivers

BOOK SIX: RIVER OF BLOOD
Lincoln and Davis, New Orleans and Vicksburg, Victory and Defeat

BOOK SEVEN: ON THE LAKE OF THE ENGINEERS
Floods Rise, Levees Rise, Dams Rise, while Mountains Fall and Grasses Sink

OLD MAN RIVER

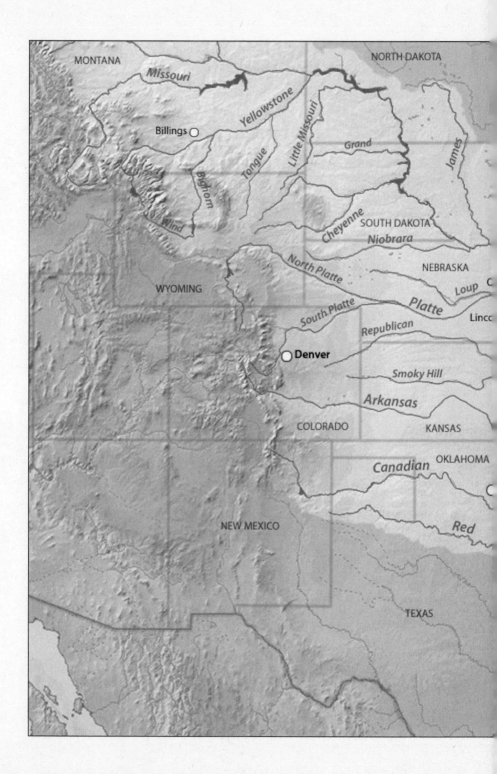

THE AMERICAN WATERSHED

It doesn't matter from what perspective you look at the river in the middle of the continent—geologically, ecologically, prehistorically, ethnographically, economically, industrially, socially, musically, literarily, culturally, or over the gunnels of your canoe midstream. It's impossible to imagine America without the Mississippi. The river's history is our history.

Similarly, just as a tree without branches and roots is merely lumber, it is pointless to separate the Mississippi from its tributaries. The upper Mississippi River, as the river above St. Louis is known, rises near the Canadian border at Lake Itasca in Minnesota. That stream has pride of name, of course, but the Missouri, which begins some nine thousand feet above sea level in the Rocky Mountains of Montana and joins the upper Mississippi at St. Louis, is a far longer river. The Arkansas River, which rises near Leadville, Colorado, and joins the Lower Mississippi halfway between Memphis and Vicksburg, is also longer than the Upper Mississippi. So is the Red River of the South, which rises in the Texas Panhandle. The relatively short Ohio, meanwhile, which rises in western Pennsylvania and Virginia and joins the Upper Mississippi at Cairo, Illinois, to form the Lower Mississippi, brings more water to the party than any two other tributaries combined. The truth is that any moving water south of the Great Lakes and between the Appalachians and the Rockies—with the exception of a few relative trickles—is going to

Louisiana. The Mississippi, the Mississippi watershed, the Mississippi basin, the Mississippi catchment—41 percent of the continental United States—it's all one river.

Parts of the river are older than the Atlantic Ocean. Parts of it were created yesterday. The Mississippi and its tributaries were the routes by which the first humans explored North America, and the earliest evidence (for the time being) of human habitation of the continent is in a rock shelter overlooking a small tributary of the Ohio in Pennsylvania. Agriculture developed independently in the Mississippi River basin, and with it, surplus food for artists, warmongers, shamans, and potentates. For millennia, cultures rose and fell in the watershed, often leaving behind elaborate earthworks and exquisite artifacts but just as often disappearing without leaving much behind. Eventually the greatest pre-Columbian city in North America was built beside the Mississippi River at Cahokia, in Illinois.

The corpse of the first European known to have explored the interior of North America—Hernando de Soto—was sunk in the Mississippi River nearly five hundred years ago. Two hundred years later George Washington got his first taste of battle during an engagement in the watershed over whether Britain or France would control the river. That skirmish started the Seven Years' War, the first global war, which Americans know as the French and Indian War.

In many ways, the story of the Mississippi basin since the end of the French and Indian War is also the story of the federal government of the United States. The taxes that American tea-partiers revolted against were levied to pay for Britain's wars in the watershed. King George's attempts to control the pace of settlement across the Alleghenies was one of the intolerable acts of 1774 later cited in the Declaration of Independence.

After the American Revolution, the one tangible asset the national government owned was the land west of the Appalachians. The first war fought by the newly independent United States was therefore to convince the resident Indians of that new political and military reality. The first road financed by the federal government of the United States was built to get to the watershed; the first civil works built by the Army Corps of Engineers was to improve navigation in the watershed; the first scientific publication by the Smithsonian Institution was a study of the archaeology of the watershed; the first request for federal disaster relief came from

Missouri, after the New Madrid earthquakes on the Mississippi River in 1811; the first efforts by the national government to impose safety regulations on a private industry were the steamboat acts of 1838 and 1852.

The Civil War was largely about who would control the lands west of the river: slave owners or Free-Soilers. John Brown lost one son in "Bloody Kansas" before losing another at Harpers Ferry, and *Uncle Tom's Cabin*—the book by "the little woman who started this big war"—is about a slave sold "down the river" from Kentucky. Ulysses S. Grant and William T. Sherman both came to President Lincoln's attention after their successes on the Mississippi River, and the siege of Vicksburg was a major turning point of the war, splitting the Slave States and giving undisputed control of the river to the North. After the Civil War the struggle for the watershed continued in an endless series of small and ugly campaigns against various Native American resisters. The last pitched battle fought between Native Americans and the United States Army was near the top of the river at Leech Lake, Minnesota, two years before the twentieth century.

Jazz was born in New Orleans, and zydeco in the bayou. The blues originated in the delta, while rock and roll poured out of Memphis and bluegrass and country music trickled down the Tennessee and the Cumberland Rivers. Cowboy tunes floated off the plains via the Red River, the Platte, and the Arkansas. The river had one Mark Twain, though it's worth remembering that Melville also wrote a novel about the Mississippi. Riverboats and pirates, gamblers and slaves, hustlers and landscape painters, loggers and catfishers, tourists and missionaries: it is a river of stories and a river of myth. It's Paul Robeson sitting on a cotton bale, Daniel Boone floating on a flatboat, and Paul Bunyan cutting trees in the neighborhood of *Little House in the Big Woods*.

The oil industry was hatched in the headwaters of the Ohio, and the steel industry at Pittsburgh. The Rust Belt, in many ways, is synonymous with the Ohio and upper Mississippi Rivers in part because the first heavy industry was building steamboats. Lead and zinc in world-leading quantities came out of Missouri, Kansas, and Arkansas. The river is still today the busiest waterway on the planet, with more than half a billion metric tons of grain, coal, petroleum, sand, salt, chemicals, and other products moving up and down the world's largest plumbing project, into which, for better or worse, the river has been transformed by the Congress of the United States.

It is tempting to think of the river as a caged animal, locked behind several centuries' worth of public works. My guess is that the Mississippi itself doesn't really care about such things any more than it cared about the Pleistocene's mile-high walls of ice, which first sent its northern sources southward. Or the rising of the Rocky Mountains half a billion years ago, hemming it in on the west. Or the volcanoes and asteroids that rained ash and dust into its waters. This is not at all to say that there are not real and serious consequences to our compulsive tinkering with the Mississippi. Nor is it to turn a blind eye to the noxious soup of fertilizer and pesticides that our addiction to cheap food and ethanol has made of the lower river. It is only to say that long after we the people reap what our congresses have sown, for good or ill, the Mississippi River will be there.

Is there. Make the effort to get your feet muddy and you'll find that the Mississippi is a very real river of water that will bring you joy and adventure if you step away from your vehicle and experience it wherever you find it. It is a magnificent creature of unsurpassed beauty, and it's sliding past Natchez and St. Louis as you read these words in the dark or in daylight. It's at Davenport and Pittsburgh, Minneapolis and Little Rock. It's trickling off of the Sangre de Cristo Mountains of New Mexico heading for Texas, and past the Seneca Indian Casino in western New York State. It's sitting as snow up in Jackson Hole, boiling up in great swirls around Tower Rock, Illinois, and licking at the levees by the aquarium in New Orleans. The river is always a willing traveling companion.

Go down to the water, whether it be the main stream at Venice, Louisiana, or the creek outside Brown's Cave in southern Missouri, or even the dry bed of the Cimarron up near Clovis, New Mexico. The longer you spend on the river, the more likely it is that the stream will draw out of you what needs to be drawn out. Not to replace it with something else; unlike lakes, rivers are never about accumulation. The flow itself is the thing that will catch your conscience like a fallen leaf.

Near the end of the process of writing this book I met a woman in Jeanerette, Louisiana, who thought she knew me, though she did not. It was an early Sunday morning in June, and I was canoeing down the Bayou Teche with a good friend from high school, Loren Demerath. Three thousand years ago the Bayou Teche was the main route of the Mississippi River, and history suggests that in some distant future it will surely regain that distinction. Today, however, Bayou Teche is a small distributary stream carrying a tiny share of the Mississippi basin's waters from Port Barre, Louisiana, through the heart of the Cajun country roughly 125 miles to the Gulf of Mexico below Morgan City. I wanted to explore it for those reasons, of course, but also for the zydeco nights in small towns along the way, gorging on jambalaya and crawfish.

It was the prospect of finding a legendary local bakery that brought Loren and me to shore in Jeanerette that morning. Le Jeune's Hot French Bread was closed, however, and we were walking empty-handed back down the empty Main Street when a lone woman yelled from across street, "Hey I know you! I know you!"

"I know you. You're from around here. Have you seen my friend?" she asked when she caught up with us. We apologized. She seemed a bit out of sorts, as if perhaps she was struggling with her sense of reality. But she was friendly, and gregarious, and said several times, "I know I've seen you two around here. You must know my friend Tim. Have you seen my old friend Tim Landry?"

"I'm sorry, we don't know anyone here," Loren explained. "We're just paddling down the bayou in a canoe and stopped here in town for breakfast."

"What?" she hollered, and instantly began to sing at the top of her lungs:

"Goodbye Joe, me gotta go, me oh my oh . . ."

The woman was dancing in the street in the morning sunshine, plumb crazy with her own brand of river madness. We couldn't help but laugh and sing along, however, trying our best to keep up with the old Hank Williams lyrics she obviously knew by heart.

Son of a gun, we're going to have some fun on the bayou.
Jambalaya, a-crawfish pie and-a file gumbo
Son of a gun, gonna have some fun on the bayou.

We walked away down Main Street toward our canoe and her voice faded off in the distance as she went looking in the opposite direction for Tim Landry. We heard her again, however, an hour later as we paddled through the warming hours of midmorning. She was up on the bank somewhere in the shade where we couldn't see her, but there is no doubt it was she. All of a sudden her voice rang out like a bayou siren: "Son of a gun, gonna have some fun. . . ." She was accompanied this time by a happy-sounding man, and they both serenaded us from the canopy of trees until we were around the corner and out of sight.

Only later still, when Loren and I were laughing and retelling each other the day's wacky turn did I realize with a start that Tim Landry was the name of my very first friend in life, a fun-loving water rat of a kid whom I haven't seen or thought of in forty years or more. By the time I remembered old Timmy and his leaky little rowboat, however, it was much too late to turn around and paddle back up the once and future Mississippi.

BOOK ONE

RIVER OF GIANTS

. . .

Continents Collide, Glaciers Recede,
Mastodons Bellow, and Humans Arrive

Sit by a river long enough and you are certain to see your enemy float by.

—JAPANESE PROVERB

1

ICE ON THE ROCKS

The Mississippi River was old long before the first giant sloth faced down a dire wolf or the last short-faced bear stood up to her full thirteen feet and bared her teeth to an eight-foot-long beaver. It was old before the first woman to see it got her feet muddy. The river is older than the entire fabulous menagerie of strange and outsized mammals that roamed the watershed during the two-and-a-half-million-year Pleistocene epoch, which ended about twelve thousand years ago with the most recent retreat of the glaciers. It was that most recent ice, however, that sculpted the northern features of the Mississippi River watershed into their current forms.

All across the top of the continent, the ice dammed up the northward progress of prehistoric rivers and sent them south, into the Mississippi watershed. The melting ice sheets didn't drain into the Gulf of Mexico in any kind of measured or consistent pattern but rather in fits and starts, and floods of diluvian scope. For several thousand years, when the ice had retreated into Canada, but not far enough to allow the northern rivers to flow into Hudson Bay and the Arctic Ocean, a gigantic lake covered northern Minnesota, western South Dakota, and most of central Canada. This prehistoric Lake Agassiz, named for the nineteenth-century Swiss-born geographer who pioneered the radical idea of prehistoric ice ages, was larger than all of the Great Lakes combined, larger than the

Caspian Sea. When at last it broke through the moraine of glacial rubble that was its southern boundary and drained for a time through Minnesota and Wisconsin, it carved the outsized gorge between those states through which the upper Mississippi River now flows. The Minnesota, Illinois, Ohio, and Wisconsin Rivers all flow through valleys that are far broader than the present water levels could have carved.

None of this is to say that the last ice age created either the Mississippi River or the land across which it meanders. The northern boundary of the watershed was shaped by glacial ice, which measures its workday in tens of thousands of years. The eastern and western walls, however, were caused by the drift of continents, which operates over hundreds of millions of years. Beneath all the lists of clay, most of the basin rests on top of some of the oldest rocks on earth. This shield of granite and gneiss known as the North American Craton, or Laurentia, has been drifting around smashing into, and breaking away from, other ancient pieces of the earth's crust for more than two billion years. During that span Laurentia has been a component of more than a half-dozen supercontinents, including the all encompassing Pangea, which formed out of a series of titanic collisions that began five hundred million years ago.

When continents collide, oceans slowly disappear and mountains creep upward; the formation of Pangea eventually threw up a mountain range along one side of Laurentia that was higher than the Himalayas are today. Remnants of that Central Pangean Range still exist, in the Anti-Atlas Mountains of Morocco and the Scottish Highlands. Much of what is left of the old Pangean Range, however, is now the Appalachian Mountains of North America—in other words, the eastern boundary of the Mississippi River basin.

Some rocks, when they are formed, align their internal magnetism with the earth's poles, allowing paleomagnetologists to say with a surprising degree of confidence that those vertiginous peaks of the Central Pangean Range half a billion years ago ran roughly east-west, rather than north-south as the Appalachians do today. Rain nonetheless fell on those same slopes that would become Kentucky and Tennessee. Rain fell in showers and torrents and began the long work of tearing down the range and carrying it to the sea. Mountain brooks seem so ephemeral when approached on foot in a dry summer, or when buried under the ice and snow of winter, at least when compared with grand continental currents such as the Mississippi, the Missouri, the Ohio, and the Arkansas. But they are not.

Bounded as they are by metamorphic walls high above the rise and fall of the seas—what geologists call basement rocks—those tiny seasonal alpine rills are more permanent in their ways than the mightiest lowland rivers. The latest sediment of the day can be found on the soles of your shoes by the banks of Old Man River, but geologists know to look for the truly ancient up in the hills. The oldest river in America, and possibly the oldest in the world, is the ironically named New River. It flows off the western slopes of the Appalachians in North Carolina through a corner of Virginia and West Virginia, where it merges with the Gauley to form the Kanawha, which joins the Ohio at Point Pleasant, West Virginia, and then the Mississippi at Cairo. The New River is older than the Atlantic Ocean, older than the dinosaurs.

Roughly two hundred million years ago the supercontinent of Pangea began to stretch and rift apart, tearing its central mountain range into pieces. The first break occurred between New Jersey and Morocco, slowly opening what became the Atlantic Ocean between Trenton and Marrakech; between, if you will, the Appalachian Mountains of the explorer Daniel Boone and the Anti-Atlas Mountains of the explorer Abu Abdullah Muhammad Ibn Abdullah Al Lawati Al Tanji Ibn Battuta; between "Dueling Banjos" and *The Sheltering Sky*. Laurentia drifted away from the rest of Pangea at a rate of several centimeters a year, which suggests that for many thousands of years what would become the Atlantic Ocean was strictly a tidal creek. Meanwhile, rain that fell on those proto-Appalachian ranges gathered into rivulets and brooks, and into streams and rivers, from which thirsty triceratops quenched their dry throats.

The water flowing off the Central Pangean Range did not, however, gather itself into a single proto-Mississippi. With no Rocky Mountains to corral them at the other side of the continent, various streams and rivers wound their way independently across a vast, flat, and periodically marshy land populated by the familiar cast of hulking dinosaurs and skulking mammals of the late Triassic and early Cretaceous eras. Along the way, Europe and Asia broke off from New England and drifted toward their current positions, and an upwelling of magma known as the Bermuda hotspot split the Ouachita Mountains off from the main branch of the Appalachians and sent them toward their current location in Arkansas. The new ocean widened, as the Atlantic is still widening today. What would become the Pacific shrank, as it still is shrinking today.

Finally, some hundred million years ago the ocean floor to the west of Laurentia began to slide under the crust of the neighboring plate, pushing up ranges along the leading edge of the drifting continent including, most importantly, the Rocky Mountains. The familiar pieces of North America were coming together: an older, decaying range of mountains running up its eastern coast and a younger, sharper, taller spine of ranges rising in the west.

Instead of a river between them, there was a sea. The lowlands between the new Rocky Mountains and the old Appalachians initially buckled downward, the way a piece of cardboard might pop down in the middle if pressure is exerted along two sides. Into these lowlands salt water flowed from both the Arctic Ocean and the Gulf of Mexico, creating a vast, shallow sea that, at its largest, stretched the entire distance between the two great ranges. For forty million years this "Western Interior Seaway" was a warm and fertile place, full of whale-size toothy mosasaurs, along with sharks and rays, finny fish, horseshoe crabs, and clams. Rockhounds today find shark teeth a thousand miles from the nearest salt water in the watershed.

Ultimately, however, the colossal uplift that forged Pikes Peak and the Grand Tetons, and lesser ranges as far east as the Black Hills of South Dakota, raised the land between the Rockies and the Appalachians. The sea retreated, until by sixty-five million years ago the mouth of what can now rightly be called the Mississippi was around Memphis. North America was just beginning to look recognizably like itself, with mountains to the left and mountains to the right and a big winding river coming down the middle when a massive meteor struck the Yucatán Peninsula, just across the Gulf of Mexico. This set in motion the great extinction of the dinosaurs and 75 percent of the other species around the globe, and gave the skulking mammals their opportunity to evolve: into mammoths, sloths, and, eventually, archaeologists and anthropologists.

2

THE MISSOURI LEVIATHAN

Someone was the first person to peer through the tall grass at an immense mammoth lumbering down to the water and think, "If we could stab that thing with a sharp rock on the end of a stick, we could light a fire and have one hell of a roast." That much, at least, is now certain about the lives and times of men, women, and mammoths in the Mississippi River basin during the waning centuries of the most recent ice age. In the past seventy-five years, Clovis and Folsom points—stone spearheads named for the towns in the headwaters of the Arkansas River where they were first identified—have turned up in hundreds of archaeological sites throughout the watershed. They have been found embedded in the bones of mammoths, mastodons, giant sloths, and bison. In 1841, however, no one believed the St. Louis impresario Albert Koch when he claimed to have found a rose-colored spear point embedded in a gigantic leg bone he had just dug up in Missouri.

It was hard enough for most people to admit that there had once been strange and gigantic beasts on the land. Today, when dinosaurs stalk the cinemas and parliaments debate the economic value of polar bears, it's almost quaint to think that extinction was once a newfangled and vaguely heretical idea. The prevailing Christian view was of a perfect creation in which none of God's creatures could possibly cease to exist. Extinction, which suggested a flaw in God's plan, was theoretically impossible.

As early as 1569, the Englishman David Ingram claimed to have walked all the way across North America from the Gulf of Mexico to Canada and seen evidence of elephants along the way, but his bizarre claims were soon filed away with the unicorns, the island of California ruled by women, the seven wandering Portuguese bishops, the people with dog faces, and a hundred other myths and rumors about the New World. Then, in 1705, a farmer in the Hudson River valley happened upon a five-pound molar, which he sold to a local politician for a half-pint of rum. The big tooth made its way to New York City and into the hands of the governor of the colony, who packed it off to the Royal Society in London with the memorable identification: "tooth of a giant."

This was a solid artifact that demanded an explanation, and Cotton Mather, the New England theologian and witchcraft expert, believed he had it. The tooth, he said, proved the existence of biblical giants, and biblical history in general, and was "an admirable obturation on the mouth of Atheism!" He solved the problem of extinction by suggesting that the giants—who he calculated were nearly seventy feet tall—were born of "parents not exceeding the common stature." These giant offspring were sent by God to punish their wicked parents, which one imagines they certainly would do. When they had done their job, they were exterminated in Noah's flood, and their perfect species—normal-size humanity—continued on.

The atheists, perhaps typically, were not long quieted. An occasional mammoth molar might look vaguely similar to a human tooth, but giant bones of all sorts were beginning to turn up in a wide range of places, particularly in the Mississippi watershed. At a place called Big Bone Lick, in the Ohio River valley, the massive ribs and tusks sticking out of the river mud were clearly not from humans, and discovering the nature of the mysterious beasts grew into something of a national obsession. Benjamin Franklin, Thomas Jefferson, and George Washington, among others, collected bones and promulgated theories about what came to be known as the American incognitum. Scientists and philosophers on both sides of the Atlantic traded teeth and picked apart one another's theories on whether the beast was a gentle grazer or a vicious carnivore. Did the tusks of the incognitum curl up? Or did they curl down? Or perhaps, as some thought, one tusk curled up and one curled down? Whatever the incognitum was, people also wondered where living specimens of it might be found.

Native American rumor suggested the incognitum might still be alive somewhere. A delegation of Indians from the Ohio valley told Thomas Jefferson "that in ancient times a herd of these tremendous animals came to the Big-bone licks, and began a universal destruction of the bear, deer, elks, buffaloes, and other animals, which had been created for the use of the Indians." The giant beasts were killed off by lightning bolts, they said, except for one that "bounded over the Ohio, over the Wabash, the Illinois, and finally over the great lakes, where he is living at this day."

The idea of giant people was laid to rest for good in 1804, when the painter Charles Wilson Peale and his son Rembrandt cobbled together the first complete skeleton of a mastodon and displayed it in their family's Philadelphia Museum. With his tusks inserted so that they pointed down in the manner of a terrible carnivore, the incognitum turned out to be an outsize cousin to the elephant rather than the big brother of Goliath. More important, as far as Albert Koch was concerned, the Peales' skeleton was by all accounts the first blockbuster exhibition in American museum history and made a small fortune for its owners. Fossil hunting was Koch's life's passion, but his business was entertainment.

There were plenty of the usual river town diversions available in St. Louis when Koch arrived at the confluence of the Mississippi and the

St. Louis, 1840, by John Casper Wild.

Missouri as a young German immigrant in 1836. It was a frontier boom-town, full of rowdy river boys, loose women, bad whiskey, bear baiting, marked cards, and public executions. But Koch, who had always been a collector of curiosities, saw an opportunity for more refined entertainments and opened the St. Louis Museum.

There, his visitors gawked at wax versions of well-known and exotic people, such as the Seminole hero Osceola, a "Chinese Lady," and the famous Siamese Twins, Chang and Eng Bunker. They gaped at mummies, both Egyptian and Native American, and gasped at a diorama of hell called the "infernal regions." On some evenings "The GREAT PERSIAN KOULAH" presented his program of "splendid and very unique ASI-ATIC ENTERTAINMENTS." Koch even had live alligators, until they got into a scuffle and fell out of the window, whereupon he stuffed them.

"These are the alligators which had a tremendous battle, in which the smallest, having been overpowered by his antagonist, broke through the window, leaped over the iron balcony in front of the museum and broke his neck," he wrote in a newspaper advertisement in 1838. "The other died a few days after, in consequence of the wounds received in the fight. Both are represented in the attitude of fighting—blood flowing from their wounds, their jaws locked in a deathly embrace, and the whole representing the ferocious nature of the animals."

"The ferocious nature of the animals" was a phrase that might have raised eyebrows in the settled cities and towns of the Atlantic coast. There, the leading transcendentalists preached of the universal goodness of nature and humanity, and it was more comforting to picture the world in the romantic light of the Hudson River School paintings, which typically depicted a melancholy but benign transition from the "savage state" to the "arcadian state." On the frontier up and down the Mississippi River, on the other hand, boatmen brawled in the streets for the pure pleasure of breaking their knuckles against another fellow's nose. Rumors of mass murderers, slave insurrections, and bloodthirsty pirates competed with the endless wars of eviction against the various Native groups for public attention.

From Koch's perspective, violence sold tickets, and ticket sales paid for fossil hunting. Nothing could stop him when he got wind of a find. "I was still lying on my sofa, suffering from a shivering fit," he said about the state of his health when the tip came about the bones on the Pomme de Terre River. Yet "the possibility of a find such as I had not yet had, and which naturally could not be mine if I did not overcome my physical weakness and go immediately on the long and difficult trip" was too much to resist.

He pulled himself together and boarded a steamboat the next day, the twenty-fifth of March 1840. He was gone from St. Louis for four months. It took the better part of a week just to get to the spot, but after harrowing crossings of both the Osage and Pomme de Terre Rivers at high water, he arrived and was overjoyed to find massive femurs and tusks sticking out of the riverbank. Nothing else went according to plan: his crew quit after two days of work, and a second bunch of locals he hired didn't stick around much longer. The excavation site repeatedly flooded, while his own health seesawed. When at last the bones were out of the mud, the river was too low to float the massive dugout canoes he had constructed. He built oxcarts.

It was all worth it. When Koch unpacked the crates in St. Louis and put the bones together—along with six extra vertebrae, a couple of extra ribs, and some rather thick ersatz cartilage made from wood—he had a thirty-two-foot-long, fifteen-foot-high, one-tusk-up one-tusk-down monster. What's more, when he lifted the femur of the Missourium out of the mud and saw an oversize flint point below it, he knew that he had made a major archaeological discovery. "These arrow-heads are indisputably the work of human hands," he wrote in his *Description of the Missourium*. "I examined the deposit in which they were embedded, and raised them out of their embedment with my own hands."

"Citizens of Missouri," he announced in an advertisement. "Come and see the gigantic race that once inhabited the space you now occupy, drank of the same waters which now quench your thirst, ate the fruits of the same soil that now yields so abundantly to your labor. To you stranger, I say, come and see the wonderful productions of unknown ages which are no where to be found but in the humble abode of the St. Louis Museum."

They did come, lining up outside the museum to buy tickets. The Missouri Leviathan was a money machine that made the stuffed alligators and the Great Persian Koulah look like kids' stuff. Yet no one paid any attention to the showman's big claim that he had discovered proof that there were people who hunted the giant beasts. He printed a scientific pamphlet explaining his findings, hoping thereby to gain the respect of the intellectual lights of the East Coast university, and in Europe. But he was greeted with silence. Indians simply could not have existed before Noah's flood because they were not mentioned in the Bible.

Ticket sales to see the Missourium were netting Koch more money than he ever imagined he would make, and he was happy enough to let the issue of who had killed the beast drop for a while. When the local crowds began to thin, he sold his museum and took the fabulous bones on a steamboat down to New Orleans, then to Philadelphia, and finally to Europe. The Missourium was a hit in London's Piccadilly Square for eighteen months, after which he sold it to the British Museum. Returning to the United States, he excavated and assembled two more fabulous skeletons, both of an extinct whale now commonly called a zeuglodon. The first of these he assembled into a 116-foot sea serpent that, after the usual world tour, he sold to the king of Prussia for the Royal Anatomical Museum in Berlin. The second wound up in a museum in Chicago. Neither of these later skeletons was outright an fraud—the fossils were real enough—but both were ultimately judged by anatomists to be incorrectly assembled out of the bones of multiple creatures. The explanation—bamboozlement or ineptitude—depended on one's opinion of Albert Koch.

The showman died on December 28, 1867, at the age of sixty-three, and nearly sixty years would pass before mainstream archaeology came to embrace the implications of his greatest find. His Missourium is still on display at the British Museum in London, though it turned out to be "just" a mastodon once his erroneous additions of vertebrae and ribs were subtracted. His other major finds were both destroyed by fires: the hydrarchus in the Allied bombing of Berlin in 1945 and the zeuglodon in the Great Chicago Fire of 1871. The spear points that he found in association with the Missourium have similarly slipped from public view. There is a secondhand report from the 1890s that the Missouri State Historical Society had an unusual "fluted" point that was purported to be the one Koch found near the Pomme de Terre River, but the historical society today has no record of it.

As for the scene of Koch's discoveries, it too is gone. I wanted to visit the Pomme de Terre River and try to find the "romantic valley" he described, with its wooded banks and clinging vines. Or walk where the

Missourium met its end at the hands of the Paleo-Indians that everyone now agrees were indeed living and hunting by the Mississippi River and its tributaries ten thousand years ago. But the whole region is at the bottom of the largest lake in Missouri, inundated not by Noah's deluge, or by the terminal moraine of a long-gone glacier, but by the Harry S. Truman Dam, which the Army Corps of Engineers completed on the Osage River in 1979.

3

BONES AND STONES

The bones that finally convinced even the most skeptical archaeologists that people lived alongside and hunted the extinct animals of North America during the late Pleistocene era were not found by a professional archaeologist from one of the great institutions of higher learning but by a legendary cowboy and bronco buster. George McJunkin was born a slave on a cotton plantation in Texas in 1851, but by 1908 he'd taught himself to read, write, play the fiddle and guitar, speak Spanish, and hunt buffalo. Like Albert Koch before him, he was something of a self-taught naturalist—enough of one, at any rate, that he knew the immense ribs he discovered sticking out of a washed-out arroyo in Folsom, New Mexico, were from a bigger animal than anything he'd seen out on the prairie.

The bones were exposed by a deadly 1908 flood, in which what the newspapers called "the heaviest rain ever known here" fell on Johnson Mesa and roared down the normally dry arroyos that make up the head-waters of the Cimarron River. The rain collected itself into such a torrent as it hurtled down toward the town that entire families were drowned when their houses were washed away in an instant. The local telephone operator, a woman named Sarah Rooke, stayed too long at her post, frantically trying to warn her fellow townspeople of the coming deluge. Her body wasn't found until the following spring.

Not long after the floods, McJunkin, who was the foreman at a ranch nearby, saddled up and rode out to check the fence lines, repair breaks, and look for stray cattle. It's spectacular country, overshadowed by the long dark line of Johnson Mesa on the west, fringed with ponderosa pine. Eastward spread rolling grasslands, cut here and there by erosion. In one arroyo, the floodwaters had carved out new deep walls, the customary occupation of rivers. Jutting out of the fresh soil McJunkin saw the gigantic bones. He took a few home, which were later identified as remnants from an extinct species of giant bison that, like the mammoth, mastodon, sloth, and a host of other large mammals, was common in Pleistocene North America.

What McJunkin himself collected from the site is unclear. The important thing is that he knew enough not to disturb the site further and got word out that there was something in the northeast corner of New Mexico that archaeologists might find interesting. For years, however, no one paid much attention to the cowboy's find. It wasn't until 1926, four years after McJunkin's death, that a team from the Colorado Museum of Natural History finally decided to excavate the site. The two men in charge, Jesse Figgins and Harold Cook, weren't specifically looking for evidence of humans when they showed up at Folsom. They just wanted a giant bison skeleton for their museum.

In the sixty years that had passed since the death of Albert Koch, others had discovered what they believed was evidence of human activity in North America at the end of the ice age or even earlier. In 1896 on a tributary to the Smoky Hill River in western Kansas, researchers found a spear point lying under and touching the scapula of an extinct bison, only to have it stolen from a public lecture before any of the claims could be verified. In 1902, a couple of farm boys digging a root cellar near a tributary to the Missouri River ran into human skeletons seventy feet into a hillside and twenty feet under the surface. There were others, but one by one their claims were discounted and disregarded.

During the first decades of the twentieth century, Aleš Hrdlička of the Smithsonian Institution traveled to virtually every new claim of ice-age humanity in North America and found reasons to disagree about the age of the site. Hrdlička, who was born in Bohemia, was an early proponent of the idea that the first Americans arrived on the continent from Asia. That theory is nearly universally accepted today and is supported by a broad range of evidence including DNA. Hrdlička did not, however, believe the Indians came over the thousand-mile-wide land bridge that periodically opens between Asia and North America during ice-age events. He thought they came much later, in kayaks across the Bering Strait.

"The population of America," he summed up, "has been established in the course of only a few thousand years, probably no more than 5,000."

Case closed, in his mind. The debate by this time was not so much about the possibility of human existence on the planet before biblical times: by the twentieth century it was accepted that Neanderthals and other early hominids lived in Europe, Asia, and Africa. A sympathetic explanation of Hrdlička's intransigence on the subject of ice-age Americans, therefore, is that he was convinced that bones from the Pleistocene must necessarily look like the Neanderthal bones that had turned up in Europe. "Only if they spoke of an anatomically distinct pre-modern human could they be Pleistocene in age," wrote one of the current deans of American archaeology in defense of Hrdlička. "His true allegiance was to the bones."

Hrdlička loved bones almost as much as Albert Koch had, and he wasn't squeamish about where he got them either. In 1902, he visited the scene of a recent massacre of three hundred Yaqui men, women, and children by the Mexican army at the Battle of Sierra Mazatan and removed a dozen heads with his machete. He boiled them and picked them clean and sent the flensed skulls to his sponsors at the Museum of Natural History in New York, along with a papoose board from which he had apparently dumped the infant's body. More than a century later the museum was compelled to apologize and send the bones back to the Yaqui, but in his own day Hrdlička's battlefield scavenging in Mexico landed him an appointment as the first curator of Physical Anthropology at the Smithsonian Institution.

In that capacity, for nearly four decades, he traveled the world measuring foreheads, earlobes, cranial cavities, and thumb joints and made some startling discoveries. In 1921, he announced to the Second International Congress of Eugenics that third-generation European-Americans were evolving into a recognizable American "type" but that the men, in his opinion, were faring better than the women. "The body proportions of the men were good," he said, "but in women there was a tendency to flatness of the chest." Sixteen years later he told the Boston Women's Republican Club that the city's older families were comprised of "excellent, healthy white stock," and that "it is something of a pity that they can't be kept in an Eden and stay there forever."

The odor of racism in Hrdlička's dogged insistence on a relatively short occupation of the Americas by the Native Americans is no surprise, therefore. Whenever anyone in the country claimed to have found evidence for an early occupation of North America, Hrdlička was sure to show up with all the prestige of the Smithsonian Institution behind him and dispute it. His usual complaint was that the human artifacts had been removed from the surrounding strata in which they were found and could not therefore be trusted to be in layers of soil laid down in the ancient past. Or he disagreed about what the surrounding strata implied. Or he was certain the artifact had washed into older layers by erosion, or was buried particularly deeply by more recent Indians. Or the excavations were not done in a professional manner. Or it was a hoax.

In fairness, even today, with dozens of high-tech tools that were unavailable to investigators in the 1920s, archaeology is at best an interpretive science, as it is not possible to replicate most findings in a laboratory or field experiment. There were plenty of false claims, and members of the fraternity—archaeology was still almost exclusively a men's game at the beginning of the twentieth century—felt they had to be constantly on guard against premature conclusions. It all added up to a blanket rejection of the notion that humans were wandering the Mississippi watershed or anywhere else in North America at the same time as the great mammals of the late Pleistocene.

When a large, well-crafted spear point turned up among the certifiably ice-age bison bones in Wild Horse Arroyo, therefore, Figgins and Cook ordered that all work at the site stop immediately. They sent telegrams around the country to the top experts, including Hrdlička; "Another arrowhead found in position with bison remains at Folsom, New Mexico. Can you personally examine find?" Hrdlička couldn't make it in person this time, but he sent a deputy. Over the next few weeks a stream of "several of the best men in the country" came and looked at the fluted point wedged in the dirt between a pair of eleven-thousand-year-old ribs.

Whoever it was 10,500 years ago at Wild Horse Arroyo didn't kill just one of the animals, but drove a small herd of some thirty giant bison

From the Collections of the Center for the Study of the First Americans, Dept. of Anthropology, Texas A&M University

Clovis point with *Bison antiquus* ribs.

up into the arroyo and killed them all. The bellowing fury of the beasts would have been something to see in any eon. Individual *Bison antiquus* were about 25 to 50 percent bigger than the familiar American bison of today. With horns regularly reaching three feet across, they stood eight or nine feet tall at the shoulders. The archaeology suggests that *Bison antiquus* gathered in smaller herds of tens or hundreds, rather than blackening the plains in herds of thousands or even millions, as later buffalo *(Bison bison)* did. In other ways, though, the behavior of the big bison is assumed to be similar to their modern counterparts, which can run up to thirty miles an hour and are notoriously moody and violent, prone to stampeding but ready to attack with horns and rear hooves should it come to that.

How long had the band at Wild Horse Arroyo planned for the bison roundup and kill? How many times had they tried and failed? How hungry were they? This was not a regular occurrence at this particular spot—all of the bison were killed in a single incident and there is no sign of a similar killing there in the intervening millennia. Neither was it just a lucky bonanza for a local community, however. Of the more than twenty stone points of varying sizes and states of repair that have been found at the Folsom site by a series of excavations, most were knapped from stone that originated two hundred miles away in the ancient quarries along the Canadian River in the Texas Panhandle. A couple more were made of "Black Forest" petrified wood and one may have been "Dakota" quartzite.

In other words, the weapons were not made from local sources. It's possible that either the raw materials or the points themselves were exchanged through trade, but archaeologists think it more likely the people who killed the herd of buffalo at Folsom were nomadic. There is no sign of tools having been manufactured at Wild Horse Arroyo, and despite two more digs at the site, most recently in 1999, no one has discovered where the people camped while in the area. There is no sign either of the "high-utility" parts of the animals. The bones relating to the choicest cuts of meat all are missing from the kill site.

There are only the spear points lying among ice-age buffalo ribs, but these were enough. Almost without exception, "the best men in the country" of 1928 went away convinced at last that somebody had lived in North America at the end of the last ice age, after all, and that they had hunted prehistoric prey more than ten thousand years ago. The exception, reliably, was Hrdlička. When the Folsom findings were presented in New York in 1928, Hrdlička sniffed that the exquisite flint points found in contact with prehistoric buffalo bones "cannot be linked with Paleolithic culture or with geological antiquity." This time, though, the old Bohemian was unconvincing to his colleagues.

The door was open, if only a crack, and crowds of prehistoric people almost immediately pushed through and are still pushing through. It wasn't too many years later that an even older site was found not far away near the headwaters of another tributary to the Arkansas and Mississippi. In a gravel mine in Clovis, New Mexico, lanceolate points made upward of thirteen thousand years ago turned up with the bones of a mammoth. Like those from Folsom, the Clovis points are notable mostly for a distinctive single large flake that was removed longitudinally from quite near the tip of the point to its base on both sides. Because of the resulting shallow groove running down their length, both styles are called "fluted" points. Clovis points are somewhat larger, broader, and in some opinions less elegantly crafted than Folsom. Both Folsom and Clovis people apparently loved exotically colored agates, however, and the points can be quite beautiful. What's more, no one has discovered a practical advantage for the distinctive shape, suggesting that the points were fluted ten thousand years ago precisely to make them beautiful.

The giant bison and mammoths already mentioned were not the only prey hunted by the Clovis and Folsom people. Points have turned up among the remains of the eight-hundred-pound sloths that Thomas Jefferson named *Megalonyx*, for their giant claws. They have been found with prehistoric North American musk ox, camels, horses, bears, pronghorn, mountain sheep, peccary, tapir, deer, rabbit, and virtually anything else that could be killed and eaten. Appropriately enough, the proof that Clovis people hunted mastodon as well as mammoth came in 1980 from a site in Kimmswick, Missouri, where Albert Koch loved to collect fossils.

But how was it done? Throwing a spear down into the bellowing mass from the relative safety of the steep sides of the arroyo would have been magnificent and terrifying, but the "kill area" is too large for the hunters to have merely hurled their spears from above. With the scantest of clues—how far apart the carcasses lay, how many presumably valuable points were lost for archaeologists to find—the researchers continue to debate whether the spears were thrown or stabbed from close range.

If the spears were thrown rather than stabbed, most likely it was done with the aid of an atlatl. An atlatl is essentially a shaft with a notch or socket at one end into which the butt of the spear or dart fits. By effectively making the thrower's arm longer, it gives a tremendous mechanical boost to the velocity with which the spear can be thrown. Just as a lacrosse stick allows a skilled player to throw a ball faster and farther, an atlatl in the right hands can drive a stone-pointed spear into the heart of a bison—or even, as Koch discovered, the leg of a mastodon. Atlatls were the weapon of choice in North America until the adoption of the bow and arrow many thousands of years later, and survived in some cultures well into the historical period.

Killing big game with an atlatl would seem to be a lost art, but you can watch videos online of Paleo-enthusiasts throwing flint-tipped spears at feral hogs and emus. There is even an astonishing video of a seven-year-old bringing down a whitetail deer with an atlatl in Pennsylvania. Of course, a whitetail deer is nowhere near the size of a mammoth, or even an extinct *Bison antiquus*. Even after it was generally accepted that ice-age people killed and ate the giant Proboscidea (trunked beasts) of North America, some questioned their methods. Frozen carcasses found in Siberia showed that mammoths had exceptionally thick and woolly hides; for a long time it was standard wisdom that the Paleo-Indians were primarily hunters of incapacitated beasts stuck in bogs and sinkholes.

This stereotypical image from old textbooks and museum dioramas of a gang of loinclothed longhairs pitching boulders and spears at a bogged-down victim didn't sit well with an anthropologist at the University of Wyoming named George Frison. What's more, he was certain that the loinclothed longhairs wouldn't have liked it either. "True hunters would be offended deeply if they were accused of resorting to this kind of hunting strategy," he wrote in an influential article in *American Antiquity* without really explaining how he knew the Paleo-Indians were "true hunters." More convincing than Frison's presumed indignation of the ice-age indigenes was his practical observation that "butchering and recovering the meat in edible condition from an animal mired in a bog is difficult at best."

Not content to rest his argument on words alone, he went hunting for African elephants in Zimbabwe with Clovis-style weapons. For two seasons, he and some spear-throwing graduate students traveled with game wardens who were culling a herd that had overpopulated its range (which is a polite way of saying the surrounding humans had overpopulated *their* range). The fact that the wardens shot the elephants with high-powered rifles first made the exercise somewhat less than a "true hunter" experience, but Frison proved to his own satisfaction that if you are willing to get within fifty or sixty feet of an angry (or in their case already mortally wounded) elephant, it is possible to strike a lethal blow with an atlatl and a Clovis point.

"The third cull was especially satisfying because a presumed-dead, mature female actually was only crippled and managed to get back on her feet while the shooters were pursuing part of the group that had split and run away," he gushed. "This provided a broadside at the rib cage. The animal was hit at the right elevation and far enough forward so that the projectile had to pass through some of the fleshy part of the front quarter. Even so, penetration was to the distal end of the mainshaft and into the lung cavity, producing a potentially lethal wound. At this point, the animal dropped on all fours."

The best available database of Paleo-Indian sites now includes nearly twelve thousand fluted points from thousands of sites across North America. When plotted on a map, there are surprisingly few sites in California west of the Sierra Nevada, but there is a healthy smattering throughout the basin and range country between the Rocky Mountains and the Sierras. When there was ice over Canada the jet stream was diverted south, and that country wasn't the arid place it is today. It was instead a kind of Serengeti of the woolly mammoth, a well-watered and grassy savanna with the easy-to-follow game highways that Proboscidea are known for making. There are also many Paleo-Indian sites east of the Appalachians and all the way down into Florida.

The heartland of the Paleo-Indians—at least if judged in a thoroughly unscientific manner by looking at a map of where they left behind things that archaeologists have found—appears to have been the Mississippi

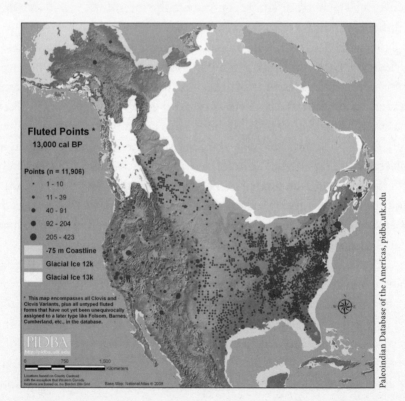

Paleoindian Database of the Americas, pidba.utk.edu

River basin. There are dense clusters of sites along the Tennessee and Ohio Rivers that give way to an even scattering of sites all over the high plains. There is not a significant blank spot in the Mississippi River watershed where fluted points from the late Pleistocene have not been found. This doesn't mean that there were ever Paleo-Indian people spread all over the watershed at any one time, of course. It means only that in three thousand years or more of stalking around after prehistoric game, the Paleo-Indian hunters got virtually everywhere.

Despite such widespread evidence of their presence, only small fragments of the Clovis and Folsom ways of living in the Mississippi River basin can really be parsed out. In Wyoming, on the Bighorn River, at least eight mammoths were killed and some of the butchered meat was piled into cold-weather meat caches. A quartered beast was placed beneath the carefully laid out long bones of several other mammoths and a skull, unbutchered, was carefully laid on top. The band returned to one of the two caches, but the other lay undisturbed until it was discovered in 1962. Some twenty caches of points and unfinished stone have been found, often near the junctures of rivers in the watershed. These were presumably memorable spots where bands of people stopped carrying around their heavy raw materials and extra weapons and stored them for their next passage through the region. But the people never came back, or they forgot the location.

Sparse as the details of their practical lives are, the emotional, artistic, and ceremonial lives of the Clovis and Folsom hunters who roamed the Mississippi basin are even more shrouded. Red ocher, a clay-based pigment that is still used in some Native American ceremonies, already held meaning ten thousand years ago: in Montana, up between the Crazy Mountains and the Belt Mountains on a tributary to the Shields and Yellowstone Rivers, the bodies of two children were prepared with ocher. Also buried with them were a collection of tools and fluted points.

4

BROKEN ARROWS

I found a fluted point on the bank of Bryant Creek, which, like every other flowing water in the state of Missouri, winds up in the Mississippi. I was walking with my mother, looking for a cave where my great-grandfather hid out from the law after stealing a horse from a man who called himself "the Christ who will never die." My mother grew up by the Mississippi River in St. Louis, the daughter of a long line of Ridgways and Ridgeways and Vogts and Voughts and Lakeys and Lakys and others, most of whom got to the state by the usual routes, over the Appalachians and down the Ohio in the decades before the Civil War.

All I know of the affair with the cave is that sometime around 1908 Harv Vogt joined up with the followers of a now-forgotten would-be messiah and took his wife, Elzina Lakey, with him. Harv and Elzina were poor young lovers, with a baby on the way, trying to figure out a future in the hot sticky Ozarks. Whatever drew Harv to the preacher's preaching wore off quickly for Elzina, however, and she soon demanded to be taken home. Caught between the messiah and the missus, Harv knew which of the two was the stronger force of nature. He "borrowed" the messiah's horse and wagon one night to take Elzina home, where-upon "the Christ who will not die" called in the law. Harv was thrown into the county jail, where he lasted less than a day before tunneling out and heading for the cave.

The old path to the cave was dappled and lovely, winding through mossy woods and occasional meadows. At a sunlit corner we stopped to rest and listen to the bugs making their noises, something I learned to do from my mother that I believe she learned to do from her mother. There were many creeks to cross—cricks, my mother would say—and at one small stream I looked down to find my footing. There, directly in front of my left foot, lay a thumb-size point of yellowish flint.

I was well into my forties at the time and had never seriously thought about arrowheads. Arrowheads were some kind of myth from another time, like circus trains and Wild West shows, like dial-up telephones must seem to my own son—like dial-up telephones are beginning to seem to me. Not that I don't come home from nearly every walk with something. I live near the sea and have a garage full of old fishing lures and rusted iron ship fittings. I have a surplus of sea-worn bricks that are looking for a better home than the bucket they're currently in. Mostly, though, I pick up bones, which are a particular gift of the sea as they come clean and white and sculptural and not at all in need of boiling and picking like the heads of Yaqui Indians that Hrdlička found on the killing fields of Sonora. But no arrowheads; generally speaking beaches aren't the place to find sharp objects.

It's more than location, however: arrowheads present themselves to some people and not to others. My niece Tybout found an exquisite quartzite arrowhead in some eroding sand dunes, not far from where I found my favorite piece of ship's iron. Another friend of mine finds arrowheads by the dozens, along with shark's teeth, which I do sometimes find, and old coins, which I do not. Henry David Thoreau once walked with a friend who complained that he never found an arrowhead and Thoreau looked down to his feet and said "here is one, take it." Another time, Thoreau wrote in his journal that he was out with a friend and on the way home "broke forth into an extravagant eulogy on those savage times." The crazy bard of Concord waved his arms around and pointed to imaginary places around them where Indian lodges had stood, and feasts had taken place, and so on. "'Here,' I exclaimed, 'stood Tahatawan; and there . . . is Tahatawan's arrowhead.'"

"We instantly proceeded to sit down on the spot I had pointed to, and I, to carry out the joke, lay bare an ordinary stone, which my whim had selected, when lo! *the first I laid hands on, the grubbing stone that was to*

be, proved a most perfect arrowhead, as sharp as if just from the hand of
an Indian fabricator."

Good for Thoreau. I, on the other hand, never found anything resembling an arrowhead until that day in Missouri. Even as I bent to pick up
the point, I simply didn't believe the rock at my feet could be more than
a "ventifact," something created by wind and weather that just looked
surprisingly like something made by human hands. I say "point" and
not "arrowhead" because it has a very obvious "flute" that runs nearly
from the tip to the base, a feature that disappeared from North American stone tools long before the advent of bows in North America. It's not
particularly elegant and may have been only a humble hand tool rather
than a projectile point because it is "unifacial," which is to say sharpened
only on one side. It may, in fact, have been a failed attempt that was abandoned when it broke during manufacture: a piece of lithic litter.

The point I found is a modest artifact, at best, but I was flooded with
excitement and happiness when I held it in my closed hand and called
my mother over to see it. Back home, when I began to research the first
Americans I dug it out of a box where it had been keeping company with
a whale knuckle and a trilobite. I put it directly beneath my computer
screen, where I could pick it up and turn it over in my hand, or rub my
thumb along the still sharp edge as I read about Albert Koch and his
fabulous creatures, or Aleš Hrdlička and his bizarre theories. It was a
piece of the ancient Mississippi basin and it kept me good company until
one day it disappeared.

This naturally sent me into an unnatural funk, but upon reflection it
was not really surprising. I've never lost a bone or a fossil or a piece of sea
glass. I still have the ID card that I carried in college and a necklace I
briefly wore in high school. Truth be told, I have a stupid amount of old
mementos squirreled away in corners and coffee cans. But I realized,
while groping the trash bag for the missing fluted point, that I have lost
a series of things with real or imagined connections to Native America.

For several years I had a beadwork pendant that a friend on the Rose-
bud Reservation in the headwaters of the Missouri River gave me. I was
up there for a magazine, writing a report about multinational trash cor-
porations putting their dumps on the reservation. The pendant was a
palm-size blue and white design on a backing of suede. I never wore it,
but hung it instead on a doorknob to my office, where I'd notice it occa-

sionally and remember what it was like to stand in the wind on Horseshoe Butte overlooking the rolling Missouri River valley prairies with Oleta Mednanksy and a couple of other Lakota folks laughing ironically about the old antilittering commercials with the crying Indian.

"Ho Mitakuye," Oleta's neighbor taught me to say before we crawled into his sweat lodge on a night when sparks from the fire traveled straight up and seemed to join the stars in the sky. He was the one who gave me the pendant before I left South Dakota.

"It means 'all my relatives,'" he said as he moved white-hot rocks from a fire outside the low, somewhat tattered-looking lodge to the pit at its center. "And whenever anyone says, 'Ho Mitakuye,' we open the lodge and go out and cool off. It's not a competition to see who can get themselves overcooked. So if you want air, just say, 'Ho Mitakuye.' Okay?"

I nodded.

"And if you can't remember that, say, 'All my relatives.'"

"Ho Mitakuye," I'd still sometimes say years later when I saw the pendant hanging there by my door, or on the rare occasion that I found myself in a sauna or steam room. And once, a few years ago, when my sister and I camped out under the stars on open prairie of Badlands National Park in South Dakota and awoke to see an enormous bison eyeing our spot from about thirty yards away, I said, "Ho Mitakuye." And also "Holy shit . . ." The beast ambled off.

I don't have the pendant anymore. At some point I must have moved it from its place on the door handle, or it moved itself, and I haven't seen it in years. The same can be said of a curiously worn shell I picked out of the roots of an immense tree that had recently blown over in a storm after growing for several hundred years on top of an obscure shell mound in Florida that I knew was originally built by the now "extinct" Tocobaga Indians. And a small, vaguely circumcised-looking rock from Martha's Vineyard that I believe was at one time hafted to make a nice hammer suitable for cracking oysters or lobsters. Whether these were real artifacts or not doesn't really matter: I thought they were, and they are all gone, along with a shard of pottery from up past the headwaters of the Arkansas River that was my favorite of them all.

Harv Vogt never did get hanged for stealing the horse and wagon from Jesus Christ who will never die, which is a fortunate thing for me and the rest of his offspring. He got out of the cave, and the law never caught up with him. He and Elzina went on to have a few more children, including the grandfather I never met. "Harv lived there for a long time in that cave," one of his other children told my mother. "Elzina's mother brought him food and water every day."

Every day, for a long time, in other words, my great-great-grandmother may have walked right past the fluted point I found. That's assuming, of course, that she walked the same path in 1908 to the cave, and that my mother and I had the right cave to begin with. It assumes as well that the point had lain where I found it for eight thousand years until I picked it up; that it hadn't been found by someone else, in other words, and re-lost. It's assuming that *Elzina Lakey herself* didn't pick it up somewhere else and drop it here while pausing to get a cool drink at the stream.

I have to believe that's possible. After all, I am walking near it today as I go back and forth from my office to my house, for it can't have gone far. It's right around here somewhere, and it is also lost forever.

Thoreau predicted my loss and, I discovered later, even preempted what I thought at the time was my own great revelation that maybe the point had been found and lost repeatedly in the previous eight thousand years. Thoreau didn't just find arrowheads, he "harvested" them.

"As sportsmen go in search pursuit of ducks—& gunners of musquash and scholars of rare books—and travelers of adventures & poets of ideas—& all men of money—I go in search of arrowheads when the proper season comes round again," he wrote in his journal on March 28, 1859.

But he knew better than to think that he possessed them in any real way.

"When you pick up an arrowhead and put it in your pocket, it may say: 'Eh, you think you have got me, do you?'" he wrote in his journal. "'But I shall wear a hole in your pocket at last, or if you put me in your cabinet, your heir or great-grandson will forget me or throw me out the window directly, or when the house falls I shall drop into the cellar and there I shall be quite at home again. Ready to be found again, eh? Perhaps some new red man that is to come will fit me to a shaft and make me do his bidding for a bow-shot. What reck I?'"

So too, I guess, with ideas and meanings. Perhaps even with rivers. What reck indeed? But I want my fluted point back.

5

MAMMOTH SEASON

Before the flood up in the headwaters of the Arkansas wiped out most of Folsom, New Mexico, and uncovered the bison bones and fluted points in Wild Horse Arroyo, the town's main claim to fame was that it was there in 1899 that the outlaw Black Jack Ketchum tried to hold up a train all by himself. Black Jack, whose real name was Tom, and his older brother, Sam, were among the most successful train robbers of their day, and this was the same train in about the same place that various members of their Hole in the Wall Gang had hit at least twice before. By August 1899 the gang was on hard times, however. Unbeknownst to Jack, his brother's luck had run out entirely a few weeks earlier when he died from gunshot wounds he received in a fight with lawmen up the river in the town of Cimarron. With the rest of the gang similarly dead or lying low in parts unknown, Jack decided, either out of desperation or bravado, to try to repeat the robbery without a crew.

On the appointed night he hid in a cave near Folsom until he heard the train approaching in the dark. Spurring his horse to a full gallop, he came alongside the locomotive and grabbed ahold and swung himself aboard. Guns drawn, he forced the engineer and fireman to stop the train. All was going according to plan until the conductor, Frank Harrington, who had been robbed by Ketchum before and was not amused to be made the fool twice, grabbed a shotgun and went after Black Jack

PD-US

Postcard of the hanging of Black Jack Ketchum.

in the mail car. Ketchum fired first, but uncharacteristically missed. Harrington blasted back with the shotgun and nearly blew off Ketchum's arm. The now one-armed bandit fled, but in his condition he didn't get far and was arrested a few days later and sentenced to hang.

Not many people would try to rob a train single-handedly, and Black Jack Ketchum was flamboyant to the end, which got both him and Folsom in the news across the country. He wrote jailhouse letters to President McKinley, claiming to have committed crimes for which others were serving time. He said he wasn't the real Black Jack but had turned to crime because he looked so much like the "real" Black Jack that he had no choice but to become an outlaw since everybody thought he must be one. He told reporters that he had instructed his famous pals from the Hole in the Wall Gang to get revenge on Harrington and the two lawmen who arrested him.

"I smuggled a letter out," he said, "and those three men are marked."

His last day alive, when it came, was a suitably boisterous affair. A stockade set up ostensibly to protect the proceedings from the Hole in the Wall Gang also handily allowed local lawmen to make some money selling tickets to come inside for the execution. There was a photographer present.

"Good-bye," Ketchum said on the scaffold on April 26 of 1901. "Please dig my grave very deep."

The executioner pulled the black hood over his head, paused, and yelled, "Let her go!"

They did, but the rope was too long. Ketchum's head snapped clean off at the neck, which made for a popular postcard of the hanging.

That was Folsom, New Mexico, before the flood, a picturesque pocket of the Old West at the beginning of the twentieth century. Since the flood, on the other hand, the words "Folsom" and "Clovis" bring up images not of the Old West of cowboys and Indians, but of the *very* old watershed of Paleo-Indians and incredible animals that all—apparently relatively suddenly—died out. The mammoths, mastodons, gigantic beaver, ground sloths, glyptodonts, camels, and proto-horses had all survived multiple ice ages and warming periods in the past hundred million years. Then, they disappeared. Thirty-three genera of large North American mammals went extinct during the same couple of thousand years that the folks who made Clovis and Folsom spear points arrived on the scene. So while no one much argues anymore about whether prehistoric Americans lived with and hunted now-extinct ice-age creatures, they argue instead about whether the Paleo-Indians killed them all.

The evidence against the Clovis hunters is largely circumstantial and on its surface quite convincing. The hunters didn't have to kill them all, the argument goes. The biggest animals were slow to reproduce and had a long gestation period: computer models show that a rise in mortality of only 1 or 2 percent can, over the course of several thousand years, drive the largest species to extinction. What is more, top tier species such as mammoths and mastodons don't exist in an ecological vacuum but are crucial to the maintenance of the habitat that supports a broad range of species. Take enough of the giant species out of the ecosystem and a more general collapse follows, driving some animals extinct that weren't necessarily preyed upon by humans.

The only thing different about the end of the most recent ice age from that which preceded it, according to this argument, is that people arrived with fluted points and atlatls. Just as in Australia and Europe and Siberia, anatomically modern humans arrived and within a relatively few thousand years most of the biggest beasts disappeared.

The argument that something else must have at least contributed to the demise of the Pleistocene megafauna, as the missing giant mammals are generally called, is more along the "reasonable doubt" lines. By this reasoning, the fact that numerous species in North America that were not hunted by humans also disappeared suggests that humans were not the primary cause of the extinctions. What's more, there were many species that the Paleo-Indians did hunt that have survived. The fact that large mammoths also disappeared in Asia and Europe around the same time as they disappeared from North America, even though humans got there earlier, is similarly seen as evidence that the big North American game didn't succumb because of the sudden arrival of humans across the Bering land bridge. The Paleolithic Siberians built their houses out of mammoth bones, and the Mal'ta Venus, a generously proportioned female figurine found at Lake Baikal in Siberia, was carved from mammoth ivory some twenty-three thousand years ago. The mammoths didn't disappear for another ten thousand years or more.

Those who doubt humans were the culprits also point out that the most recent ice age ended in a particularly erratic fashion, with an extremely sudden return to Arctic conditions for about 1,300 years beginning 12,900 years ago. The Arctic cold snap was most likely triggered when the massive Lake Agassiz that had flooded most of Canada finally burst through the retreating ice into the North Atlantic through the St. Lawrence, effectively shutting off the Gulf Stream. The process of warming, which had already disrupted and stressed the continental ecosystem, was slammed into reverse, putting some species over the edge into extinction. Also, a thin layer of sediment in the strata may suggest that a meteoric impact or a period of intense volcanic activity took place. A very small increase in mortality can lead to the extinction of a species over a long period, these arguments agree, but there were causes of their extinction other than early hunters.

The most significant chink in the reasoning that sudden human over-harvesting of unwary mammals led to their demise may be the growing body of evidence that the Clovis hunters were not, in fact, the first people to arrive in North America. At the Meadowcroft Rockshelter, overlooking a tributary to the Ohio in western Pennsylvania, an unfluted spear point and other artifacts have been found in strata dated to as early as 16,250 years ago.

The significance of Meadowcroft and other pre-Clovis sites isn't that they push the date of human presence back significantly—after all, the modern human species in Africa goes back two hundred thousand years. The slow acceptance of ever-earlier arrival dates for humans in North America—and people who did not make fluted points and specialize in big-game hunting—does suggest that the North American megafauna were not caught dumbly lumbering along by an invading horde from Siberia who arrived when the ice-free corridor from Alaska to the Mississippi River basin opened.

Whether or not a human being killed the last mammoth or mastodon will never be known. There is no doubt, however, that someone, or some band of someones, were the last people ever to kill a North American mammoth. Someone ate a mammoth steak as a child and never tasted it again. Someone told their children about a gigantic animal their fathers and mothers had known but no one had seen since. Someone wondered where they went. Someone may even have wondered if they had done something wrong, either by the mammoth or by the universe.

An old Japanese proverb says that if anyone sits by a river long enough they are certain to see the body of their enemy float past. This might easily be interpreted as a vaguely Buddhist rumination about living in the present: "don't worry so much about your enemies," in other words, "if you are at peace with yourself watching the river go by, the river will take care of them." You can imagine the bloated bodies of romantic rivals and evil samurai drifting downstream toward and past some peaceful philosopher-shogun, who sits by a river in the delicious shade of a bodhi tree. This interpretation seems suitably Asiatic, like the ancient wanderers who came over from Siberia with their chipped rocks and their taste for big game.

There is another possibility, however. The enemy floating by is time, as time is the notion that invariably lurks somewhere in every river proverb. Marcus Aurelius, the philosopher-king of second-century Rome, dispensed with riddles altogether when he wrote that "time is a sort of river of passing events, and strong is its current; no sooner is a thing brought to sight than it is swept by and another takes its place, and this too will be swept away."

Marcus Aurelius composed most of his meditations not on the Tiber River, as one might expect for a Roman emperor, but far away on the much larger Danube. He was there fighting the Germanic tribes, and he vanquished them, though everyone knows the babbling barbarians came back to haunt his grandchildren and sack Rome eventually. What's more, he wrote not in the Latin language of his own doomed empire but in the Greek language of the already fallen Athenian one.

"Some things hasten into being," he wrote, "some hasten to depart; some even that are coming into being are already in part extinct. These fluxes and changes continually renew the world, just as the constant flow of time ever renews eternity. What is there among the things swept along by this river of being, on which there is no abiding, that one can value? It would be like falling in love with a sparrow as it flies by us, and in an instant is out of sight."

For the mammoths and their fellow giant mammals, the hundred-million-year moment by the Mississippi had run out. Even the river itself was much smaller now, as the ice had retreated far enough to allow most of the rain that fell over Canada to flow north and east toward the Gulf of St. Lawrence and Hudson Bay rather than south into the Mississippi and the Gulf of Mexico, as it had during much of the ice age. The mammoths were gone, not just from the vast savannas and woodlands of the Mississippi River basin, but all over the world.

The people who had hunted them with fluted points, on the other hand, were still around. Killing mastodons and mammoths had become an unsustainable way of life and they turned to a new one: killing bison and deer.

BOOK TWO

RIVER OF MOUNDS

. . .

*The Rise and Fall, and Rise and Fall, and
Rise of Native America*

No one tests the depth of a river with both feet.

—ASHANTI PROVERB

6

AMONG THE EFFIGIES

I didn't know that I was in the presence of bears until suddenly the inescapable essence of bearness was all around me.

I was walking a small path, high on a bluff above the upper Mississippi River in the northeast corner of Iowa. The river there is very wide and shallow, with a myriad of islands and marshes, small pools and larger lakes, crowded with birdlife. It's one of the very wide places in the upper river that Mark Twain may have been thinking about when he wrote of the Mississippi that "it is a remarkable river in this: that instead of widening toward its mouth it grows narrower; narrower and deeper."

The land along the banks in this section, meanwhile, is dramatic and tall, giving up grand views of the river. This is the "driftless area," an anomalous pocket of geography that was not covered by ice in the last glaciation, though the width of the riverbed itself is largely a work of the ice-age-swollen Mississippi. As a result, the surrounding hills were not shaved by the advancing ice, and the valleys were not filled with "drift" during the long glacial retreat. The Mississippi and its tributaries flow in this region through steep, incised, almost canyonesque valleys. "The high hills are perceptible on both sides," Zebulon Pike said of this stretch of the river in 1805, "but on the west [the ridges] almost border the river the whole distance." It is breathtaking country, in other words.

Maiden Rock, Wisconsin, 1856.

Across the river lay Wisconsin, to which my great-grandparents on my father's side immigrated in the first years of the twentieth century. They were part of the wave of middle-European migration in the decades before the First World War, a deluge of Lutherans and Catholics that filled the upper Mississippi valley with Swedes and Norwegians, Germans and a few Czechs. In the 1960s and '70s my parents regularly packed my sisters and me into VW buses or Chevy vans and took us from Massachusetts out there, where we rode ponies, baled hay, milked cows, and argued with our Winger cousins about whether the Schneiders were just an offshoot, or legitimately part of the main stem of things in Wisconsin.

Sixty-five years after leaving the state, Wisconsin is still in my father's blood more than any other place is, I believe. "Black loam energy stirs," he wrote once about the coming of early spring along the fence lines of his parents' farm. "Snow slips away to the Mississippi." For me, though, it's just another place my "people" have been.

I arrived at the river this time not from the ancestral farmlands over in Wisconsin but from a series of explorations farther upstream in Minnesota, toward St. Paul and Leech Lake and beyond. Once off of the water, I sped south, happy with the memory of recent adventures but eager to be elsewhere. After any extended period inland, even on a river as marvelous and wild-seeming as the upper Mississippi, I yearn for salt, and I was in a hurry to get back to the sea and to my family. I gunned my rental car down Highway 76. When I passed the sign for Effigy Mounds, however, I pulled over, because I invariably stop for mounds.

As landscape sculptures go, effigy mounds are unassuming. They come in a wide variety of shapes, most notably the outlines of animals, but they are rarely more than thigh-high at best, and most are substantially lower than that. If you came upon an effigy mound unmarked and overgrown—an unlikely event in our century, but not impossible—you might not even know it was something other than a natural feature of the land. You might be excused for thinking it an unusual deposit of sediment created by some odd eddy of silty water beneath the retreating ice; an esker of some sort. You would be mistaken, however. Over the course of five centuries, beginning about thirteen hundred years ago and ending about eight hundred years ago, thousands of effigy mounds of all shapes and sizes were constructed by a now-mysterious people who lived and hunted along the routes between the Great Lakes and the upper Mississippi.

"To a certain extent in Michigan, Iowa and Missouri, but particularly in Wisconsin, we find a succession of remains, entirely singular in their form, and presenting but slight analogy to any others of which we have an account, in any portion of the globe," wrote Ephraim Squier and Edwin Davis in their 1857 masterpiece *Ancient Monuments of the Mississippi Valley.* "The larger proportion of these are structures of earth, bearing the forms of beasts, birds, reptiles, and even of men; they are frequently of gigantic dimensions, constituting huge basso-relievos upon the face of the country. They are very numerous and in most cases occur in long and apparently dependent ranges."

As Squier and Davis suggested, what effigy mounds of the upper Mississippi River watershed lack in elevation, they make up for in scale and in frequency. Near the shore of Lake Mendota, not far from Madison, Wisconsin, is a straight-winged eagle effigy with a wingspan of 620 feet. It is larger than two of its companions only by a matter of degree. Two of its *many* companions: in the surrounding four-lakes area, there were at one time some twelve hundred effigy mounds. Statewide there were ten times that number. Iowa and Minnesota were less richly landscaped by the effigy builders, but both states once had mounds numbering in the thousands. The single site where I pulled off, Effigy Mounds National Monument in Harpers Ferry, Iowa, once had nearly nine hundred earthen sculptures associated with it.

Squier and Davis's *Ancient Monuments of the Mississippi Valley* is something of a monument itself, not least to the ambitions of the fledgling Smithsonian Institution, which commissioned the work as its first publication on any subject. Full of elaborate plates showing surveyors' plans of mounds and monuments of all kinds, it is filled with drawings and descriptions of places built over the course of seven thousand years in almost every corner of the Mississippi watershed. Already by the middle of the nineteenth century, however, the earthworks of the previous millennia were rapidly disappearing beneath the plow and factory, which gives the book an elegiac quality.

"The little town of Alexandersville is laid out over a portion of the smaller circle," reads a typical sentence, in this case about a "sacred enclosure" near Dayton, Ohio. "The clay composing the embankments is now much used in the manufacture of bricks, and but a little time will elapse before the work will be entirely obliterated."

For the effigy mounds of the upper Mississippi, destruction more often came less intentionally, as successive decades of tilling slowly reduced their contours until at last there was no distinguishing the "bassorelievos" from the surrounding prairie. For half a millennium near Prior Lake, Minnesota, a flock of five bird effigies, each with a wingspan of about 150 feet, flew, so to speak, across the prairie toward the Minnesota River. The "five hawks" were there in the 1880s when a young archaeologist named Theodore Hayes Lewis set out from nearby St. Paul to survey some seven thousand mounds of Minnesota. "It is hardly possible for the reader, even with the aid of faithful diagrams, to form an adequate idea of the beauty and symmetry of the effigies as they appear to the eye in their undisturbed state," he wrote in 1888.

When the Minnesota Department of Anthropology visited the location of the "Five Hawks" in 1960, however, they met an old farmer whose father had been a farmer in the same location. He was, he claimed, "the son of the original owner" of the land, apparently with no sense of irony given that the anthropologists were looking for ancient artworks twice the size of his barn. The anthropologists consulted Lewis's old maps. They walked the farmer's fields. They triangulated from Lewis's landmarks. But the birds were gone. Every year for two generations the land had been cultivated, the farmer explained. There was evidence under the soil that the effigies had indeed been there, but there was nothing left to save. "It was found that there is not surface indication as to where the mounds had been originally nor their relationship to the highway right of way," the archaeologists wrote in their report to the state highway department.

Today, even the farm is long gone, and whatever subterranean evidence remains of the lead hawk lies directly beneath the four lanes of Highway 13, with its 100-foot wings spread and heading toward the parking lot of the Tractor Supply Company outlet. The rest of the flock are under the tidy row houses and backyards of Willowood Street, just east of a cul de sac called Peregrine Circle. A similar story could be told of the 225-foot bird effigy that was once in Hokah, Minnesota, or the 110-foot-long fish that swam the land beside the Mississippi River in Dakota, Minnesota. Remarkably, every single animal-shaped effigy mound in Minnesota has disappeared back into the earth over the course of the last century. Fortunately, though, Wisconsin and Iowa had many more effigy mounds to start with, and so more survived, including those on the ridges where I was drawn off the highway.

When you first approach an effigy mound, it is not always possible to discern its shape from merely looking at it. Without the helpful sign placed by the National Park Service, it wouldn't have been obvious in the failing light what manner of beasts lay before me. It was not quite dusk, but glowing the way early evenings sometimes do in the vicinity of water. Gloaming. The park closes at nightfall, but it was late autumn and the place was empty. Without thinking, really, I began to walk around one of the ten great bear mounds that lie nose to tail along the ridge over the river.

What is it about bears? Wherever they dwell or have dwelt, which is to say all the way around the Northern Hemisphere, they are deeply symbolic beasts to traditional cultures. They are carriers of meaning well beyond what their economic value as food or fur might seem to warrant. How ancient this veneration is, is a matter of debate; circles of fossilized bear skulls in European caves have led some to argue for the existence of a bear cult among the Neanderthals one hundred thousand years ago. That bear veneration in North America predated the arrival of Europeans is

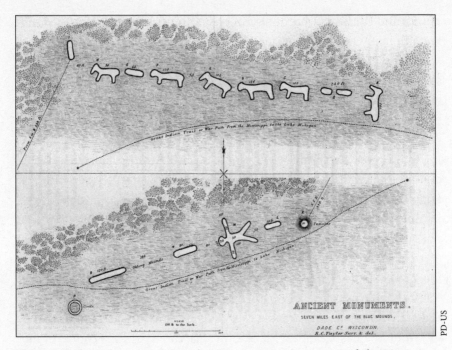

Illustration from Squier and Davis's 1848 *Ancient Monuments of the Mississippi Valley* plotting the locations of bear mounds in Wisconsin.

obvious from the existence of the mounds, but whether bear mythology arrived in the Mississippi watershed with the first humans from Asia, whoever they were and whenever that was, is less clear. What can be said, at least by laypersons, is that there are remarkable similarities of bear-related practices on both sides of the Pacific and Atlantic.

Also open to speculation are the reasons for such a widespread habit of treating bears differently than most other animals. The bear's ability to walk and run on two legs is commonly mentioned, as is the fact that bears give birth in womblike dens during hibernation. Hibernation itself is mysterious: "A bear is wiser than a man because a man does not know how to live all winter without eating anything," an Abnaki elder explained to one researcher. Anthropologists point out that the skinned carcasses of bears look disconcertingly human in proportion. Bears are also unpredictable and omnivorous masturbators, who might become enraged when attacked or might sit back and whine and shed tears. Bears are natural carriers of human symbolism, in other words, because they seem in many ways quite human themselves.

Stories of bears becoming human and vice versa are common wherever bears have lived. The Cherokee tell of a young man who didn't like village life and moved into the woods and became the first bear. The Penobscot tell of a boy who was lost and adopted by bears, and founded the bear clan. Bears are the primal ancestors of the Ute people, something the bears also know. Waiabskinit Awase, or the Great White Bear of the Menominee people of Wisconsin and the western Great Lakes, is capable of shape-shifting from human to bear form at will.

Across the Pacific, Korean mythology tells of a mother bear who eats twenty-one cloves of garlic and is transformed into a beautiful woman (with dubious breath), from whom all Koreans are descended. From India comes Jambavan, the king of bears, and his daughter, Jambavati, who becomes one of Krishna's wives. In Ancient Greece Zeus's lover Callisto is transformed into a bear by Hera, who is in a jealous rage at the birth of Callisto's son Arcas. Arcas in turn very nearly kills his mother during a hunt, not knowing she is a bear, a tragedy only averted when Zeus transforms both mother and child into the bear constellations, Ursa Major and Minor.

There are also people around the globe who, while not quite shape-shifting into bears, are nonetheless associated with the animal. In most Native American cultures the bear represents one of the most powerful clans. From Norway, there are the Berserkers, who wore bear shirts and were transformed into ravenous bear-men. There is also Beowulf, whose name, the bee wolf, means bear, and King Arthur, whose name also derives from Arcas, or bear. And Orson, who was raised by bears and served in the court of Charlemagne. Bjorn means "bear" and its common usage in Scandinavian countries attests to an ursine past. More recently, some large hairy gay and transgender men identify themselves as "bears."

Wherever you are, don't call a bear a bear to its face. The most unifying feature of global bear veneration throughout history is the taboo against calling a bear by its real name. In North America the Abnaki people called a bear "cousin" and apologized when killing it. To the Penobscot, Ojibwa, Tsimshian, Tahltan, and the Tete de Boule he was "grandfather," and to the Luiseno a bear was "great grandfather." If you were a Montagnais-Naskapi of Labrador and you tried unsuccessfully to call a bear out of its den three times using "grandfather," you could always change to "grandmother" and out she would come so you could knock her on the head with your club. An unseen bear, meanwhile, must not be called anything but "black food" or "the one who owns the chin," to avoid offending it, though you might also speak of "old porcupine" or the "lynx-like creature."

Out on the plains of the western half of the Mississippi watershed, the Cree spoke of the "four-legged human," or "chief's son," while the Sauk addressed a bear as "old man." "Elder brother" is how he was known to the Menominee, while the Blackfoot might say "unmentionable one" or "that big hairy one."

Traditional Siberian peoples on the other side of the Pacific also do not call a bear by his or her real name, preferring "the little old man," "the respected one," "the wise one," "my cousin," or simply "that's him." The Lamut, when they called a bear out of its den to be killed, would say: "Grandfather, Old One, Our Grandmother, and the older sister of yours, Dantra, ordered you saying, Do not frighten us! Die of your own choice." In Kolyma they say "grandfather," "great man," and "owner of the earth," while the Ainu of Sakhalin Island, who are perhaps the most famous bear venerators of all, speak of the "dear little divine thing who resides among the mountains." Until well into the twentieth century, when the practice was suppressed by the Soviets, the Ainu captured cubs in the spring and raised them, sometimes with human wet nurses, for later sacrifice at a great bear festival.

You can't say "bear" in the Ural Mountains of Russia and Kazakhstan, where the Amur people called bears "chief" and the Yakut called him "worthy old man." The Vogul people called him "the venerable one," and the Votyak, "Uncle of the woods," while Hutsul of the Carpathian Mountains in Ukraine call him "the big hairy one." The Lapps of Lapland called bears "the old man with the fur garment," while Swedish herd-girls would not speak of bears directly lest they attack the cows, and might say instead, "golden feet" or "twelve men's strength." The relationship between unmarried women and dead bears is also tricky around the world; women are often not to look at a bear, and sometimes the dead bear's eyes were covered or sealed, lest he turn his gaze at the young women.

Veneration did not stop any of the cultures from hunting bears, of course. In both Asia and America bears were often spoken to before killing, and apologized to. On both continents blame for the killing was sometimes ritually explained away as the work of enemies: the Siberians blamed the Russians and the Abnaki blamed the English. On both continents meals were offered to slain bears, and the meat was only eaten with great ceremony.

Even when the feast was over there was still ceremonial work to do. Bear remains could not be left for dogs or scavengers, presumably to avoid insulting the bear spirits. There are mass graves of bears from five thousand years ago in the Ohio River valley. Skulls were commonly hung high on posts or trees in a village, or just outside it. Bear teeth were extracted and drilled for necklaces for shamans and warriors. Of course the furs were tanned and treasured.

In all the world of bear veneration, however, only the effigy mound people of the upper Mississippi River gathered together at sacred times of the year and constructed vast ground sculptures of bears. From archaeological excavations it appears that individual mounds were usually built in a single outpouring of effort, obviously by a fairly large group of people who had gathered at the site in a particular season of coming together and socializing. The remains of great feasts that attended the construction have been found. There would have been music, one suspects, and dancing, but whether these rituals took place on the mound or around it, who knows? Also unknown are the uses of mounds built in previous seasons or by previous generations. What is the meaning of ten bear mounds in a row, seemingly walking head to tail along a ridge, traveling in the general direction of downriver? Why, in fact, do the majority of effigy mounds—whether bird, bear, or water spirit—point downriver?

Taken together, the effigy mounds of the upper Mississippi River valley were the largest-scale collection of sculpture of any kind in the world. More than art, though, the landscape of the upper river valley was the spiritual expression of a civilization that left almost nothing else behind in the way of material artifacts. Many of the mounds contain a few graves, but there are plenty of effigy mounds with no burials associated with them. The graves that do occur seem almost incidental—a juvenile here, or a few bodies there—so that some have suggested they may have been people who merely happened to pass away during the season of mound building. More telling, they were not buried with the kind of ornaments and other goods that connote either a high level of social stratification or a strong belief in a material afterlife. The mounds have a meaning of their own, seemingly separate from either the social structure of the builders or their burial practices. But what is that meaning?

And where did the mound builders go? After five hundred years of effigy mound construction, the practice simply stopped. More than stopped: sometime before AD 1300 the people of the Effigy Mound region abandoned their sacred landscape altogether. For several centuries after that, the archaeological record for the heart of the effigy mound region is a total blank. The people, it seems, were gone, and the forest returned over the mounds that were not on the prairie, and the grass grew thick again on the paths around those that were.

At first I walked somewhat quickly around the shape in front of me, on a path that obviously has been walked by tourists before me. I didn't think about the meaning of bears or even the fate of the builders; my mind was still where I had come from that morning and where I wanted to get to that evening. I wondered, too, whether a ranger was going to come and kick me out, as the park closes at sundown and it was late. I was nonplussed by the mound. Humph, I thought with a shrug, bear.

When I moved on to the second beast in the row, though, I unconsciously slowed down and became, as a result, more conscious. The path turned sharply left, then right, then right again, then left as I walked around first one bear leg, then another. Then along the long belly of the beast. When I completed my circuit of the third mound, for some reason I didn't move on but began again down the same great neck to the grass-furry paw. I walked myself into a trance.

Whether walking the outline of an effigy mound was part of the original rituals practiced by the builders I couldn't say, but it felt reflexively correct. As ceremonial practices go, walking where others have walked before has to be at least as ancient as sticking bear skulls up on tree posts. There's the ceremonial avenue from the river Avon to Stonehenge, and the sacred ceques of the Inca, and the route of Paul Revere's ride, and the walk down the aisle to be married, and ten thousand parade and carnival routes all over the globe. There are the ceremonial wanderings of Australian Aborigines, not to mention a million years of migrations from winter food to summer forage. It stands to reason that the

Clovis people and their predecessors followed the mammoths back and forth across the continent on the same trails a thousand thousand times, like remora behind a whale. "The more I read," said Bruce Chatwin, "the more I became convinced that nomads were the crankhandles of history."

Tracing the outline of a knee-high bear in the dimming light above the Mississippi River felt less a pilgrimage than some kind of devotional act. I was going around in circles, after all, not to some holy place. Ancient Druids circumambulated their temples, as did ancient Greeks and no doubt a hundred other lost peoples, not to mention the Hindu circumambulations, the Zen Kinhin, the Christian Stations of the Cross, labyrinths, the Freemasons, and the Wiccans.

I don't currently practice any circumambulation regularly, other than taking two trips around every new rental car to make sure there are no dings or dents before leaving the parking lot. Truth is I don't take part in much organized ceremonialism of any sort, thank God. Whether this makes a person more or less vulnerable to surprise attacks from global bear spirits, I have no way of knowing, but I do know that on my fifth trip around the third bear, what hair there is on the back of my neck stood up and would not stand back down.

A braver man than I am might have stayed on for a few more laps around the grassy beast, would have tested the waters with both feet, as the Ashanti might say. But I got the hell out of there before old Uncle-Big-Hairy-Black-Food-Honey-Paws-Chin-Face-Lynx-like-Porcupine ever saw me.

He or Mr. Ranger, sir.

7

POVERTY POINT

The history of humans piling up dirt in the Mississippi watershed didn't begin with the bears, snakes, and thunderbirds of the effigy mound builders any more than it is likely to end with the levees and earthen dams of the United States Army Corps of Engineers. It's almost as if something about the absurd wealth of soil in the basin compels humans to rearrange it. "In short, they occupy the entire basin of the Mississippi and its tributaries," is how Squier and Davis put it in 1858. Earthworks come in all shapes and sizes, most of them built by cultures that, like the effigy mound builders, flourished in a particular corner of the watershed for several centuries or a thousand years, and then declined or evolved into something unrecognizable in the archaeological record.

The "oldest" is always a moving target, but some seven thousand years ago at Watson Brake, on a former channel of the Arkansas-Ouachita River, a society of "Middle Archaic hunter-foragers" spent five hundred years constructing a rough circle of mounds enclosing what is assumed to be a sacred space of some sort. Archaeologists don't know much about the Watson Brake builders, except that they ate virtually anything they could get their hands on, including their pet dogs. In the middens are the bones of fish from the river—three species of gar, three species of sucker, five species of catfish, and various bass, drum, and crappie—but also the remains of deer, opossum, moles, voles, various mice and rats, pocket gophers, gray squirrels and fox squirrels, cottontail and swamp rabbits, beaver, raccoon, muskrats, otters, turtles of all kinds, snakes, alligators, frogs, toads, geese, ducks, turkeys, grouse, and eighteen different species of river mussel.

Then, times changed. A thousand years after their first appearance, the Watson Brake people were gone.

A lot can happen in a few thousand years. By the time the next major phase of mound building began, some groups in the Mississippi watershed had taken the revolutionary step of not just camping near where the plants they liked to eat grew. The lower Mississippi River valley is one of only a handful of places in the world where agriculture developed entirely independently of outside influence. Wild gourds were used as containers and food by North Americans as early as eight thousand years ago, but at a five-thousand-year-old habitation site on the Pomme de Terre River in Missouri—not far from where Albert Koch dug up his Missourium— archaeologists found seeds of pepo (acorn) squash and bottle gourd that are larger than the seeds that either wild plant could have produced. The people who lived near the confluence of Caney Creek and the Duck River in Tennessee forty-eight hundred years ago raised sunflowers. Up along the lower Illinois someone was planting marsh elder about forty-four hundred years ago, and goosefoot—a kind of North American quinoa— was cultivated near the rock shelters of Kentucky thirty-seven hundred years ago. Small amounts of maygrass and barley were also grown. If the usual divisions of labor within nonagricultural societies existed, with male hunters and female gatherers, it seems likely the revolution was fomented by women.

None of these domesticated North American plants transformed hunter-foragers into midwestern farmers, but the wheels were in spin. The invention of agriculture, and to a lesser degree the creation of pottery, mark the transition from what archaeologists call the "Archaic" to the "Woodland" period that extended to the arrival of European people and diseases.

By the Bayou Macon in northeastern Louisiana, about fifteen miles west of the current location of the Mississippi River, a society of people who lived mostly on nuts and fish but also raised squash took up the mound-building habit and created six concentric earthen crescents. They began the work roughly thirty-five hundred years ago, and continued to modify the landscape for the next five hundred years. Like the later effigy mounds of the upper stretches of the river, the ridges at Poverty Point are not particularly tall—probably a little over six feet originally—but they are remarkably large. The longest is longer than thirteen football fields. They vaguely surround a thirty-seven-acre plaza, in which there is a platform mound on which wooden buildings once stood. Another, much larger mound overlooks the whole from just outside the concentric ridges.

Standing in the plaza of Poverty Point, even mingling with the busloads of schoolkids on a field trip, it's easy to imagine all manner of woodland majesty and pageantry going on in the broad space between the ridges and the riverside—music and dancing, howling and cheering, living and dying and loving. Were there dwellings on the ridges? Were there potentates or shamans with secret knowledge at the top of "mound A," as it's blandly called today.

It's all easy to imagine, impossible to prove. As befits a Stone Age society in a land of mud, the people of Poverty Point liked pretty rocks: one of the hallmarks of sites from that period are artifacts made from exotic stone from far up the river and its tributaries. These stones—fancy flints, sandstones, hematites, soapstones, galena, quartzes, schist, basalt, ocher, greenstone, hornblende, limonite, and granites—must have come in the hands of immigrants, some archaeologists say. The earthen rings are therefore a symbolic map of the known world at the time, built by members of "a cosmopolitan society, a people of vast cultural connection." The river, in this telling, was what it always has been, a highway for ideas, products, and immigrants.

Other scientists argue that while the Poverty Point people were admittedly well traveled, they were more likely an artistic local bunch who traded for raw materials, either through trips of their own or through intermediaries. The rings of earth are not a map of the world, these scientists would tell you, they are a map of the local hierarchy in a culture that stretched up the Lower Mississippi on both sides from New Orleans to above the Arkansas River.

Whoever they were, their Poverty Point culture "reached its zenith" around three thousand years ago. The rings around the plaza were finished, or at least no more were constructed. Trade carried on, as did ceremony and music. And fishing. And rock chipping. It all carried on for twenty more generations—about the amount of time that English-speaking people have now been in North America.

Then, like Clovis and Folsom and Watson Brake, and like the effigy mound builders, the Poverty Point culture disappeared from the archaeological record. By twenty-five hundred years ago they were gone. Down the river, up the river, or with the wind. No one knows.

8

60,000 PEARLS

I once met a Mingo named Dallas, while inspecting an obsidian phallus. That's not really right. It was a ceremonial arrowhead the size of a plantain, and I didn't once meet a Mingo as much as he once met me. I was minding my own business in the middle of Ohio, which is always a good policy for a New Englander, looking at the absurdly long ceremonial arrowhead that is kept behind glass at the Hopewell Culture National Historical Park. Dallas, on the other hand, was being loud in the corner.

"The people who built this place were long before my people," he said. He said this to no one, or to me, since only he and I were in the room and I was obviously trying to get a good look at the glassed-in glass blade in front of my studiously glassy face.

"It's amazing," Dallas hollered at a similarly glass-enclosed diorama. "But these people were long, long before my people."

Long before me too, I thought, and looked even harder at the blade. There is something subversive about fine objects made by people who disappeared a long time ago. People who knew exactly what they were doing, and how to do it with materials that nobody uses anymore. The big obsidian blade in the national park museum is almost obscenely beautiful. You might bury such a thing with your grandfather's bones at the bottom of a shapely mound, or figure out a way to give it to your grandchildren without paying taxes. You might take it to the *Antiques Roadshow*

and have Busby give you a quote. But you would never put such a thing
in the backseat of the car and take it to the thrift shop along with some
candelabra from a catalog that you once thought might look good on
the dining-room table.

"Long before my people," Dallas was still saying when I fled to the
earthworks outside.

After the fading of Poverty Point, the center of landscaping activity
in the Mississippi basin moved upriver and into the Ohio Valley. Agriculture was more common now, though still limited to North American
crops as opposed to the maize and beans that were creeping north from
Mexico. Pottery was also old news by then, though people were beginning to do interesting new work with textiles pressed into the clay before
firing. Depending on which archaeologist you talk to, some groups may
have been experimenting with newfangled bows and arrows, though
the atlatl was still the hunting weapon of choice among the people of the
river basin. "Arrows and bows will never catch on," I like to think of the
old atlatl crowd saying around the fire.

Beginning about twenty-five hundred years ago along the river in Kentucky, West Virginia, and Ohio, the people now known as the Adena began
to bury their dead with more ceremony and artifacts than did their predecessors down the river in Louisiana. Conical and oval-shaped mounds
made by the Adena people along the Ohio and its tributaries have been
stripped by thieves and scientists of beads made of shell from the ocean a
thousand miles away, bracelets and breastplates of pounded copper from
the Great Lakes, carved stone effigy pipes and tablets, mica cutouts of
hands and other shapes. There are dozens of variations on the form, but the
Adena often buried their dead flat on their backs, in small wooden crypts
that were then covered with earth, which built up into impressive mounds
over decades or centuries as new layers and bodies were added.

The Adena and their contemporaries lived and died this way for
thirty-five generations—seven hundred years—before their culture was
supplanted in the eyes of the experts who sort people out by pottery
fragments and mortuary fashions. The culture now called the "Hopewell
interaction sphere" overlapped with the final centuries of the Adena
and rose to prominence roughly two thousand years ago. The Hopewell
were even more worldly in their trade and skilled in their artistry than
the Adena, and they occasionally buried spectacular caches.

Squier and Davis's illustration of the Marrietta earthworks, 1848.

"The mounds in that valley are sacred mounds," Frederic Ward Putnam of Harvard's Peabody Museum told a gathering in Cleveland in
1887. He was speaking in particular of Hopewell mounds in the valley of
the Little Miami River, which enters the Ohio just upstream of Cincinnati. "On these mounds fires were kindled and sacrifices made—not
human sacrifices, but sacrifices to the fire. In one of these mounds we
found terra-cotta figures beautifully carved and perfect representations
of people in a perfect attitude of rest; there was nothing to suggest action.
There were beside these stone images of fine shape. There were copper
pendants and thousands of copper beads. Many earrings were found of
copper covered with native silver, and over 60,000 pearls."

Putnam was the most distinguished and most experienced archaeologist in North America at the time, yet even he was amazed at the wealth.
"It seemed as if all the pearls of all the tribes had been cast upon this
altar," he said.

It wasn't all the pearls, however. There were fifteen thousand pearls in
another mound; fifty copper breastplates and ear spools in another; there

was the "great mica grave," and so on. From one Hopewell mound came a collection of 136 carved stone platform pipes, the bowls of many of which were effigies that faced the smoker: crow, blue jay, kingfisher, quail, crane, heron, owl, parakeet, hawk, eagle, toad, turtle, squirrel, wolf, fox, deer, mink, rabbit, dog, otter, beaver, opossum, porcupine, raccoon, wildcat, mountain lion, and, of course, bear.

The Hopewell built many mounds, but they are best known for sprawling geometrical earthworks, such as the one in Chillicothe, Ohio, that Dallas and I chose to visit at the very same time on the very same day. Before arriving at Chillicothe, I spent the early morning hours in solitude hiking up to, and then bushwhacking my way around, the mile and a half of Hopewell walls that encircle a hilltop in Hillsboro, Ohio. Fort Hill is my kind of ruin, overgrown with mature trees and vines and giving the impression of being forgotten, even though it is part of a state park and there is a small museum at the bottom of the mount that was closed for the season. The walls were constructed in several stages out of earth and quarried sandstone, but two thousand years later you might not even recognize them as human work if you weren't looking for them.

I traipsed around happily for hours, inspecting the holes left by freshly fallen trees to see what they might have dug up (a trick I learned from Florida mound hounds) and trying to divine some sense of what the place might have meant to the people who created it. There was nothing in the holes to find and re-lose, but while circumambulating the perimeter wall I found the place where Lynda and Mike carved their initials into a sycamore in 1964, and where at the opposite end of the enclosure for a couple of years in the late 1980s it was a tradition of sorts for locals to carve their names into a rock outcropping. The names were almost lost already, filled in many cases with thick lichens and mosses. This hill, it seems, is well practiced in the art of erasure.

Archaeologists and sociologists debate virtually everything, from the meaning of a misplaced rock to the age of a given fragment of charcoal, to whether the various "hilltop enclosures" of the Ohio Hopewell were primarily defensive or sacred. No one argues, however, with the obvious truth that the mounds and earthworks of the Mississippi basin were communal expressions and markers. My personal preference for visiting them alone at the end of the day or the crack of dawn is, therefore, something of a modern affectation, and when I saw Dallas walking slowly in my direction across the well-clipped grass of the thirteen-acre mound-studded plaza at Chillicothe, I resisted the temptation to duck behind the nearest dirt pile and waited for him.

"Pretty amazing place, isn't it?" I said when he got to where I was standing.

"Sure is, but it's long before my people," he said reliably.

I asked him the obvious follow-up.

"I've got Mingo blood in me, or at least that's what my grandfather always said it was. Chief Logan was a Mingo, you know, you can look that up."

He was right about Logan and about his chronology. The Mingo—which comes from an Algonquin word, "Mangwe," and means something like "treacherous and probably cannibalistic Iroquois"—are an offshoot of the Iroquois League who arrived in the Ohio River valley from their ancestral lands in upstate New York during the eighteenth century. They were on the move as part of the great upheavals caused by the arrival of French and English colonists along the Atlantic coast. The Hopewell trading networks and mound builders, on the other hand, were largely gone by the fifth century AD.

"I've got emphysema," Dallas went on. "And I'm not supposed to be off of my oxygen. But I find if I get out and walk around I can breathe better. I don't have to wear the tank even though I'm not supposed to go without it. So I just come out here to walk around."

He reminded me of an uncle of mine who has passed away, a man who also liked to talk, and I liked him.

"Yeah, well it's a strangely powerful place," I said, not certain if he was saying that walking generally did him good or walking among the ancient mounds did him good. It was the former.

"I'm part Mingo," he said, "but every time I try to mess around with any of that Indian stuff it brings me bad luck. I like to play with my grandkids, we had a tipi and stuff with them, but I don't get into that Indian stuff because of the bad luck."

When I asked him for specifics he wouldn't elaborate. "Just bad luck," he said.

"I was listening to a preacher I listen to on the radio and it turns out there's something called the mark of Cain. And that maybe that's a part of what it is or was with all the bad things that happened to the Indians, and it's all tied up with Israel today and all those problems they're having over there, and . . ."

He talked on, but my eyes followed the national park ranger on a big sit-down mower as he drove in circles around one of the mounds in the distance. The park service does a very good job of mowing the mounds and walls of the Hopewell Culture National Monument, and as Dallas talked and the ranger mowed, I thought about the odd history of this particular site, which was extensively surveyed by Squier and Davis in the 1850s. Chillicothe was their base of operations during the writing of *Ancient Monuments of the Mississippi Valley*, and Mound City—as it was known then—was one of the inspirations for their monumental effort. During the First World War, however, the land became Camp Sherman, presumably because the lumpy real estate was less valuable than the surrounding farmland. The army leveled most of the mounds, and they were only restored by the park service after the Second World War with the help of Squier and Davis's plans and large earthmoving equipment. So Mound City today is really sort of a monument to a monument, or a reenactment of a ruin.

Dallas changed the subject.

"You don't have any Indian blood in you, I don't suppose?" he said.

"No," I answered, and then said, "Well, I guess it depends on who in the family you ask."

Dallas the Mingo nodded as if he were familiar with the phenomenon. "So if you are or aren't Indian, what are you?"

"The usual European mix, I guess. But mostly German."

"Oh yeah, German." He laughed. "Me too. We all got that."

9

THE MISSISSIPPIAN MOMENT

In the spring of 1542 a messenger brought news to Quigaltam, the supreme leader of a people whose ancestors for seven hundred years had built mounds and dwelt along the bayous and cutoff channels of the Mississippi and Yazoo Rivers. The message came from a strange new headman named Hernando de Soto, who had recently come down the Arkansas River with his warriors and was now occupying the town of Guachoya, up near the confluence of that river with the Mississippi.

According to the messenger, this new leader claimed to be "the son of the sun and that wherever he went all obeyed him and did him service." De Soto furthermore hoped that Quigaltam would "choose his friendship and come there where he was, for he would be very glad to see him; and in token of love and obedience that [Quigaltam] should bring him something of what was most esteemed in that land."

Quigaltam lived in a place that was also called Quigaltam, and that was most likely the Lake George site, an imposing, fifty-five-acre compound of mounds and plazas about thirty-five miles northeast of Vicksburg, Mississippi. Wherever it was, Quigaltam the leader was not amused by the temerity of this self-proclaimed son of the sun, and he sent the messenger immediately back with explicit instructions.

"With respect to what he said about being the son of the sun," Quigaltam told the messenger to say to Hernando de Soto, "let him dry up the great river and he would believe him."

To Quigaltam, the Spaniard must have seemed like some kind of freak of nature. He and his army of strange-colored men and fantastic deer, on which some of them rode, were to be regarded with wariness. Some word or rumor of their marauding on their way up from Florida, through Tennessee, and eventually across the Mississippi to the Arkansas had surely reached Quigaltam. They were not by any means to be feared in some existential way or kowtowed to as "sons of the sun," however.

"With respect to the rest," Quigaltam told his messenger, de Soto should be informed that Quigaltam "was not accustomed to visit anyone. On the contrary, all of whom he had knowledge visited and served him and obeyed him and paid him tribute, either by force or of their own volition. Consequently if [de Soto] wished to see him, let him cross there. If he came in peace [Quigaltam] would welcome him with special good will; if he came in war, he would await him in the town where he was, for not for [de Soto] or anyone else would [Quigaltam] move one foot backward."

It was not the answer that the conquistador was looking for.

What Quigaltam didn't say, perhaps couldn't even have known, was that the culture to which he was the principal heir was in decline long before the first Europeans arrived in the hemisphere. The last great flowering of monumental Native American landscape architecture is known today as the Mississippian Cultural Tradition because its greatest centers were built in the river valley starting around a thousand years ago. By the time Quigaltam was lecturing de Soto about the proper way to approach a Mississippian king in 1542, however, many of the largest centers of Mississippian power had already been abandoned.

By far the most magnificent of these was Cahokia. Situated on the Illinois side of the river just downriver from the confluence with the Missouri, which is to say directly opposite the current location of St. Louis, Cahokia was the largest pre-Columbian city ever to have existed in North America. At its peak around AD 1200 there were roughly 120 mounds of various shapes and sizes in Cahokia, along with thousands of rectangular residences constructed out of pole and thatch and arranged into neighborhoods that may have been clan based.

There were massive temples in places, and gigantic upright marker posts the symbolism of which is unclear, but probably had to do with the status of individuals. Some compounds had walls, even bastioned palisades. At some point a neighborhood of dwellings was displaced by the construction of an immense circle of cedar trunks. Now referred to as "woodhenge," the 150-foot-diameter circle may be the earliest and largest example of a sun-dance arbor. The central feature of Cahokia, however, was (and is) the massive earthwork known as Monks Mound, a flat-topped pyramid that covered seventeen acres at its base and rose 100 feet over a perfectly leveled plaza.

Evidence from a gigantic waste trench not far from the central plaza suggests big parties: "At each public event several hundred to several thousand deer were consumed, several hundred to several thousand pots were broken (intentionally or accidentally), and several thousand or hundreds of thousands of tobacco seeds were dropped and left behind," wrote a leading archaeologist of the site, Timothy Pauketat. Native tobacco, it's worth pointing out, was significantly stronger than modern varieties, to the point of being hallucinogenic. "Hundreds to thousands of people, crowds worthy of the Grand Plaza, probably attended these rites."

Cahokian arts and crafts, meanwhile, were distributed widely, either as trade items or as gifts or distributions to people who attended the ceremonies. They have been found from Lake Superior to the Gulf of Mexico. The Cahokian national obsession was a game called Chunkey, in which spears were thrown at rolling disks, and it, too, spread far and wide as other people were drawn into the cultural orbit of Cahokia.

Cahokia was the largest of several centers in the immediate vicinity of the Mississippi's confluence with the Missouri. There were another fifty earthen pyramids with their associated temples and residences a few miles down Cahokia Creek, in what is now East St. Louis, while across the river in St. Louis proper were another twenty-six arranged around a large plaza. Cahokia itself rose rapidly around AD 1000 and then declined almost as precipitously for reasons that are not yet clear. By the beginning of the 1300s the city was virtually abandoned.

By then, though, other Mississippian centers had developed at various locations up and down the river and its major tributaries. Some have suggested that there was a Cahokian diaspora of sorts, with clans or subgroups of the Cahokian center moving north and south to set up new

Creative Commons

Mississippian pipe bowl showing a chunkey player.

centers along the river and its tributaries. Archaeologists are "reasonably confident" that the Cahokians spoke a Siouan language, and the oral histories of the Siouan Osage, Kansa, Ponca, Omaha, and Quapaw peoples in particular tell of splintering off from a homeland near the confluence of the Mississippi and Ohio Rivers. Mississippian culture eventually spread eastward, out of the watershed entirely, into Georgia, the Carolinas, and northern Florida.

Besides the grandeur of their plazas and the popularity of their arts, games, and rituals, two technologies in particular set the Mississippians apart from their middle and late woodland predecessors such as the Hopewell and Adena: they hunted with bows and they grew corn and beans, crops originally from Mexico. Most communities grew at least three varieties of maize, which ripened at different times in the season. As late as 1753, a French missionary in Louisiana wrote that "it is useless for me to enter here in detail all the different ways in which maize may be treated," and then went on to discuss breads, porridges, smoked dishes, hominy, gruels, and other preparations. Mississippians invented a new style of pottery, tempered with seashell, which allowed them to make new styles of cookware to accommodate their corn diet including cazuela bowls for stews and flat ceramic griddles for cooking pancakes in bear grease. Served with the corn were all manner of fish, game, nuts, berries, and wild salads, as well as cultivated squash, beans, goosefoot (quinoa), and sunflower seeds.

The rise of the Mississippian lifestyle has been implicated in the disappearance of the effigy mound builders who created the bears and birds of the upper river. Sometime between AD 1050 and 1100, during the heyday of Cahokia, a group of Mississippians moved into the heart of the effigy mound region of southern Wisconsin. They came from somewhere in southern Illinois, possibly Cahokia itself, and built a classic Mississippian town on the banks of the Crawfish River. Azatlan, as the place is now called in mistaken homage to the Mexicans, had large temple mounds, stockades, and other fortifications. It had corn and Mississippian pottery. The effigy mound builders came to trade, and some eventually stayed. Old ways began to fade under the influence of the new.

Distribution of Mississippian culture groups.

"Under Mississippian influence, the Late Woodland became Oneota," wrote Robert Birmingham of the process by which the effigy mound builders may have given up their own traditions and adopted a version of the new that was not quite Mississippian but also not what it had been.

The image is oddly foreboding, a premonition of things to come. The late woodland people of the upper river, who for more than four hundred years had been fully engaged in a beautiful cultural project of turning their landscape into a vast cathedral of animal shapes, now began to succumb to the cheap food and trinkets being offered up by the newcomers down at the fort. The people who made the effigy mounds had their own pottery, but the stuff being made by the people from Illinois was tempered with seashells and was therefore thinner and more beautiful, stronger and cheaper. And who could argue with corn? Maybe someone from the late woodland effigy mound culture even made the canoe trip down the river to the great city of Cahokia and came back with tales of the current king of corn, who lived on top of his giant pyramid of Mississippi mud. It wasn't always a peaceful transition, and by 1300 the effigy mound builders were entirely gone and Cahokia itself was nearing the apogee of its power.

Even to casual visitors a thousand years later, the great pyramids and plazas of Cahokia and other Mississippian centers whisper of political stratification and concentration of power in a way that lower mounds— even the most sprawling ones—do not. Wandering around the plaza of Cahokia today, the power of the place is palpable, but it's not the mysterious energy of the bears and birds of the upper river or the enigmatic draw of the arcs at Poverty Point. It is political power, almost familiar.

That aura becomes clearer still when you add the knowledge that archaeologists have uncovered mass graves of executed or sacrificed women in Mound 72 at Cahokia—nineteen daughters carefully laid side by side in one trench, twenty-two side by side in another, fifty-three bodies side by side in a third, and so on. There were beheaded and handless men buried in Mound 72, and at least one who appeared not to be fully dead when thrown in, along with thirty-nine people who were "probably executed on the spot." Generally speaking, it was better to be a paramount Mississippian chief than to serve one.

It would be a grave mistake, however, to let a little human sacrifice overshadow the cultural achievements and influence of Cahokia. Around the same time, the fair-haired Swedes at the Temple of Uppsala were sacrificing people to Odin (and building mounds), while the rest of Europe was gearing up for an orgy of witch-hunting and inquisitions that would eventually burn or hang a hundred thousand or more, usually for the benefit of the crowd. In the universe of officially sanctioned homicides, the Cahokians were small-time practitioners. Human sacrifice was even less important or nonexistent in later Mississippian polities, such as the one led by Quigaltam.

Decline is a relative thing. Various late-Mississippian leaders destroyed not one but two great armies of the apparently ascendant Spanish who came to North America having already conquered the Incas and the Aztecs. In 1528 the Apalachee of the Florida Panhandle drove the army of Pánfilo de Narváez—a former conqueror of Jamaica and Cuba—into the sea. Twelve years later de Soto, who made his fortune with Pizarro in the conquest of Peru, landed in Florida and caused havoc during a three-year march throughout the southeastern quarter of the continent until he arrived in the Mississippian heartland. By the time de Soto insulted

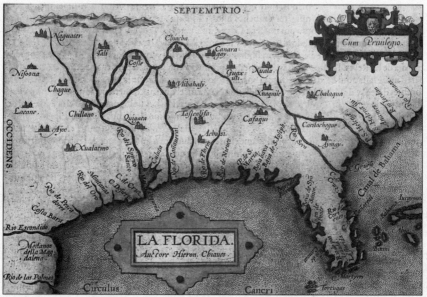

Map from 1584 based on the de Soto expedition.

Quigaltam, he was beyond caring much about the honors of being "first" anywhere and was merely hoping to stay alive long enough to get out of the country. Within two weeks his fever-wasted corpse was secretly sunk with rocks in the Mississippi by his men, lest the Indians of the river learn of his death.

When the remnants of de Soto's army tried to escape down the river in roughly constructed ships, Quigaltam's people chased them in giant canoes, "some of which held sixty or seventy Indians, and those of the principal men with awnings, and they [the principal Indians] with white and colored plumes of feathers as a device." The Gentleman of Elvas, a survivor, told the story, which began with de Soto's successor in command, Moscoso—"the Governor"—sending several canoes with twenty-five armored conquistadors to try to chase Quigaltam's navy away. These men were all quickly killed, when the Indians overturned their canoes and their heavy armor carried them to the bottom.

> The Indians, on seeing that they had gained the victory, were so greatly encouraged that they went out to engage the brigantines which they had not dared to do before. First they went to that in which Calderon was captain. It was going in the rear guard. At the first flight of arrows twenty-five men were wounded. In the brigantine were only four men with armor. These were stationed at the side in order to defend it. Those who had no armor, seeing that they were being wounded, abandoned the oars and hid away below the covering. The brigantine began to run crosswise and to go whither the current of the water might bear it. . . .
>
> Having left that brigantine they [the Indians] went to another and fought against it for half an hour. And in this way they circulated from one to another of them all. The Christians had brought mats to put under themselves which were doubled and very close and strong so that the arrows did not pierce them. As soon as the Indians gave them time, the brigantines were hung with them. The Indians seeing that they could not shoot direct shot their arrows haphazardly into the air which fell down into the brigantine and wounded some of the men. . . .
>
> And now, finding themselves so closely pursued by [the Indians] and so tired out that they could not endure it, they resolved to travel all that night following, thinking that they would pass by the land of Quigualtam and that [the Indians] would leave them. But they were going along

more unworried, thinking that they had already left them, they heard very loud cries hard by, which stunned them. In this manner, they followed us that night and the next day, until noon, when we had now reached the land of others whom they advised to treat us in the same way; and so they did.

Those of Quigualtam returned to their own lands, and the others in fifty canoes continued to fight us for a whole day and night. . . .

What might be called the first battle in what was to be a very long war for control of the Mississippi watershed ended with the courageous knights of Spain huddled behind grass mats, drifting down the river under a rain of arrows. It was a war that began with de Soto's arrival in the Mississippian heartland in 1540 and continued with various intermissions and a shifting mix of Native and European parties for 350 years until it officially ended with 153 Siouan-speaking Miniconjou and Hunkpapa thrown into a mass grave by the United States Cavalry at Wounded Knee, far up in Missouri River country.

10

THE GREAT SERPENT

Quigaltam and the other Mississippians so thrashed the armies of Hernando de Soto and Pánfilo de Narváez that the Spanish all but gave up on North America. It wasn't just the Mississippians, either: in 1521 the Calusa of Charlotte Harbor shot Juan Ponce de León in the buttock and sent him home to Puerto Rico to die; in 1526 the coastal people of Georgia destroyed Lucas Vázquez de Ayllón's attempt to found a "New Andalusia" there; in 1539 the Apache, various Caddo groups, the wide open spaces, and a great loneliness for his wife sent Francisco Vásquez de Coronado back to Mexico with a broken ankle and a severely sprained reputation.

More than a century passed between Coronado's departure from the Arkansas River and the next known visit to the watershed by a European. Two centuries passed before French and English explorers and traders established any sustained presence in the basin. Three centuries passed before the flood of Anglo immigration spilled into the watershed via the Susquehanna, Allegheny, Tennessee, and other tributaries to the Ohio.

Time, however, did not stand still.

The Spanish left behind pigs, horses, and, most of all, diseases that ravaged Native populations. With mortality as high as 80 or 90 percent in some places, old top-down modes of social organization disintegrated and Native Nations of the sort that built the great Mississippian mound centers re-formed into other tribes and nations that did not, as a rule, build large civic works. The arrival of the English and the French brought another series of epidemics and caused further dislocations as displaced coastal Indians dispersed into the hinterlands ahead of the frontier. Add the possibility that mound building in North America was entering one of its cyclical hiatuses with the decline of Mississippian culture, and it's understandable that by the 1600s even most of the Indians themselves didn't know who had piled up the dirt so artfully.

As with the great debates over what manner of beast was the mammoth, and whether the ancestors of Indians could have hunted them, the origins of the various prehistoric earthworks in North America was a source of consternation to generations of racist European Americans who couldn't quite believe that they were built by Native North Americans. Nature, or the Mexicans, must have done it, some suggested. Others argued that only the Danes could have achieved such a feat, or perhaps the Tartars. Some said the Spanish themselves built the mounds, and that the accounts given by de Soto and Narváez expedition survivors of powerful kings and queens carried in litters by their adoring and occasionally uppity vassals were vastly overstated. Whoever built the mounds, the thinking went, must have been run off by invading hordes of the current Indians.

"There are several ancient remains in Kentucke, which seem to prove, that this country was formerly inhabited by a nation farther advanced in the arts of life than the Indians," wrote John Filson in a typical example from his 1784 *The Discovery, Settlement and Present State of Kentucke.* "These are there usually attributed to the Welsh, who are supposed to have formerly inhabited here; but having been expelled by the natives, were forced to take refuge near the sources of the Missouri." Filson had it on very good authority that there were still Welsh-speaking Indians living in Montana.

One earthwork in particular, was so spectacular that some argued in good faith that it must have been placed in the Ohio Valley by none other than God, to mark the entrance to the Garden of Eden. Curving and undulating over a quarter of a mile, the Great Serpent Mound is the most famous effigy mound in the world. It lies on a curving tongue of land that was itself blown above the surrounding countryside by a deep

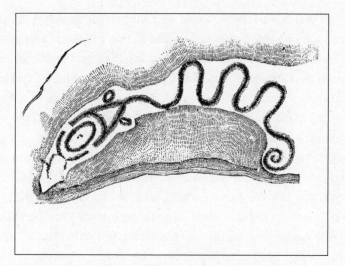

Squier and Davis's survey of the Great Serpent Mound, 1848.

underground explosion of gas two hundred million years ago, and winds back and forth on itself in a series of undulations that nearly touch one another. It looks as much like a river of oxbows as it does a snake, until you get to its mouth, which is open and seemingly carrying an egg.

What is it about snakes? Without going into bearish detail, it's safe to say that serpents are the equals of old honey paws, and probably surpass bears in the symphony of global mythological overtones. To the Mississippians, and to the effigy mound builders of Wisconsin, and to many later and earlier Native American cultures, the snake—sometimes with a salamander's legs—represented the underworld of water. And also, particularly for Mississippians, they signified women and fertility.

"The most prominent of these [Cahokian motifs] is the symbolic depiction of a female mythological character associated with fertility, regeneration, water, serpents and feline monsters, and the Underworld," wrote the archaeologist Thomas Emerson in a study of Mississippian shamanism. Snakes, women, water, and alligators: all are linked, say Emerson and other students of the late woodland nations, to the various Earth-Mother myths, including Corn-Mother, Old Woman, and Snake Mother. Like so many of the largest effigy mounds, the Great Serpent was almost destroyed in the nineteenth century. It was saved, appropriately enough, largely through the efforts of the pioneering female ethnologist

Alice C. Fletcher. Fletcher is more well known for her work among the Sioux and the Omaha, but when she heard that the Great Serpent was in danger of being sold and leveled, she took it upon herself to raise the funds from the women of Boston to purchase it for the Peabody Museum.

Interestingly, the Great Serpent Mound is not in the effigy mound region of the upper Mississippi, or in the neighborhood of Cahokia. It is instead almost solitary as far as animal effigy mounds go, on a small tributary of the Ohio. Also enigmatic is the time in which it was built. Long thought to be several thousand years old, carbon dating of charcoal found near the serpent puts its construction at no earlier than AD 1050. Which is to say, it was built when Cahokia was near its apex and the Mississippians were spreading up the tributaries and down the main stem.

By the time I got to the Great Serpent Mound I believed I was well traveled in the world of American land sculpture. I had read widely on the serpent mound, was familiar with its contours from aerial photos and Squier and Davis's diagrams. I knew of the debates about whether the oval in the serpent's mouth was an egg or just the mouth.

I knew as well from experience that the power of earthen sculptures—even the largest of them such as Monks Mound—doesn't really draw from first impressions. In our day of landfill mountains that rise above the skyline, even a million baskets of dirt doesn't amount to a hill of beans.

Still, I was not fully prepared for the Great Serpent Mound, for the way the beast lounges over an undulating hillside. Like any serpent in repose, I suppose, it doesn't present itself with ostentation, but lies low on the ground and is comfortable with its magnificence. All mounds today, including the serpent, are mysterious due to the simple fact that they endure against all odds—maybe with a fence around them, or with a couple of Civil War–era graves sticking akimbo out of their sides such as the one I visited in Piketon, Ohio. They are graves in their way, even those that hold no bodies.

But the serpent is also simply beautiful.

I timed my visit perfectly, arriving near dusk in the fall when there were sure to be no crowds. I had the beast to myself and spent a long time with her. I walked down below, to the stream, where there are great sycamores, but not great enough to remember when the serpent was imagined before it was laid out and built. Big beautiful trees they were, but just flickers on the land, waiting for the nearby river to undercut them and lay them down in the current.

When I got back to the top of the ridge, and to the Serpent, two people had arrived: a man and a woman, Anglo and Asian, dressed in black and in blue, taking pictures of each other with an iPhone and an Android. I offered to take a picture of the two of them together and they smiled and said, "Yes, thank you, we'd like that."

When I handed the camera back, the man asked me, "How did you hear of the Serpent Mound?"

"Oh," I said, caught a little off guard by the unusual question. "I don't know. I've just always read and heard about it and was in the area and decided to come and see it." I didn't want to spoil my mood by going into details about why I visit mounds in the Mississippi River basin.

"Ahh, I see," he said, and she smiled, and we parted. I began walking down the path toward the serpent's tail, thinking I'd take one last circumambulation before leaving and secretly hoping they were on their way to the parking lot so I could have the serpent to myself again. I didn't get far, though, before something about the way he asked me the question made me want to turn back up the body of the snake to ask the same thing.

I caught up with them near the fifth coil.

"Excuse me," I said. "I'm just curious because you asked me. How did you hear about the Great Serpent Mound?"

"Us?" he began. "We saw a documentary called *Ancient Aliens* and this is one of the places they were talking about. Where it might have happened. We came to see what all the fuss was about."

BOOK THREE

RIVER OF FORTUNE

· · ·

*The Spanish Exit, the French Arrive,
the Iroquois Take Action*

Follow the river and you will find the sea.

—FRENCH PROVERB

11

BONJOUR GREAT KHAN

Everything about the French arrival in the Mississippi watershed was stylistically different from the Spanish entrada of a century before. The Spanish came on horseback from the south; the French came in a couple of native canoes from the north. The Spanish came in armies that numbered in the hundreds and marched in relative formation with attendant slaves and retainers from the Caribbean and Africa; the French party consisted of six fur traders and a priest. The Spanish arrived in what they called La Florida fresh from their stunning victories over the great civilizations of South and Central America, victories that had produced fleets full of gold; the French had spent the previous century trading for beaver pelts and the eternal souls of Indians on the Great Lakes. The Spanish came looking for cities like those they had found in South America; the French were mostly trying to figure out if the "Great River" the Indians of Wisconsin kept talking about ran to the Gulf of Mexico or veered west, perhaps to the Pacific. The Spanish mostly feared winter and the awesome archery of the Mississippian warriors; the French were worried they might run into the Spanish.

French interest in North America had deep roots. Fishermen from Normandy, the British Isles, Portugal, and elsewhere almost certainly visited the North American coast for decades before Columbus's game-changing voyage of 1492. After Columbus, however, their governments rapidly became more actively involved in the exploration efforts. In 1497, Henry VII of England sent the Italian navigator John Cabot off on two voyages out of Bristol, and he explored from Hatteras to Greenland. In 1500, King Manuel I of Portugal sent Gaspar Corte-Real on a similar mission. There may have been a brief attempt at a permanent French colony at Sable Island in 1518, but more well known is that in 1524 François I of France sent yet another Italian navigator, Giovanni da Verrazzano, on a voyage to explore the coast of North America.

It wasn't until the voyages of Jacques Cartier of the 1530s, however, that France began the process of exploration and colonization of Canada that ultimately led, among other things, to French names up and down the Mississippi River from La Crosse and Prairie du Chien in Wisconsin, to St. Louis and Ste. Genevieve in Missouri, and to New Orleans and Louisiana. Cartier's own attempts to establish a year-round presence came to naught, but with growing confidence and knowledge of the coastline, the fishermen from Brest and elsewhere began to supplement their seasonal earnings by trading for furs at informal posts set up near the mouth of the St. Lawrence.

From the St. Lawrence, on which Samuel de Champlain founded Quebec City in 1608, the French eventually arrived at the Great Lakes, which flow into the sea via that river. Priests and fur traders—the legendary Black Robes, voyageurs, and coureurs de bois—hopscotched one another deep into the North American interior. Their lives today seem almost impossibly violent and hard; the *Jesuit Relations*—the annual reports and correspondence of the Catholic missionaries, from which comes most of what we know—are full of tales of beards plucked out hair by hair, reeds shoved under fingernails, digits sawed off with seashells, and other pleasantries. One who seemed to thrive in the New World, however, was a translator named Jean Nicolet, who arrived in the colony in 1618 at the age of twenty and was promptly sent out by Champlain to spend the winter alone with the "Island Algonquins" and learn their language.

"He tarried with them two years, alone of the French, and always joined the Barbarians in their excursions and journeys," wrote Barthélemy Vimont in a posthumous tribute to Nicolet in 1643. "He often passed seven or eight days without food, and once, full seven weeks with no other nourishment than a little bark from the trees."

While living among the "Island Algonquins" Nicolet traveled with a delegation of four hundred of their warriors and leaders to make peace with the Iroquois. Long before the arrival of Europeans there had been no love lost between the mostly Algonquin-speaking peoples of the Great Lakes and the five-nation Iroquois League, whose own homeland was centered in what is now upstate New York. When the French first arrived in the New World, one of the Huron and Montagnais Indians' first requests to their new friend Samuel de Champlain was that he bring his French soldiers and guns and help attack the powerful and "bloodthirsty" Iroquois League to the south.

Champlain obliged them in 1609, going with some Hurons down to Lake Champlain. "I rested my musket against my cheek, and aimed directly at one of the three chiefs," Champlain later wrote in his journal about the resulting battle. "With the same shot, two fell to the ground; and one of their men was so wounded that he died some time after. I had loaded my musket with four balls."

Champlain's Algonquin allies raised a tremendous cheer, but the standard wisdom is that the Iroquois, being Iroquois, never forgot. "It was an evil hour for Canada," wrote Francis Parkman, the greatest chronicler of the forest wars that burned off and on for the next century and a half. "My pen can no longer express the fury of the Iroquois," wrote the French missionary Father Ragueneau to his superiors in France in 1650, "it shrinks from the repeated portrayal of such scenes of cruelty, to which our eyes cannot become familiarized any more than our feelings."

Champlain's hasty intervention in the ancient rivalry was ill-advised, but the Iroquois had better reasons than revenge for contesting French influence. For nearly as long as the people of the Great Lakes and the St. Lawrence had been trading with the French, the Iroquois had been selling furs to the Dutch. In 1609, *Half Moon*, a small ship owned by the Dutch East India Company, sailed up the river now named after its captain, Henry Hudson. They anchored near Albany, which was as far as was possible to sail on the incoming tide.

"The people of the Countrie came flocking aboord, and brought us Grapes and Pompions [pumpkins], which wee bought for trifles," a crew member named Robert Juet noted in his journal. "And many brought us Bevers skinnes, and Otters skinnes, which wee bought for Beades, Knives, and Hatchets. So we rode there all night."

The Indians who greeted *Half Moon* were almost certainly from the easternmost Iroquois nation, who called themselves the kaynekero-nu, or "people of the place of flint." The Massachusett nation called them the Mohawks, the name that ultimately stuck, and meant "man-eaters." In 1614, the Dutch established their first permanent trading post at Albany and trading began in earnest. From that point on, any pelt going down the Mohawk River in Iroquois canoes to the Dutch on the Hudson River was one not going down the St. Lawrence River in Huron canoes to the French, and vice versa.

This all seems a long way away from the Mississippi. Neither the Hurons nor the Iroquois lived primarily in the basin, and the negotiations that Nicolet facilitated most likely took place in a longhouse at the Iroquois League's "capitol," Onondaga, in upstate New York. In ways that none of the participants could have imagined at the time, however, the parley was an early act in a long drama that would ultimately determine the political future of the Mississippi basin and, with it, North America. The homeland of the Iroquois League put them within easy range of five

John Carter Brown Library, Providence, R.I.

Sa Ga Yeath Qua Pieth Ton, Iroquois leader who visited England in 1710.

great American waterways: the Great Lakes; the Mohawk River, which flows east into the Hudson; the upper Susquehanna, which flows south into the Chesapeake; the Delaware, which flows south into Delaware Bay; and the Allegheny, which flows west via the Ohio into the Mississippi. This strategic position gave them tremendous reach in the competition for furs, which could be exchanged for guns and other European manufactures. The Dutch were soon replaced by the English, but the balance of power between the Iroquois and Algonquin and a shifting mix of European clients and partners—be they French, Dutch, British, or American—was the hinge on which the fate of the Mississippi swung until well after the American Revolution.

The temporary peace that Nicolet brokered between the Iroquois and Algonquin allowed the French explorations on the Great Lakes to continue unabated. Nicolet went to live among the Nipissing on the Ottawa River, where, according to the *Jesuit Relations*, "he passed for one of that nation, taking part in the very frequent councils of those tribes, having his own separate cabin and household, and fishing and trading for himself." While living there, he heard stories of a strange nation of people far to the west who were neither Algonquin speakers, like the Huron and the Nipissing, nor Iroquoian, like their enemies. The Hurons told Nicolet that these people lived near stinking water, or "Winnebago," and called them such.

The Hurons probably knew more about the Winnebago than they were letting on. The trade in seashells and coastal products for copper and other exotics from the interior was ancient, and long before the French or Dutch arrived on the scene the Huron had controlled the steady flow of goods. Champlain discovered this himself when he first made his way up the Ottawa River to the Huron Country in 1615. The Hurons, he said, "go in troops to various regions and countries, where they traffic with other nations, distant four or five hundred leagues."

The French fantasized that perhaps at last this stinking water of the Winnebagos would turn out to be salt water. From the *Jesuit Relations*: "some of the French call them the 'Nation of Stinkards,' because the Algonquin word 'ouinipeg' signifies 'bad-smelling water,' and they apply this name to the water of the salt sea,—so that these peoples are called Ouinipigou because they come from the shores of a sea about which we have no knowledge; and hence they ought not to be called the nation of Stinkards, but the nation of the sea."

Despite the fantastic wealth of furs that the discovery of the Great Lakes had afforded the French, there was an ongoing sense of disappointment in Quebec and Paris that each of the enormous bodies of water they discovered in their explorations proved to be freshwater. Just as the grand Spanish invasions of the previous century were driven by a plausible but ultimately chimerical notion that another Inca or Aztec empire lay waiting for them in North America somewhere, the French were obsessed with the idea of a northern sea passage to Asia. Champlain wasted little time, therefore, when he got wind of the Stinkards. Though he had stopped his own exploring in 1620 to administer the colony from his fort at Quebec, in 1634 he sent Nicolet to find this "nation called People of the Sea."

Nicolet "embarked in the Huron country, with seven Savages; and they passed by many small nations," is how the *Jesuit Relations* describes Nicolet's long canoe voyage from Quebec some twelve hundred miles west to Green Bay (or, possibly, through Sault Ste. Marie to the eastern end of Lake Superior). "When they arrived at their destination, they fastened two sticks in the earth, and hung gifts thereon, so as to relieve these tribes from the notion of mistaking them for enemies to be massacred."

The people in question naturally didn't call themselves the Stinkards any more than the Mohawks called themselves the Cannibals. They called themselves the Hochungara or O-chunk-o-raw (today's Ho-Chunk), which means "speakers of the parent language." The parent language they spoke (and speak) was from the Siouan family, and the Ho-Chunk are related to the Iowa, the Omaha, the Oto, and the other probable Lakota heirs to Cahokia and the Mississippian culture. Some have suggested as well that the Ho-Chunk may be descendants of the effigy mound builders, who were gradually "Mississippianized" by the Cahokian outposts at Azatlan and elsewhere. That the Ho-Chunk knew of European trade goods before Nicolet's arrival is evident from the *Jesuit Relations*, which point out that they were excited to hear from Nicolet's advance man that an actual European was approaching.

"They dispatched several young men to meet the Maitouirinious,—that is to say, 'the wonderful man.' They meet him; they escort him, and carry all his baggage."

In the hope that he would, with luck, find China somewhere in Wisconsin, Nicolet had packed suitably for a potential audience with the

Great Khan. "He wore a grand robe of China damask, all strewn with flowers and birds of many colours." He also packed two handguns, which he apparently fired in the air soon after disembarking from his canoe. Metal trinkets and knives the Ho-Chunk may have seen, but firearms were another matter.

"No sooner did they perceive him than the women and children fled, at the sight of a man who carried thunder in both hands,—for thus they called the two pistols that he held. The news of his coming quickly spread to the places round about, and there assembled four or five thousand men. Each of the chief men made a feast for him, and at one of these banquets they served at least six score Beavers."

Once again, Nicolet managed to broker a peace between the Algonquin Hurons and their neighbors, improving the prospects for trade for the French colony. He did not, however, make it across the divide to whatever mysterious water—stinking or otherwise—lay to the west. Just as important to those in Quebec and Paris who held out hope for a northwest passage, however, Nicolet did not find proof that the longed-for sea did *not* exist.

"I will say, in passing, that it is highly probable one can descend through the second great lake of the Hurons, and through the tribes that we have named, into this sea that he was seeking," wrote the head of the French Jesuit mission to his superiors some six years later. "Sieur Nicolet, who has advanced farthest into these so distant countries, has assured me that, if he had sailed three days' journey farther upon a great river which issues from this lake, he would have found the sea. Now I have strong suspicions that this is the sea which answers to that North of New Mexico, and that from this sea there would be an outlet towards Japan and China"—in other words, the Pacific.

Most historians assume the three-day journey that Nicolet spoke of, but did not take, was up the Fox River out of Green Bay. This leads over the divide between the Great Lakes system and the Wisconsin River, which flows into the Mississippi. Some argue that Nicolet's proposed route may have been farther west on Lake Superior, to a dead end. There's no way to know for sure, however, because Nicolet's own journals were lost in a canoeing accident in 1642 in which he himself drowned. Despite a lifetime on the lakes, he never learned to swim.

12

IN THE IROQUOIS LONGHOUSE

After Nicolet's initial foray west, the Iroquois League made sure that no one else from New France would manage to get back to Green Bay and over the divide into the Mississippi basin for another thirty-five years. They attacked their northern neighbors in earnest in the early 1540s, as part of an ongoing campaign to expand their trapping territory and control the fur trade generally. With the added power of guns bought from the Dutch in Albany, they had already all but eliminated the Mahican tribe on their eastern frontier in Connecticut. With their Hudson River homeland nearly trapped dry of beaver, in 1538 the Iroquois drove the Wenro out of the Allegheny River area on their western frontier. The remnants of both of these former neighbors of the Iroquois tribes fled north to the Great Lakes and west into the Mississippi watershed.

It's important to remember that only one side—the French—took notes, but the *Jesuit Relations* of the years of the "Beaver Wars" are singularly gruesome and detailed. The case of Father Joseph Bressny, who was captured by the Iroquois along with several Huron, is perhaps extreme, but not unique in the annals. Once the raiders had their prisoner safely away:

The Father was stripped quite naked; and when the Savages had ranged themselves in two lines, facing each other, and armed with cudgels, he was ordered to march the first of all through the ranks of the band. No sooner had he lifted his foot than one of the Iroquois seized him by the left hand, and with a knife inflicted a deep gash between the third and the little fingers; and then the others discharged on him a shower of blows with cudgels, and led him thus to the cabins.

There they made him ascend a scaffold (raised about six feet from the ground),—quite naked, bathed in his own blood, that flowed from nearly every part of his body, and exposed to a cold wind that congealed his blood on his skin; and they ordered him to sing during the feast that they gave to those who had brought in the prisoners.

When the feast was over, the warriors withdrew and left the Father and his companions in the hands of the young men, who made them descend from the scaffold, whereon they had stood for two hours, exposed to the jeers of these Barbarians. When they had come down, they were made to dance, after their fashion. But, as the Father did not do it well, they struck him, goaded him, and tore out his hair.

The burning and poking and hair-pulling and finger-chopping went on day after day for more than a month, all carefully cataloged in the Jesuit report. Father Bressny was hung upside down from trees by his feet, and forced to eat filth, and "made to suffer in places and ways concerning which propriety will not allow us to write."

All these sufferings reduced him to such a state that he became so offensive and noisome to the smell, that all kept away from him as from carrion and approached only to torment him. He was covered with pus and filth, and his sores were alive with maggots. With all this, he could hardly find any one who would give him a little Indian corn boiled in water. The blows that he had received caused an abscess to form on his thigh, that allowed him no rest,—which was, moreover, difficult to obtain on account of the hardness of the ground, on which he stretched his body, that was only skin and bone.

He did not know how he could succeed in opening his abscess, but God guided the hand of a Savage—who wished to stab him three times with a knife—so that the Savage struck him directly on the abscess, whence flowed an abundance of pus and blood, and thus he was cured.

Eventually Bressny's captors got bored and gave him to an old woman whose son had been killed in the wars by the Huron allies of the French. Her daughters, however, were horrified at the sight of him. What's more, with no fingers he was fairly useless, so she sold him to the Dutch, which is how his story got out.

The Jesuits didn't expend as many words in their annual reports on the treatment afforded Iroquois prisoners taken during the Beaver Wars. They didn't pretend their allies were any kinder to prisoners, however. Of an Iroquois prisoner taken by the Hurons, all that is said in the *Jesuit Relations* is "they commenced to treat him in a barbarous manner." Suffice it to say that neither side was queasy when it came to violence, or cuisine or medicine:

> It was quite true that one of those three Iroquois, on being captured, had stabbed with his knife the Huron who had seized him; and that the wound was considered mortal. But it was not so, although his lung was badly injured, and a portion of it protruded. The surgeon cut this off; and, strange to say, when he threw it on the ground, a Huron picked it up, roasted it, and gave it to the wounded man to eat. He swallowed it, singing: "That is very strange medicine."

By all rights, the Iroquois League should have been easily subdued. They were surrounded on all sides by Algonquin-speaking enemies that often outnumbered them. Perhaps because of their underdog status, however, the Iroquois were incredibly brave and, thanks to the Dutch, they were far better armed than the Hurons and other Algonquin peoples of the Great Lakes. As important, they were organized. Though the five nations didn't always agree with one another on policy or strategy, they were better able to coordinate their efforts than their enemies. Finally, the strategic location of their homeland on so many waterways gave them an ability to strike at will over large distances.

The Iroquois' usual method of warfare was a blitzkrieg-style surprise attack, after which they would disappear—until the next raid. By the end of the 1640s, they had fairly well destroyed the Huron, completely erasing major villages and taking prisoners by the thousands. Prisoners—particularly women and children—were often assimilated into the Iroquois, while the rest of the once-great nation was driven into exile in

Wisconsin. By the end of the 1650s, the large Erie and the Neutral nations were similarly dispatched with, as were the Petun and the Tobacco. The once lightly populated region of Wisconsin and the upper Mississippi River valley was becoming something of a refugee territory. In the 1660s and '70s the Iroquois concentrated their efforts on the Miami and Shawnee of the Ohio River valley, driving most of them across the Mississippi and leaving the Ohio Country largely underpopulated.

Only the Susquehanna Nation, to the south, seemed able to resist the Iroquois and even push back against them. Part of the Susquehanna's success against the expanding empire of the Dutch-armed Iroquois was thanks to help from the expanding empire of the English. Specifically, the colony of Maryland supplied the Susquehanna with arms and ammunition as a bulwark against the Iroquois. Of even greater consequence to Iroquois aspirations, the English in 1664 took possession of New York. Now cut off from their Dutch arms dealers, the Iroquois made peace with the French—at least temporarily, that is, until they could engineer some kind of workable arrangement with the new power at the mouth of the Hudson.

The French, meanwhile, had become somewhat more assertive. Louis XIV, who had been on the throne of France since the age of four, took the reins of control into his own hands in 1661 and let it be known that he was willing to back up his imperial ambitions with a few troops. Expeditions under the command of fur traders were sent to the far corners of the Great Lakes in search of mines and other potential industries, but all they came back with were more rumors of a big river on the other side of the watershed.

The Jesuit missionaries, too, had followed their refugee flocks west. One in particular, Father Claude-Jean Allouez, sent back an interesting report of his trip to the "Bay of Stinkards," in 1669. When he arrived at the Fox River, which flows into the head of Green Bay, a feast was given in his honor. The mood was not joyous, however, for even though the nearest European settlement was a thousand miles away, the signs of dislocation were everywhere.

When all were seated, and after some had filled a dish with powdered tobacco, an Old man arose and, turning to me, with both hands full of tobacco which he took from the dish, harangued me as follows: "This is well, black Gown, that thou comest to visit us. Take pity on us; thou art a Manitou; we give thee tobacco to smoke. The Nadouessious and the Iroquois are eating us; take pity on us. We are often ill, our children are dying, we are hungry. Hear me, Manitou; I give thee tobacco to smoke. Let the earth give us corn, and the rivers yield us fish; let not disease kill us any more, or famine treat us any longer so harshly!" At each desire the Old men who were present uttered a loud "Oh!" in response.

The priest hastened to tell the gathered that not he, but perhaps his God in heaven, could cure the disease, end the famine, and turn back the Iroquois. He gave them some hatchets and knives and beads and taught them to pray.

"These people are settled in a very attractive place, where beautiful Plains and Fields meet the eye as far as one can see," Father Allouez reported. "Their river leads by a six day's voyage to the great River named Messi-Sipi."

This is the first known mention of the river by the familiar name in a European document. The word, in Ojibwe/Algonquin, does not mean "Father of Waters," but rather something closer to "big long river." Another report from the time, one that did not call the river by any name, painted an intoxicating picture of the lands to be found down the river, particularly for a colony like New France, where the winters were so long and harsh that raising enough food to be self-sufficient was a constant problem.

It is a country which has none of the severity of our winters, but enjoys a climate that is always temperate—a continual Spring and Autumn, as it were. The soil there is so fertile that one could almost say of it, within bounds, what the Israelite discoverers said of the Promised land; for, to mention the Indian corn only, it puts forth a stalk of such extraordinary thickness and height that one would take it for a tree, while it bears ears two feet long with grains that resemble in size our large Muscatel grapes. NO Moose or Beavers are seen there, as they live only in cold countries; but, to make up for this, Deer, Buffalo, wild Hogs, and another Species of large animal wholly unknown to US, inhabit those beautiful forests, which are like so many Orchards, consisting almost wholly of fruit-trees.

But where this Messi-sipi went, no European could say for sure. "Their villages are situated along a beautiful river which serves to carry the people down to the great Lake (for so they call the Sea), where they trade with Europeans who pray as we do, and use Rosaries, as well as Bells for calling to Prayers," reported Father Hierosme Lalemant in 1662. "According to the description given us, we judge them to be Spaniards. That Sea is doubtless either the Bay of St. Esprit in the Gulf of Mexico, on the coast of Florida; or else the Vermilion Sea [Sea of Cortés], on the coast of new Granada, in the great South Sea [Pacific]."

The idea that the Mississippi flowed into the Pacific was not as far-fetched as it sounds today. No European had seen the Rocky Mountains north of New Mexico or Arizona by that point. The de Soto–inspired maps of the period, meanwhile, showed mountains running east to west across the middle of the continent. On most of these the Rio Espiritu Santo, as the Spanish called the Mississippi, entered the Gulf closer to Galveston than to its true location. Whether Father Lalemant had heard somewhere that a great river flowed into the head of the Vermilion Sea, as the Colorado River does, is unknowable, but it was well known that the Spanish were already on the Pacific, so the presence of fellow Catholics at the mouth proved nothing.

In Quebec, the idea that one might sail unimpeded to the Pacific via the Great Lakes was by now largely discredited. The western outlines of the Great Lakes were fairly well known by that point. There was also no practical way to sail directly from the North Atlantic into the Lakes at their eastern end, due to rapids and Niagara Falls. Still, the possibility of a river route to the Pacific from somewhere near the western end of the lakes was tantalizing both from the point of view of a trade route to Asia and for the potentially vast new farming and fur-trapping territory that such a discovery would open up. There were also the usual rumors of "numerous gold mines."

With that in mind, Louis XIV's royal representative in Quebec, Jean Talon, asked a Canadian-born trader named Louis Joliet to put together a private expedition to find out more. Specifically, he was "to discover the sea of the South by way of the country of the Mashoutins and the great river which they call Michissipi which is thought to empty into the sea of California."

Though the trip was officially sanctioned, the crown invested no

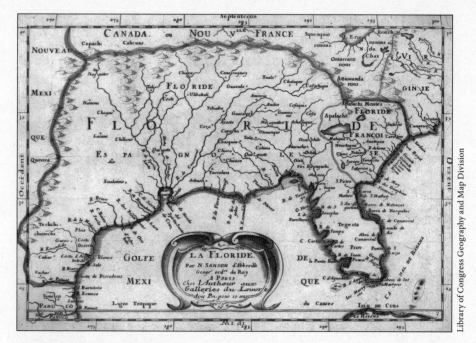

Map from 1657 of the watershed.

money in the operation and it was entirely funded by Joliet and his seven partners. They were expected to make a profit on whatever furs and other wealth they might bring back from the unknown river, but Joliet may have had other motives as well. His older brother, Lucian, also a fur trader, had disappeared in the western wilderness and a desire to find his lost sibling may have driven Joliet to take on the assignment. Among the seven voyageurs he took with him was his younger brother, Zacharie. After a late start from Montreal, the eight canoe men arrived in Michilimackinac—Mackinaw, in the straits between Lakes Huron and Michigan—on December 8 and informed the Jesuit father Jacques Marquette that he was ordered to accompany them.

Despite the power of the Jesuits, or more likely because of it, there was ambivalence in the halls of power in Paris about the religious order. The king's powerful minister of finance, Jean-Baptiste Colbert, advised the monarch "to diminish quietly and imperceptibly the religious of both sexes, who produce only useless people in this world, and very often devils for the next world." Still, Jesuit power in New France was such that it was inconceivable to leave them out of such an important project as Joliet's.

Joliet's own attitude toward the Black Robes is enigmatic. At the age of seventeen he entered the Jesuit order, with an apparent intention to become a priest. He spoke and read Latin and was a church organist by the age of nineteen. When he turned twenty, however, he withdrew from the seminary for reasons that are unknown. What is known is that the bishop of New France lent him the money to get started in the fur trade—to become a coureur de bois, or woodland runner—an occupation that in reputation is as far from the pious "cross-bearing" of the priests as can be imagined.

"The life of the coureurs de bois is spent in idleness and dissolute living," wrote a colonial official. "They sleep, smoke, drink brandy whatever its cost, gamble, debauch the wives and daughters of the Indians. They commit a thousand contemptible deeds. Gambling, drinking, and women often consume all their capital and the profits of their voyages. They live in complete independence and account to no one for their actions. They acknowledge no superior, no judge, no law, no police, no subordination."

For his part, Father Marquette was thrilled to join the expedition to the Mississippi. He had, on his own, been trying to figure out a way to make a trip to preach among the Illinois Indians, some of whom he had met during his travels on the Great Lakes. Michilimackinac lies at the great crossroads of the upper Great Lakes, and while Joliet and Marquette waited for spring, they questioned the Indians of various nations who came through. (Marquette spoke six native languages, and Joliet and some of the other voyageurs spoke a few more.) From all that they gleaned, they made a crude map and decided their best route was through Green Bay and up the Fox River.

Finally, on May 17, 1673, the ice was gone and they were ready to go. "Indian Corn, with some smoked meat, constituted all our provisions," wrote Marquette. "With these we Embarked—Monsiur Jollyet and myself, with 5 men—in 2 Bark Canoes, fully resolved to do and suffer everything for so glorious an Undertaking." Spirits were high: "we Joyfully Plied our paddles on a portion of Lake huron, on That of the Illinois [Lake Michigan] and on the bay des Puants [Green Bay]."

Like Nicolet before him, Joliet's journals and notes were lost in a freak canoe accident after the expedition, though he himself was unhurt. Most of what is known about the voyage, therefore, comes from Marquette's reports to his superiors. Fortunately, he is an observant traveler,

Courtesy of the Metropolitan Museum of Art, New York, Gilman Collection, ART 348816

Kno-Shr, Kansas Chief, by John H. Fitzgibbon, 1853.

both of native custom and of geography, and a good storyteller. At the head of Green Bay he reported on wild rice harvests, snake cures, and rumors of river monsters to come. The village of the Maskoutens, like much of Wisconsin, had become a hodgepodge of refugee nations living together, and he reported that the Miamis "are the most civil, the most liberal, and the most shapely," while the Kikabous and Maskoutens, by contrast, "seem peasants." They hired two guides to show them the portage route.

"On the following day, the tenth of June, two Miamis who were given us as guides embarked with us, in the sight of a great crowd, who could not sufficiently express their astonishment at the sight of seven frenchmen, alone and in two Canoes, daring to undertake so extraordinary and hazardous an Expedition."

At the headwaters of the Wisconsin River the two guides turned back, "leaving us alone in this Unknown country," wrote Marquette. "Thus we left the Waters flowing to Quebec, 4 or 500 leagues from here, to float on Those that would thenceforward Take us through strange lands."

They paused at the edge of the new watershed and said good-bye to the guides. They prayed together to the Virgin Immaculate, asking that she protect them and give them success.

"And, after mutually encouraging one another, we entered our Canoes."

13

THE AMERICAN BOTTOM

My son and I put our kayaks into the Mississippi not far from the great mounds of Cahokia on a splendid mid-June morning, not knowing precisely how far we were going to go down the Father of Waters. We didn't know whether we were going to camp every night on islands and sandbars, or stay in the small towns the maps suggested were along the way. We didn't know whether we were going to paddle hard to put miles under the hull like the lapsed novitiate Joliet (him?) and the earnest Marquette (me?), or whether we would just drift along like Huck (him?) and Jim (me?).

It didn't matter, we figured. We hadn't come to the Mississippi to prove or conquer anything, but to see the great mounds at Cahokia and the Gateway Arch of St. Louis, to genuflect up in Hannibal at the various shrines to Twain, and to see a little minor league baseball in Davenport. Mostly, though, we came to see where the biggest river in America would take two generations of supplicants in plastic boats with a couple of summer weeks in which to explore.

The Old Man, of course, was rolling on toward New Orleans and beyond, but we had no intention of going even a tenth that far. I had a vague goal of getting to Cairo and the mouth of the Ohio, or maybe beyond to Quigaltam and Natchez. All we knew for certain was that we were headed toward that next corner there, and then around it to whatever might lie beyond. With our holds full of power bars and instant oatmeal, we were hoping for sunshine but ready for rain.

Usually with human-powered trips, be they walking, hiking, paddling, or cycling, there's an extended warm-up period—hours or days, even—where you are getting into the rhythm of the trip, letting go of where you came from, falling into the vibe. The process can be slow. "I am alarmed when it happens that I have walked a mile into the woods bodily, without getting there in spirit," Thoreau wrote in "Walking." "But it sometimes happens that I can not shake off the village."

Such is not the case, however, with launching a small boat on the Mississippi, at least if you put in below St. Louis where the river is at last set relatively free from the upstream dams of the Army Corps. As soon as you are in the coffee-colored water, you know immediately that you belong to the Mississippi River.

It commands every sense. There's the sound a truly big river makes— not loud but nonetheless vast and soothing, more like wind over grasses than a waterfall. There is an odor to the river as well, vaguely sweet and earthy, though oddly more like the sea than like a mountain stream or a woodland lake. In no time, it seemed that Cahokia and St. Louis were lost far behind us, as if removed not just geographically but in time as well. We were away.

Three sounds regularly punctuate the background music of the river. The least common is the wail of the freight trains hauling their loads along the tracks that run parallel to the river on the Missouri side. The arrival of trains in the nineteenth century is often said to have been a death knell for the era of fabulous steamboats. Today the songs of the trains are neither unpleasant nor particularly lonesome; with miles of riverbank on both sides undisturbed by houses or other visible signs of human impact, the occasional passing trains seem to be friendly, if oblivious, fellow travelers.

The same could be said for the much more common barges that ply the river in both directions loaded with grain, gravel, giant rocks, oil, and other bulk commodities. Visions of these football-field-size beasts swamping and slap-chopping our tiny boats had cost me sleep in the weeks leading up to our trip, and I certainly would not advise playing chicken with a sixteen-barge tow in a fog, or traveling around a bend in midchannel. But without diminishing the importance of vigilance and common nautical sense, there is nothing in their wakes to alarm a moderately experienced kayaker. A canoeist might be advised to spend some time on his or her knees, however.

The most common sound is the surprisingly loud complaining of the river when it drops over and around the various contrivances of the Army Corps. There may be no dams across the Mississippi below St. Louis, but there are thousands of other manipulations installed over the years as part of the effort to keep the channel open to barge traffic. We had been advised before putting in to wait for the river to drop below fifteen feet at the St. Louis gauge, which would have brought most of the groins and revetments to the surface, but we were happier with a reading of eighteen feet because the higher water covers the miscellaneous rock works, giving the visual impression of a free river. What's more, the quickening drop over the structures, followed by the clot of whirlpools and eddies, are interludes of adrenaline, which is to say fun.

The water was not so high, however, that the long sandbars at the downstream ends of islands were covered. Late in the afternoon on most days we pulled our boats up on a likely point and spread a large tarp to serve as a first defense of sorts against the thin layer of Mississippi mud that lay caked over virtually everything. We pitched our tent and gathered firewood for a small fire that served more for atmospheric purposes than warmth on the long summer evenings. Books came out of dry bags, and a journal, but mostly I found it difficult, even after a long day spent on the water, to take my eyes off the river. It slid on by us on both sides, leaving the odd impression at times that the islet itself might be moving upstream, as if we had pitched our homes on the stern of a cosmic canoe headed north.

In the mornings, when we rose and rekindled the fire, the river was still there of course, flowing as if nothing had changed and no one had one less day in which to live in this hypnotic world of green and blue than he did the day before. "C'mon, let's go, time's wasting," the river murmured, a glib and sarcastic chorus, it seemed to me, for an immortal to sing out as it passed continuously by us without ever passing us by.

The best thing about the water level that June was that the chutes and sloughs that pass behind and around the various islands had adequate water for passage, and it was in those narrower places—though they were often big enough to be important rivers in any other part of the country—

that we occasionally spotted deer, beaver, small water snakes, large herons, and birds of prey. We looked for, but never saw, the coyotes we heard howling at night, one time much closer to our campsites than we might have liked. We did, however, surprise a family of local catfishermen—the only other recreationalists we saw on the entire voyage.

"Hey, come on over," they called out from their campsite. "We got fresh fish frying and cold beer," a very good sounding combo indeed.

"You ever fish in those boats?" "You want a cigarette?" "You're from where, you say?"

14

THE ILLINOIS COUNTRY

Not far upstream from where we sat in our kayaks trading news with the friendly locals onshore, Joliet and Marquette saw their first signs of the Illinois Indians that Marquette, in particular, was hoping to find. For the first 180 miles from the mouth of the Wisconsin River, the expedition saw buffalo and sturgeon and catfish and wildcats, but no signs of human habitation. Then somewhere just above the confluence with the Missouri, which Marquette called the Pekitanoui—or muddy—they stopped to look at a path leading from the water's edge into the prairie. Joliet and Marquette left the rest of the men with the canoes, went ashore, and followed the path until they could see the village. In the distance they could see another village, and another beyond that.

By that time 130 years had passed since the last documented European visit to the river had ended with de Soto's army fleeing downstream under a hail of arrows. In the intervening years war, trade, disease, and dislocation had redrawn large portions of the map of the upper Mississippi and Ohio valleys. Yet the watershed had remained entirely a Native American world, albeit with an increasing supply of European weapons, booze, clothing, and trinkets in the mix. Now, though, there were two canoes of Frenchmen floating down out of Wisconsin, and there would be no such hiatus following the return to Quebec of Joliet and Marquette. It was the beginning of direct contact.

Father Marquette was surprised and pleased that even here on the previously unvisited Mississippi, the Indians seemed to recognize the newcomers. "On hearing the shout, the savages quickly issued from their Cabins," he wrote later, "having probably recognized us as Frenchmen, especially when they saw a black gown."

But the celibate man in the long black skirt could not make any sense of the Illinois men who dressed like women, sang but didn't dance, and were highly esteemed spiritual leaders in the councils of the powerful.

> I know not through what superstition some Ilinois [sic], as well as some Nadouessi, while still young, assume the garb of women, and retain it throughout their lives. There is some mystery in this, For they never marry and glory in demeaning themselves to do everything that the women do. They go to war, however, but can use only clubs, and not bows and arrows, which are the weapons proper to men. They are present at all the juggleries, and at the solemn dances in honor of the Calumet; at these they sing, but must not dance. They are summoned to the Councils, and nothing can be decided without their advice. Finally, through their profession of leading an Extraordinary life, they pass for Manitous,—That is to say, for Spirits,—or persons of Consequence.

Most of the time, however, Father Marquette refrained from passing overt judgment and described the people he met on the Mississippi River in 1674 with a degree of subtlety that was no doubt a product of his long years of experience living among other Native Americans along the Great Lakes. His description of the first group of Illinois they met is a rare image of life on the river before the deluge of Europeans.

> Having no cause for distrust, as we were only two men, and had given them notice of our arrival—they deputed four old men to come and speak to us.
>
> Two of these bore tobacco-pipes, finely ornamented and Adorned with various feathers. They walked slowly, and raised their pipes toward the sun, seemingly offering them to it to smoke—without, however, saying a word. They spent a rather long time in covering the short distance between their village and us. Finally, when they had drawn near, they stopped to Consider us attentively.

I was reassured when I observed these Ceremonies, which with them are performed only among friends; and much more so when I saw them clad in Cloth, for I judged thereby that they were our allies. I therefore spoke to them first, and asked them who they were. They replied that they were Ilinois; and, as a token of peace, they offered us their pipes to smoke. They afterward invited us to enter their Village, where all the people impatiently awaited us. These pipes for smoking tobacco are called in this country Calumets. . . .

At the Door of the Cabin in which we were to be received was an old man, who awaited us in a rather surprising attitude, which constitutes a part of the Ceremonial that they observe when they receive Strangers. This man stood erect, and stark naked, with his hands extended and lifted toward the sun, As if he wished to protect himself from its rays, which nevertheless shone upon his face through his fingers. When we came near him, he paid us This Compliment: "How beautiful the sun is, O frenchman, when thou comest to visit us! All our village awaits thee, and thou shalt enter all our Cabins in peace."

Having said this, he made us enter his own, in which were a crowd of people; they devoured us with their eyes, but, nevertheless, observed profound silence. We could, however, hear these words, which were addressed to us from time to time in a low voice: "How good it is, My brothers, that you should visit us."

After We had taken our places, the usual Civility of the country was paid to us, which consisted in offering us the Calumet. This must not be refused, unless one wishes to be considered an Enemy, or at least uncivil; it suffices that one make a pretense of smoking. While all the elders smoked after us, in order to do us honor, we received an invitation on behalf of the great Captain of all the Ilinois to proceed to his Village where he wished to hold a Council with us. We went thither in a large Company, For all these people, who had never seen any frenchmen among Them, could not cease looking at us. They Lay on The grass along the road; they preceded us, and then retraced their steps to come and see us Again. All this was done noiselessly, and with marks of great respect for us.

When we reached the Village of the great Captain, We saw him at the entrance of his Cabin, between two old men,—all three erect and naked, and holding their Calumet turned toward the sun. He harangued us. In a few words, congratulating us upon our arrival. He afterward offered us his Calumet, and made us smoke while we entered his Cabin, where we received all their usual kind Attentions.

Marquette had been in enough lodges and camps to know the etiquette of oratory and gift giving that such occasions required. When their host had finished his welcoming words, therefore, it was his turn to speak and offer gifts. He had four gifts, most likely beads, hatchets, or knives. With the presentation of each one, he made a separate statement.

With his first gift he wanted the gathered Illinois people to know that he and Joliet and their company were traveling peacefully down to the sea. Second, he had been sent by "God, who had created them," to come and teach them the new religion and that "It was for Them to acknowledge and obey" God. Third, he hoped they understood that it was the king of France who had "restored peace everywhere" and "subdued the Iroquois."

"Peace everywhere" was an extremely optimistic reading at best of the current situation south of the Great Lakes, but one that the Illinois apparently were too polite to dispute at such a solemn occasion. Marquette himself knew better, noting later in his report that the Illinois were in the business of slave trading and that they had guns, "which they buy from our savage allies who Trade with our French. They use them especially to inspire, through their noise and smoke, terror in their Enemies; the latter do not use guns, and have never seen any, since they live too Far toward the West."

They are warlike, and make themselves dreaded by the Distant tribes to the south and west, whither they go to procure Slaves; these they barter, selling them at a high price to other Nations, in exchange for other Wares. Those very Distant Savages against whom they war have no Knowledge of Europeans; neither do they know anything of iron, or of Copper, and they have only stone Knives.

When the Illinois depart to go to war, the whole village must be notified by a loud Shout, which is uttered at the doors of their Cabins, the night and The Morning before their departure. The Captains are distinguished from the warriors by wearing red Scarfs. These are made, with considerable Skill, from the Hair of bears and wild cattle. They paint their faces with red ocher, great quantities of which are found at a distance of some days' journey from the village.

When Father Marquette presented his last gift to the leaders of the Illinois nation he made a simple request. He hoped his new friends would tell them all they knew about the river downstream.

After Marquette was finished, the "Captain" of the Illinois Indians thanked him with another elaborate recitation of how the river had never been calmer, the crops never so healthy, the tobacco never so tasty, or the sun ever as bright as it was now that "thee, Black Gown, and thee, O frenchman," had visited. He offered the travelers one of his sons, to be their slave, and presented Marquette with "an altogether mysterious Calumet, upon which they place more value than upon a Slave." The pipe itself was of carved red stone, probably in the shape of an animal, and the stem was ornamented with feathers and the heads and necks of birds with bright plumage.

> There is nothing more mysterious or more respected among them. Less honor is paid to the Crowns and scepters of Kings than the Savages bestow upon this. It seems to be the God of peace and of war, the Arbiter of life and of death. It has but to be carried upon one's person, and displayed, to enable one to walk safely through the midst of Enemies—who, in the hottest of the Fight, lay down Their arms when it is shown.
>
> For That reason, the Ilinois gave me one, to serve as a safeguard among all the Nations through whom I had to pass during my voyage. There is a Calumet for peace, and one for war, which are distinguished solely by the Color of the feathers with which they are adorned; Red is a sign of war. They also use it to put an end to Their disputes, to strengthen Their alliances, and to speak to Strangers.

After the leader of the Illinois had presented the peace pipe he told the French they were insane to try to go farther down the Mississippi, and announced that it was time to eat. It was, said Marquette, "a great feast, consisting of four dishes, which had to be partaken of in accordance with all their fashions." The first course was a giant platter of sagamité, or corn porridge seasoned with bear fat. When it arrived "The Master of Ceremonies filled a Spoon with sagamité three or 4 times, and put it to my mouth As if I were a little Child. He did The same to Monsieur Jollyet."

Then came a fish course, with three roasted choices on a wooden platter. The third course was "a large dog, that had just been killed; but, when they learned that we did not eat this meat, they removed it from before us." The final course was roasted buffalo. In each case, the guests were hand-fed the best morsels before anyone else partook.

Overall Marquette was impressed with the lifestyle along this stretch of the river:

They live by hunting, game being plentiful in that country, and on indian corn, of which they always have a good crop; consequently, they have never suffered from famine. They also sow beans and melons, which are Excellent, especially those that have red seeds. Their Squashes are not of the best; they dry them in the sun, to eat them during The winter and the spring.

They are liberal in cases of illness, and Think that the effect of the medicines administered to them is in proportion to the presents given to the physician. Their garments consist only of skins; the women are always clad very modestly and very becomingly, while the men do not take the trouble to Cover themselves.

The houses, he said, were "very large," with thatched roofs and floors covered with mats made of woven rushes. There were at least three hundred dwellings in the main town, and many other towns scattered around the surrounding prairie. Everywhere they went the people came out and offered them "Belts, garters, and other articles made of the hair of bears and cattle, dyed red, Yellow, and gray." Both men and women had "shapely" bodies, though some of the women appeared to have been mutilated.

They have several wives, of whom they are Extremely jealous; they watch them very closely, and Cut off Their noses or ears when they misbehave. I saw several women who bore the marks of their misconduct.

More than almost any other feature of the Illinois culture, at least judging from his report back to France, Marquette was fascinated by the dancing he saw and the singing he heard. In particular, he was moved by

Calumet stem decorated with feather.

the ceremony associated with the calumet, or tobacco pipe. It was, in his opinion, as good as any ballet he had seen in France.

The Calumet dance, which is very famous among these peoples, is performed solely for important reasons; sometimes to strengthen peace, or to unite themselves for some great war; at other times, for public rejoicing. Sometimes they thus do honor to a Nation who are invited to be present; sometimes it is danced at the reception of some important personage, as if they wished to give him the diversion of a Ball or a Comedy. In Winter, the ceremony takes place in a Cabin; in Summer, in the open fields.

When the spot is selected, it is completely surrounded by trees, so that all may sit in the shade afforded by their leaves, in order to be protected from the heat of the Sun. A large mat of rushes, painted in various colors, is spread in the middle of the place, and serves as a carpet upon which to place with honor the God of the person who gives the Dance; for each has his own god, which they call their Manitou. This is a serpent, a bird, or other similar thing, of which they have dreamed while sleeping, and in which they place all their confidence for the success of their war, their fishing, and their hunting.

Near this Manitou, and at its right, is placed the Calumet in honor of which the feast is given; and all around it a sort of trophy is made, and the weapons used by the warriors of those Nations are spread, namely: clubs, war-hatchets, bows, quivers, and arrows.

Everything being thus arranged, and the hour of the Dance drawing near, those who have been appointed to sing take the most honorable place under the branches; these are the men and women who are gifted with the best voices, and who sing together in perfect harmony.

Afterward, all come to take their seats in a circle under the branches; but each one, on arriving, must salute the Manitou. This he does by inhaling the smoke, and blowing it from his mouth upon the Manitou, as if he were offering to it incense. Every one, at the outset, takes the Calumet in a respectful manner, and, supporting it with both hands, causes it to dance in cadence, keeping good time with the air of the songs. He makes it execute many differing figures; sometimes he shows it to the whole assembly, turning himself from one side to the other.

After that, he who is to begin the Dance appears in the middle of the assembly, and at once continues this. Sometimes he offers it to the sun, as if he wished the latter to smoke it; sometimes he inclines it toward the earth; again, he makes it spread its wings, as if about to fly; at other times, he puts it near the mouths of those present, that they may smoke. The whole is done in cadence; and this is, as it were, the first Scene of the Ballet.

The second consists of a Combat carried on to the sound of a kind of drum, which succeeds the songs, or even unites with them, harmonizing very well together. The Dancer makes a sign to some warrior to come to take the arms which lie upon the mat, and invites him to fight to the sound of the drums. The latter approaches, takes up the bow and arrows, and the war-hatchet, and begins the duel with the other, whose sole defense is the Calumet.

This spectacle is very pleasing, especially as all is done in cadence; for one attacks, the other defends himself; one strikes blows, the other parries them; one takes to flight, the other pursues; and then he who was fleeing faces about, and causes his adversary to flee. This is done so well—with slow and measured steps, and to the rhythmic sound of the voices and drums—that it might pass for a very fine opening of a Ballet in France.

The third Scene consists of a lofty Discourse, delivered by him who holds the Calumet; for, when the Combat is ended without bloodshed, he recounts the battles at which he has been present, the victories that he has won, the names of the Nations, the places, and the Captives whom he has made. And, to reward him, he who presides at the Dance makes him a present of a fine robe of Beaver-skins, or some other article.

Then, having received it, he hands the Calumet to another, the latter to a third, and so on with all the others, until every one has done his duty; then the President presents the Calumet itself to the Nation that has been invited to the Ceremony, as a token of the everlasting peace that is to exist between the two peoples.

When Joliet and Marquette took their leave of the Illinois village and set off downriver, six hundred townspeople came down to the banks to see them off and wish them well.

15

ADRIFT

We might have seen more wildlife had we gotten up with the dawn and paddled till dusk, but we chose instead to read into the nights by the lights of our headlamps and often slept late in the shade of our tent. Whether this was the influence of my teenaged companion or the lull of sleeping beside the siren song of the river, I can't say.

"One cannot see too many summer sunrises on the Mississippi," Mark Twain wrote, however, and more than once I woke with the dawn and let the boy sleep while I sat by the river to watch the day arrive.

"The dawn creeps in stealthily; the solid walls of black forest soften to gray, and vast stretches of the river open up and reveal themselves; the water is glass-smooth, gives off spectral little wreaths of white mist, there is not the faintest breath of wind, nor stir of leaf; the tranquility is profound and infinitely satisfying," said Twain of his days as a pilot on the early shift. "Then a bird pipes up, another follows, and soon the pipings develop into a jubilant riot of music. You see none of the birds; you simply move through an atmosphere of song which seems to sing itself."

We also might have covered more miles with a stricter schedule, but we stuck instead to our plan of no plan and dawdled with abandon. We slipped down off the continent, along with all manner of everything else that the Mississippi had picked up along the way and brought to where we were at any given moment.

Shoving off in the morning after days on the river and nights on a sandbar is qualitatively different from putting your boat in for the first time. The river plays tricks with your sense of perception: all the previous evening and morning you have been sitting like Buddha under his tree, observing the river roll by against an unmoving backdrop of limestone bluffs and evening or morning sky. The giant barges come and go in both directions, but the motion of the river, from the perspective of your house pitched on sand, seems immutable and constant.

The moment you shove off, however, it is suddenly the land that scrolls by while the water immediately around your hull is strangely still. Apply yourself adequately to the paddle and even the water beneath your hands appears to flow backward, though not as fast as the land onshore. As if attached to a single moving particle of water in the river by some stretchy cord or yoyo string, you zoom ahead during daylight and it all catches up with you overnight. On land the river moves forward; on the river the land scrolls back.

One of the great attractions in the middle of the nineteenth century

Midstream below St. Louis.

Author's photograph

was to pay a fee and go to a dimly lit theater on the Atlantic seaboard, or in Europe, and take a virtual trip up or down the Mississippi via a gigantic panoramic painting that slowly scrolled past the viewer. There were at least five different versions on tour during the 1850s, each claiming to be longer than all the others. Leviathan Panorama of the Mississippi River announced itself as more than four miles long. Grand Panorama of the Mississippi, on the other hand, was "the largest picture ever executed by man," and Mammoth Mississippi Panorama was supposedly three times bigger than all the others.

None were close to as large as advertised, and unfortunately none of the giant scrolls has survived. But from descriptions, it's clear that all were allegorical masterpieces of a sort, full of scenes from history and myth—the Mormon war at Nauvoo, the Trail of Tears, the Indian maiden We-No-Nah who died for love. All the panoramas were also imbued with a triumphal and inevitable vision of American progress, duly narrated and accompanied by music. The river was a metaphor for the young nation to which settlement and "civilization" were coming as surely as middle age follows youth.

Even Thoreau got caught up in the heroic moment. In "Walking," the same essay that begins with the memorable "I wish to speak a word for Nature, for absolute freedom and wildness, as contrasted with a freedom and culture merely civil," and contains the famous dictum "In wildness is the preservation of the world," he also wrote:

> Some months ago I went to see a panorama of the Rhine. It was like a dream of the Middle Ages. I floated down its historic stream in something more than imagination, under bridges built by Romans, and repaired by later heroes, past cities and castles whose very names were music to my ears, and each of which was the subject of legend. . . . They were ruins that interested me chiefly. There seemed to come up from its waters and its vine-clad hills and valleys a hushed music of Crusaders departing for the Holy Land. I floated along under the spell of enchantment, as if I had been transported to an heroic age, and breathed an atmosphere of chivalry.
>
> Soon after, I went to see a panorama of the Mississippi, and as I worked my way up the river in the light of today, and saw the steamboats wooding up, counted the rising cities, gazed on the fresh ruins of

Nauvoo, beheld the Indians moving west across the stream, and, as before I had looked up the Moselle, now looked up the Ohio and the Missouri and heard the legends of Dubuque and of Wenona's Cliff,—still thinking more of the future than of the past or present,—I saw that this was a Rhine stream of a different kind; that the foundations of castles were yet to be laid, and the famous bridges were yet to be thrown over the river; and I felt that this was the heroic age itself, though we know it not, for the hero is commonly the simplest and obscurest of men.

Without diminishing either the wisdom of the bard of Concord or the achievements of the castle builders and bridge engineers to come, Henry was closer to the Mark, I think, when he said, "Everyone must believe something. I believe I'll go canoeing."

Some time during our third morning on the river—or was it the fourth day, or the second afternoon, or fifth . . . ? I'd lost myself again in a silent reverie, allowing the kayak to spin lazily along the great river's western shoreline, like a bright yellow leaf with some kind of exotic beetle perched in a life vest in the middle of it. With the underlying current that was so obvious from shore now masked by our own movement upon it, and with the land scrolling peacefully by on both sides, what came into relief were the counterpoint harmonies within the general flow. There are countless undulations and eddies, boils and bubbles rising up from somewhere—from some *thing*—unseen below the surface of the Mississippi.

The current turned the bow first toward the unbroken line of trees and the muddy banks covered with mysterious animal tracks. Then to the downriver view, with my son's kayak on its own gyre a hundred yards ahead, beneath the limestone bluffs of the Missouri shore. Then across the not-quite-mile-wide river—a line of hazy sky and glassy black water with a thin band of flat green on the far side that looked more like my imagined images of the Amazon than my assumed images of Illinois. Countless swallows dipped and dove. How much time had passed on this particular spiral drift? A half-hour? A million years? Who knew? Who cared?

"Peace, like a river," goes the old hymn.

Until a formerly upstanding tree caught my eye out there in the current of the main channel, about seventy-five yards away. The Mississippi is full of driftwood, large and small, though nowhere near as much as it used to be. Wood falls from any of a thousand million trees up a hundred thousand streams. Father Marquette in 1673 remarked that the Missouri River in particular was a veritable fountain of logs pouring into the Mississippi: "an accumulation of large and entire trees, branches, and floating islands, was issuing from The mouth of The river pekistanouï, with such impetuosity that we could not without great danger risk passing through it. So great was the agitation that the water was very muddy, and could not become clear."

Marquette was not the last navigator to worry about logs. Trees, whether floating, still attached by the roots or otherwise stuck in the riverbed, bobbing up and down, or traveling in great clots—were among the gravest threats to travelers on the river until relatively recently. This stretch my son and I were on, between St. Louis and Cairo, was known in the 1870s as "the graveyard" because there were so many steamboat wrecks, many of them caused by "snags."

It's not every day that you find yourself jealous of a piece of flotsam, but I thought I recognized this particular log from the day before. Something about its stumpy broken-off root sticking up aft and a smaller one forward had made me smile due to its sullen resemblance to the George Caleb Bingham painting "Fur Traders Descending the Missouri." The extent of my early art history education was playing the board game Masterpiece with my sisters, and I'd always bid high for "Fur Traders" just because it was my favorite painting in the game. I thought the person in the middle of the boat was a girl—maybe the trader's girlfriend even—which only made the painting more enticing to my junior high sensibilities.

I now know that Bingham himself titled the painting "French Trader and His Half-Breed Son," and have read several long (winded) essays attesting to the fact that it is as loaded with nineteenth-century metaphors about progress, race, and civilization as any self-respecting half-mile of panorama. I still love it, however, with its strange catlike bear-cub creature chained by a thread in the bow.

Not everything is moving toward the all-consuming sea at the same speed, it turns out, and now this uppity stump with artistic pretensions had somehow found a sweet line of lesser resistance in our mutual slide.

Fur Traders Descending the Missouri by George Caleb Bingham, 1845.

It was cruising right on past me and my son out there in midriver, as if it was late for a board meeting down in Memphis or Baton Rouge. I had no such appointments and had counseled myself by the morning campfire specifically to let go of measuring my existential progress by triangulating the relative position of my fellow drifters in the big river of life. I could not resist the bait, however, and I dug in with my paddle.

"Come on," I said as I passed both son and log, "let's put some muscle into it for a while."

With surprisingly little effort, barely more than letting the weight of the paddle fall into the water on either side, a sea kayak can be kept fairly ripping along in the Mississippi current at a very satisfying seven miles an hour or more. That's faster than a jog and much easier on the knees. In no time the fur-trading log was far behind us and we were speeding on toward . . . toward . . . ?

The satisfaction in outracing a log is rather slim, as it turns out, and after some undeterminable passage of time we declared victory and stopped to take a close look at a long row of boxcars on a siding that appeared to be literally hanging over the bank. There was no one in sight and we could see up and down the river for miles. There was no reason we could think of, in other words, not to beach the kayaks, climb the ladder, and

run along the top of the cars. High over the Mississippi in the June sunshine my boy and I ran the length of the engineless train, jumping the
gaps like Ernest Borgnine and Keith Carradine in *Emperor of the North*
while down below that old man river rolled by. "Above all," Thoreau
wrote near the end of "Walking," "we cannot afford not to live in the
present."

We stopped as often as we wanted to along the river. On the Missouri
side of the river we stopped once to check out whether a dark spot in the
bluff was the opening to a cave—it was not. We paddled up a creek to
Herculaneum, Missouri, and bought ham sandwiches at the general
store there. We spent a day hiking the trails of Trail of Tears State Park
and another morning trying unsuccessfully to catch catfish.

On the Illinois side, we stashed our kayaks partway up One Mile
Race Creek and walked along the levee, with wide views of the rich farmland and distant bluffs that are not visible from river level.

"The finest country in the world," said a French missionary in 1680 of
the Illinois prairie lands once a person hiked through the bottomland
forests next to the river. "Our hunters, French and Indians were delighted
with it. For an extent of at least two hundred leagues in length and as
much in breadth, as we were told, there are vast fields of excellent land,
diversified here and there with pleasing hills, lofty woods, groves through
which you might ride on horseback, so clear and unobstructed are the
paths. These little forests also line the rivers, which intersect the country
in various places, and which abound in fish."

He described a sort of American Serengeti: "The fields are full of all
kinds of game, wild cattle, stags, does, deer, bears, turkeys, partridges,
parrots, quails, woodcock, wild pigeons and ring-doves. There are also
beavers, otters, martens . . ." And an American Garden of Eden: "The
peach trees are quite like those of France and very good; they are so
loaded with fruit that the Indians have to prop up those they cultivate in
their clearings. There are whole forests of very fine mulberries, of which
we ate the fruit from the month of May; many plum trees and other fruit
trees, some known and others unknown in Europe; vines, pomegranates
and horse chestnuts are common . . ."

The land is still astoundingly beautiful, though tilled now and set back
from the river by the long mound that is the levee. According to my
notes from that day, I was thinking to myself that the levee is a thousand-

mile homage to the Great Serpent Mound. I was wondering if it would be possible to take a truly long walk along the levee someday, maybe from New Orleans to St. Paul, when we saw our destination. Down within a grove of trees, where the Army Corps' great serpent levee curved off to the left, sat the boxy gray remains of Fort Chartres, the former military and administrative center for what was the breadbasket of French colonial activity in North America.

First constructed in 1755 to replace a series of earlier, wooden forts, the eighteen-foot walls originally formed a complete polygon nearly two thousand feet in circumference. "This Fort is situated on a plain, near the River Mississippi, which breaks in upon it so fast that it will soon be in great danger of falling into it," said John Jennings, an English traveler who visited the fort in 1766. "It's built with a high Stone Wall, about eighteen inches thick, four Square, with four Bastions, full of Loop holes, port holes for Cannon, & a ditch round it, hath very good Barracks, The Gate fronting the river makes a very good appearance."

That gate is long gone. Jennings was right about the foolishness of the location; the western half of the fort eventually fell into the river, though the river has since changed course. There was a prison and a bake house, a commandant's house and a ninety-foot-long storehouse, a pigeon house, a coach house, and various other buildings. What remains has been partially restored and is fortified against further damage from the river by the levee, which is a happy irony, I suppose.

A week before we got there, Fort Chartres had been stuffed to the turrets with "living historians" dressed up as fur traders, Native trappers, and French infantry come for the annual jamboree. When we scrambled down the steep side of the levee and came in through the back of the fort, however, the place was deserted. With Chartres to ourselves, we wandered around peering through loopholes and into the dark powder magazine.

In the small gift shop we called hello and eventually a friendly woman appeared from somewhere and sold us ice-cold Sprites and told us about her technique in the tomahawk-throwing competitions of the previous week.

"Really?" we asked. She seemed like a nice middle-aged farmwife who had taken an interest in the local historical society and had volunteered to run the gift ship in the middle-of-nowhere fort for a few afternoons a week. "You throw tomahawks?"

"Oh sure," she said as if it were a silly question. "Pretty much everyone around here throws a little tomahawk."

Hearing that, we ducked out, kept low, headed back to the river, and slipped away downstream.

16

THE INCOMPARABLE LA SALLE

Joliet and Marquette didn't make it all the way to the Gulf of Mexico. Somewhere past the mouth of the Ohio they met a large band of Indians who were even better equipped with European weapons and trade goods than the Illinois had been. "They have guns, hatchets, hoes, knives, beads, and flasks of double glass, in which they put their powder," said Marquette. "They wear their hair long, and tattoo their bodies after the hiroquois fashion. The women wear head-dresses and garments like those of the huron women."

Who exactly these people were is unclear, though some have suggested they may have been Tuscarora, the Iroquoian nation that were in North Carolina when Europeans began settling there in the 1650s but gradually migrated north and joined their Iroquois cousins as the sixth nation in the League. The source of their trade goods is also a bit mysterious, though the mere fact that people on the river were so well equipped as early as the 1670s is perhaps more important than where they shopped. The Indians themselves said the goods came from the east, which would imply the English via the Ohio River. They also said the Europeans had rosaries and occasionally dressed like the Black Robe, however, which implied the Spanish at the mouth of the river.

The assurances from the Indians that they were only ten days' travel from the sea "animated our courage and made us paddle with Fresh ardor," said Marquette, and they pushed on until they reached the vicinity of the Arkansas River. They were, in fact, still nearly six hundred river miles from the sea, in the neighborhood where de Soto's army had run into Quigaltam 130 years before.

When the residents of a village called Mitchigamea first saw the two canoes full of Frenchmen, they launched their flotilla of giant dugouts, as their predecessors had when they chased the Spanish downriver. Someone threw a war club, which missed, and others swam toward the French canoes. The attack was suddenly called off, however, by a pair of elders onshore, who, according to Marquette, finally noticed that the Black Robe was wildly waving the peace pipe he had received from the Illinois. Finding someone who knew a little bit of the Illinois language—one of the six that Marquette spoke—they were able to ask a few questions and were directed to continue downstream to the main town called Akamsea.

The heirs to Quigaltam had come down in the world. They were surrounded now by enemies who possessed guns and who made it a policy to prevent them from trading with the Europeans and getting their own guns. They were even afraid to go out and hunt buffalo, as they used to do, and were living on corn and watermelons. The sea was not that far away, they told Joliet and Marquette, but to go farther was madness "on account of the continual forays of their enemies along the river,—because, as they had guns and were very warlike, we could not without manifest danger proceed down the river."

The French considered their options. They hadn't gotten all the way to the mouth of the river, but they were now certain that the Mississippi did not veer either west to the Gulf of California nor east to the Atlantic. "Beyond a doubt," Marquette wrote later, "the Missisipi river discharges into the florida or Mexican gulf." If they continued forward, even if they survived the gauntlet of well-armed Indians, the Spanish would most likely arrest them for trespassing and thus prevent them bringing the news back to New France.

They turned around and paddled upstream. On the way home their friends the Illinois told them about a shortcut, and after passing the mouth of the Missouri they took a right turn up the Illinois River. "We have seen nothing like this river that we enter, as regards its fertility of soil, its prairies and woods; its cattle, elk, deer, wildcats, bustards, swans, ducks, parroquets, and even beaver," said Marquette. As beautiful as the

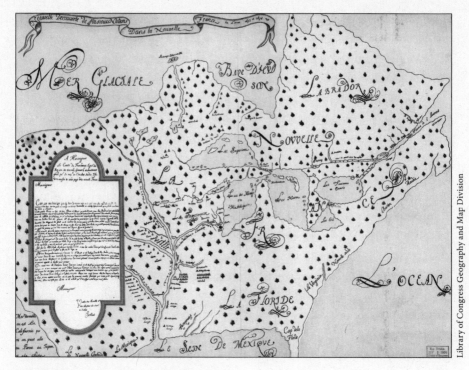

Louis Joliet's map of Nouvelle France, 1674.

river was, even more important was the relatively easy portage to Lake Michigan at a place called Checagou. This crossing was previously unknown to Europeans, and by the summer of 1674, Joliet was back in Montreal, with news of the new portage and of the Great River to which it led. Five years later, in November 1679, René-Robert Cavelier, Sieur de La Salle, arrived at Chicago with four canoes and a plan to build an empire.

La Salle dreamed up his idea of a string of forts controlling the Mississippi watershed for France even before Joliet had returned from his voyage, and there is some evidence that he explored the headwaters of the Ohio in 1669, three years before Joliet crossed into the watershed. He is indisputably one of the great epic characters of the age of European exploration, the protagonist in a tale full of absurdly grandiose plans, treacherous partners, international intrigue, and almost unbelievable feats of survival in an unknown and largely hostile land. Like de Soto, he obtained a license from his king to develop a continent but no royal cash to help make it real. Unlike de Soto, La Salle planned to conquer the watershed for God, king, and self not with an army of conquistadors but with a small company of voyageurs, a handful of priests, and a changing cast of Native American allies.

René-Robert Cavelier was born in Rouen, France, in 1643 and, like Joliet, studied for a time with the Jesuits but left the order before becoming a priest. His brother was a priest with the Jesuits' rivals, the Sulpician order, stationed at Montreal, and La Salle followed him to Canada. He arrived in 1668 and, presumably through his brother's connections, received a valuable tract of land from the Sulpicians controlling the portage around the Lachine Rapids in Montreal. The location of the rapids, just downstream from the confluence of the Ottawa and St. Lawrence Rivers, gave La Salle a bottleneck on the Great Lakes fur trade.

He promptly set about making money, friends, and enemies. He built a fort and a trading post and studied the languages of the Native travelers who passed through. Had he kept his estate, he might have built a great fortune without much risk to life or limb, but when he learned from a party of Seneca Iroquois about a large river in their country that ran eventually to the sea, he sold Lachine and made plans to head west. He gathered a party of five canoes loaded with fourteen voyageurs and trade goods. The Sulpicians, who were always on the lookout for souls that had not yet been harvested by the Jesuits, sent along two canoes with seven men of their own. The Seneca, in two more canoes, agreed to guide them at least as far as their village on Lake Ontario. From there, La Salle's plan was to travel inland and portage over to the mysterious river.

"This river is called, in the language of the Iroquois, 'Ohio,'" wrote René de Bréhant de Galinée, one of the Sulpician priests who accompanied La Salle on this voyage. "On it are settled a multitude of tribes, from which as yet no one has been seen here, but so numerous are they that, according to the Indians' report, a single nation will include fifteen or twenty villages. The hope of beaver, but especially of finding by this route the passage into the Vermillion Sea, into which M. de la Salle believed the River Ohio emptied, induced him to undertake this expedition, so as not to leave to another the honor of discovering the passage to the South Sea, and thereby the way to China."

Galinée's implication that La Salle's motive was primarily his own sense of personal glory was not an unintentional slight. It comes very shortly after the priest has pointed out that he and the other clerics, by contrast, were risking their lives in "labor for the salvation of the Indians." He goes on to say that the governor of New France had supported the expedition because "M. de la Salle showed him some probability by a great number of fine speeches, of which he has no lack."

La Salle's gift for convincing the powerful was matched only by his talent for alienating colleagues, subordinates, and priests. Father Galinée was sent along on the expedition, he said, because he had traveled in the backcountry and his superiors were afraid that La Salle might "abandon our Gentlemen, and that his temper, which was known to be rather volatile, might lead him to quit them at the first whim, perhaps when it was most necessary to have some one with a little skill in finding his bearings for the return journey."

La Salle had little in the way of inland experience at that point, and Galinée was downright scornful of his fitness to command such a dangerous mission. "M. de la Salle, who said that he understood the Iroquois perfectly, and that he had learned all these things from them through his perfect acquaintance with their language, did not know it at all, and was embarking upon this expedition almost blindly, scarcely knowing where he was going." As insurance, Galinée hired his own interpreter, a Dutch trader who spoke fluent Iroquois. Unfortunately, however, the man did not speak French.

It was an inauspicious beginning, but on July 6, 1669, the little flotilla of birch bark canoes set off from Montreal. By the middle of August—sick, hungry, and wondering if the fragile new peace between the Iroquois and the French would really protect them—La Salle and company were at the palisaded Seneca village in the Finger Lakes region of New York. The Iroquois lived in long, multifamily structures called longhouses: their name for themselves, Haudensaunee, means "people of the longhouse." The French visitors were given lodging in a longhouse, and after they were made comfortable, fifty or sixty Seneca elders gathered from the four main towns to hear from La Salle why he had come to their country.

"Their custom is, when they come in, to sit down in the most convenient place they find vacant, regardless of rank, and at once get some fire to light their pipes, which do not leave their mouths during the whole time of the council," Galinée recalled. "They say good thoughts come whilst smoking."

The Iroquois were and are famous orators: "The Senators of Venice do not appear with a graver countenance, and perhaps do not speak with more majesty and solidity than those ancient Iroquois," recalled the Franciscan father Louis Hennepin, who visited the Seneca in the 1670s. But when it came time for the French to say why they had come to the Senecas' country, there was an awkward silence.

"It was then M. de la Salle admitted he was unable to make himself understood," said a disgusted Galinée. The Dutch interpreter also demurred, saying his French wasn't good enough. The whole council might have broken down completely if not for the fact that an earlier delegation of Jesuits had left behind a translator who stepped into the breach.

As was the custom, La Salle presented a series of gifts, each attached to a message. The first was a double-barreled pistol, to symbolize their friendship. The second gift included six kettles, six hatchets, four dozen knives, and a large bag of glass beads to confirm the peace between New France and the Iroquois. The third gift was similar, but came with a request for a slave or guide who could take them to the Ohio River. The elders listened, accepted the gifts, smoked their pipes, and told La Salle they would think about it.

The following day the elders filed back in and lit their pipes. The "head chief among them" presented La Salle with wampum belts to symbolize the peace between the Seneca and the French. You need to be patient, he said, it might take some time. Much of the nation was away at Albany, trading, but when they returned they would give La Salle a slave from one of the Ohio tribes.

A week went by with no slave appearing, then a few more days. The season wore on, but still the Seneca produced no guide to the Ohio Country. At last a war party returned from a raid with a prisoner who might have been suitable as a guide for La Salle, but he was instead given to a woman whose son had been killed during the raid. This was a traditional practice, and the family of the lost warrior could choose to adopt the prisoner, which was usually done with women and children. Or they could kill the prisoner as retribution for their loss. They chose the latter.

Galinée said the execution ritual that followed was "the saddest spectacle I ever saw in my life." The prisoner was first tied to a stake and slowly burned over his entire body with red-hot gun barrels. This took six hours, after which, they "required him to run six courses through the square where the Iroquois awaited him armed with large flaming brands, with which they kept urging him on and knocking him down when he would come near them. Many took kettles full of coals and hot cinders, with which they covered him the instant that, by reason of his exhaustion and weakness, he wished to rest for a single moment." Finally they killed him with a rock and, according to Galinée, ate him. "Several presented portions of his flesh to the French," he said, "but no one would try the experiment."

Some in La Salle's party began to lose their nerve for continuing into the interior. Others began to wonder if the Seneca had any real intention of ever producing the promised guide. Some of the elders had told the Dutch translator that they were worried about supplying a guide to the Ohio. If the French were killed during their harebrained adventure, an outcome the Seneca were all but certain would be the case, the Seneca nation would be blamed and the peace with New France would be jeopardized.

Besides, the Seneca said truthfully, there was a much shorter route to the Ohio from down on Lake Erie. La Salle agreed to go there, and a guide who could take them up the Niagara River was rapidly provided. Though they didn't see the magnificent falls as they portaged around, they became the first Europeans to report back about them. At last, from an Iroquois village near the entrance to Lake Erie, La Salle was given two slaves to act as guides into the interior and the Ohio. By then, however, the priests had had enough of him. For reasons long brewing, and never explicitly explained in the record, Galinée and the other priests took one of the guides and continued on around the Great Lakes and never reached the Mississippi watershed.

La Salle, on the other hand, took the other guide and plunged south. Nothing is known with certainty about where he went during the winter of 1669–70, how he survived, or how far he got; he simply disappeared. He did not, as is occasionally suggested, get all the way to the Mississippi. He may well have reached the Allegheny River, as he later implied, and traveled down as far as the Falls of the Ohio, at the present site of Louisville. What's clear is that when La Salle reappeared in Montreal and Quebec in 1672, he was no longer a novice woodsman, no longer in need of translators, and utterly convinced that the Ohio and Mississippi were the keys to a continent-wide empire.

His legendary powers of persuasion were, if anything, increased by the addition of actual woodland experience to his résumé. He became a close ally of the ambitious new governor of New France, Louis de Buade de Frontenac. He went to Paris and charmed King Louis XIV and his powerful finance minister, Jean-Baptiste Colbert, who rewarded him with title—Sieur de La Salle—and feudal control of Fort Frontenac at the head of the St. Lawrence River. Once again with a bottleneck on the Great Lakes fur trade, money poured into La Salle's coffers. Money isn't glory, however, and in 1677 he was back in Paris negotiating with Colbert for a five-year contract to develop the Ohio and Mississippi basins. Typically of European monarchs of the period, the Sun King was happy to oblige, as long as he got his cut and didn't have to put up any money of his own. In May 1678 letters patent were issued to La Salle giving him a five-year monopoly, and "the seignory of the government of the forts which he should erect on his route."

For their part, Louis XIV and Colbert were interested in the Mississippi primarily as a strategic outpost, rather than a purely economic wager. There was still some possibility that a western tributary might lead to the Pacific, but by that time almost everyone was convinced the Ohio flowed into the Mississippi and that the Mississippi flowed into the Gulf of Mexico. La Salle's main mission, therefore, was to claim the region for France and thus control the continent. As he himself explained, Colbert was interested in "finding a port where the French might establish themselves and harass the Spaniards in those regions from whence they derive all their wealth." The notion that controlling the watershed would also hem in the English and Dutch colonies on the Atlantic seaboard was not unnoticed either.

That the watershed was already a part of the expanding Atlantic economy is obvious from the guns and trinkets that Joliet and others had seen far inland from any European settlement; during the 1690s roughly three hundred thousand North American beaver pelts were sold in Europe every year. With La Salle's license directly from the king of France, however, a new phase began. Going forward, whether La Salle succeeded or failed in his grand ambition was beside the point: the Mississippi basin was now on the European map of the world, as it were. The river was in play in the global scramble for empire.

It never seems to have occurred to La Salle that he wouldn't succeed. Before leaving Paris he borrowed as much money as he could. He hired thirty carpenters, shipwrights, sailors, and mechanics to come to Canada with him. You can never have enough capital or skilled labor when you're speculating on a continent.

17

NOUS SOMMES TOUS SAUVAGES

One who came to La Salle looking for work was an Italian soldier of fortune named Henri de Tonti. "After having been eight years in the French service, by land and by sea, and having had a hand shot off in Sicily by a grenade, I resolved to return to France and look for work," he recalled after the whole grim Mississippi River adventure was over. Tonti got in touch with his friend Prince Conty, who landed him a job as La Salle's lieutenant.

On January 20, 1679, Tonti and La Salle and the thirty carpenters arrived at the mouth of the Niagara River. A small crew that included the Franciscan Louis Hennepin was already at work building a small fort and storehouse. Everything went well, until bit by bit nothing was going according to plan. Not surprisingly, the Iroquois were unhappy with the prospect of a French fort controlling the Niagara portage and demanded that it be scaled back. Then the ship bearing all the carpenters and tools was lost due to pilot error and, though no one died, only a small amount of the equipment was salvaged. Worst of all, perhaps, it was the middle of winter.

Nonetheless, La Salle and his men managed to portage what gear they had salvaged around the falls and found a place to begin construction of a small sailing ship. This was to be the first of two planned barks—one for the Great Lakes and one for the Mississippi. Along with the boat he already had on Lake Ontario, these were to be the supply chain between La Salle's planned network of forts. Leaving Tonti in command, La Salle headed back to Fort Frontenac to replace the supplies lost in the ship-wreck.

It seemed almost as insane then as it does now: to walk in midwinter from somewhere near the present site of Buffalo, New York, across the entire length of Lake Ontario to Kingston. "He undertook this journey afoot, over the snow, having no other provision but a little sack of roasted Indian corn," recalled Father Hennepin. "However, he got home safely . . . with two men and a dog, who dragged his baggage over the frozen snow."

When La Salle returned the following summer, Tonti had succeeded in launching the sixty-ton *Griffin* under the watchful eyes of a band of disapproving Iroquois. "We made all haste we could to get our ship afloat, though not altogether finished to prevent their designs of burning it," said Hennepin. "We fired three guns and sung Te Deum; and, carrying our hammocks aboard, the same day were out of reach of the savages."

These were glorious days for La Salle, his new ship relatively flying across the distances that once seemed so appallingly large. They sailed west the length of Erie in only three days, and passed up the Detroit River, through Lake St. Clair and up the St. Clair River, without incident. There was a nasty storm at the bottom of Lake Huron that had them all on their knees praying; "except our pilot, whom we could never oblige to pray," said Hennepin, "and he did nothing all that while but curse and swear against M. de la Salle, who had brought him thither to perish in a nasty lake and lose the glory he had acquired by his long and happy navi-gations on the ocean." But with the storm passed, they sailed on to Michilimackinac, where virtually no one was happy to see them.

"No vessels had yet been seen sailing on the lakes," said Zenobius Membre, another Franciscan in the expedition. "Yet an enterprise which should have been sustained by all well-meaning persons for the glory of God and the service of the king had produced precisely the opposite feelings and effects."

Everyone in the squalid trading village where Lakes Huron, Michi-gan, and Superior intersect was threatened by the prospect of a fur trade dominated by a series of forts and a fleet of sailing vessels controlled by one man. The voyageurs who made their living transporting goods via canoe—both Native and French—didn't like the ship for obvious reasons. The trappers and traders in Michilimackinac found no comfort in the fact that the terms of La Salle's contract with the king forbade his interfering in the Great Lakes fur trade, perhaps because they knew such technicalities meant nothing so far away from Paris or Montreal. The Iroquois, as already mentioned, resented the control of important portages that the forts implied, and the other tribes were similarly skeptical. Even the Jesuits were alarmed by La Salle's alliance with Franciscans such as Hennepin. The hostility was so palpable that La Salle's own men, whom he had sent ahead, had fled town. He dispatched Tonti up to Sault Ste. Marie to find them.

Unwelcome where he was, La Salle sailed for Green Bay at the beginning of September and loaded the *Griffin* with furs. He gave the captain orders to take the ship back to Niagara and use the cargo to pay off some of his creditors. He and thirteen men would continue on in four canoes to the Chicago portage. The *Griffin* was then to return to Chicago as quickly as possible, but she was never seen again.

"They sailed the 18th with a westerly wind, and fired a gun as taking leave," remembered Hennepin. "It was never known what course they steered, nor how they perished; but it is supposed that the ship struck upon a sand and was there buried. This was a great loss for M. De la Salle and other adventurers, for that ship and its cargo cost above sixty thousand livres."

By the time La Salle learned about the wreck of the *Griffin*, it was merely the most devastating in a mounting string of disappointments. The canoe trip from Green Bay down to Chicago lasted six weeks, most of them starving and cold. They lived at times on carrion stolen from ravens and eagles, and according to Hennepin were grateful for that: "the rudest of our men could not but praise the divine Providence who took so particular a care of us."

What kept them going was the knowledge that Tonti would be waiting at the Chicago River with fresh men and supplies. When at last La Salle and his companions stumbled up to the site of the camp, however, Tonti was nowhere to be found. Worse, when Tonti did arrive after a series of mishaps of his own, he had neither the supplies nor men. All he had was the news that the *Griffin* was lost.

Without provisions, there was no hope of spending the winter on the howling lakeshore. Their only chance of survival lay with the villages on the Illinois River that Joliet had reported befriending on his return voyage six years before. "As soon as I arrived we ascended 25 leagues, as far as the portage," Tonti recalled. "We made the portage, which extends about two leagues, and came to the source of the Illinois River."

Some of the men grumbled about deserting, until they realized it was so cold that they stood no better chance of surviving by going back. About 250 miles down the river the bedraggled party came at last to a large Illinois town of four hundred multifamily lodges. It was only a summer residence, empty in winter when the residents went downriver to hunt. There was a stash of corn, however, to which the French helped themselves before moving on.

It was a tense moment a few days later when they paddled right into the middle of the large Illinois village of Peoria. The town occupied both sides of the river, and the French were in the middle of it almost before they realized it was there. The Illinois likewise were equally startled by the sudden appearance of an armed party of thirty strangers in a flotilla of canoes coming down the main avenue of town.

"The Sieur de la Salle had a calumet of peace, but would not show it, not liking to appear weak before them," recalled Father Membre. "As they were soon so near that they could understand each other, they asked our Frenchmen who they were. They replied that they were French, still keeping their arms at ready, and letting the current bear them down in order, because there was no landing place till below the camp."

The Illinois were not as concerned about who showed whom their pipe first and held out three calumets. "Our people at the same time presented [ours]," said Membre, "and, their terror changing to joy, they conducted our party to their cabins, showed us a thousand civilities and sent to call back those who had fled."

Nothing in the Mississippi basin went unnoticed by the various players in the fur trade, whether Native American or European. The night La Salle and company arrived in town, an emissary sent from the neighboring Miami and Maskouten nations snuck into town and held a secret midnight council with the leaders of Peoria. La Salle, he warned them, was really an agent of the Iroquois, who were at that moment on their way to attack the Illinois. "He caballed even the whole night, speaking of the Sieur de la Salle as an intriguer, a friend of the Iroquois, coming to the Illinois only to open the way to their enemies," said Father

Membre. "The next day the Illinois chiefs were found completely changed, cold and distrustful, appearing even to plot against our Frenchmen, who were shaken by the change."

La Salle's powers of persuasion were apparently transnational. "It was easy for me to destroy all these falsehoods," he wrote later to Governor Frontenac, noting that by the end of his speech it was the intriguer Monsoela whose life was in danger. "Had I not interposed, the Illinois would have killed [him]."

With the crisis averted, at least temporarily, La Salle took his men a little downstream and began the construction of a fort he named "heartbreak." Father Membre said Fort Crevecoeur was so named "on account of the many disappointments he had experienced." Father Hennepin echoed that it was "because the desertion of our men, with the difficulties we labored under, had almost broken our hearts." Some scholars have suggested that the name was in homage to Tonti's participation in a siege in Holland before coming to North America, but whatever the original inspiration, it was an apt name for what was still to come.

As soon as Fort Crevecoeur was habitable, La Salle put some of the men to work building the boat that was supposed to have been the Mississippi River sister ship to the *Griffin*. The loss of the *Griffin* still haunted him, and in March he left Tonti in charge of the ship building and with five men returned to Fort Frontenac on Lake Ontario for fresh supplies. At the same time he sent Father Hennepin and one man down the Illinois River with orders to turn north when they got to the Mississippi and look for the Sioux. Hennepin, who later wrote a stream of half-true best sellers about his travels, eventually got as far north as the present site of Minneapolis. There he (re)named the great waterfall after Saint Anthony of Padua.

La Salle wasn't gone long before all but six of the men he had left behind on the Illinois River deserted. They demolished Fort Crevecoeur and the half-built boat and ran off with most of the tools and supplies.

"They left me with two Recollets and three men, newly arrived from France, stripped of everything and at the mercy of the savages," said the ever-loyal Tonti, who wasn't at Crevecoeur at the time of the desertion. He had gone downriver to begin the construction of yet another fort, this one at Kaskaskia, and only discovered the treachery after the perpetrators were long gone. With the supplies destroyed or missing, once

From Louis Hennepin's 1699 bestselling account of
his travels in the New World showing a figure with a
peace pipe.

again the remnant party's only hope for survival lay in moving back in
with the friendly Illinois. Before leaving the ruined fort and the half-built
boat, Tonti had one of the priests write the date, April 15, 1680, on one of
the planks, along with the inscription *"Nous sommes tous Sauvages"*—We
are all savages.

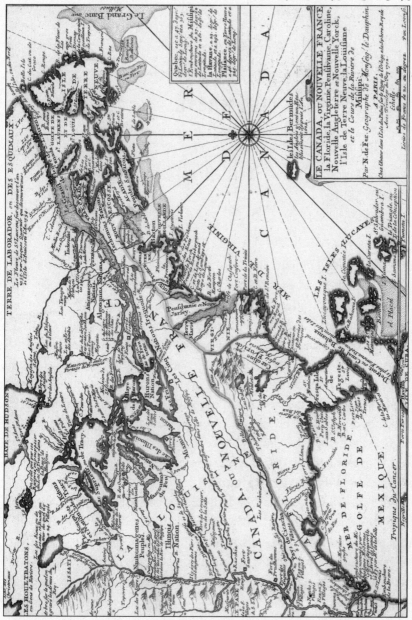

From Nicolas de Fer's 1702 map of Nouvelle France.

18

THE WRATH

Tonti and his five compatriots were still living with the Illinois a few months later when six hundred Iroquois and allied warriors appeared across the river. This attack by the Iroquois army confirmed the Illinois Indians' worst fears about the duplicity of their French houseguests; they had been assured, after all, that the French could protect them from the Iroquois League. To placate their hosts, Tonti and Father Membre took a necklace of wampum across the river and tried to negotiate a cease-fire. Their plan was to tell the invaders that to attack the Illinois would break the truce between the Iroquois and New France, bringing on the wrath of the French. Before they got a chance to say much, however, some hot-headed warriors stabbed Tonti in the chest and stuck his hat on the end of a gun and started waving it around.

"They immediately surrounded him and wished to carry him off; but when, by his ears, which were not pierced, they saw that he was a Frenchman, one of the Iroquois chiefs asked loudly what they had meant by striking a Frenchman in that way, that he must be spared, and drew forth a belt of wampum to staunch the blood and make a plaster for the wound," recalled Membre.

Tonti, for his part, remembered sitting in shock after the stabbing, bleeding profusely, while two Iroquois chiefs debated whether or not to scalp him. "There was a man behind me with a knife in his hand, who every now and then lifted up my hair," he said.

The Seneca chief, Tégantouki, argued that since the French were seen shooting at the Iroquois in the battle that was going on around the village, they should roast Tonti. The Onondaga chief, Onnoutagues, on the other hand, was a friend of La Salle's and won the day. Tonti and Membre were released and sent back to the Illinois. The Iroquois did not end their siege, however, and the Illinois ultimately fled their town, whereupon the Iroquois promptly moved in and built themselves a stockaded compound. They made it clear to Tonti that now might be a good time for him to leave the area as well.

Tonti did not need to be asked twice, and the six remaining members of La Salle's advance team fled back to the Great Lakes. Long before they got there, one of them, Father Gabriel, was shot full of arrows by a wandering band of Kickapoo teens out looking for Iroquois scalps. It may have been a blessing for the sixty-three-year-old missionary, who had barely survived the hard trip down the lake the previous winter. Father Membre, at any rate, didn't think Father Gabriel would have survived the next weeks. They nearly starved, nearly froze, nearly died of food poisoning, and spent days walking in circles trying to find their way out of the Illinois Country.

"We supported this remnant of a languishing life by the potatoes and garlick and other roots that we found by scraping the ground with our fingers," said Membre. "We were all like skeletons, the Sieur de Tonty extremely sick." Eventually, however, they made their way to Green Bay, where the Jesuit missionaries nursed them back to health.

La Salle, meanwhile, was not doing much better. His own passage back to Niagara and Fort Frontenac for supplies had been harrowing. It rained and sleeted without end, and his party was continuously hounded by hostile bands who suspected them of being Iroquois allies. "We followed the shore of Lake Erie on foot until the Indian and one of my men succumbed to the toil of walking continually in water, the constant rain and the great thaw having flooded nearly all the woods," La Salle recalled later. His men "were attacked by a very violent fever with an inflammation of the lungs, bringing up blood."

What's more, when they finally made it all the way back to Fort

Frontenac and Montreal, the news was uniformly grim. The *Griffin* had not been seen, several other cargoes of furs and supplies had similarly been lost, and creditors had seized much of his Montreal property. What's more, the mutineers who had abandoned Tonti had also destroyed the fort at the head of the Chicago portage and stolen the cache of furs La Salle had left in a warehouse at Michilimackinac. All La Salle had left, really, was his alliance with Governor Frontenac, two more years on his license from the king, and the loyalty of Tonti.

La Salle had no way of knowing that Tonti and the others had already fled the Illinois Country, and he believed that their lives might depend upon his bringing fresh supplies. There was nothing to do but borrow yet more funds from somewhere, load up a convoy of canoes, and set off back to Fort Crevecoeur. He arrived at the first Illinois village in December 1580 to find a hellish scene. "There remained standing only some charred stakes, showing what had been the extent of the village," he wrote in his official report, which refers to himself as LaSalle or in the third person:

> Upon most of these stakes the heads of the dead had been fixed to be devoured by the crows. There were more skulls at the gates of the Iroquois fort, with a mass of burnt bones and some remains of French utensils and clothing, which he perceived by certain signs to have lain there for some time. In fields were to be seen many carcasses half gnawed by the wolves; tombs were demolished, bones dragged from the graves and scattered about the plain; the trenches wherein the Illinois hide their utensils when they go away to hunt all opened; their kettles and their pots all broken. Most of the Indian corn was still standing and in various parts half burnt heaps of it were seen. The horror of the scene was increased by the howls and screams of the wolves and crows.

La Salle wandered around the devastation, looking for clues about the fate of his most faithful comrades.

> One after another he inspected the heads of the dead, which he recognized by the hair to be the heads of women or of Savages, whose coarse hair is worn close-cropped. It was not pleasant business, but he was bound to do it in order to learn the fate of M. De Tonty and his men.

La Salle didn't find their bodies, of course, but he was fairly certain they must be dead. Leaving some of his men behind, he headed downriver in search of clues. In six places along the Illinois River were versions of the same thing: an abandoned Illinois town on one side of the river and an empty Iroquois war camp directly opposite it. When he got to the ruined Fort Crevecoeur, his boat was lying in pieces on the ground, all the nails having been pulled out by the Iroquois on their way through. The board where Tonti had written "We are all savages" was broken.

Continuing down the Illinois River to the Mississippi, it seemed the camps were fresher. No rain had fallen on the ashes, and he figured he was about two weeks behind the war. Near the mouth of the river, on the north bank, across the prairie, he saw what looked like people, only motionless:

> Going ashore to examine these things more closely, he found all the grass trodden down, and a little on one side, the body of a woman half burnt and eaten by wolves. From this beginning he could easily infer the rest and could judge the outcome of the war.

From what La Salle saw and later learned from conversations with survivors on both sides, after Tonti and the French had fled the town the Iroquois had begun a cat and mouse siege of the Illinois nation. Outnumbered, but better armed and far better fighters, the Iroquois never attacked outright as they slowly herded the Illinois down the river toward the Mississippi. When they all arrived at the big river, most of the Illinois fled across and south, to join up with the Osage. About seven hundred of the Tamaroa clan—mostly women and children—tarried, however, and paid the price. La Salle had wandered into a killing field:

> This whole plain was covered with horrible traces of Iroquois cruelty. It would be impossible to describe the ferocity of those madmen, and the tortures they had inflicted upon the miserable Tamaroas. Parts of bodies had been left in kettles over fires that had afterward died out. The Iroquois had put these hapless people to death by rending out their sinews, by mutilating, by flaying, and by a thousand tortures besides. What had been observed from a distance proved to be heads and entire bodies of women and children, empaled and roasted, and then set up in the field.

Again La Salle looked among the bodies for his friends, "but after a careful and sorrowful search, he found nothing to lead him to think that the Frenchmen had been involved in this disaster," he reported. "Nevertheless, to neglect nothing that might afford a clue, he went as far as the Great River, finding no trace of either the French or the Savages." The Iroquois, having made their point about who was in control of the trade with the Europeans south of the Great Lakes, had headed home to New York via the Ohio River.

This was not how La Salle had imagined his first view of the Mississippi would have come about. Standing there looking at the object of his desire—the "River Colbert," as he and other French called it in honor of Louis XIV's minister—he paused. His comrades wanted to continue downstream now that they were finally at the Mississippi, but he knew that it was folly to go farther with such a small crew. "Their action would be judged the fruit of rashness or despair," he told the men.

More important, La Salle would not "abandon the search for M. De Tonti without learning what had become of him." They turned back toward the Great Lakes on December 7, 1680. "He was very glad to see us again," said Tonti, recalling the moment La Salle paddled up to the trading post Michilimackinac and found his deputy still alive, "and notwithstanding the many past reverses, made new plans to continue the discovery which he had undertaken."

Whatever weaknesses La Salle had as a leader and empire builder, persistence and creativity were not among them. Success, he now realized, depended at least as much on Indian relations as it did on supplies and ships. On his return from the devastation of the Illinois River he had not gone directly to Michilimackinac but had spent several months shuttling among a handful of nations. He brokered a grand alliance among the Miami Indians—usually a client state of the Iroquois—the Shawnee, and the remnant Illinois Indians. He also wooed a half-dozen refugee tribes from New England—where King Philip's War had ended only a few years previously—and from New Amsterdam and Virginia. He "pointed out to them the fertility of the Miami and Illinois prairies, the abundance of beaver, of wild cattle, and of all kinds of game and fish; assured them that they would here enjoy perfect peace, far from their enemies, the English, and under the protection of the greatest King in the world."

La Salle also shifted his geographical focus from the Chicago portage to the mouth of the Mississippi, where he had not yet been. A port on or near the Gulf coast would eliminate the need to traverse the frozen lands of the north, which were deadly cold and controlled by the Iroquois and the Jesuits. He told the gathered New England Indians that "as soon as he should have discovered the mouth of the Great River, he would furnish them with all sorts of goods very cheaply, and that he would introduce cattle, horses, and all the other commodities they had had in New England." A downriver route would also minimize or even eliminate his need to deal with Michilimackinac, Montreal, and Quebec, all of which were infested with his creditors and other enemies.

All that remained, therefore, was to find the mouth of the river. Having at last reunited with Tonti, and having made the decision not to leave anyone behind where they might defect or cause other mischief, they set off. In January 1682, they crossed the Chicago portage one last time and made their way to the Illinois River. In the party were twenty-three Frenchmen and thirty-one Mohican and Abnaki Indians from New England, ten of whom were women and three of whom were children. At Fort Crevecoeur they found ice-free water and launched their canoes and reached the Mississippi itself on February 6.

For all the trouble it had been to get to the Great River, once they were on it the miles flowed past relatively uneventfully. They passed the mouth of the Missouri in the middle of the month and the mouth of the Ohio a week later. They made friends with the Arkansas villages by the middle of March, where it seemed they were at last out of the constant war zone of the northern fur-trading country.

"These Indians do not resemble those at the north, who are all sad and severe in their temper," noticed Father Membre. "These are far better made, honest, liberal and gay. Even the young are so modest that, though they had a great desire to see La Salle, they kept quietly at the doors, not daring to come in." La Salle made a great ceremony of claiming the land for France, and Membre planted a cross.

Farther down they feasted with the Tensaw, who from Membre's descriptions retained some of the pomp and social stratification of their Mississippian ancestors.

> The walls of their houses are made of earth mixed with straw; the roof
> is made of canes, which form a dome adorned with paintings; they have

wooden beds and much other furniture, and even ornaments in their temples, where they inter the bones of their chiefs. They are dressed in white blankets made of the bark of a tree, which they spin; their chief is absolute, and disposes of all without consulting anybody. He is attended by slaves, as are all his family. Food is brought him outside his cabin; drink is given him in a particular cup, with much neatness. His wives and children are similarly treated, and the other Taensa address him with respect and ceremony.

The Sieur de la Salle, being fatigued and unable to go into the town, sent in the Sieur de Tonty and myself with presents. The chief of this nation, not content with sending him provisions and other presents, wished also to see him, and, accordingly, two hours before the time a master of ceremonies came, followed by six men; he made them clear the way he was to pass, prepare a place and cover it with a delicately worked cane-mat. The chief, who came some time after, was dressed in a fine white cloth or blanket. He was preceded by two men carrying fans of white feathers. A third carried a copper plate and a round one of the same metal, both highly polished. He maintained a very grave demeanor during this visit, which was, however, full of confidence and marks of friendship.

The Tensaw told La Salle the names of seventy-four towns they would pass between them and the Natchez, who were their enemies. But when the French and New Englanders arrived at Natchez toward the end of March, they were again welcomed with feasts and calumet ceremonies.

On the sixth of April the expedition arrived at the head of passes, where the Mississippi divides into three distributaries. They split into three groups, and "advancing on we discovered the open sea," remembered Father Membre.

"On the ninth of April, with all possible solemnity, we performed the ceremony of planting the cross and raising the arms of France. After we had chanted the hymn of the church, 'Vexilla Regis,' and 'Te Deum,' the Sieur de la Salle, in the name of his majesty, took possession of that river, of all rivers that enter it, and of all the country watered by it."

Everyone present yelled, "Long live the king." Never mind that the Spanish had claimed the continent a century before, and that the charters of the English colonies on the Atlantic seaboard theoretically

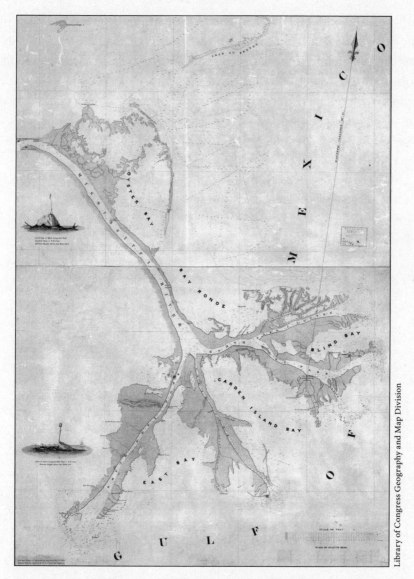

Map from 1732 of the course of the river below New Orleans.

stretched to the Pacific, and most of all that the Mississippi basin was populated with Indians who had lived there for fifteen thousand years. Those were all details that could be dealt with later. By French standards, the watershed was officially French.

The individual Frenchmen who had just traveled its entirety and had found the sea at last, however, were in the middle of nowhere surrounded by reeds and out of provisions. The pristine Mississippi delta was one of the most biologically productive places on the planet, but without fishing equipment and local knowledge, it can be a hard place to find food. Someone finally discovered a cache of dried meat left there by some unknown previous visitors to the mouth, and everybody dug in. It seemed an auspicious omen after all they had gone through to get where they were and claim a continent for God and king. Until someone else realized it was human flesh.

"We left the rest to our Indians," said Father Membre, though he noted, "it was very good and delicate."

19

IF THE RIVER DON'T RISE

My own voyage with my son through the heart of the Illinois Country ended more like Joliet and Marquette's expedition down the Mississippi than like La Salle's, thank goodness. Leaving the friendly tomahawk thrower of Fort Chartres behind, we paddled downriver about five miles to Ste. Genevieve, where we again stashed the kayaks in some woods and walked into town. Like most of the small towns we visited along the river, Ste. Genevieve appeared to have a high level of detachment toward the river that was its original reason for existence. Except for a sign showing historic flood levels, you might not know you were in a river town. We didn't care, however. We checked into a funky old hotel, took hot showers, ate big steaks followed by enormous bowls of homemade ice cream. We slept in beds, watched television, and were otherwise very well behaved for a couple of boatmen who just walked in off the river. Ste. Genevieve is a remarkably well-preserved town and as much as we loved our campsites of the previous days, we were content to be rinsed clean of silt for a day or two, wandering among French Colonial houses, antiques shops, and art galleries.

While we tarried in places like Ste. Genevieve, and the tiny towns of Tower Rock and Herculaneum, and elsewhere, the river was rising. By the time we left Trail of Tears State Park the best camping sandbars were gone. The river was up in the trees in many places, and the word from the Army Corps of Engineers Web site was that it was still coming up. Fast. When we got down below Cape Girardeau, which has a wall to keep the river out of the town, it was no longer as much fun, and I took a Greyhound bus back up to St. Louis to get our car.

Ste. Genevieve, Cape Girardeau, Fort Chartres, St. Louis, and all the other French names along the Mississippi are almost all that remains of La Salle's grand vision for the territory he named Louisiana, after his king. For more than a century, however, it appeared that his dream of a French Mississippi basin would be realized. Official and unofficial fur-trading activities started almost immediately after his voyage to the mouth of the river, with a trading post opening near Prairie du Chien during the late 1680s. In the traders' wake Catholic missionaries took up residence among the Illinois Indians living at Cahokia and in 1703 at the larger Illinois town of Kaskaskia. French voyageurs, meanwhile, explored the major western tributaries: Louis Antoine Juchereau de St. Denis ascended the Red River and crossed over to the Rio Grande in 1713; in 1743 La Vérendrye traveled mostly overland, sometimes accompanied by thousands of Cheyenne and Pawnee warriors, to the upper Missouri country later reexplored by Lewis and Clark.

In the beginning, the French presence on the Mississippi consisted primarily of rowdy fur-trading outposts, where voyageurs fell in love with and/or mistreated their Native wives, and where low prices were generally facilitated by frontier brandy. With the founding of Natchez in 1716 and New Orleans in 1718, and with the establishment of Fort Chartres in the Illinois Country, however, agriculture grew in importance. Organized in the manner of a medieval French village, with habitants and their slaves raising crops in narrow strips of land within a commonly held field that was surrounded by a single fence, Ste. Genevieve, in particular, was a breadbasket for the territory.

La Salle himself, however, did not live to see any of these facets of his grand plan come to fruition. By the time he and his expedition made it back up the river to the Great Lakes, his primary ally, Governor Frontenac, had fallen from power and been recalled to France. La Salle's enemies were firmly in control of the fur trade, and his storehouses at

Niagara and Fort Frontenac had been seized. His outposts and forts in the Illinois Country, meanwhile, were systematically starved of the trade goods needed to maintain relations with his new Native Alliance. Against such a reversal of political winds, only the king himself could help. He sailed for Paris.

As usual, he charmed Louis XIV and his ministers. They sent word to Quebec to give La Salle back his storehouses and trade goods. Even better, the king authorized him to go back to the mouth of the Mississippi by sea—via the Gulf of Mexico—with a fleet, no less. There he was to found his own colony, free of meddling from Quebec and Montreal. From that point on, however, everything that could possibly go wrong did so in spades, producing a final disaster worthy of the grandiosity of La Salle.

Four ships left France in July 1684, with 150 soldiers, a consignment of priests that included Father Membre, a collection of craftsmen and traders, a few second sons of wealthy families, eight or ten yeoman families, and a contingent of unmarried women. The crossing was storm-tossed and disease-ridden. Many of the soldiers deserted in the West Indies. Others, said one of the priests, "having plunged into every kind of debauchery and intemperance so common in those parts were so ruined and contracted with various disorders that some died in the island and others never recovered." The Spanish seized one ship.

What ultimately doomed the expedition, however, was the fact that La Salle's pilots entirely missed the mouth of the Mississippi. All they had to go on were La Salle's sketchy calculations from the voyage of four years before, and they put ashore in Matagorda Bay, Texas. This was nearly four hundred miles west of where they were supposed to be, and entirely outside of the Mississippi basin. More ominously for the short term, the landing was botched when the store ship ran aground, losing most of the provisions. The fleet, which was sent to look for the mouth of the river, abandoned the landing party altogether and never returned. Disease began to take the lives of the colonists, sometimes at a rate of four or five a day. Starvation and disillusion relentlessly descended into mutiny and madness, and on March 19, 1687, La Salle was ambushed and shot by several of his own men.

"I saw him fall a step from me, with his face full of blood," recalled

The death of Sieur de la Salle.

Father Membre. "I watered it with my tears exhorting him, to the best of my power, to die well."

———

"What are you so worried about?" said my son as I hemmed and hawed and generally bemoaned our decision to get off the river a few days earlier than we originally planned. "We thought we might explore two hundred miles of the Mississippi," he said, "and we did about a hundred and seventy. No one else we know has even done that."

He was right, of course. As usual, I might add. But later that day we drove down to Cairo and snuck into the seemingly abandoned and overgrown Fort Defiance Park, where the Ohio River comes in from the east and joins the Mississippi. Cairo is a town that doesn't look like it's been hit by the recession, it looks like it's been hit by a bomb—think Jimmy Carter in the South Bronx in 1977—but the confluence of the giant rivers is a surprisingly peaceful affair.

One river, seemingly clear and dark from the forests of the east, meets the other chalky with mud from the prairies of the west. "They do not immediately merge, however, but flow along side by side like traffic lanes on a freeway," Edward Abbey wrote of a different meeting of rivers on the far side of the Rockies. The same could be said here, and we stood there for quite some time watching the conjoined but not yet commingled serpent spirit of a river rolling on south, cafe latte Mississippi water to the right, dark and deep black-green Ohio water to the left. Looking downstream we agreed that if we could, we would come back someday soon and take another bite of the snake.

But we also looked over our shoulders up the Ohio River, which is so massive at Cairo that it makes the Mississippi look more like the nephew of waters rather than the patriarch. Up the Ohio, past the mounds of Chillicothe; past the Iroquois battlegrounds and the mammoths of Big Bone Lick; past the falls at Louisville and the mouth of the Tennessee; past the Meadowcroft Rockshelter with its Paleolithic flints and past the Ohio's own great fork at Pittsburgh. Past all of that, up the Allegheny and the Monongahela into the ancient headwaters in the western slopes of the Allegheny Mountains. There, in the same decades that the French habitants and voyageurs founded their pretty towns in the Illinois Country, the first trickles of change were already seeping in through the cracks in the wall of the Appalachians.

BOOK FOUR

RIVER OF EMPIRES

. . .

The English Enter, the French Exit,
the Iroquois Negotiate, and the Americans Take Over

Those who have one foot in the canoe and one foot in
the boat are going to fall into the river.

—TUSCARORA (IROQUOIS) PROVERB

20

THE SCRAMBLE FOR THE FORKS

Until he'd had a few drinks, Captain Philippe-Thomas Joncaire was polite but reticent toward the twenty-two-year-old soldier who arrived outside his outpost on the Allegheny River in the middle of December 1753 and introduced himself as Major George Washington. The young Virginian was tall and had a studiously polite bearing, but there was nothing particularly impressive about the company of a half-dozen half-frozen backwoodsmen and traders with whom he was traveling. Nor did Washington speak French, even though he claimed to be on an important diplomatic mission from the governor of Virginia to the commander of French forces in the Ohio River country.

Joncaire's outpost was at a place called Venango, a Delaware Indian village near the juncture of the Allegheny and French Creek, in the current town of Franklin, Pennsylvania. French Creek rises less than a dozen miles from the shore of Lake Erie and the route along it—known as the Venango Path—was a well-known portage route between the Great Lakes and the Mississippi basin for thousands of years before the French began building a string of forts on the stream in 1753. The new forts were intended to solidify France's claim to the entire Mississippi watershed, and enhance communication between Quebec and the French towns down on the Mississippi. Mostly, though, they were designed to halt the steady trickle of English settlers into the Ohio Country. The

majority of these were hunters and trappers from Virginia and Pennsylvania, along with a smattering of New Englanders and southerners. Most
arrived via the Monongahela River, which joins the Allegheny at the
"Forks of the Ohio," the present site of Pittsburgh.

By the time Washington arrived at Joncaire's door, the French had completed Fort Presque Isle on the lake at the current site of Erie, Pennsylvania,
and Fort Le Boeuf, some fifteen miles inland at a fork near the headwaters
of French Creek. The fortifications at Venango were not yet complete, but
Joncaire and two fellow officers had taken over the home of a Pennsylva-
nian fur trader. "We found the French colours hoisted at a House [from]
which they drove Mr. John Frazier, an English Subject," Washington wrote
later. "I immediately repaired to it, to know where the Commander resided."

In the previous sixty years France and England had fought three
wars, each of which included grim battles in North America. The most
recent, King George's War (1744–48), as the War of Austrian Succession
was known in the English colonies, had ended in a stalemate only six
years previously. Whatever might be going on in London and Paris, Joncaire and Washington both knew that Anglo-French tension was mounting rapidly in the Ohio valley and was, in fact, the reason both men were
at the confluence of French Creek and the Allegheny River in the winter
of 1753. The stakes were huge: Would the Ohio and Mississippi remain
French and Indian, or become English and Indian?

Joncaire told Washington that he could not accept the letter from the
English governor and that Washington must carry it to more senior officers up French Creek at Fort Le Boeuf. But as it was too late in the day to
travel farther, and England and France were technically still at peace,
Joncaire invited the Virginian and his men to stay for dinner. News in the
backcountry was still news, after all. George Washington, who had been
traveling through the snow for two weeks, gratefully accepted. Joncaire,
he said, "treated us with the greatest complaisance."

At dinner, formalities fell. "The wine, as they dosed themselves pretty
plentifully with it, soon banished the restraint which at first appeared in
their conversation and gave a license to their tongues to reveal their sen-
timents more freely," the future president reported.

Washington didn't say whether he allowed Joncaire to read the text
of the letter from Governor Dinwiddie, which was in essence an eviction
notice to the French. "The lands upon the Ohio River," it read in part, "are

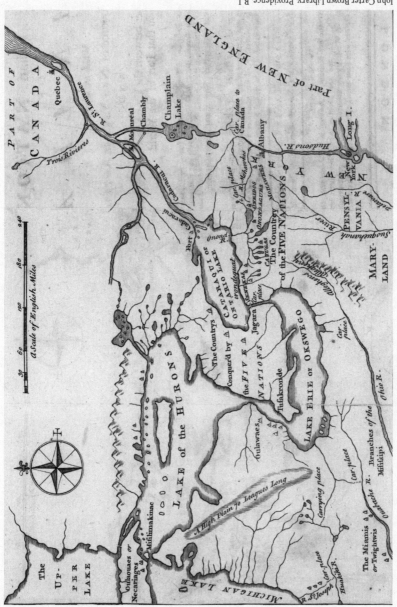

Cadwallader Colden's 1747 map of the Iroquois Confederacy.

so notoriously known to be the property of the Crown of Great Britain that it is a matter of equal concern and surprise to me, to hear that a body of French forces are erecting fortresses and making settlements upon this river, within his Majesty's domains."

The subject of whether France or England would ultimately appropriate the Ohio Country did, however, come up. "They told me that it was their absolute Design to take Possession of the Ohio, and by G—— they would do it," Washington recalled.

The French plans for the spring of 1754 were to finish the fort at the mouth of French Creek and construct a more significant one at the Forks of the Ohio. If expansionists in both the English and French colonies in North America agreed on one thing, it was that the future site of Pittsburgh held the key to the Mississippi basin. The French needed to control the forks if they were to have a prayer of keeping the burgeoning English colonies bottled up on the eastern side of the Appalachians. Powerful English forces, meanwhile, wanted it because they had no intention of staying east of the mountains. Governor Dinwiddie's primary reason for sending Washington down the Monongahela was that a consortium of land speculators called the Ohio Company of Virginia planned to build their own trading post and fort at the forks. Not coincidentally, Dinwiddie and two of George Washington's older brothers were investors.

When someone at the table that evening, perhaps Washington himself, pointed out that the English colonies were vastly more populated with potential settlers than was New France, Joncaire didn't dispute it. He knew better than most that the Ohio Country was crawling with adventurers and traders from the bulging English colonies. Unlike his youthful dinner guest, the forty-seven-year-old Joncaire had been a player in the colonial backwoods chess game for decades. He grew up among the Iroquois, at his father's trading post near the current site of Geneva, New York, and served for decades as the official French envoy to the League. In the 1730s, he lived among the Shawnees in the Ohio valley, attempting to persuade them to move west toward the Mississippi and align themselves with the French rather than with the English. During King George's War he was considered so dangerous that the British put a price on his head, which may have been one reason he was ready to move back to Montreal after the Treaty of Aix-la-Chapelle ended that war in 1748.

Joncaire's hoped-for retirement from the frontier didn't last long, however, as he was recalled only a year later to serve as a translator and expert on a new French expedition through the Ohio Country. Led by Pierre-Joseph Céloron, the mission had the usual goal of limiting English influence in the Mississippi basin and driving English traders and agents from the Ohio Country if possible. What Joncaire and Céloron discovered, however, was that most of the Indians in the region preferred the cheaper booze and better manufactures the English were offering. It didn't help that Céloron insisted on claiming everything in sight for France and burying lead plaques to that effect at important river junctures. He even posted NO TRESPASSING signs here and there on trees. The message was intended for the British, of course, but the locals were not amused. Almost all of them had been displaced by European encroachment elsewhere, and at the Lower Shawnee Town (near Portsmouth, Ohio) the signs were torn down and trampled on before Céloron and Joncaire even had a chance to move on.

At his dinner with George Washington, Joncaire was therefore well aware of the challenge facing his country in the Ohio and Mississippi valleys; New France remained primarily a skein of trade routes and missionary outposts thinly stretched over a vast territory. He also knew, however, that the Virginians, Pennsylvanians, New Yorkers, and New Englanders were as apt to squabble among themselves as they were to coordinate their efforts against the French. Sounding not unlike Britain's own frustrated colonial ministers in London during the same period, he argued that the English colonies were simply too disorganized to take advantage of their size.

"They were sensible [that] the English could raise two men for their one," Washington said, "yet they knew, [our] motions were too slow and dilatory to prevent any undertaking of theirs."

Mostly, though, Joncaire simply argued that the Ohio River and the Mississippi basin were French because the French were there first. "They pretend to have an undoubted right to the river, from a discovery made by one LaSalle 60 Years ago," Washington wrote, implying that he had never heard of La Salle. Whether he'd heard of La Salle or not, Joncaire's "we called it first" reasoning was an argument to which Washington and the other Englishmen in the room might have been expected to riposte that in 1609 *their* monarch had granted *them* an immutable charter that stretched to the Pacific.

Any scene featuring a young George Washington is ripe with portent for the future. Yet there is something singular, almost surreal, about the tableau of a world-weary French Indian agent and the unsuspecting future "Father of His Country" sitting in a dim and smoky room that used to be a fur trader's warehouse, drinking French wine and debating who "owns" the Ohio valley—especially when the practical reality on the ground was that only the Iroquois League could legitimately claim to exert any real, albeit waning, control over the current residents of the Ohio valley.

All the more interesting, therefore, to note that elsewhere in the same small village that night Tanaghrisson, one of the most important Iroquois power brokers of the Ohio valley, was having his own dinner with the resident Delaware Indians. At that party too, conversation almost certainly turned to the same subject the Europeans were debating: the limits of diplomacy and the prospect of war.

It wasn't racism or oversight that kept Tanaghrisson from Joncaire's table that night. Joncaire had known Tanaghrisson for decades and was surprised and disappointed when he found out the following day that the sachem was in town but that he hadn't come immediately to visit. George Washington, meanwhile, had gone out of his way to find Tanaghrisson at his home on the Ohio River and bring him with him to find the French, hoping that arriving with an Iroquois delegation would raise his own stature in the eyes of the French. But Washington, who spoke neither French nor Iroquois, didn't want his new Native friend and ally to get *too* friendly with the legendary Joncaire:

"I knew [Joncaire] was an Interpreter, and a Person of very great Influence among the Indians and had lately used all possible Means to draw them over to their Interest; therefore I was desirous of giving no Opportunity that could be avoided." Washington didn't invite Tanaghrisson to the dinner.

21

THE HALF KING

Tanaghrisson was not an Iroquois by birth, but had been taken from his Algonquin Catawba family as a child during one of the countless raids and skirmishes of the Beaver Wars. Some sources say he was originally captured by the French, about whom he is reputed to have later said, "they ate my father." He was ultimately adopted and raised by the Seneca, the westernmost of the five original nations of the Iroquois League.

The Seneca lived (and live) near and on the headwaters of the Allegheny River, in what is now upstate New York and Pennsylvania. Along with the Tuscarora who were coming up from the Carolinas, it was the Seneca who were the most likely Iroquois to migrate into the Ohio Country and become identified as Mingos. Exactly when Tanaghrisson moved south and settled about twenty miles below the Forks of the Ohio at Logstown (Ambridge, Pennsylvania) is not clear. Once there, however, he rose to become a leader among the Mingo, presumably through the traditional Iroquois method of being elected by the women of his town. As such, Tanaghrisson was perceived by the English as both an enforcer of Iroquois League policy among the various non-Iroquois Indians in the Ohio Country and as point man for the League in any dealings with Europeans in the valley. The English called him the "Half King," in an apparent attempt to honor his position without offending the old-guard leaders of the Iroquois League back in upstate New York.

Tanaghrisson reached the pinnacle of his influence in 1751, two years before Washington's arrival at Venango, when he unceremoniously threw Joncaire out of a diplomatic council. For several years before that, he and his fellow Mingo had been slowly testing their independence from their cousins in the old Iroquois League. Specifically, they had reached out to the government of Pennsylvania through the gregarious fur trader George Croghan in an attempt to establish a direct connection to the English suppliers of weapons and trade goods. During King George's War they ignored the official neutrality of the Iroquois League and sided with the English, attacking the French in the Ohio Country and on the shores of Lake Erie. Most symbolically of all, perhaps, in 1748 Tanaghrisson and his fellow Mingo established a new council fire at Logstown.

This was an act of hubris that could not have pleased everyone at the main Iroquois council at Onondaga. Nor for that matter would it have been welcome news among the Iroquois' traditional trading partners in the colony of New York. For a century and a half it had served both Albany and Onondaga well that the only good way inland was up the Hudson and Mohawk Rivers. On the other hand, the aspirations of the

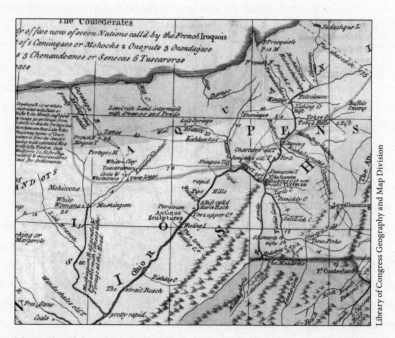

The Forks of the Ohio, circa 1771.

Library of Congress Geography and Map Division

Mingo people pleased Pennsylvania's Indian agent immensely. Conrad Weiser was happy to show up with twelve hundred pounds' worth of gifts, and when Virginia got wind that Weiser was going, the burgesses there voted to send him a little something for the Mingo that he could say came from them as well.

The French in Canada were the least pleased of all to hear of Tanaghrisson's shenanigans at Logstown. When word went out up and down the river in 1751 that the Half King was presiding over another great council fire, Joncaire—then France's premier Indian agent—made plans to attend with an ostentatious squadron of forty pro-French Seneca warriors. Early in the council, the Irish-born trader George Croghan delivered a message from the governor of Pennsylvania encouraging the Ohio Indians to resist any French advances in the valley and promising that English intentions were completely benign. He was followed some time later by a pitch from Joncaire, who urged the people of the Ohio Country to throw the English out of what he called "Onontio's land."

Joncaire's choice of words was what today would be called a diplomatic gaffe: phrasing that might have played well enough on the Great Lakes a hundred years before, but was incendiary in the Ohio valley after all the blood that had been shed. "Onontio" was the name originally given by the Hurons to the first governor of New France, and it had come to mean all governors of New France, and by extension the king of France. Tanaghrisson was livid at Joncaire's implication that the land he lived on belonged to anyone but the Mingo and the other Iroquois, and he immediately dropped the usual hyperbole and decorum of Native American speechifying.

He spoke, said one witness, with "the Air of a Warrior," and stormed right up to Joncaire. Poking him in the nose with his pointed finger, he demanded to know where Onontio thought he got the right to "Our Lands." Then he threw Joncaire out of the council and told him to paddle home. To Croghan and the other English, meanwhile, he announced that no Indian from the Ohio Country was going to demean themselves by traveling all the way to Virginia to discuss potential English forts on the river. If their governor wanted to send a message to the council at Logstown explaining English positions, however, they would listen to it. The English hurried off, promising to be back.

Despite his impressive defiance around the council fire of 1751, the

Half King's actual ability to control events in the Ohio valley at any one time is open to question. Like Wisconsin and the rest of the upper Mississippi, the region was in a state of demographic flux. A kaleidoscope of new and returning refugees and immigrants, along with a handful of English traders and French soldiers, were gradually repopulating the valley that had been largely swept of its earlier human population during the wars of the 1600s. Among these the Iroquois Mingo, and Algonquin-speaking Delaware (Lenape) and Shawnee were the most populous. All three of these peoples succeeded in maintaining much of their culture and kinship ties in the new Ohio territory. Other towns were more multiethnic, however, with smatterings of Mahican, Mesquakies, and others from all over the north and east of the continent.

As with any melting-pot culture, the material and spiritual life of the people was complex and shifting. More than a century of trade with Europeans had largely replaced traditional pottery with metal kettles and pots and recycled jugs. Firearms and metal hatchets and knives were also common, though traditional weapons persisted. Clothing was a matter of personal choice, with European jackets and hats mixing it up with traditional deerskin and beadwork. "At this time the Delawars had no King, but were headed by two Brothers named Shingas and Beaver who were dressed after the English Fashion, had silver Breast Plates and a great deal of Wampum around them," reported a Virginian who traveled to Logstown and the Forks of the Ohio in 1752.

One of the best descriptions of the people who lived near the Ohio during the second half of the 1700s comes from John Filson's 1784 "The Discovery, Settlement and Present State of Kentucke." "The Indians," he said, "take a great deal of pains to darken their complexion, by anointing themselves with grease, and lying in the sun. They also paint their faces, breasts and shoulders, of various colours, but generally red; and their features are well formed, especially those of the women."

> They are of a middle stature, their limbs clean and straight, and
> scarcely any crooked or deformed person is to be found among them.
> In many parts of their bodies they prick in gun-powder in very pretty
> figures. They shave, or pluck the hair off their heads, except a patch
> about the crown, which is ornamented with beautiful feathers, beads,
> wampum, and such like baubles. Their ears are pared, and stretched in

a thong down to their shoulders. They are wound round with wire to expand them, and adorned with silver pendants, rings, and bells, which they likewise wear in their noses. Some of them will have a large feather through the cartilage of the nose; and those who can afford it, wear a collar of wampum, a silver breastplate, and bracelets, on the arms and wrists.

A bit of cloth about the middle, a shirt of the English make, on which they bestow innumerable broaches to adorn it, a sort of cloth boots and mockasons, which are shoes of a make peculiar to the Indians, ornamented with porcupine quills, with a blanket or match-coat thrown over all, compleats their dress at home; but when they go to war, they leave their trinkets behind, and mere necessaries serve them. There is little difference between the dress of the men and women, excepting that a short petticoat, and the hair, which is exceeding black, and long, clubbed behind, distinguish some of the latter. Except the head and eye-brows, they pluck the hair, with great diligence, from all parts of the body, especially the looser part of the sex.

At Onondaga during this period, traditional percussion instruments such as drums and gourd rattles were accompanied as well by penny-whistles, violins, and Jew's harps. Even ceremonial items overlapped; the Forks of the Ohio was where the calumet—the Mississippian peace pipe described by La Salle and Joliet—overlapped with the giving and receiving of wampum belts that was more typically practiced east of the Appalachians.

Alliances and enmities were similarly fluid, as might be expected under the circumstances. The shifting intricacies of intercolonial and Native diplomacy are the subject of several good books, best among them McConnell's *A Country Between: The Upper Ohio Valley and Its Peoples, 1724–1774*. Suffice it here to say that in a world turned upside down and shaken up by the cultural, physical, and biological invasion of Europeans, there was no room for immutable bonds. Cards changed hands very quickly, and every faction and splinter group, whether Native American, European, or some mix of both, played their current draw as best they could to their own advantage. The stakes were high for all sides, but only the various Ohio Indians were in immediate danger of losing their homes, livelihoods, and cultures.

Any fantasies Tanaghrisson and his neighbors may have harbored that English intentions were somehow more benign than French intentions were scattered when commissioners from Virginia traveled to Logstown the year after Joncaire's dramatic ejection. The 1752 council began well enough, with a welcoming escort from Tanaghrisson meeting the delegation three miles from Shonassim's Town, one of the first important Delaware villages in the Ohio Country. Horses didn't exist in North America until the arrival of the Spanish in the 1490s, but two and a half centuries later they were common even in canoe country. "When they came near, all, as well English as Indians, dismounted, and the Indians having filled and lighted their long Pipes or Calumets, first smoak'd and then handed them to the Commissioners and others in their Company, who all smoked," the delegation later reported back to Governor Dinwiddie.

They passed the pipe two or three times, and then made their way to a point just outside of the town. There, the escort told the Virginians to stay behind while he rode on ahead. A few minutes later the commissioners heard a volley of guns fired into the air, a salute that they responded to in kind. The Delaware fired again, and the English responded. Two or three times, taking turns, everyone shot the sky.

The speechifying began in earnest the next day in a lodge specially prepared for the occasion, with seating for everyone of importance. "Brethren, you have come a long Journey and have sweated a great Deal. We wipe off your Sweat with this String of Wampum," the designated Delaware speaker said, and he presented the commissioners with a string of beads.

"Brethren, you are come a long Way, & we are glad to see you; we hope you will open yr Hearts to us, & speak clearly, and that you may be enabled to do it, we clear your Voices with this String of Wampum," he continued and gave another string.

"Brethren, you are come from far, and have heard many Stories & false Reports about us, your Brethren. We hope that you will not keep them in your Mind, and that you will disregard them, we give you this String of Wampum." Another string.

"Brethren, we desire you will consider our Brethren that live towards the Sun setting, & that you will give them your best Advice, upon which we give you this String of Wampum." Another string.

Eyes turned to the Virginians, whose turn it now was to respond. There was an awkward pause, however, when the visitors suddenly realized they weren't as prepared as they should have been. "The Commissioners [did not have] any Wampum strung, without which Answers cou'd not be returned." It was a bit of a faux pas, which their translator—a half-Seneca, half-Canadian named Andrew Montour—only managed to finesse by requesting a recess. The Virginians then spent their lunch break threading beads, because by afternoon they were ready to respond in kind to the Delaware welcome.

"Brethren, the Chiefs of the Delawars," they began. In conscious contrast to the French, who typically addressed the Indians as "children" and called their governor "your father," the English early on adopted a policy of implying the equality of brotherhood in their speeches. "We have had a long & difficult Journey hither to see our Brethren, but that has been sufficiently made Amends for by the kind Reception you have given us; we assure you we are glad to meet you here in Council, and present you with this String of Wampum." The commissioners presented one of their newly tied strings.

Each point that the welcoming committee had made in the morning was specifically referenced and responded to with an appropriate gift of wampum. "We did hear many Stories in our Way hither, rais'd by idle and wicked People to occasion a Difference between us, but we did not believe them, and now we are satisfied that they were false," the Virginians assured the Delawares with one string. "Brethren, in your second Speech, you clear'd our Voices, that we might speak our Minds to you," they said with another. When all of the formalities were attended to, it was at last time to move on to Logstown and the council proper.

Tanaghrisson and an official delegation from the Iroquois League were not there when the Virginians arrived, so the council was adjourned after another elaborate round of welcoming speeches. When Tanaghrisson did arrive a few days later, by canoe with a British flag flying above it, he waited nearly another week before commencing the parley. Whether this was diplomatic gamesmanship intended to make a point to the English is not clear, but there is no doubt that the 1752 Logstown Council was a highly theatrical event. Before Tanaghrisson addressed any of the various requests of the English, he staged a mock coronation of "Kings" for the Delaware and the Shawnee.

"We think proper to give you Shingas for your King, whom you must look upon as your Chief, & with whom all publick Business must be transacted between you & your Brethren, the English," he told the Delaware in attendance. With appropriate ceremony he placed a lacy European hat "on the Head of the Beaver, who stood Proxy for his Brother Shingas." A similar gift of clothing was given to the Shawnees to pass along to their leader, Cockawichy, who claimed to be sick in bed.

It's interesting that both of the new "kings" found excuses to be absent from their respective coronations. Despite Tanaghrisson's assertion that "We let you know that it is our Right to give you a King," the reality was that Mingo and Iroquois power over the other nations living in the Ohio valley was ebbing. The appointment of kings was a tacit acknowledgment that the Delaware and Shawnee could henceforth deal directly with the English rather than having to go through the Iroquois as in the past. The moment was coming when Tanaghrisson, as a leader among the Mingo, would have to decide if his loyalties lay with his Iroquois cousins in upstate New York or with his neighbors in the Ohio valley.

The English had reasons of their own to wish to sustain Iroquois hegemony over the Ohio Country. The treaty ending the War of Austrian Succession designated the Iroquois as British subjects, making any Iroquois land also the territory of King George III and not the territory of the French. More important, the Iroquois couldn't rightly sell the Ohio valley to the English if they didn't first own it, and the Virginians had come to Logstown with the audacious plan of convincing Tanaghrisson that the Iroquois League had in fact *already* sold it at a council in Lancaster, Pennsylvania, eight years previously. Specifically, the English wanted Tanaghrisson, as the Iroquois representative in the Ohio Country, to reaffirm the Lancaster terms: "recognizing the King's Right to all the Lands in Virginia, as far as it was then peopled, or heareafter should be peopled, or bounded by the King."

To the Delaware in attendance, the Treaty of Lancaster was a sore reminder of both English and Iroquois duplicity when it came to Delaware homelands. Two years prior to the Treaty of Lancaster the Iroquois had officially recognized the Penn family's earlier fraudulent taking of some sixty million acres from the Delaware in the so-called walking purchase. At Lancaster, in what could only be seen as a payback, the British Colonies had recognized Iroquois domination of the dispossessed Delaware Nation. Now the English were back, claiming they had a "right" to the Delaware's new home in the Ohio valley. All eyes, therefore, were on the Half King.

In public sessions of the council Tanaghrisson tried his best to parry the English on the issue of Lancaster by kicking the issue back up to the main Iroquois council at Onondaga. It was they, after all, who had made the agreement. He argued, correctly, that what the Iroquois had agreed to at Lancaster was a sale of lands only east of the Continental Divide and not in the Mississippi watershed. "We assure you we are willing to confirm anything our council has done in regard to land," he said diplomatically, "but we never understood, before you told us Yesterday, that the Lands then sold were to extend further to the Sun setting than the Hill on the other Side of the Allegany Hill, so that we can't give you a further answer now."

Historians today agree that Lancaster was a bait and switch agreement: "Although it is quite clear that Canastego, the Onondaga headman who negotiated on behalf of the league . . . *thought* he was giving up only a fictive Iroquois claim to the Shenandoah Valley, he was in fact trading away the whole of the Ohio Country," wrote Fred Anderson in his epic study of the Seven Years' War. "More than reticence made the

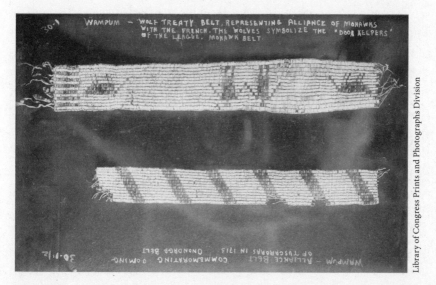

Wampum.

Virginia commissioners [at Lancaster] refrain from mentioning that their colony's charter assigned the Old Dominion a western boundary on the Pacific Ocean."

Tanaghrisson also stood firm on the other English requests. During their presentation the Virginians asked for permission to "make a settlement of British subjects on the south East Side of Ohio." The benefits to the Ohio Indians would include cheaper imports, a defensive alliance, and a government with the "authority to punish & restrain the many Injuries & Abuses too frequently committed here, by disorderly white People." There was nothing to worry about, they promised. The English king, "by purchasing your Lands, had never any Intention of takeing them from you, but that we might live together as one People, & keep them from the French, who wou'd be bad Neighbours."

> He is not like the French King, who calls himself your Father, & endeavoured about three Years ago with an armed Force to take Possession of your Country, by setting up Inscriptions on Trees, and at the Mouths of Creeks on this River, by which he claims the Lands, tho' at the Time of their Coming & for many Years before, a Number of your Brethren, the English, were residing in this Town, & at several other Places on this River.

Tanaghrisson replied that he thought a full-fledged settlement of English was more than was necessary: a single strong house at the Forks of the Ohio should be sufficient, and assured them that his Mingo hunters would keep them well fed. He agreed with the English when they said, "We earnestly exhort you not to be drawn away by the empty, deceitful Speeches of ye french, the peculiar Talent of that cunning people." But he was determined not to affirm the expanded Lancaster deed and not to sign off on any English settlement in the Ohio Country other than a strong house at the Forks.

Then, on the fourth day of the council, the Half King abruptly changed his mind.

There is no adequate explanation. The English were clearly exasperated with Tanaghrisson's intransigence. In the middle of one of his rambling speeches, they asked their translator, Montour, to pull Tanaghrisson and the other Iroquois leaders aside for a private conference with no English and no Delaware present.

What did Montour say? He is an interesting character in his own right, the son of a French trader and a Seneca mother, a man who typically dressed in European clothing but painted his face and had Iroquois-style earrings of wire and feathers. In his early remarks at the opening of the council, Tanaghrisson presented Montour personally with one of the largest belts of wampum and reminded him, "You are not Interpreter only; for you are one of our Council, have an equal Right with us to all these Lands, & may transact any publick Business in behalf of us, the six Nations, as well as any of us, for we look upon you as much as we do upon any of the chief Counsellors."

Did Montour make the seemingly obvious observation that the English were already moving into the Ohio valley with or without the permission of the Iroquois, and that it was therefore better to have at least some hypothetical control? Or that the English were prepared to cut separate deals with the Delaware and Shawnee and stop recognizing the Iroquois as supreme in the valley? Or that the English had said they would not come and fight the French if all they had in the valley was a single strong house? Or that confirming British possession of the valley was the only way to scare off the French? Did Montour and the other Iroquois press Tanaghrisson to say, once and for all, whether he and his fellow Mingo wished to be true Iroquois or wished to cast their lot with the confused lowlife of the Ohio valley?

Montour's pitch probably included some combination of all of the above, aided by Tanaghrisson's realization that whatever power he personally wielded was directly related to his ability to act as the local conduit of English gifts and Iroquois power. Whatever the argument was, it didn't take long. "They retir'd for half an hour and then return'd, & Mr. Montour said they were satisfied in the Matter & were willing to sign & seal the Writing, which was done & witnessed by the Gentlemen then present."

With the document signed—and the deed to the eastern half of the Mississippi watershed in their pockets—the English delegation quickly wrapped up business and made preparations to return to Virginia. Before going, they had one more offer for Tanaghrisson and his fellow Mingo.

Perhaps they wanted to send some of their children to a special Indian school back in Virginia where they would gain "the advantage of an English education?"

Tanaghrisson paused before answering them, apparently thinking about the implications of sending his children to a boarding school.

Thanks, said the Half King. But no thanks.

22

ADIEU NEW FRANCE

By the time George Washington showed up in Logstown the following year to enlist Tanaghrisson to join him on his errand up the Allegheny to the French outpost at Venango, the Half King's influence over his Delaware and Shawnee neighbors was nearly gone. Washington hoped Tanaghrisson could convince Shingas, the leader of the Delaware, and as many other important personages as he could find, to come along on the mission. They were to bring with them any treaty wampum they had received in earlier years in order to symbolically return them to the French, giving Washington's letter from the governor of Virginia a bit more heft. But Shingas begged off, saying his wife was sick, and no Shawnee at all could be found. In the end, Tanaghrisson could round up only Jeska-kake and White Thunder, two minor chiefs, and one additional hunter.

How much Tanaghrisson's failure to gather an impressive retinue for Washington was a result of his apparent sellout to the British the year before is difficult to say. Whatever Shingas and the other non-Iroquois leaders thought of Tanaghrisson, it's unlikely that a personal snub was at the heart of their unwillingness to accompany Washington and him. With the French and English now in an open and headlong race to control the Forks of the Ohio, it was late in the game and bluffs were being called. If the Delaware and Shawnee thought it was in their interest to accompany the youthful Virginian major, they surely would have gone, but with French troops in the valley there was nothing about Washington and his mission to make it worth staking one's own reputation on.

The sad (and sadly familiar) truth from the Iroquois and Ohio Indians' point of view is that precisely at a time when a unified response to both the English and French might have served them best, it eluded them. The new French forts along the Allegheny were a far greater insult to the Iroquois League than they were to the English, but the council at Onondaga was paralyzed by internal divisions. They rebuffed repeated requests from Tanaghrisson and others in the Ohio Country to take some action. The Delaware and Shawnee, meanwhile, with their long history of trouble with the Iroquois League, were understandably wary of making any firm alliance with the Iroquois Mingo. A similar disunion at the bottom of the Mississippi River prevented the Natchez Indians from a unified response to the encroachment of French and English invaders. The only thing that all the Native Americans of the region could agree on was that a century and a half of experience taught them that neither the French nor the English were likely to stay satisfied with any border agreement for long. Even the ancient Iroquois policy of playing the Europeans off against one another was not, in the end, preserving very much of the middle.

"We don't know what you Christian French and English together intend," a sachem at Onondaga told New York's Indian agent, when he came to ask them why they weren't doing anything about the French building forts in the Ohio Country. William Johnson was the English counterpart to Joncaire—fluent in the Mohawk language and ceremonially "adopted" by that nation. He was a flamboyant lover of life and a frontier character of the first order. He kept a council fire continuously burning at his semifeudal manor house on the Mohawk River, where he regularly threw huge bacchanals and was waited on by a team of dwarfs. He exercised his seigneurial "rights" with the farmers' daughters on his land, and apparently plenty of other women as well: the English press claimed he sired seven hundred children. His influence with the League was such that in 1746, his Iroquois friends announced that "should any French priests now dare to come among us, we know no use for them but to roast them." But in 1753 even William Johnson could not convince the League that they should trust the English over the French.

"We are so hemmed in by both [of you] that we have hardly a hunting place left," the Iroquois said. "If we find a bear in a tree, there will

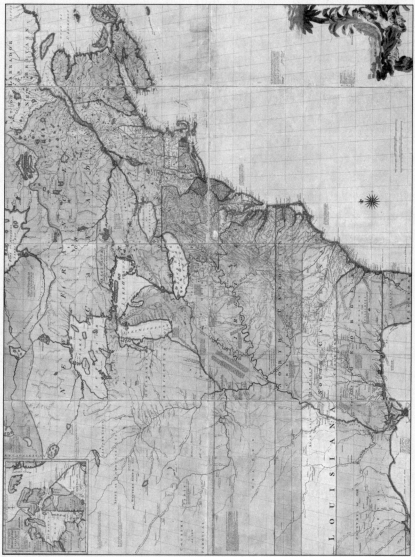

Colonial claims, 1755.

immediately appear an owner for the land to challenge the property, and hinder us from killing it."

If that was the sentiment in the still relatively protected Iroquois heartland of upstate New York, down in the Ohio Country the Natives were even more restless. There, not only were the French building forts and burying plaques, but heroic surveyors like Washington and his traveling companion, Thomas Gist, were roaming around with compasses and notebooks taking measurements. Only the wily old Joncaire, it seems, found it in his interest to be completely honest with his Indian colleagues about their prospects. A few days before Washington arrived he told a gathering of Mingo and Delaware leaders that France was likely to fight the English for three years and then defeat them. But, he went on, there was always a chance of a stalemate between the two European armies.

"If they should prove equally strong," Joncaire said bluntly, "they and the English would join to cut [the Indians] all off, and divide the land between them." It was time, in other words, for the Indians of the Ohio valley to choose their poison.

Just as Washington feared, when Joncaire found out the morning after their dinner together that Tanaghrisson was in town, he sent immediately for the Half King and put on the traditional French charm offensive. According to Washington, when Tanaghrisson and the other Mingos came in, "there was great Pleasure express'd at seeing them; [Joncaire] wonder'd how they could be so near without coming to visit him, made several trifling Presents, and applied Liquor so fast, that they were soon render'd incapable of the Business they came about, notwithstanding the Caution that was given."

Washington accomplished the rest of his errand without much drama—Dinwiddie's letter was delivered to the commandant at Fort Le Boeuf, who responded, "I do not think myself obliged to obey." The tug-of-war for Tanaghrisson's affections, however, was relentless. "I can't say that ever in my life I suffer'd so much Anxiety as I did in this Affair," Washington wrote to Dinwiddie. "I saw that every Strategem that the most fruitful Brain could invent, was practic'd, to win the Half-King to their Interest."

For his part, Tanaghrisson played both sides well. He liked the French brandy when it was offered, but never lost his wits and sobered up when there was work to do. Washington was pleased to see him rail against the

French in council and try to return their wampum to Joncaire, who refused it. But he was less happy when the Half King insisted on meeting with the French alone and accepted some guns and other gifts from them, and was even more alarmed on the return trip when Tanaghrisson insisted on staying behind with Joncaire at Venango.

"I told him I hoped he would guard against his Flattery, and let no fine Speeches influence him in their Favour," Washington recalled saying as they parted. "He desired I might not be concerned, for he knew the French too well, for any Thing to engage him in their Behalf."

The time had not yet come for the Half King to unequivocally cast his lot with one European power or the other, but when it came, George Washington would again be with him. Washington's report on the situation in the Ohio Country was alarming enough in January 1754 to goad the Virginia House of Burgesses into a rare cooperation with Governor Dinwiddie. Like many royal governors, Dinwiddie was considered by the colonists to be disrespectful of their rights and liberties. He also appeared less interested in the welfare of the commonwealth than he was in enriching himself and his fellow speculators in the Ohio Company. Both charges appear in hindsight to be largely correct, but with Washington's news that the French were advancing toward the Forks of the Ohio, Dinwiddie was able to extract from the burgesses an appropriation of 10,000 pounds to pay for two hundred men to defend the confluence of the Allegheny and Monongahela from the French. Their commander would be Washington, who was promoted to the rank of lieutenant colonel.

It took Washington until April to get under way, and during the intervening months various representatives of the Ohio Company who were already in the territory built a small timber fort at the future site of Pittsburgh. Tanaghrisson was on hand to lay the first log on February 17, but most of the Ohio Country Indians sensibly chose to bide their time. There were fewer than fifty volunteers building the English stockade, therefore. Meanwhile, a sizable army of well-trained French soldiers with a flotilla of canoes and pirogues were merely waiting for the ice to go out of French Creek and the Allegheny to come down the river in force.

Five hundred French soldiers arrived at the stockade only a few hours after the English had hung the gate and closed themselves inside. Peering out between the logs of Fort Prince George, as they had named the place, the English could see the French ranks setting up in formation, aiming their big guns toward the pathetic wooden walls. There was no hope of reinforcements. Washington and his paltry militia weren't even over the Alleghenies and into the watershed yet. Tanaghrisson was on hand, but hardly any other Indians were willing to fight alongside the English in such a lopsided battle. Even the other employees of the Ohio Company up the Monongahela sent word that they weren't likely to come down the river to help anytime soon.

The choice given by the French was straightforward: get blown to bits by the cannons, or surrender and have a pleasant dinner provided by the French that evening. The English would be allowed to leave in the morning with whatever possessions they could carry and their colors and honor. It didn't take long for the English commander Ensign Edward Ward to make up his mind.

Tanaghrisson fumed and fulminated against the French as the English vacated Fort Prince George and marched off up the Monongahela the next morning. The retreat was a personal disaster for him, exposing how pathetic his friends the English were. Not only were the Delaware and Shawnee disgusted, but even his own Mingo people were as well. There was nothing the Half King could do about the situation, however, but wait for George Washington to arrive and hope that the forces he brought with him would be adequate to drive the French out.

Tanaghrisson was sorely disappointed, therefore, when Washington arrived in the watershed in mid-May having only managed to enlist about 150 men. What's more, the Virginia militiamen were poorly trained and outfitted and had not been adequately provisioned for their march west. There was no possibility, in other words, of Washington and his puny force directly retaking the Forks of the Ohio. The French were already busy replacing the paltry stockade built by the Ohio Company with a proper stone fort, which they would name Duquesne, after the governor of New France.

There was, however, a good possibility of sparking a major war between France and England. There's little reason to think the young George Washington had any intentions beyond following his orders and impressing the governor of Virginia, but Tanaghrisson was ready to roll the dice. On May 28, at a place now called Jumonville Glen near the Monongahela River, he led Washington and forty Virginian soldiers and a dozen Mingo fighting men on a rain-soaked overnight march to a hollow where a small party of French soldiers were just waking up. The French were under the command of a thirty-six-year-old officer named Joseph Coulon de Villiers de Jumonville, who had been sent out from the Forks of the Ohio to find Washington and ask him to leave the watershed. The small size of Jumonville's company—just thirty-five men—almost certainly indicates that the commander at Fort Duquesne did not want to threaten or alarm Washington's larger force.

What exactly happened in the first fifteen or twenty minutes after the awakening French crawled out of their tents and realized that a larger English force was looking over its gun sights at them is a source of enduring debate. Somebody shot first—whether French or English is unclear, though no account suggests it was the Mingo. Washington, who had never before been in the heat of battle as a soldier, let alone as a commander, then ordered his entire force to open fire on the disorganized French. Several French soldiers were killed immediately, perhaps as many as ten, and Jumonville may have been wounded as well, but he was not killed. Others fled into the hollow behind the camp, only to encounter a flanking force consisting of Tanaghrisson and his Mingo, who drove them back toward the English.

This was the age of muzzle-loading flintlocks, so there was a built-in pause in action after the first flurry of musket fire. The French called out asking for quarter and announced that they were bearing a diplomatic message for Washington. He apparently ordered a cessation of hostilities so he could study the message, but during the lull in the activity Tanaghrisson came up to the wounded Jumonville and spoke to him.

"Tu n'es pas encore mort, mon père,"—You are not yet dead, my father—a witness recalled the Half King saying in his flawless French. It was almost certainly intended sarcastically, a reference to the countless speeches about the great French Father that the Half King had endured over the years, for no sooner had he said it than he split open Jumonville's skull with his hatchet.

"He then took out his brains and washed his hands with them and then scalped him," another soldier later reported.

In the mayhem that followed, more French soldiers were killed and scalped. The details remain murky, but in the end a dozen French colonials and soldiers were dead compared to one English casualty.

Washington was somewhat circumspect in his report about when, exactly, most of the killing took place so as not to leave the implication that the battle of Jumonville Glen was the massacre that most historians believe it was. What seems certain about the incident is that the young officer lost control of the situation and, in so doing, helped set the world on fire. The incident didn't cause the Seven Years' War; but it was the spark that set off a well-primed fuse that almost certainly would have ignited somewhere else eventually. Before the war was over, there were battles on four continents—North America, Africa, Europe, and South Asia—and at sea in the Caribbean, the South and North Atlantic, the Mediterranean, and the Indian and Pacific Oceans.

As its name implies, the Seven Years' War took a good deal longer than the three years that Joncaire had predicted to Tanaghrisson and the Mingo that the fighting would last. In the Ohio Country, the Battle of Jumonville Glen was followed six weeks later by the Battle of Fort Necessity, at which Jumonville's older brother surrounded and defeated Washington and obliged him to sign a document in French that admitted to having "assassinated" Jumonville. A year later the British general Edward Braddock, with now Colonel Washington in tow, was similarly defeated on July 9, 1755, at the Battle of the Wilderness in a disastrous effort to wrest the Forks of the Ohio from the French. In 1756 the Pennsylvania militia attacked without warning and destroyed the Delaware village of Kittanning on the Allegheny River, one of many bloody raids carried out by Europeans and Indians on both sides during what the English colonists came to call the French and Indian War.

In the North American theater, the shifting calculus of the various Indian nations remained central. Finally, in November 1758, having at last made peace with the Western Delaware Indians, an English army of some six thousand men under the command of General John Forbes occupied the smoldering ruins of Fort Duquesne, which the French had blown up before retreating from the Forks of the Ohio. One of the first to enter what remained of the fort was George Washington.

No one in the Ohio Country at the start of the conflagration could have imagined that the impact of the Seven Years' War would be as sweeping as it turned out to be. When the Peace of Paris was concluded in 1763, France was not just out of the Ohio valley but out of North America entirely. The treaty stipulated "for the future, the confines between the dominions of his Britannick Majesty and those of his Most Christian Majesty, in that part of the world, shall be fixed irrevocably by a line drawn along the middle of the River Mississippi," implying that France would continue to have a presence in the western watershed. In reality, though, France had already secretly transferred its claims west of the river to Spain. New Orleans had also been transferred to Spain, specifically to keep it out of British hands.

Tanaghrisson did not live to see his beloved Ohio Country turned over to the English. A few months after the Battle of Jumonville, he fell ill with pneumonia and died. Joncaire, who was born in New France and had spent his life in the service of the colony, was naturally heartbroken by the outcome of the Seven Years' War. Rather than live under English rule, he retired to France and took what consolation he could from being knighted in the order of Saint Louis. He died in 1766.

George Washington, of course, emerged from the war as the most experienced commander among the colonial militias.

23

THE AMERICAN WATERSHED

From this period it remained concealed till about the year 1767, when one John Finley, and some others, trading with the Indians, fortunately travelled over the fertile region, now called Kentucke, then but known to the Indians, by the name of the Dark and Bloody Ground, and sometimes the Middle Ground.

—JOHN FILSON, 1784

The connection between the Anglo-French competition for the Ohio and Mississippi Country and the Founding Fathers of the United States is more than merely coincidental. As Fred Anderson shows in his majestic history of the conflict, *Crucible of War: The Seven Years' War and the Fate of Empire in British North America*, the lust for Indian land in the Ohio Country and the rest of the Mississippi watershed following the removal of the French was a significant factor leading up to the American Revolution. The taxes the American colonists famously refused to pay were levied by London explicitly to fund the continuing military actions against Native Americans in the Mississippi basin, ranging from the Cherokee in the south to Pontiac in the Ohio Country and on the Great Lakes. The same was true for the troops the colonists resisted quartering. As Anderson put it: "The regiments were being stationed in America to protect Americans. Justice, no less than economic realism, decreed that the colonies should contribute modestly from their prosperity to relieve the burdens under which the metropolis now groaned."

Even more alarming than taxes to those colonists wealthy enough to be speculating on land deals west of the Alleghenies, George III appeared to believe his paternalistic responsibilities as monarch extended to the Indians. "It is just and reasonable, and essential to our Interest, and the Security of our Colonies, that the several Nations or Tribes of Indians with whom We are connected, and who live under our Protection, should not be molested or disturbed in the Possession of such Parts of Our Dominions and Territories as, not having been ceded to or purchased by Us, are reserved to them," the king announced in 1763.

That kind of royal verbiage was bland enough to be ignored by everyone, but Mad King George went on to get very specific: "No Governor or Commander in Chief in any of our other Colonies or Plantations in America [shall] grant Warrants of Survey, or pass Patents for any Lands beyond the Heads or Sources of any of the Rivers which fall into the Atlantic Ocean from the West and North West, or upon any Lands whatever, which, not having been ceded to or purchased by Us as aforesaid, are reserved to the said Indians, or any of them."

No surveyors across the Appalachians? In plain English, as opposed to the king's, George III seemed to be announcing that the entire French and Indian War had been fought to protect the Mississippi watershed as a hunting preserve for the Delaware, the Mingo, and the rest of the savages. No subdividers, speculators, or settlers were authorized to cross over the hills from anyplace that drained into the Atlantic to anyplace that drained into the Mississippi. The king's concern for the welfare of the Indians was only half sincere at best, as the caveat "until our further pleasure be known" shows. His true motive in the proclamation was a short-term desire to quell Pontiac's rebellion and other uprisings in newly acquired territories, a goal that distributing smallpox-infested blankets from the infirmary at Fort Pitt on the Forks of the Ohio had so far not succeeded in achieving.

No one really believed that the king wanted to stop westward expansion altogether, but he clearly intended to regulate the future appropriation of Indian land himself, rather than through the various colonial governments. Even worse, when George III did discover his "further pleasure" regarding the Ohio Country in 1774, he lumped everything north of the Ohio River into the compliant Province of Quebec rather than with the increasingly uppity colonial legislatures to the south. Two years later, the list of grievances against George III in the Declaration of Independence included that he was "raising the Conditions of new Appropriations of Lands."

The royal ban on traveling into the Mississippi watershed was honored only in the breach. In the 1770s "long hunters" and prospectors from Virginia, Pennsylvania, and the other colonies were everywhere. Both the Iroquois League and the Cherokee had officially relinquished their Ohio Country claims in treaties like the one to which Tanaghrisson had capitulated. As usual the people who actually lived in the affected region—mainly Shawnee, Delaware, Miami, and Mingo—were left out of the deal making. They did not, therefore, feel obliged to welcome the first settlers who arrived over the mountains from Virginia in 1773 with a hunter named Daniel Boone.

"I sold my farm on the Yadkin, and what goods we could not carry with us; and on the twenty-fifth day of September, 1773, bade a farewell to our friends, and proceeded on our journey to Kentucky, in company with five families more, and forty men that joined us in Powel's Valley, which is one hundred and fifty miles from the now settled parts of Kentucky," Boone wrote in his memoir. "This promising beginning was soon overcast with a cloud of adversity; for upon the tenth day of October, the rear of our company was attacked by a number of Indians, who killed six, and wounded one man. Of these my eldest son was one that fell in the action. Though we defended ourselves, and repulsed the enemy, yet this unhappy affair scattered our cattle, brought us into extreme difficulty, and so discouraged the whole company, that we retreated forty miles, to the settlement on Clinch River."

This raid on Boone's little company of settlers is considered the beginning of Lord Dunmore's War, which Governor Dunmore of Virginia instigated against the Ohio Indians in 1774 to punish them for resisting the advance of settlers into their hunting grounds. It was symbolically far more than that, however. Boone's first company of settlers retreated back over the Appalachian Divide to the Clinch River, but the deluge was only temporarily postponed. The following year, Boone was hired by a consortium of speculators to blaze what became "the wilderness road" through the Cumberland Gap and down to the Kentucky River. Ten years later, there were some thirty thousand non-Indian settlers living in "Kentucke." Most were whites, including a sizable contingent of Scots-Irish Presbyterians and Calvinists whose English and

Scottish ancestors had previously colonized the Irish province of Ulster and were now seeking full religious freedom on the American frontier. There were also both free and enslaved blacks among the newcomers to the Ohio Country, however, as a gruesome incident from the period attests:

> In October following, a party [of Indians] made an excursion into that district called the Crab Orchard, and one of them, being advanced some distance before the others, boldly entered the house of a poor defenseless family, in which was only a Negro man, a woman and her children, ter-rified with the apprehensions of immediate death. The savage, perceiv-ing their defenseless situation, without offering violence to the family attempted to captivate the Negro, who, happily proved an over-match for him, threw him on the ground, and, in the struggle, the mother of the children drew an ax from a corner of the cottage, and cut his head off, while her little daughter shut the door.
>
> The savages instantly appeared, and applied their tomahawks to the door. An old rusty gun-barrel, without a lock, lay in a corner, which the mother put through a small crevice, and the savages, perceiving it, fled. In the mean time, the alarm spread through the neighbourhood; the armed men collected immediately, and pursued the ravagers into the wilderness. Thus Providence, by the means of this Negro, saved the whole of the poor family from destruction.

Independence in 1783 found the new national government saddled with debt and burdened with myriad claims of various state legislatures and speculators to Indian lands in the West. (Not surprisingly, perhaps, most of the Indians of the Mississippi watershed who paid any attention to the war had sided with the British; the king was untrustworthy, but he offered the only, albeit slim, hope of containing the burgeoning colonial populations.) In response to both problems, Congress passed the North-west Ordinance in 1787, establishing the new lands north of the Ohio and east of the Mississippi as United States territory. The language of the Northwest Ordinance included the usual promises to the Indians about never depriving them of their homelands, but the real intent was appar-ent to everyone. The Ohio Country in particular could now be granted to veterans, sold to speculators, and otherwise used to fund the new republic's national aims.

With the land rush officially under way, wealthy and well-connected speculators gathered in all their usual haunts, including the Bunch of Grapes tavern in Boston, where General Rufus Putnam and other Revolutionary War heroes formed the Ohio Company of Associates over glasses of beer. In April 1788, Putnam and forty-seven other settlers laid out Marietta, Ohio, the first permanent American settlement in the Northwest Territory. (First by a hair: Cincinnati was also founded in 1788 and rapidly grew to be the largest town on the river.) It was a milestone for the watershed with an ironic twist given the outsize role the permanent Army Corps of Engineers would play in the future of the river: Rufus Putnam was George Washington's chief of army engineers, a job he resigned when the Continental Congress refused to establish a permanent corps of engineers.

Across the Ohio, in Kentucky, the freshet of settlers had already swelled to a flood. "Numbers are daily arriving, and multitudes expected this Fall; which gives a well grounded expectation that the country will be exceedingly populous in a short time." wrote John Filson in 1784. "The inhabitants, at present, have not extraordinary good houses, as usual in a newly settled country."

Filson, who initiated the legend-making around Daniel Boone by including an "autobiography" of Boone in the appendix of *The Discovery, Settlement and Present State of Kentucke*, also attempted to compile a list of the various Indian nations he knew of that were still living in the eastern half of the watershed. Using his spellings for nations and rivers, he began with the Cherokee on the Tennessee River. He mentioned the Chicamawgees (also Cherokee), downriver at a rapid called the Boiling Pot, and the Dragomonough. The Cheegees and the "middle-settlement" Indians were related to the Cherokee. The Chicasaw were at a place called the French Lick on the Cumberland River (Nashville). The Choctaw were down the Cumberland River from the Chicasaw. Across the Ohio the Lenai Lenape (Delaware) were on the Muskingum River while most of the Mingo were on the Scioto. The Shawnee villages were mostly on the Little and Great Miami Rivers. The Piankashaws were 160 miles up the Wabash River and farther up that river were the Vermillion Indians and the Wyahtinaws. The Isle-River Indians were on a tributary to the Wabash. There were the Osaw (Osage) on their river, and the Kakasky Nation on the Mississippi. The Illinois and the Poutawattamies were on the Illinois River, and the Illinois were also on the Mississippi. The Seneca of the Iroquois League were on the headwaters of the Allegheny.

Filson's list isn't complete by a long shot, and doesn't even attempt to cover the upper Mississippi, the Missouri, the Platte, the Arkansas, the Red, and all the other rivers of the western half of the basin. It's more interesting for what it says about how much a motivated person in the year after the American Revolution could already know about the various cultures still inhabiting the valley. Filson's list is also a useful reminder that even though the various descendants of the mound builders and mammoth hunters of North America were on the cusp of losing control of almost all of their inherited watershed, they did not "disappear," as the literature and art of the following century suggested. Of his list, only the Piankashaws, the Wyahtinaws, and the Kaskasky are no longer in existence as recognized tribes or nations. Even they are not gone, however, having almost certainly melded into the larger Miami and Illinois Nations.

Most of the nations of the eastern watershed ultimately joined the nations of the western watershed, migrating or being forcibly removed to Oklahoma and elsewhere during the nineteenth century. But not all. In particular, the Haudenosaunee of the Iroquois League are still primarily located in their historic heartland, straddling the country between the Allegheny, Lake Erie, the Hudson, and the Susquehanna. Some of the Ho-Chunk, or Winnebago, are still in Wisconsin, where they were when Joliet put his paddle into the Wisconsin River in 1673. The Ojibwa are still on Leech Lake, at the headwaters of the river. The Tsalagiyi Detsadailvgi, or Eastern Band of Cherokee Indians, are still in the Great Smoky Mountains on a tributary to the Tennessee River.

It is far beyond the scope of this book to chronicle the filling in of the lands of the watershed with people of European and African stock—and eventually of people from all corners of the globe—but a partial list of the remembered wars and skirmishes gives an idea of the magnitude of the endeavor. In the eastern half of the watershed, the American Revolution didn't end with the peace between England and the United States in 1783. The Lower Cherokee and a coalition of fugitive blacks and Shawnee and others resisted American sovereignty over the Tennessee valley in the Chickamauga Wars until 1794. The same thing happened in the northern Ohio Country, where the Shawnee, Miami, Delaware, Wyandotte, and others under the leadership of Little Turtle denied American claims to control the valley until defeated at the Battle of Fallen Timbers in 1793. A young Shawnee soldier named Tecumseh saw his first action at that battle, as did a young American warrior named Zebulon Pike.

The Shawnee and others picked up the resistance again in the Indiana Territory in 1811, where Governor William Henry Harrison was eager to attract enough settlers to qualify for statehood and where the now battle-hardened Tecumseh rallied his people by asking, "Where today are the Pequot? Where the Narragansett, the Mohican, the Pokanoket, and many other powerful tribes of our people?" And answering: "They have vanished before the avarice and oppression of the white man, as snow before a summer sun."

Tecumseh's war merged into the War of 1812, which was as bloody on the western frontier as had been the American Revolution and the French and Indian Wars. From Britain's perspective the war was a side theater to the Napoleonic Wars; for the United States, it was a second War of Independence. For the Indians of the Mississippi watershed, however, it was business as usual in a struggle that by now had burned off and on for two centuries.

As they had so many times before, native nations chose sides after a grim calculation of the odds of preserving their own homes and lifestyles. As with the American Revolution, most looked across the Appalachians to the primary source of white and black settlers, and allied themselves with Britain. In the 1813 American victory at the Battle of the Thames, in Ontario, Tecumseh was killed and his alliance disintegrated. Another casualty of that same battle was Zebulon Pike, who, in the twenty years that had passed since the last time he and Tecumseh faced each other in battle, had explored more of the Mississippi watershed than anyone else.

In many ways the War of 1812 closed a chapter for the Mississippi and its tributaries, cementing the United States' relatively new claims to control the entire watershed. Access in and out of the Mississippi River via New Orleans was universally considered to be vital to the aspirations of the new American settlements in the upper valleys, and in 1802 Thomas Jefferson had sent James Monroe and Robert Livingston to Paris with the authority to pay up to $10 million to France for the city. France, under Napoléon Bonaparte, had only recently reacquired the city from

Spain, a development that caused President Jefferson to lose sleep. It seemed obvious that Napoléon was intending to rebuild France's North American empire.

"The cession of Louisiana and the Floridas by Spain to France works most sorely on the U.S.," Jefferson wrote to Livingston in Paris on April 18, 1802. "I cannot forbear recurring to it personally, so deep is the impression it makes in my mind. It completely reverses all the political relations of the U.S. And will form a new epoch in our political course."

> There is on the globe one single spot, the possessor of which is our natural and habitual enemy. It is New Orleans, through which the produce of three-eighths of our territory must pass to market, and from its fertility it will ere long yield more than half of our whole produce and contain more than half of our inhabitants. France placing herself in that door assumes to us the attitude of defiance. Spain might have retained it quietly for years. Her pacific dispositions, her feeble state, would induce her to increase our facilities there, so that her possession of the place would be hardly felt by us, and it would not perhaps be very long before some circumstance might arise which might make the cession of it to us the price of something of more worth to her. Not so can it ever be in the hands of France. The impetuosity of her temper, the energy and restlessness of her character, placed in a point of eternal friction with us, and our character, which though quiet, and loving peace and the pursuit of wealth, is high-minded, despising wealth in competition with insult or injury, enterprising as any nation on earth, these circumstances render it impossible that France and the U.S. can continue long friends when they meet in so irritable a position.

Jefferson was not mistaken about Napoléon, who did indeed have a grand plan to reestablish a large French presence on the Mississippi. Just as La Salle had envisioned a Mississippi breadbasket for Canada, Napoléon saw the river as a supply chain for France's fantastically profitable sugar-, coffee-, and chocolate-producing colonies in the Caribbean. Foremost among these was the future country of Haiti, where some 450,000 enslaved Africans under the brilliant leadership of Toussaint

L'Ouverture were rebelling against their forty thousand French masters. In December 1802, Napoléon sent more than thirty thousand troops to restore French rule and, secretly, to reestablish slavery. Despite early military successes, a year later there were fewer than ten thousand French troops still alive. Most had succumbed to yellow fever, the perennial scourge of the region, but Napoléon's army had also been soundly defeated by the rebels. In Europe, meanwhile, war with England loomed and Napoléon was certain that one of the first moves London would make would be to grab New Orleans and Louisiana. With Haiti all but lost, there was little reason to keep New Orleans and plenty of reason to keep it out of London's hands. As a result, Napoléon was in a mood to sell not just the city; he wanted out of North America entirely.

"They ask of me only one town in Louisiana; but I already consider the colony as entirely lost," he told his ministers on April 10, 1803,

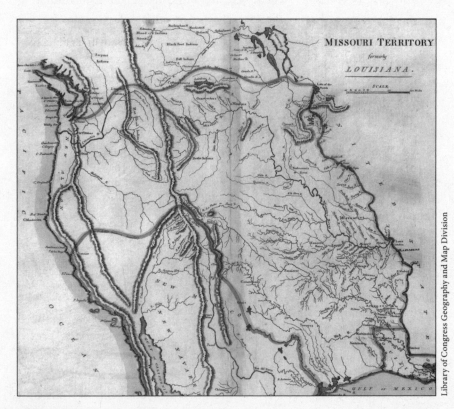

The Purchase.

which was Easter Sunday. By the following morning he had made up his mind.

"I renounce Louisiana," he said. "It is not only New Orleans that I cede; it is the whole colony, without reserve. I know the price of what I abandon. I have proved the importance I attach to this province, since my first diplomatic act with Spain had the object of recovering it. I renounce it with the greatest regret; to attempt obstinately to retain it would be folly."

Strictly speaking, Napoléon had no legal right to make the sale, and Jefferson had no constitutional right to agree to buy, but after several days of furtive negotiations the Louisiana Purchase was made and the United States found itself in possession of the entire Mississippi basin. The country was surprisingly torn in 1805 over whether to ratify the treaty, with certain Anglophile New Englanders in particular threatening to leave the Union. Napoléon, on the other hand, appears to have known exactly what he was doing by creating a great power in the Western Hemisphere.

"This accession of territory affirms forever the power of the United States," he memorably said after the sale, "and I have given England a maritime rival who sooner or later will humble her pride."

The chief American negotiator had a similar sense of the importance of the acquisition of the western watershed for his young country. "We have lived long but this is the noblest work of our whole lives," said Robert Livingston, who earlier in his life had been one of the drafters of the Declaration of Independence. "The United States take rank this day among the first powers of the world."

Andrew Jackson, who owned the future site of Memphis, summed up the feelings of the residents of the river when he wrote to Jefferson: "on the Joyfull event of the cession of Louisiana and New Orleans, every face wears a smile and every heart leaps with joy."

Jackson's bloody victory over the British in the Battle of New Orleans in 1815 tragically took place after the Treaty of Ghent had officially ended the War of 1812, but that city was nonetheless a symbolically fitting location for the final battle of the conflict. Had England won the war, or even had lost it on terms more to her liking, Kansas and Montana might today be in Canada. As it turned out, however, the American victory ratified the Louisiana Purchase and marked the virtual end of European competition to control the basin. Except for a relatively small section along the border with Canada, the entire Mississippi River basin was within the United States of America. Forever . . . or at least until the Civil War.

This is not to say that the warfare with the Native American inhabitants of the river valley ceased. Why would it? The Civil War came and went, but the wars against the Indians continued unabated for more than another century. A partial list of the wars between the United States and the Indians of the Mississippi watershed includes:

- The Arikara War of 1823, which was the first of the wars with the various nations west of the Mississippi.

- The Winnebago War of 1827 began near Prairie du Chien in Wisconsin with the murder of a French Canadian and his Indian wife by a band of Ho-Chunk raiders, followed by a similar murder of an African-American settler and a raid on two keelboats heading down the Mississippi.

- Black Hawk's War of 1832 included an eight-hour massacre of Indians who were waving a white flag on the banks of the Mississippi in Illinois. "The Inds. were pushed literally into the Mississippi, the current of which was at one time perceptibly tinged with the blood of the Indians who were shot in its margin & in the stream," wrote the Indian agent Joseph Street.

- The First Sioux War of 1854 started when a Brulé warrior named High Forehead shot an ox that belonged to a passing Mormon immigrant in the Platte River valley.

- The Dakota War of 1862 started as an Indian uprising along the Minnesota River that in one day left some five hundred settlers dead, spread throughout the upper plains, and continued for eight years.

- The Colorado War of 1863–65, in which a former Methodist minister named John Chivington declared to his men that "he believed it to be right and honorable to use any means under God's heaven to kill Indians." The "fighting parson" then surrounded a village of Cheyenne and Arapaho on a tributary to the Arkansas River in Colorado called Sand Creek. The village had already surrendered, and the chief, Black Kettle, ran an American and a white flag up his tipi, but to no avail, and within minutes two hundred Cheyenne were dead, most of them women and children. A white interpreter later testified: "They were scalped, their brains knocked out; the men used their knives, ripped open women, clubbed little children, knocked them in the head with their guns, beat their brains out, mutilated their bodies in every sense of the word."

- The Powder River Invasion of 1865 was a punitive action taken after some three thousand Teton Sioux and Cheyenne warriors overran a military installation on the North Platte River.

- Red Cloud's War of 1866–68, which Crazy Horse and Red Cloud won, extracting a treaty from General Sherman on their own terms.

- The Comanche War of 1867–75, in which George Armstrong Custer surrounded a sleeping village of Cheyenne on the Washita River in Oklahoma and attacked at dawn. One soldier recalled: "We had just reached the edge of a shallow ravine beyond which we could see the clustered tepees, situated among wide-branching cottonwood trees, when a shot was fired in the village, and instantly we heard the band on the ridge beyond it strike up the familiar air 'Garry Owen' and the answering cheers of the men, as Custer, and his legion came thundering down the long divide, while nearer at hand on our right came Benteen's squadron, crashing through the frozen snow, as the troops deployed into line at a gallop, and the Indian village rang with unearthly war-whoops, the quick discharge of fire-arms, the clamorous barking of dogs, the cries of infants and the wailing of women."

- The Great Sioux War of 1876, in which Custer was defeated and killed at Little Bighorn.

- The Buffalo Hunter's War of 1877, which started with a series of Apache and Comanche raids against white buffalo hunters in the upper Red River valley in the Texas Panhandle.

- The Crow War of 1887, which was the last Indian war in the state of Montana.

- The Ghost Dance War of 1890–91, which included the massacre of 153 Lakota at Wounded Knee Creek.

- The Battle of Sugar Point in 1898 took place not far from the headwaters of the Mississippi in Cass County, Minnesota, in part because

Courtesy Minnesota Historical Society

Ojibwa women, Leech Lake, 1896. By Edward Augustus Bromley.

the Pillager band of the Ojibwa Nation were weary of lumbermen encroaching on what was left of their land.

• The Crazy Snake Rebellion in Oklahoma in 1909 started with a piece of stolen jerky and ended up with three people dead.

It's a long list to which some would also add the Wounded Knee Incident of 1973, in which two FBI agents were shot and Leonard Peltier was convicted on bad evidence. It doesn't include the countless unnamed raids and ambushes by belligerents and brigands on both sides, the massacres and cabin burnings, the rapes and abductions. It doesn't include the revenge or the regret. Or the stolen land that didn't cost lives but was part of the process. Or the lost memories, forgotten place-names, dead myths, and extinct languages. The violence in the valley most certainly didn't end with the War of 1812, but from that point onward the watershed was not Native or European, but some strange pemmican called American. New names and memories were added to those old ones that remained. New myths acquired lacquer; new songs were sung around new hearths and campfires.

Another age was passing—not disappearing, but morphing, making accommodations and adjustments that are still ongoing but that were irreversible. Into the watershed had come people from across the oceans with new tools and new amusements, new drinks and new religions. They brought new diseases and new weapons—new greed, some might say, and new ideas about private landownership and large-scale slavery. For centuries they had come in small batches of adventurers and traders, but now these new people—free and enslaved—poured into the Mississippi watershed. They came from the east via the Ohio, from the south via New Orleans and the Gulf, and from the north via the Great Lakes. The future of the river lay with them.

24

ALLEGHENY MORNINGS

I left the Atlantic coast one morning with a boat on the roof of my car
and crossed the watershed into the Mississippi basin late that same afternoon. This surprised me when I figured out it was possible. In this age of
speed the world usually presents itself less as the wide, round place that
it is than as a string of discrete scenes separated by air-conditioned intermissions, and I would have guessed that the Mississippi was farther away
from home. But Coudersport, Pennsylvania, where the Allegheny seeps
out of a spring in the woods above town, is less than three hundred miles
from New York City. From Plymouth Rock, nearer to where I live, it is
less than five hundred miles. It took a century and a half for English
colonists to beg, buy, bully, and brave their way to the Ohio Country, but
I got there from Cape Cod before sundown.

I didn't embark on the river that day, however. The Allegheny in
Coudersport is too small to paddle, at least in the relatively low water of
late September. Plus, I wanted to poke around a bit, look for the spring
and find the places where the merry little brook that grows into the largest source of water for the Mississippi gurgles under farm-road bridges.
These are places that, unless you are going slowly and looking for them,
you will never see. I stopped in a field to watch a wooden waterwheel go
round and round at what must be the first impoundment not made by
beavers on the entire watershed. Not far from there I stopped to talk to a

pair of farmers—one young and one older, one named Erricson and the other Dunn, though which was which I can't decipher from my journal of that trip. They were repairing a baler.

"His family's been there since the eighteen hundreds," said the younger man. "His granddaddy lost both his legs in the Civil War, isn't that right? Tell him."

"No, wait a minute," said the older fellow, laughing. "It better not have been my granddaddy. I'm in pretty good shape if my granddaddy was in the Civil War. How old you think I am, anyway? Ha ha ha. It was my great, my great-great, maybe. But he did lose his legs, that part is true. I guess my family came here sometime in the early eighteen hundreds or so."

I asked about getting on the river.

"Heck, you can't barely spit in it here," said one. "Some people came through here who waded the whole thing, just to start at the top, but you better go on down a ways if you want to float."

"All them rivers start right around here," said the older fellow. "The Allegheny there starts right up the road a ways and then if you go a bit further that way you get to the Genesee and the Susquehanna."

"You going all the way to New Orleans?" said the younger farmer, looking at my trusty beat-up yellow kayak on top of my trusty beat-up black pickup truck.

"I wish," I said, "but not this time. Maybe Pittsburgh if I get that far. And maybe down the Ohio a ways. I'll just go until I run out of time and have to turn around."

"Time," I thought I heard the older fellow say under his breath to no one. He looked at his baler and then up to me a moment and then said, "Well, you have a nice ride. Don't go over the Kinzua Dam."

I did have a nice ride, and not only because I didn't go over the 179-foot dam, which would certainly have spoiled the fun. There is no need, fortunately, to rank the places of the watershed in terms of loveliness. I will say, though, that I would be as happy to find myself again sliding down that stream as almost anywhere I have been before or since. Not for nothing did the Seneca and their Mingo cousins keep this stretch of country secret as long as they could:

"There is an old agreement that no white men should pass through their country for fear of spies to see their land," said John Hays, who tried to travel the Allegheny in 1760 and was unceremoniously turned back.

At the Allegheny River Campground ten miles downriver from Coudersport, the stream still looked too small to be fun. I walked the river
along the campground, which was sparsely occupied by motor homes
and trailers, and could see that even drawing only two inches of water, I
was going to be getting in and out of my boat most of the time. One of the
drawbacks of traveling by kayak as compared to a canoe is that the latter
is much easier to jump in and out of when you need to drag in shallow
water or around fallen logs. The coolness of the fall weather told me to
push on farther: I didn't come to wade in the water.

I stopped to talk with the boy who was minding the counter in the
little campground store. He told me that in the spring and early summer
people sometimes ride inner tubes down from the campground to Port
Allegany, or even on to Turtle Point. Turtle Point is about five miles past
Port Allegany and I asked him about the river below there. He looked at
me blankly, as if the thought had never occurred to him.

"I don't know where it goes from there," he said.

Driving on in search of deeper water, I thought about his innocent
comment. This boy lived by the river every day of his life, old enough to
mind a store but not knowing from where the Allegheny came or where
it goes. Was he too young? Or too incurious? Too innocent? Or too content to care? I, on the other hand, had seen where the Allegheny seeps out
of a hillside and held in my mind a map of where it meets the Monongahela to become the Ohio, and where it goes from there all the way down
to the Gulf of Mexico.

I knew where the Allegheny goes, so what more did I expect to discover by finding out how it gets there? Would I, once I pulled my boat
out downstream somewhere, know any more about the river than an
old farmer or a young boy or anyone else at any point along its
banks? "A man's ignorance sometimes is not only useful, but beautiful," Thoreau said, again in "Walking." The Eastern proverbs about sitting beside a river generally promise wisdom and serenity; the European
proverb about going downstream promises only the deeper conun-
drum of the sea.

At Turtle Point I dropped the boat under a bridge in the middle of
nowhere and went to park the truck near the general store nearby, which
was closed, so I left a note on the windshield explaining that I had gone
on down the river and would return eventually. When I got back to the

kayak a woman was there, probably in her fifties, give or take a decade, smoking a cigarette and inspecting the boat.

"Hello," I said.

"Hello," she replied. "Have you come down the river?" She had a German accent, which only heightened her out-of-place Marlene Dietrich aura.

"No," I replied, "just setting off."

"I come down here sometimes at my lunchtime just to sit and see the water go by," she said.

As beautiful as the Allegheny River is, this wasn't to my mind the loveliest place to pay attention to it, what with the uninspired bridge so close, adorned with the usual profane graffiti and littered here and there with bottles. The river is about twenty yards wide there, and overhung with dense vines and scrubby river brush.

"The kids they write sometimes terrible, terrible things on the bridge," she said as if reading my mind. "It's too bad, but that always happens."

It took me a few minutes to get my gear stowed the way I like it, and I realized for the first time that packing a boat is an oddly personal endeavor better accomplished without a beautiful stranger watching me obsessively rearrange my water bottles, navigational gadgets, and whatnot. I got the feeling that she, too, was not altogether thrilled to be sharing her private time by the river with me.

"You are from Germany?" I asked after I had gotten into the kayak and was pushing my hands into the sand beneath the hull, sliding the boat backward into the six-inch-deep channel.

"Yes," she said, "a long time ago." She named a city and a river, the Rhine or the Elbe, I can't remember which.

"What brought you all the way here to western Pennsylvania?" I asked. I was floating slowly backward now. Neither of us was moving a muscle, but I was drifting away from her.

"Marriage," she said, like that, one word with no particular inflection good or weary.

"Oh, that will do it," I said, and smiled.

"Yes, it will," she said, and smiled too, for the first time in our conversation.

Then I was around the corner.

One morning on the river I startled a young buck and doe in the dawn light by the side of the river, in a scene that almost made me laugh as it was so perfectly romantic, not as in love, but as in a gilt-framed Hudson River School painting or the cover of an old recording of a Beethoven symphony. I slid quietly up on the opposite bank until the deer were only forty yards away. Then, huffing and snorting, they bounded up the banks and away.

There were eagles overhead almost all the time, and ducks behind every corner—or, it seemed the same ducks were continually spooking downriver, where they waited for me to reappear and re-startle them so they could squawk on farther down. The river in many places was just barely wider than the trees that have fallen into it, and occasionally I had to paddle over submerged branches or logs. Even where the river widened out, it was shallow and shoaly, making me glad my boat was plastic and not birch bark, and allowing a good view of large muskie and pike, and once of a giant hellbender salamander—an "Allegheny Alligator"— that looked to be almost two feet long.

"Few rivers and perhaps none excel the Allegheny for the transparency of its water, or the beauty of its bottom, having a fine gravelly bed, clear of ricks and uninterrupted by falls," Zadok Cramer wrote in the 1817 version of *The Navigator, Containing Directions for Navigating the Monongahela, Allegheny, Ohio and Mississippi Rivers; with an Ample Account of These Much Admired Waters, from the Head of the Former to the Mouth of the Latter.* With its long, winding subtitle, Cramer's guide was a bible of sorts for the rising tide of settlers, containing detailed notes about currents, cargoes, and the various settlements along the rivers.

It is the opinion of a friend of mine who lives in Minneapolis that cities on the Mississippi are more like one another than they are like the hinterland cities and towns within their own states. Minneapolis is more like St. Louis than it is like Rochester, Minnesota, for instance. And St. Louis is more like Memphis and New Orleans than it is like Springfield, Missouri. From my experience of those places, I know what he means. "A river touching the back of a town is like a wing," Thoreau wrote in his journal on July 2, 1858. "River towns are winged towns."

Small river towns throughout the watershed also share a certain kinship with one another, though the ties are looser the higher up into the tributaries you travel. Most of the settlements have long since divorced from their first love, the river, and are defined instead by whether they were favored or scorned, first by the railroad and more recently by the interstate highway. Up on the Allegheny, the old days when the river was the reason for the towns lurk mostly in the occasional old saloon facing the stream, sometimes with rooms still available for rent upstairs if you are brave enough to venture up there.

The biker bar next to the bridge in the town of Allegany, which doesn't have rooms to let, felt weirdly like a throwback to rough old river days. A tall, tattooed bartender, with her hair dyed jet black and a friendliness that belied her tough look, maintained order. "You're not from around here," she even said to me at one point, like a line out of a spaghetti western. The old drunk to my left had been blabbering racist garbage in my ear, inspired by something he saw in the football game on the screen behind the bar.

"No," I said. "I'm not from around here."

"I could tell," she said. "Your burger will be out in a little bit, hon." It wasn't flirtation, really, it was just a statement of something apparently obvious to her, though what made it so obvious I couldn't say. Could it be because I was dressed head to toe like a Florida fishing guide, in quick-dry microfiber khaki—my usual uniform when traveling by river?

The river. After a few days of travel, watching it widen and grow from something awkward and crooked into something curving and lovely, it took a part of me. "Where have you been?" the Allegheny seemed to whisper whenever I returned from lunch or a night in town. "I know, I'm sorry," I whispered in return as I pulled my boat out of the weeds where I had stashed it. "But I'm back."

Downstream from Allegany, the blue jays were screaming at an immature bald eagle, who was nonplussed. A mile down from them, a pair of ruddy ducks startled and took off, one heading upriver, the other down.

Then the drake, realizing his mistake, turned around and followed his mate upriver, quacking plaintively as he veered over my head.

The Seneca Allegany Casino is a suitably fabulous tower hotel rising over the river in Salamanca, New York, and I hope the Seneca Iroquois are getting as rich as the Mohegans and don't go broke like the Pequots might. I wandered in from the river and headed for the buffet, which was an astonishing thing to behold after a week of power bars and bar-room burgers: there was rotisserie chicken, mashed potatoes, cornbread muffins, BBQ wings, Asian noodles, egg rolls, spicy beef stir-fry, roast beef, roast turkey, Caesar salad, coleslaw, beet salad, six other salads, shrimp bar, weird Chinese dumpling-like devices, cheese, soft ice cream, pies, cookies, pizza—on and on and on it went. There were whole bays of foods I didn't even look at.

Strangely, though the food was attractive, none of it made me hungry. The more I looked, in fact, the less hungry I became. My misgivings about coming in weren't really about the food; when I did load up a plate, it was edible enough, though surprisingly all tasted somewhat the same. I sat by myself in a vast dining room, surrounded by sweeping murals with various Native American themes—happy Indians in the old (old old old) days—and tried to eavesdrop on the conversations next to me, but on both sides no one was talking to their dinner companions.

I don't have a problem with other people going and having their fun, and I like a friendly game of poker now and then. But for all the posters of fabulously beautiful people in states of hyper-happiness on the billboards, whenever I set foot in a casino, all I ever see are lonely-looking senior citizens in front of slot machines. Sometimes they have their plastic buckets of quarters or tokens, but more often nowadays they are wired to the machine by something attached to their neck.

There are no windows anywhere in the casino because, I presume, the Seneca don't want anyone looking outside when they should be gambling. "No white man should see their country . . ." Sitting there picking at my Chinese dumplings, I knew I did not want to paddle thirty miles down the half-full reservoir in order to drag my kit around the big dam. Not when I could call a cab to take me back to Turtle Point to get my truck, come back here and fetch my kayak from its hiding place among the reeds and rushes, and drive around the reservoir and put back in below Kinzua.

The spell was broken. Hurtling through the towns that it had taken me the better part of a week of paddling to pass through on the river took less than an hour in the cab. Places I had approached at the river's pace now flashed past with barely enough time to register. "Look, there's the funky bar and hotel, and, oops, that was the mystical bridge ruin, and . . ." Boom boom boom—I was back at my truck fishing my keys from their hiding place.

The river below the dam was determined to make me pay for my unfaithful act of bypassing the reservoir, as if to say, "What kind of friend are you to love me when I am free and abandon me when I am jailed by the dam builders?" I put back in on the Conewango, just upriver from its confluence with the Allegheny in Warren, Pennsylvania, and all went well for the first five hundred yards. As soon as I got to the confluence with the main river, as if on cue, my little GPS device fell overboard. Normally, I religiously attach its lanyard to the deck bungee to prevent just such a fiasco, but for some reason this time I had failed to do so, and it sank to the bottom like a lost bowie knife.

The river here was less than knee deep and, as the GPS was waterproof, I quickly beached the boat and waded around for twenty minutes under the monstrously huffing and puffing tanks of an oil refinery. But it was gone, along with all my tracks and waypoints, average speed, maximum speed, time moving, time resting. Very important statistics indeed!

There was something oddly familiar about the incident: years before, while traveling around Nantucket on foot I accidentally erased all the data from a dozen or so research trips. That time, I waxed on in my journal for several pages about the meaning of my technological obsession with charting my progress. This time, however, I just swore out loud, thought, "Thank God it wasn't my iPhone," got back in my boat, and paddled away. It was just one less thing to carry into towns from the river at night, and now that the Allegheny had requisitioned my gadget as the price for skipping the reservoir, I was permitted to proceed.

I didn't miss the GPS. After all, it wasn't as if the destination and route were complicated. I was floating down the river. I floated past the first oil wells in the world, and past Babylon Hill, where the ladies of the Tidioute evening used to entertain the roughnecks. In the early days, wooden barrels filled with the new "earth-oil" were simply pitched into the river to be picked up downstream. The forest of rickety wooden derricks is gone now, replaced by a forest of third-growth trees, many of them showing their yellow and scarlet fall colors.

I floated past Buckaloons and Kittanning, and the other old Indian towns. And the place where George Washington tried to convince the Half King to trust the English more than the French. And past the funky RV parks on bits of land, the flatness of which was exactly why the Delaware and Mingo also camped there in the 1740s. I paddled past miles of exquisite national forest. I slid past Oil City toward Pittsburgh. Toward Wheeling and Cincinnati, Louisville and Cairo. Sliding toward the big Mississippi, Memphis, Vicksburg, Baton Rouge, and New Orleans.

With no compass, even, I could have slid all the way from Kinzua Dam to the Gulf of Mexico without ever getting lost. I was happy and free beneath the eagles and above the salamanders, singing to myself the old Smothers Brothers version of "Hey ho, boatmen row, Sailing down the river on the O-hi-o."

BOOK FIVE

LIFE ON THE MISSISSIPPI

· · ·

Flatboats and Keelboats, Steamboats and
Showboats, Songsters and Soul Drivers

The turd is proud that the river will carry it.

—SPANISH PROVERB

25

DOWN A LAZY RIVER

"Yes Ma'am I know a lot about boats," said George Taylor Burns to a historian from the Works Progress Administration. "My first memories are filled with boats. My babyhood was passed in Missouri where my master kept a wood yard. Boats of every kind stopped there, for no coal was used to fire the boilers. The slaves worked from morning until late at night piling and sawing and hauling wood to sell the boatmen."

Burns was born around 1833 in Gregory Landing, Missouri, on the Mississippi River just south of the border with Iowa. At that time the color of a person's skin had different consequences depending upon which side of which river you were on. Indians from the eastern half of the watershed were being forced west across the Mississippi, in the wake of Andrew Jackson's ethnic cleansing. Runaway slaves tried desperately to get north across the Ohio—the River Jordan—to the free states. Or even better, once the Supreme Court allowed slave hunters to prowl the North at will, all the way up the Mississippi to Canada. Only whites were truly free to go where they wanted, unless they got caught helping fugitive slaves across the Ohio.

Gregory Landing is 350 river miles north of the mouth of the Ohio River—the putative line between enslaved and free states—but it's on the west side of the Mississippi, in the slave state of Missouri, which was bad luck for Burns. "Father was black," he said, "but my mother was a bright mulatto." Not that Burns knew either of his parents very well. One of his earliest memories was of his mother led away in a long line of chained slaves, sold down the river one winter after the owner of the woodlot died. His father was apparently already gone, to a similar fate. Not yet seven, George Taylor Burns was a motherless slave in the Show Me State with a view across the river to the Land of Lincoln.

The geography of race before the Civil War was so convoluted in that great crossroads of the watershed that even some of the owners of slaves got confused, which is how Burns ended up a river man. The winter his mother was sold, he slept alone in the slave quarters. Never very big or strong, one night he froze so solidly into his bed that he was unable to get out when the breakfast horn called him to come and begin another day of hauling wood for the steamboats.

"Old Missus went to the Negro quarters to see what was wrong," Burns later said, and "she was horrified." She carried him into her house and managed to warm him up, but all of his toes fell off. She paid the local cobbler to make some special shoes for her young property, but it was obvious his days of hauling wood were over. He was soon taken to Indiana by a relative of "Old Missus" who didn't realize she wasn't going to be allowed to keep a slave in that state. She could own a slave as an investment, however, and she leased Burns out to do dishes on an Ohio River flatboat.

"I was still a young child, possibly seven years of age when we came to Indiana," explained Burns. "That may have been in the year 1839 or 1840, but within one month after landing at Troy, I had been indentured to a flat-boat captain and my life for the next 70 years was spent on the different rivers."

"I worked on many boats in the Ohio River when I was such a little child that I had to stand up on a soap box to wash dishes," he said. "Even then I was a river-rat."

People have always traveled in boats in the watershed, and there have always been proud river rats among them. For ten thousand years or more the primary vessel was a dugout, which could range from crude solo fishing crafts that weren't much more than logs to the enormous and ornate cypress war canoes with awnings and seventy paddlers that chased de Soto's men down the river in 1542. In the far north there were bark canoes, though those are more often associated with the Great Lakes. In the bayou there were dugouts with platforms at the stern, from which to spear fish or alligator.

The first few centuries of European contact didn't change river navigation much. The rough ships built by the remnants of de Soto's fleeing army were forgotten as soon as they passed out of the river into the Gulf of Mexico and limped away. La Salle's ship never made it off of its blocks beside the Illinois River. In the mid-1700s, French voyageurs began to use long, slender keelboats to explore the western watershed, but most of the traffic was still carried on in bark and dugout canoes, or in pirogues, which were essentially cypress dugouts with flat bottoms and sharper chines, though sometimes pirogues were made beamier by combining logs into a catamaran or trimaran.

With the arrival of the Americans in the watershed, however, the baroque era of river traffic began. Decades before Americans began to speak of their "manifest destiny" to control the continent from sea to sea, the Mississippi watershed assumed a mythical status in the self-identity of the young nation. "No country perhaps in the world is better watered with limpid streams and navigable rivers than the United States of America," crowed the 1817 edition of Zadok Cramer's *Navigator*. "And no people better deserve these advantages, or are better calculated to make a proper use of them, than her industrious and adventurous citizens."

The watershed was America's future, but only if Americans could get there. In 1806 President Jefferson authorized the first federal highway project, improving the old Braddock Road that ran from Cumberland, Maryland, to the Forks of the Ohio and extending it down to Wheeling, (now West) Virginia. That section of what eventually became known as the National Road was built between 1811 and 1818 and became a principal route to the Ohio. From there, anyone with any sense continued their journey to the far corners of the basin by water. In the early decades it wasn't the iconic steam-powered paddle wheelers so associated with the Mississippi of the mid-nineteenth century; it was virtually anything that would float.

"The first thing that strikes a stranger from the Atlantic, arrived at the boat-landing, is the singular, whimsical, and amusing spectacle, of the varieties of water-craft of all shapes and structures," Timothy Flint wrote home from Pittsburgh to his brother in Massachusetts in 1824. Flint, who first traveled out to the Ohio and Mississippi Country as a missionary in 1815, left behind one of the best memoirs of life on the river in the first half of the nineteenth century.

Aside from small skiffs, pirogues, and canoes, the most common boat on the river in the early nineteenth century was the flatboat. These were also sometimes called "Kentucky flats," though the majority of them were built in Brownsville, Pennsylvania, on the Monongahela. Brownsville, which grew rapidly into a major center of riverboat construction, is considered the birthplace of the flatboat because it was there in 1782 that a farmer named Jacob Yoder invented the form. He took a crop of grain to New Orleans, where he earned a tidy profit from the sale of both it and the wood from which his boat was built.

"Invented" might be stretching the level of nautical innovation involved in Yoder's design. A flatboat was not much more than a rectangular box of planks, fifteen feet wide and up to a hundred feet long, caulked with pitch or tar. There was a large steering oar at the stern and two smaller oars at the bow, which resembled antlers when not in use and gave flatboats the nickname "broadhorns." Most flatboats had a shed at the back, but not all. Flint described the flatboat as "a species of ark, very nearly resembling a New England pig-stye."

After a painting by George Caleb Bingham showing men on a flatboat.

There were floating blacksmiths and floating general stores. There were floating sawmills and gristmills that anchored up in the current and drove their machinery with the current. There were floating bars, theaters, and circuses loaded with exotic animals. There were, said Flint, "monstrous anomalies, reducible to no specific class of boats, and only illustrating the whimsical archetypes of things that have previously existed in the brain of inventive men, who reject the slavery of being obliged to build in any received form. You can scarcely imagine an abstract form in which a boat can be built, that in some part of the Ohio or Mississippi you will not see, actually in motion."

Enormous rafts of logs came down the rivers from anywhere there were trees to cut. As early as 1812, according to Cramer's *Navigator*, seven million board feet of lumber passed Pittsburgh from the Allegheny and Monongahela. The most spectacular log runs, however, were later in the century when the loggers sank their crosscut teeth into the ancient forests of Wisconsin and Minnesota. Constructed entirely of logs, usually

Minnesota logjam, by John D. McCall.

only one deep, these rafts eventually grew to fifteen hundred feet long and could cover as much as six acres. Until the advent of steam tows in midcentury, both barges and log rafts were kept in the current by teams of twenty men or more, using enormous sweeps in the bow and a gigantic stern oar that took a team of ten men to handle.

For a while there were even oceangoing sailing ships on the upper river. Not everyone who joined the rush to the Ohio and Mississippi Country was a small-time pig farmer, after all, content to drift down the river in a flat-bottomed box. Admiral Abraham Whipple of Rhode Island joined his daughter and son-in-law at the new settlement of Marietta not long after its founding in 1788. Whipple was a bona fide old salt. During six months as a privateer in the French and Indian War, Whipple, along with his crew on the *Game Cock*, captured twenty-three French vessels. Like many in Marietta, he was also a hero of the American Revolution. In 1772, Whipple led a small band of Rhode Island Sons of Liberty out to the HMS *Gaspée*, a British customs schooner that had run aground in Narragansett Bay. Claiming to be the "Sheriff of Kent," Whipple took the entire crew prisoner and burned the *Gaspée* to the waterline, which didn't please the Admiralty.

"You, Abraham Whipple, on the 17th day of June, 1772, burned his majesty's vessel, the Gaspée, and I will hang you on the yard-arm," Captain James Wallace of the HMS *Rose* wrote to him. To which Whipple famously wrote back: "Sir: Always catch a man before you hang him."

Hang Whipple, Wallace never did, and after the war Whipple sailed to London on the *George Washington* and unfurled the first American flag seen on the Thames. Whipple was a hero on the East Coast, but the land that the new national government was giving away to Revolutionary War veterans was in the West, so he moved to Marietta intending to live out his days as a farmer. In 1800, however, the old lure of the sea and profits induced him to help build an oceangoing schooner and load it with locally produced pork and flour. He sailed the vessel from Marietta to Havana, Cuba, where he traded the cargo for sugar to take back up the coast to Philadelphia. There, he sold the ship, along with its cargo, and returned overland to Ohio.

For a decade or more after Whipple's pioneering voyage, others emulated his success. "The ship 'Pittsburg' and the schooner 'Amity' . . . cleared from this port, the former for Lisbon and the latter for St. Thomas, loaded with flour," the *Pittsburgh Gazette* reported on the last day of December 1802. "The 'Pittsburgh' registered 270 tons, the largest boat built thus far on western waters." Given the hazards of taking deep draft ships down the shoaly river, the practice of taking oceangoing vessels down the Mississippi didn't last. The business of selling produce from the watershed abroad, however, was just getting going. Today more than 90 percent of the agricultural exports of the United States—five hundred million tons a year—goes down the river to the world.

The most elegant boats in the watershed, at least until the arrival of steam, were the long, slender keelboats. These first appeared on the rivers with the French and Anglo traders of the second half of the 1700s. "It was a well-modeled craft, sixty to eighty feet long, and fifteen to eighteen feet wide, sharp at both ends, and often with fine lines," remembered George Byron Merrick, who grew up in Wisconsin in the 1840s and worked the river in almost every capacity before becoming a newspaper editor after the Civil War. "In its day and generation it was the clipper of the western river to which it was indigenous."

Keelboats were what the professionals traveled in: half-mythical, half-

Small keelboat on the New River, 1872.

Library of Congress Prints and Photographs Division

real boatmen with names like Mike Fink and Davy Crockett. Washington Irving described them as "a singular aquatic race that had grown up from the navigation of the rivers—the 'boatmen of the Mississippi,' who possessed habits, manners, and almost a language, peculiarly their own." Henry Adams wrote that along with squatters on Indian land boatmen "were perhaps the most distinctly American type then existing, as far removed from the Old World as though Europe were a dream." Until the Civil War, jolly bare-knuckled boatmen—not the squinty-eyed gun-toting cowboys who replaced them—were the quintessential American folk heroes. Besides boating, drinking, singing, and womanizing, what the boatmen were most famous for was brawling and bragging. Adams recounted a quarrel overheard in Natchez in 1808:

"I am a man; I am a horse; I am a team," cried one voice; "I can whip any man in all Kentucky, by God!"

"I am an alligator," cried the other; "half man, half horse; can whip any man on the Mississippi, by God!"

"I am a man," shouted the first; "have the best horse, best dog, best gun, and handsomest wife in all Kentucky, by God!"

"I am a Mississippi snapping-turtle," rejoined the second; "have bear's claws, alligator's teeth, and the devil's tail; can whip any man, by God!"

"And on this usual formula of defiance the two fire-eaters began their fight, biting, gouging, and tearing."

The "half alligator–half horse" or "half alligator–half man" was a standard trope of the myth of Mike Fink and the life of the river people. There is a whiff of Egypt in the myth, in keeping with place-names on the river such as Memphis, Cairo, Thebes, Karnak, and Alexandria. "Fink was a manifestation of Seek, the Egyptian half-man, half-crocodile god of the Nile," notes Thomas Ruys Smith in *River of Dreams: Imagining the Mississippi before Mark Twain*. It wasn't just the Nile that brought Egypt to mind for nineteenth-century Americans, of course, but bondage—and Monks Mound and the other great pyramids of the Mississippians.

The half-alligator was not purely an import, however. When the French explorer Jean Bossu traveled among the Arkansas Indians in 1777, he wandered into a temple filled with broken clay pots and the remains of tobacco and incense that had apparently been offered to a goddess with a familiar form.

Fifty steps from there we found that for which we searched. The idol was placed upon a kind of altar made of rough stone. It was made of wood which grows in the Bay of Campeche, and which serves the Europeans in making dye. It is extremely hard. They had painted their idol with vermillion to give it a very terrible air. The upper half of its body was in the form of a woman and the bottom half represented that of a cayman; she wore a pair of wild goat horns on her forehead; she held a rattlesnake in her right hand, and in her left, an arrow; she had on her back wings of parchment which were painted black and made in the form of a bat's; the altar was covered with honey, dried fruit, maize, millet, and smoked buffalo tongue.

Whether steered by half an alligator or guided by the spirit of a manitou, every boat of whatever design on the river was a little bit different, just as every bend in every stream in the basin is unique. A flatboat might be loaded down with apples from an orchard planted by John Chapman in central Ohio: he established his earliest nurseries on the Allegheny at Venango, where Washington and Joncaire had their dinner debate, but by the 1820s, like everyone else "Johnny Appleseed" was down in the Ohio Country heading for the Mississippi. Or the apples may have already been converted into cider or applejack. A keelboat could be carrying corn, corn whiskey, or manufactures from New England that had been hauled overland to Brownsville or Wheeling along the National Road. A pirogue of pelts could be floating down the Platte or Missouri from the west.

Anything that anybody might buy, in other words, was on the river somewhere. "Hoop-poles and punkins,—in the slang of the day," said Merrick, meaning everything that might be traded for something else somewhere along the line. Andrew Jackson arrived in Natchez in 1789 with "cotton, furs, swan skins and feathers for bedding, lime, pork, beef, boats and slaves."

Or a boat could be loaded with people. Often an entire family farm made its way west on the water highway, usually in a flatboat. This was part of the astonishing migration that brought the American population of the Mississippi valley from one hundred thousand in 1790 to more than eight million by 1848: an eightyfold increase.

"Some of them, that are called family-boats, and used by families in

Flatboat and keelboat.

descending the river, are very large and roomy, and have comfortable and separate apartments, fitted up with chairs, beds, tables and stoves," Flint wrote to his brother. "It is no uncommon spectacle to see a large family, old and young, servants, cattle, hogs, horses, sheep, fowls, and animals of all kinds, bringing to recollection the cargo of the ancient ark, all embarked, and floating down on the same bottom."

Late spring was the best season for travel down the river, when the water was sure to be high and the current swift, but the danger of extreme floods or excessive ice floes was (one hoped) past. Dozens of flatboats might set out the same day from Brownsville, or Pittsburgh, or Wheeling, all heading down the Ohio at the current's pace. More boats of all sorts would come in as each tributary was passed. By one estimate some three thousand flatboats a year were traveling down the Ohio in the first decades of the nineteenth century. Inevitably, with so many vessels drifting on the same current, boats ended up traveling together for days or weeks on end. Skiffs ferried visitors from boat to boat, or two or more vessels might simply tie together. Then, "Halloo, I know you" might bring another boat on over.

"I was once on board a fleet of eight, that were in this way moving on together," Flint recalled. "It was a considerable walk, to travel over the roofs of this floating town. On board of one boat they were killing swine. In another they had apples, cider, nuts, and dried fruit. One of the boats was a retail or dram shop. It seems that the object in lashing so many boats, had been to barter, and obtain supplies. These confederacies often commence in a frolic, and end in a quarrel, in which case the aggrieved party dissolves the partnership by unlashing, and managing his own boat in his own way."

Days on the river began with a bugle call and ended with fiddle tunes, particularly on nights when there was no town nearby and the boats had to make their own music in the moonlight. "Almost every boat, while it lies in the harbor has one or more fiddles scraping continually aboard, to which you often see the boatmen dancing," said Flint.

There were countless songs to choose from, with endless personal variations by every boat and performer. A fiddle song that started out as a Scotch-Irish reel from Ulster might be passed on along the river to a German fiddler from Mannheim, or a Bohemian Jew, or even a wayward Brahmin from Boston. An attempt to archive the fiddle tunes in the Ozarks alone in the early twentieth century produced a list of nearly five hundred titles. Among the songs starting with a W, there was "Wagoner" and "Wake Snakes." There was "Wake Up Jacob" and "Walls of Jericho," "Walk Along John," "Walk in the Parlor," "Walking to the Pasture," "Way Down Yonder," "Weavering Way," "Weaving Way," "Wednesday Night Waltz," and "What Makes a Nigger Love 'Taters So." There was "Wheel Buzzard Wheel," and there was "Whipples' Hornpipe," "Whistling Reuben," "Whistling Rufus," "White River," "White River Charley," and "White River Shore." There was "Who's Keeping Tally" and the "Wiggle-Ass Jig." There was "Wild and Wooly," "Wild Goose A-Flying," "Wild Hair Frolic," "Will Your Mule Carry Double," "Wilson's Clog," "Wind on the Wabash," and "Woozy Creek." There was "Where Is My Pants At."

There had always been music on the river. "Here is one of the songs that they are in the habit of singing," said Father Marquette after staying with the Illinois Indians on the banks of the Mississippi in 1674. "They give it a certain turn which cannot be sufficiently expressed by note, but which nevertheless constitutes all its grace: Ninahani, ninahani, ninahani, nani ongo." Farther down the river, several decades later, Antoine-Simon Le Page du Pratz lived among the Natchez for eight years and described a night full of singing and dancing, accompanied by drums and calabash maracas:

Upwards of two hundred torches of dried canes, each of the thickness of a child, are lighted round the place, where the men and women often continue dancing till day-light; and the following is the disposition of their dance. A man places himself on the ground with a pot covered with a deer-skin, in the manner of a drum, to beat time to the dances; round him the women form themselves into a circle, not joining hands, but at some distance from each other; and they are inclosed by the men in another circle, who have in each hand a chichicois, or calabash, with a stick thrust through it to serve for a handle. When the dance begins, the women move round the men in the centre, from left to right, and the men contrariwise from right to left, and they sometimes narrow and sometimes widen their circles. In this manner the dance continues without intermission the whole night, new performers successively taking the place of those who are wearied and fatigued.

Many of the early French voyageurs and traders on the upper Mississippi and Missouri Rivers married into local nations and adopted the Native American "dip dip and swing" habit of singing to pass the time, and apparently never shut up. "In all canoe journeys undertaken by Canadians, songs follow the paddle, beginning as soon as it is picked up," said one early-nineteenth-century traveler, who described the voyageurs' songs as "gay, often a trifle more than gay." The songs were often ribald, as befitting the artistic output of twenty men a thousand miles from any woman they knew. "Somewhat smutty, but never intolerable," said one traveler. "Chansons profanes," said a missionary to the Hurons in 1615. The traditional ending to any song was a "piercing Indian shriek."

Musical influence came from all corners. After France transferred Louisiana to Spain at the end of the French and Indian War to prevent it from falling into English hands, colonists came to the Louisiana bayou country from Málaga, Spain, on the Mediterranean coast, bringing their songs and festivals with them. There were sacred songs sung in Latin by priests and Ursuline nuns in New Orleans, and Methodist revival hymns that could loosen the tent stakes along the Tennessee.

And of course there was a very strong flow of musicality from Africa. Africans, both free and enslaved, arrived in the Mississippi basin with the first Europeans. Some were brought directly from the slave markets of Africa—primarily from the Senegal River—to those of New Orleans.

Mardi Gras, 1867.

Library of Congress Prints and Photographs Division

Others had been in the Americas for generations before coming to the watershed, either in the various English colonies on the Atlantic coast, or Spanish colonies in Florida, or the various colonies in the Caribbean. Notably, the Haitian Revolution of 1804 resulted in a dramatic influx of both white and free black Haitians into New Orleans over the following decade. Others came from Cuba. Every migration, whether free or enslaved, brought with it a boatload of melodies, rhythms, riffs, and traditions. The Mississippi River was where it all got mixed and remixed, nowhere more than in New Orleans. "Basin Street is the street" goes one version of the song about New Orleans that Louis Armstrong made famous a century later, "where all the white and black folks meet."

New Orleans was already well on its musical way by the time the Americans took over in 1804. Particularly during Mardi Gras: as early as 1781, town government took up the issue of free and enslaved blacks who "mask and mix in bands passing through the streets looking for dance-halls." There was a motion "to prohibit all kinds of masking, and nightly dancing by the negroes; also those dance halls where a fee is collected at the door." It wasn't just the blacks, either, though they doubtless faced particular discrimination. White dance halls also ran afoul of city government when they got too rowdy, as a Spanish club owner named Filberto Jorge found out when he was shut down in 1792. The problem was never so much the music in the dance halls as it was the ruckus in the streets as people wandered from party to party. New Orleans then, as now, was unlike any other city in North America.

"It was impossible not to stare at a sight wholly new even to one who has traveled much in Europe and America," wrote Benjamin Latrobe, who arrived in New Orleans by sea from Baltimore in January 1819. Like Flint, he mentioned the collection of boats "unlike anything that floats on the Atlantic side of our country." He noticed as well a group of Choctaw women—the heirs to Quigaltam—sitting on the dock. One of these was "a stark naked Indian girl, apparently 12 years old, with a monstrously swelled belly." Whether she was pregnant or starving Latrobe could not tell, or did not say.

It was the market on the New Orleans waterfront, however, that thoroughly astounded Latrobe. It extended along the levee as far as he could see in one direction, and almost that far in the other direction, with two rows of sellers. Some of these had stalls and tables, others had awnings to offer respite from the tropical sun. Most, however, spread their inventory out on the ground on a piece of canvas or a bed of palmetto leaves, off of which they sold "innumerable wild ducks, oysters, poultry of all kinds, fish, bananas, piles of oranges, sugar cane, sweet & Irish potatoes, corn in the Ear & husked, apples, carrots & all sorts of other roots, eggs, trinkets, tin ware, dry goods, in fact of more & odder things to be sold in that manner & place, than I can enumerate. The market was full of wretched beef & other butchers meat, & some excellent & large fish. I cannot suppose that my eye took in less than 500 sellers & buyers, all of whom appeared to strain their voices, to exceed each other in loudness."

Varied as the goods for sale were, the variety of the sellers seemed even greater. "White men and women, & of all hues of brown, & of all classes of faces, from round Yankees, to grisly & lean Spaniards, black negroes & negresses, filthy Indians half naked, mulattoes, curly & straight-haired, quarteroons of all shades, long haired & frizzled, the women dressed in the most flaring yellow & scarlet gowns, the men capped & hatted."

After he was in town a little more than a month, Latrobe wandered into what was then known as Congo Square or the Place des Négres

(Beauregard Square), where the African-American population of the city gathered on Sunday afternoons to play music and dance. Following his ears, he arrived at the square to find a crowd of more than five hundred people. Despite his inability to appreciate the subtleties of the performances—which were largely of Bambara/Senegal River origins—and his typical racism of the time, his is one of the best available descriptions of what many scholars believe to be one of the birthplaces of jazz.

"I went to the spot & crowded near enough to see the performance. All those who were engaged in the business seemed to be blacks. I did not observe a dozen yellow faces," he said. "They were formed into circular groups in the midst of four of which, which I examined (but there were more of them), was a ring, the largest not 10 feet in diameter."

In the first were two women dancing. They held each a coarse handkerchief extended by the corners in their hands, & set to each other in a miserably dull & slow figure, hardly moving their feet or bodies. The music consisted of two drums and a stringed instrument. An old man sat astride of a cylindrical drum about a foot in diameter, & beat it with incredible quickness with the edge of his hand & fingers. The other drum was an open staved thing held between the knees & beaten in the same manner. They made an incredible noise. The most curious instrument, however, was a stringed instrument which no doubt was imported from Africa. On the top of the finger board was the rude figure of a man in a sitting posture, & two pegs behind him to which the strings were fastened. The body was a calabash. It was played upon by a very little old man, apparently 80 or 90 years old.

The women squalled out a burthen to the playing at intervals, consisting of two notes, as the negroes, working in our cities, respond to the song of their leader. Most of the circles contained the same sort of dancers. One was larger, in which a ring of a dozen women walked, by way of dancing, round the music in the center. But the instruments were of a different construction. One, which from the color of the wood seemed new, consisted of a block cut into something of the form of a cricket bat with a long & deep mortice down the center. This thing made a considerable noise, being beaten lustily on the side by a short stick. In the same orchestra was a square drum, looking like a stool, which made an abominably loud noise; also a calabash with a round hole in it, the hole studded with brass nails, which was beaten by a woman with two short sticks.

New Orleans was the undisputed Queen of the River Towns, but there were other contenders upriver that were also growing fast. Most towns on the river had split personalities. Wealthy planters and trades-people lived on the higher and drier lands of the bluffs, which had attracted the first settlers and immigrants, while a rowdy red-light zone carried on down on the waterfront. "Natchez under the Hill," as the por-tion of that town down by the river was called, was legendary for its good times at bars and bordellos, often accompanied by music, not to mention brawls, duels, and random murders of passion. "Vicksburg under the Hill" was a variation on the same bawdy theme. Both on the bluffs and under them, river towns were home to a relatively diverse lot, thanks in large part to the communication with the outside world afforded by the river. For instance, Vicksburg's population of just under five thousand in 1860 was about one-quarter slave, one-third Southern-born whites, and the rest split between European and Northern state immigrants. The town had six newspapers, several churches, and a synagogue.

The truth was that any town large enough to sell whiskey was large enough to draw travelers ashore in search of music and fun. The nature of drifting together on the same river with the same current meant that scores of boats that had been traveling along vaguely together might arrive for the night at the same town. Flint, in one of his most memorable passages, recalled the scene in New Madrid, Missouri, where as many as a hundred boats at a time gathered in the late afternoon or early evening.

> In one place there are boats loaded with planks, from the pine forests of the southwest of New York. In another quarter there are the Yankee notions of Ohio. From Kentucky, pork, flour, whiskey, hemp, tobacco, bagging, and bale-rope. From Tennessee there are the same articles, together with great quantities of cotton. From Missouri and Illinois, cattle and horses, the same articles generally as from Ohio, together with peltry and lead from Missouri. Some boats are loaded with corn in the ear and in bulk; others with barrels of apples and potatoes. Some have loads of cider, and what they call "cider royal," or cider that has been strength-ened by boiling or freezing. There are dried fruits, every kind of spirits

manufactured in these regions, and in short, the products of the inge-
nuity and agriculture of the whole upper country of the west.

They have come from regions, thousands of miles apart. They have
floated to a common point of union. The surfaces of the boats cover
some acres. Dunghill fowls are fluttering over the roofs, as an invari-
able appendage. The chanticleer raises his piercing note. The swine
utter their cries. The cattle low. The horses trample, as in their stables.
There are boats fitted on purpose, and loaded entirely with turkeys, that,
having little else to do, gobble most furiously.

The hands travel about from boat to boat, make inquiries, and
acquaintances, and form alliances to yield mutual assistance to each
other, on their descent from this to New Orleans. After an hour or two
passed in this way, they spring on shore to raise the wind in town. It is
well for the people of the village, if they do not become riotous in the
course of the evening; in which case I have seen the most summary and
strong measures taken. About midnight the uproar is all hushed. The
fleet unites once more at Natchez, or New Orleans, and, though they
live on the same river, they may, perhaps, never meet each other again
on the earth.

Next morning at the first dawn, the bugles sound. Everything in and
about the boats, that has life, is in motion. The boats, in half an hour,
are all under way. In a little while they have all disappeared, and nothing is seen, as before they came, but the regular current of the river.

In an age before broadcasting, before recording, when even decent
roads were a rarity, the Mississippi and its tributaries were unique in
the world as a conduit in which so many musical traditions of several
continents collided in real time and were remixed for the listening audience. It's no surprise, therefore, that so many of the important strains of
American music of the twentieth century originated in the Mississippi
basin. Ragtime and jazz were born in the ferment of New Orleans and
soon headed upriver to St. Louis, Kansas City, and beyond. Cajun and
zydeco—white and black cousins to each other—bubbled up in the
bayou and lay low like alligators. The blues were born in the delta, out of
a tradition of work songs and field hollers. The roots of black gospel, and
of soul are there, too. Rock and roll eventually burst out of Memphis
while early bluegrass and country trickled down mostly from the

Tennessee and the Cumberland Rivers, along with white gospel. Cowboy and western music floated off the plains via the Red River, the Platte, and the Arkansas.

Every song, verse, and beat was potentially up for grabs and reinterpretation and in some cases outright appropriation by anyone who heard it and liked it well enough to learn it. One of the most well known songs of the river in the early nineteenth century drifted down to New Orleans where it was lucky enough to be employed by sailors, who took it out to sea and apparently kept it.

> Oh Shenandoah, I long to see you
> A-way, you rollin' river
> Oh Shenandoah, I long to see you
> A-way, we're bound away
> Across the wide Missouri . . .

That song is now more associated with Yankee clipper ships and other seafaring vessels than it is with the keelboats and flatboats where it was almost certainly first sung. It's usually listed as a sea chantey, and so it did become. "Shenandoah," said the playwright Eugene O'Neill when he put it in the mouth of an old sailor in his play *Mourning Becomes Electra*, "more than any other holds in it the brooding rhythm of the sea."

Perhaps, but it was composed on the river where American music was born.

26

I LONG TO SEE YOU

Easy as the life seemed, at least when viewed from shore, there were a
thousand things that could go wrong on a boat going down the river. You
could run aground on a bar and be stuck for days or weeks. Some of these
were permanent features of the river, with names such as Big-Bone, Pig's
Eye, Beef Slough, and Scuffletown. Other sandbars came and went, particularly in the lower Mississippi or up on the Missouri, where the channel was constantly cutting away the land on one side and depositing it
somewhere else. There were long sandbars known as "reefs," and there
were "ripples" and "shoals" where the sand or gravel bars came in quick
succession, usually in a place where the river dropped more steeply than
average. If you ran aground on a sandy bar and didn't get off quickly
enough, the river might load more sand around the hull, making you
even more stuck than you originally thought. The Mississippi rises and
falls on a daily basis with the supply of water coming from rain or snow
that may have fallen a thousand miles upstream, and God forbid you
fetched up on a sandbar with a boat full of hungry swine when the river
was dropping fast.

There were also, in places on the upper river and tributaries, "chains"
of rock shoals that could rip the bottom of a boat. The biggest of these
created rapids or "falls," the most notorious of which were the Falls of
the Ohio at Louisville, the Des Moines Rapids and Rock Island Rapids

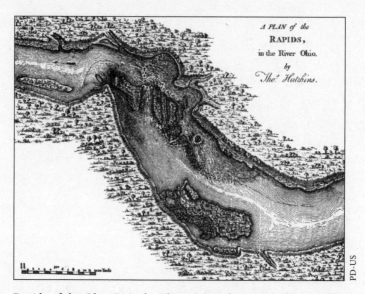

Rapids of the Ohio River by Thomas Hutchins, site of Louisville, 1778.

on the upper Mississippi, and the thirty-seven-mile-long Muscle Shoals on the Tennessee River. About the only good thing about the shoals and falls is that they didn't move around.

Except once. In December and January 1811–12 a series of earthquakes struck the corner of Missouri and Arkansas, some of which were strong enough to ring the church bells in Boston. The New Madrid earthquake, as it is now known, was one of the most powerful series of quakes ever to strike the North American continent. Eliza Bryan, who lived in New Madrid, Missouri, at the time, remembered the scene on the river during one of the largest tremors, when what might be called an inland tidal wave made the Mississippi appear to change direction.

At first the Mississippi seemed to recede from its banks, and its waters gathering up like a mountain, leaving for the moment many boats, which were here on their way to New Orleans, on bare sand, in which time the poor sailors made their escape from them. It then rising fifteen to twenty feet perpendicularly, and expanding, as it were, at the same moment, the banks were overflowed with the retrograde current, rapid as a torrent—the boats which before had been left on the sand were now torn from their moorings, and suddenly driven up a little creek, at the mouth of which they laid, to the distance in some instances, of nearly a quarter of a mile.

The river falling immediately, as rapid as it had risen, receded in its banks again with such violence, that it took with it whole groves of young cotton-wood trees, which ledged its borders. They were broken off with such regularity, in some instances, that persons who had not witnessed the fact, would be difficultly persuaded, that is has not been the work of art. A great many fish were left on the banks, being unable to keep pace with the water.

The devastation was biblical in scope, and the loss of human life was only limited by the sparseness of the population.

"The shaking would knock you loose like knocking hickory nuts out of a tree," said George Crist, who lived near Louisville, Kentucky, when the quake hit. "I don't know how we lived through it. None of us was killed—we was all banged up and some of us knocked out for awhile and blood was every where."

"The screams of the affrighted inhabitants running to and fro, not knowing where to go, or what to do—the cries of the fowls and beasts of every species—the cracking of trees falling, and the roaring of the Mississippi . . . formed a scene truly horrible," said Bryan.

New Madrid was virtually flattened. Fissures opened in the ground from which "sulpherious vapor" spewed, along with sand and, in some places, coal. Some lakes, raised as much as fifteen feet above their former level, drained and disappeared. In other places new lakes appeared where the land sagged. Islands in the Mississippi that had seemed permanent disappeared entirely. Most alarming, if you were unfortunate enough to be traveling on the river in the winter of 1811–12, the quake created two roaring waterfalls on the lower Mississippi River. They didn't last long, but it only took a few seconds of disbelief and indecision on the part of a flatboat crew to result in disaster.

"The river was literally covered with the wrecks of boats," remembered Eliza Bryan. "And 'tis said that one was wrecked in which there was a lady and six children, all of whom were lost."

The aftershocks went on for months, driving some of the people on land to wit's end. "If we do not get away from here the ground is going to eat us alive," George Crist wrote in February 1812. "We had another one of them earth quakes yesterdy and today the ground still shakes at times. We are all about to go crazy—from pain and fright." A month and a half later he was still traumatized and wrote: "I do not know if our minds have got bad or what. But everybody says it. I swear you can still feel the ground move and shake some."

A month later still and he was gone, moved to Pigeon Roost, Indiana, where the quake had been less violent but where other troubles haunted him.

> We lived to make it to Pigeon Roost. We did not lose any lives but we had aplenty troubles. As much as I love my place in Kentucky—I never want to go back. From December to April no man—woman or animal if they could talk would dare to believe what we lived through. From what people say it was not that bad here—They felt the ground move and shake but it did not destroy cabins and trees like it did in Kentucky. I guess that things was as bad here but at least they could see the enemy. On 3 September 1812 the Shawnees that William thought was friendly went crazy and them savages killed twenty-four people. . . .

For travelers on the various rivers of the basin, the aftershocks of the New Madrid earthquake probably went by unnoticed except to the degree that they caused a few more trees than normal to lose their grip and fall into the flow. Earthquakes come, and earthquakes go, but fallen trees were the implacable and constant enemies of wooden boats. They fell (and fall) into the river and its tributaries anywhere that the current erodes away the banks and undermines the forest. "The continuous falling of trees on some of the bends makes a noise resembling the distant roar of artillery," reported the chief of army engineers about a particularly active section of the Red River in 1873. The Red River was especially notorious for logs: in the early 1800s the "great raft," a semipermanent clot of logs, jammed the entire river for more than 160 miles.

Most dangerous among the fallen trees were those logs that in low water became partially buried in the riverbed, as if replanted. It happened whenever an otherwise buoyant log became waterlogged and the heavier stump end, which might still be loaded with dirt and gravel, dropped to the bottom. The current of the water then obliged by building up sand in the lee of the roots and left the other end angling up into the water like a spear. Usually the current swung the lighter end of the log around, and "sawyers" were snags that pointed downstream and vibrated in the current. These could be massive trunks of old-growth trees, battering rams sixty feet long, or more. The *Louisville Courier* reported in 1852 that the snag that destroyed the steamboat *Banner State* "went up through the starboard guard, turned eight passengers out of their beds, and the same time bursting the state rooms into splinters, and then continuing its course upward through the hurricane roof, cut the Texas [wheelhouse on top deck] in two, and disappeared over the other side of the boat."

Snags that pointed upstream were called "preachers" and were even more dangerous because they bowed up and down in the current, as if baptizing their business end. Suffice it to say, you didn't want to hit a preacher or a sawyer. "As she struck a sawyer one night we all ran like mad to make ready to leap overboard," wrote the ornithologist John James Audubon in a letter to relatives in 1843. "But as God would have it, our lives and the *Gallant* were spared—she from sinking, and we from swimming amid rolling and crashing ice. The ladies screamed, and the babies squalled, the dogs barked, the steam roared, the captain (who, by the way, is a very gallant man) swore—and all was confusion and uproar. Luckily we had had our supper, as the thing was called aboard the *Gallant*, and every man appeared to feel resolute, if not resolved to die."

Even floating logs could be dangerous, particularly when they traveled in committees, creating "floating islands" that could literally crush a flatboat or keelboat that got tangled up in them. Ice jams did the same thing, only they were colder and larger, sometimes trapping numbers of boats at a time and slowly devouring them.

"The night of the 18th to the 19th of December was a terrible one for us," said the fossil hunter and museum impresario Albert Koch, who traveled on the steamboat *Palestine* in 1844 when both it and the *Allegheny* became trapped in ice on the Mississippi below St. Louis. "At one o-clock at night a dull rumble, like distant thunder, was heard," he wrote.

This ceased but was repeated toward five o'clock, when it was joined from time to time by a certain cracking noise. Now the whole frightful mass of ice moved; our boat trembled and moved slowly forward straight toward the other steamboat, which lay at a right angle before us, and which we would have shattered if the mighty force of the ice had not also dragged it along and stopped us at the moment of greatest danger. But as soon as we stood still again the ice floes threatened to crush the boat. The sight was indescribably dreadful for there was no thought of escape unless the ice closed up again, which fortunately happened shortly. All anxiously awaited the dawning day, and when it finally came everybody tried to save himself before the ice broke loose a second time. The first who walked over the ice to shore were passengers of our unlucky neighboring boat, which had already sprung a leak.

Not all the dangers facing travelers on the river were the work of Mother Nature. "I met a slave who was a cousin to my own mother," George Taylor Burns said. "His fingers were badly mangled and he was scarred from burns received when he had been taken a captive at Cave In Rock." Cave-in-Rock, an arched cavern overlooking the Ohio River on the Illinois side about halfway between Evansville, Illinois, and Paducah, Kentucky, was one of the most notorious haunts for river pirates.

"The slave man declared that three men who had been captured by the outlaw gang, hiding at Cave In Rock had been burned at the stake," said Burns. "His captain had been put to death by a knife thrust from a ruffian and he alone of all the crew of a captured boat had made his escape by swimming from the rocks. He believed that the pirates believed him to have committed suicide when he jumped from the rocks and therefore made no effort to recapture him."

Cave-in-Rock was the perfect spot for a lair, with a good view up the river so boats could be seen coming before the people in them could see the cave. According to Otto Rothert, who wrote the definitive history of the cave in 1923, passing boats were usually hailed from shore by one or more gang members, preferably attractive female gang members.

"These decoys pleaded to be taken aboard, claiming they were alone in the wilderness and wished to go to some settlement down the river, or that they desired to purchase certain necessities which they lacked," said Rothert. "If the boat was thus enticed ashore, the crew saw their cargo unloaded and plundered, or beheld their craft continue its course down the river in the hands of the enemy, themselves held as hostages or murdered."

Tales of the cave are many and tall. Most sources agree that the Cave-in-Rock itself was less often the actual scene of a crime than a kind of jolly social club for a revolving syndicate of river bandits and counter-feiters, under the leadership in the early days of Samuel Mason. Mason, who had fought in the Revolutionary War, went under numerous aliases, including Wilson, and in the last few years before 1800 there was a large painted sign hanging outside the opening to the cave that read WILSON'S LIQUOR VAULT AND HOUSE FOR ENTERTAINMENT. Between the sign and the waving women, unsuspecting flatboats were drawn to the cave like flies. Occasionally victims might be dispatched right at the cave: either forced to join the gang or, if they refused, killed outright. More often, though, to preserve the good name of Wilson's Liquor Vault and House for Entertainment, boat crews were sized up in terms of fighting ability and wealth and sent on their way toward Hurricane Island, where the dirty work was done by a crew of as many as forty brigands. The boat, under a pirate crew, would be taken to New Orleans and sold.

Mason had a lucrative, if bloody, business going in a good location, but it all caught up with him when he was arrested in Spanish Missouri in 1803 in the company of Wiley "Little" Harpe. Wiley Harpe and his older brother, Micajah "Big" Harpe, were notorious serial killers from Kentucky and Tennessee. By all accounts Big Harpe truly was a giant man, with an oversize and ruddy face framed by jet-black, curly hair, while Little Harpe was smaller, with light hair and blue eyes. The Harpe brothers mostly killed travelers on land, but there was no real pattern to their crimes, other than bloodthirstiness. They murdered women and children they came across in isolated cabins, sometimes after accepting a night's hos-pitality. Often they gutted their victims' bodies with bowie knives, in order to load the carcasses with rocks and dump them in the nearby river.

Two sisters named Susan and Betsey Roberts were lovers of Big Harpe and traveled with the gang, as did a Baptist preacher's daughter named Sally Rice who was Little Harpe's wife. The only time they were all jailed, the two brothers escaped before the trial, leaving the three women behind in another cell. All were pregnant at the time, and after each gave birth in prison, they were released by a sympathetic jury. The three new moth-ers insisted that all they wanted to do was get away from their terrible lovers and start new lives, but as soon as they were free they set off in a canoe with their babies for a two-hundred-mile paddle down to Cave-in-Rock. Somewhere along the way, probably at the cave, they were reunited with the Harpe brothers.

For a while, the other bandits at Cave-in-Rock accepted the Harpe gang into their rarefied society. In the end, however, the brothers' appetite for wanton brutality was too much even for the murderers and thieves of Cave-in-Rock. When the Harpes tied a naked hostage to a horse and drove both horse and human over the cliff in front of the cave for no purpose other than some kind of sick amusement, they were expelled.

In 1799 a posse had finally tracked the Harpes down for a second time, and though Little Harpe escaped, Big Harpe was shot and the Roberts sisters were recaptured. Moses Stegal, a member of the posse whose wife and only child had been killed recently by the Harpes, executed the wounded outlaw and cut off his head with a hunting knife.

"I want to preserve that for a trophy," he said, and handed it by the hair to Harpe's new widow, Susan. She carried it along the road toward Henderson, chanting, "Damn the head, damn the head, damn the head," as she trudged along between the men on horses.

According to Lyman Draper, who interviewed members of the posse, the enormous head was eventually put into a saddlebag and then onto a tree as a warning to other brigands. (The place, at a crossroads near the Pond River in Kentucky, became known as Harpe's Head.) Whether this was done out of pity for Susan Roberts or because the men of the posse were weary of listening to her grim mantra, Draper doesn't say. At trial, however, the jury once again took pity on the women of the Harpe gang and found them not guilty. This time, though, none of them tried to follow Little Harpe, who had wandered west and reunited with Mason.

Mason was no longer at Cave-in-Rock, having moved down the Ohio to the Mississippi, apparently out of fear that Wilson's Liquor Vault and House for Entertainment was due for a visit from local vigilantes known as "regulators." He set up shop for a time on Wolf Island, about thirty miles down the Mississippi from the mouth of the Ohio. There, according to Audubon, "his depredations became the talk of the whole western country; and to pass Wolf Island was not less to be dreaded than to anchor under the walls of Algiers. The horses, the negroes, and the cargoes, his gang carried off and sold." Stack Island, about fifty miles below Vicksburg, was another notorious river pirates' haunt.

Author's photograph

The Ohio River from inside Cave-in-Rock.

Mason and Little Harpe also frequented the Natchez Trace, the ancient route from Natchez to Nashville that was used by flatboat crews to walk home to Kentucky after selling their boats and cargoes in New Orleans. The trace was even better pickings than the river, as most travelers on the path carried the proceeds of their recent voyages; gold was better loot than barrels of flour.

"I have received information that a set of pirates and robbers who alternately infest the Mississippi River and the road leading from this district to Tennessee [i.e., the Natchez Trace] rendezvous at or near the Walnut Hills," Governor William Claiborne of the Mississippi Territory wrote to a local militia commander in April of 1802. "A certain Samuel Mason and a man by the name of Harp are said to be the leaders of this banditti," the governor went on, promising "a very generous reward" for bringing them to justice, dead or alive.

With the public aroused and a $900 bounty on his head, Mason relocated once again, to the Spanish side of the river below New Madrid. With four sons, one daughter-in-law, three grandchildren, and a man calling himself John Taylor, Mason moved into a pair of empty houses in

Little Prairie, Missouri. All went well for a few days, but the group's strange obsession with secrecy, and the fact that they were armed to the teeth, aroused the suspicions of the locals. Eventually the commandant at New Madrid dispatched a division of regulars to the scene, and the entire clan was captured without a firefight.

At an extensive hearing in New Madrid, Mason claimed to be innocent, and tried to implicate Taylor. Taylor, who was really Little Harpe, claimed to be innocent and tried to implicate Mason. One witness said a woman in Mason's party told him she'd been forced to help dispose of a body; another witness said he was held hostage by the gang. Most damaging of all, a search of the gang's belongings turned up "twenty twists of human hair of different shades which do not seem to have been cut off voluntarily by those to whom the hair belonged"—in other words, scalps.

All the reported crimes had taken place on the American side of the river, however. The New Madrid court therefore sent the entire gang in chains to New Orleans, where the Spanish governor-general could, if he wished, turn the prisoners over to the Americans. In one of the last actions of the Spanish government in New Orleans before the Louisiana Purchase, Mason and Harpe were extradited to Natchez.

They didn't get there. About a hundred miles below Natchez, while some of the guards were ashore collecting supplies, the two bandits grabbed some guns and commandeered the boat. In the ensuing firefight Mason was shot in the head, though not fatally, and the pair made their escape. Some said that Samuel Mason never knew his compatriot's true identity, which seems unlikely. If Mason did know he was traveling with the notorious Wiley Harpe, however, he made a colossal error by turning his back on him: a few months after their escape Harpe buried a hatchet in the back of Mason's head. Along with another gang member, he decapitated Mason, wrapped the head in a ball of Mississippi River clay, threw it in a pirogue, and brought it back to Natchez to claim the reward for killing the notorious bandit king.

It was a brazen move. Craven, really. Within hours of applying for the reward, someone accused him of a recent robbery on the Natchez Trace. Within days, his red hair and grim visage caused others to wonder if he was not John Setton—his current alias—but the notorious Little Harpe. Five flatboatmen answered an advertisement and came in and identified him as such. Other witnesses from Kentucky traveled down to confirm the accusation. It was like a scene out of bad television: "if he is Harpe he has a mole on his neck and two toes grown together on one foot," said one witness, and the mole and toes on the defendant were examined and found to be as he described. "If you are Harpe you have a scar under your left nipple where I cut you in a difficulty we had in Knoxville," said another. The scar was there.

When Wiley Harpe was found guilty of highway robbery, the judge ordered that "he be taken to the place of execution and there to be hung up by the neck, between the hours of ten o'clock in the forenoon and four in the afternoon, until he is dead, dead, dead."

In Natchez and elsewhere along the river, condemned prisoners traditionally rode to their execution sitting on their own coffin in the back of a wagon. According to Rothert: "Upon his arrival the same wagon and coffin on which he rode were used as the platform and trap of his gallows. After the suspended rope was properly looped around his neck the condemned man was made to stand erect on his coffin. When all details had been attended to the horses were rushed forward, leaving the human body hung suspended in the air."

After the hanging, Little Harpe's freshly severed head was stuck on a pole along the Natchez Trace, a southern echo of his brother's rotted skull in the crux of a tree up on the Ohio. Sam Mason's mud-caked face, meanwhile, had been identified in Natchez. The most notorious killers on the Mississippi and Ohio Rivers were gone, which didn't at all mean that those traveling down the river could rest easy. Cave-in-Rock remained an occasional lair of outlaws for decades, most notoriously the Ford's Ferry gang. The same was true of many of the islands on the Mississippi, and on the Natchez Trace. Generally speaking, however, lawlessness hovered on the frontier of settlement by whites and blacks. By the middle decades of the nineteenth century, that frontier was moving out of the eastern half of the watershed and heading up the western tributaries. What had been the West was becoming the Midwest.

Even more dangerous than pirates, and more deadly than earthquakes, were the diseases that struck without warning and traveled the river. Typhus, malaria, various flus, mumps, measles, and smallpox were regular and unwelcome visitors. The worst, however, was yellow fever, known locally as yellow jack. Just the rumor of an outbreak terrified river people, and afflicted towns flew yellow flags to warn off boats. It got its name from the yellow pallor of victims, jaundiced from the damage the disease wreaked on their livers. In later stages the ill bled from their mouths, noses, eyes, and ears. The surest sign that death was near, however, was called "the black vomit."

"The patient frequently discharges a liquid similar to black vomit; but it is not the genuine article," the *New York Times* reported in 1854 under the headline "The New-Orleans Plague: Sketches of the Yellow Fever." "Instead of coming from the stomach—the seat of the real black vomit—it is a mere bloody discharge from the gums, the nostrils, and other parts of the internal system. The real black vomit comes from the stomach, and is almost identical with a mixture of blood and meiotic acid; it is thrown up in copious quantities; and if the patient ever recovers after such ejections, it is a miracle which old doctors require to see before they will believe."

Mary Harris "Mother" Jones was living in Memphis when the disease struck there in 1867. "Its victims were mainly among the poor and the workers," she wrote in her autobiography:

> The rich and the well-to-do fled the city. Schools and churches were closed. People were not permitted to enter the house of a yellow fever victim without permits. The poor could not afford nurses. Across the street from me, ten persons lay dead from the plague. The dead surrounded us. They were buried at night quickly and without ceremony. All about my house I could hear weeping and the cries of delirium. One by one, my four little children sickened and died. I washed their little bodies and got them ready for burial. My husband caught the fever and died. I sat alone through nights of grief. No one came to me. No one could. Other homes were as stricken as was mine. All day long, all night long, I heard the grating of the wheels of the death cart.

Yellow fever is transmitted by mosquitoes and struck almost every summer in the lower regions of the river, but there was little way to know if one year would be worse than the last. In New Orleans between 1845 and 1860, the average number of deaths per year from yellow fever was more than fifteen hundred, but some years fewer than twenty people died. In the epidemic of 1853, nearly eight thousand succumbed in the city. The epidemic of 1878 spread to the entire valley, killing nearly twenty thousand people.

Whatever was on board a boat, and whoever was at the steering oar, the situation facing every craft that was not steam-powered on the Mississippi was a variation on the same theme. Going downstream was dangerous for a thousand reasons, but if you didn't run aground on one of the countless and shifting sandbars, it was relatively easy to keep moving.

Going upstream, on the other hand, was dangerous for the same thousand reasons, and it was brutally hard work.

27

UP THE WICKED RIVER

Rough flatboats, such as the one that Abe Lincoln and his stepbrother built on the Sangamon River near Springfield, Illinois, and took to New Orleans in 1830, didn't even attempt to get back up the Mississippi. They were a part of the cargo, broken up and sold for lumber once they arrived at their final destination. In many cases flatboats were converted into cabins by their immigrant owners; the first schoolhouse in Cincinnati was supposedly built from the planks of a flatboat.

If a flatboat crew member wanted to get back home to Kentucky in the decades before steam, there weren't many choices. You could ride a horse or walk along the Natchez Trace, which was arguably a more dangerous endeavor than any boat trip. You could find work on an ocean vessel heading back to the East Coast, or on a keelboat heading upriver. Or you could spend your profits on passage on the same.

More than a few who came down the river simply stayed in New Orleans, which grew from fewer than five thousand people when the first flatboat arrived from Pennsylvania in the last year of the American Revolution to a city of more than one hundred thousand by 1840. People dropped off of the river and put down roots anywhere that looked promising, and once there, they multiplied. "From the cabins and houses tumble out, as you approach the shore, a whole posse of big and little boys and girls," Flint recalled of the settlements he passed in 1824. "And

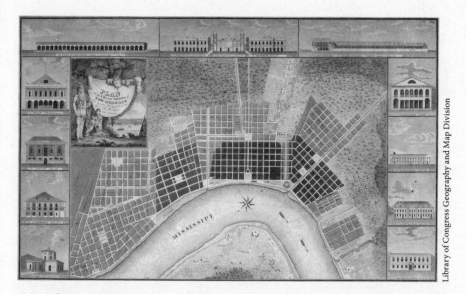

New Orleans, 1815.

Library of Congress Geography and Map Division

the white headed urchins, with their culottes gaping with many a dismal rent, stare at you as you pass. I have seen no where else such hosts of children."

Despite the tide of humanity, the view from the river was more often of a seemingly endless wilderness, particularly the farther you traveled away from Pittsburgh, Cincinnati, St. Louis, or New Orleans. As late as 1823 there was only a single log building at Cairo, the juncture of the Ohio and Mississippi. Between there and the mouth of the Missouri River there were a handful of towns with only a dozen or so families and one, St. Louis, with a population of about five thousand. Above St. Louis there were only a few more small settlements and an occasional single cabin. The population of Hannibal, for instance, was one, and no one was sure if even that person was still in residence or had moved on. With little else in the way of entertainment, river traffic was always an occasion for curiosity on the lonelier stretches of the river: the traditional greeting from shore was "Halloo the boat," to which the proper answer was "Halloo the house."

Those boats that did attempt to travel up the river in the first decades of the nineteenth century did so by sheer will and prodigious muscle power. Small boats could sometimes be paddled or rowed, and anything afloat that could hoist any kind of sail did so whenever the wind was

The river below Cairo, 1862.

remotely favorable. On a winding and shoal-filled river, however, wind could not be relied on except for an occasional boost. Anything much bigger than a canoe or skiff, therefore, needed a method other than paddling to overcome the pull of the current. Most often, this consisted of a rope tied to something onshore. Almost unbelievably, barges the size of oceangoing schooners were hauled by human power up the Mississippi and Ohio.

"I have seen them day after day, on the lower portions of the Mississippi, where there was no other way of working them up than carrying out a cable half a mile in length, in advance of the barge, and fastening it to a tree," said Flint. While the hands on board were pulling in a half mile of rope, another crew was taking another rope a half mile farther around the next oxbow so that there was as little time lost between ropes as possible. "This is the most dangerous and fatiguing way of all," said Flint, "and six miles advance in a day, is good progress."

Of the larger boats, only the keelboat was really designed with upriver travel in mind, and it was that craft that pioneered the upper reaches of the northern and western watershed. Lewis and Clark set out in a keelboat and two pirogues on their famous "Voyage of Discovery" up the

Missouri on May 14, 1804. Their keelboat was fifty-five feet long and drew about three feet of water. It had one large square sail, in the hope of wind, twenty-two oars, and no doubt as many or more poles. The bow and stern both had covered decks and the middle had lockers that were designed so they could be raised as a breastwork if they were attacked.

Designed for upriver travel did not mean it was easily or safely achieved, and Lewis and Clark almost lost their keelboat only ten days into the expedition. "We passed a very bad part of the River Called the Deavels race ground," Clark wrote in his journal on May 24. "We hove up near the head of the Sand bar, the same moving & backing caused us to run on the sand. The Swiftness of the Current Wheeled the boat, Broke our Toe Rope, and was nearly over Setting the boat."

The year after Corps of Discovery departed from St. Louis on their epic cross-country expedition, twenty-six-year-old Zebulon Pike "sailed from my encampment, near St. Louis, at 4 p.m., on Friday, the 9th of August, 1805, with one sergeant, two corporals, and 17 privates, in a keel-boat 70 feet long, provisioned for four months."

Pike's orders didn't come from President Jefferson, as Lewis and Clark's did, but from General James Wilkinson, whom Jefferson appointed in 1805 as the first governor of the Louisiana Territory. Wilkinson was also, at that time, both the commanding general of the United States' armed forces and a paid spy for the government of Spain. Though never proven, Wilkinson may also have conspired with Aaron Burr to set up a new country of their own somewhere west of the Mississippi. Frederick Jackson Turner called Wilkinson "the most consummate artist in treason that the nation has ever possessed." Another historian, Robert Leckie, dubbed him "a general who never won a battle or lost a court-martial."

Though Pike was Wilkinson's protégé, he seems to have been out of the traitorous loop and there is no whiff of foul intentions in his expedition up the Mississippi, which was a logical companion to the voyage up the Missouri. "Soon after the purchase of Louisiana by an enlightened administration, measures were taken to explore the then unknown wilds of our western country," Pike wrote in the preface to his published journals. "Meriwether Lewis, then a captain of the first regiment of infantry, was selected by the President of the United States, in conjunction with Captain C. Clarke [sic] to explore the then unknown sources of the Missouri, and I was chosen to trace the Mississippi to its source."

Specifically, Wilkinson ordered Pike to take a keelboat up the Mississippi as far as he could go in a single season and "spare no pains to conciliate the Indians and to attach them to the United States." He was also
to take note of the fur trade and scope out suitable locations for a string
of American forts and try to get permission from the Indians to build
them. He was to report on any British fur traders in the region.

Pike grew up largely in frontier outposts in the Ohio Country and
was as familiar with river navigation as anyone who wasn't a professional boatman could be. What's more, he ran a tight crew and made
good time, up to thirty miles a day when the wind allowed them to set
sail on the wide stretches of the Mississippi above St. Louis. Nonetheless,
like Lewis and Clark, he almost lost his keelboat within two weeks of
setting out.

"I arrived here [at the Des Moines Rapids] this day, after what I have
considered as rather an unfortunate voyage, having had a series of rainy
weather for the first six days, by which means all our biscuit was more or
less damaged, they being in very bad and open barrels," he wrote. "And
our having twice [gotten stuck] so fast on forked sawyers or old trees as
to oblige me partly to unload, and staving in a plank on another [saw-
yer], which nearly sunk our boat before we got on shore."

A keelboat always had a steering oar at the back, but it was usually
propelled upstream by a crew of some twenty men armed with twenty-
foot-long ash poles that were tipped with iron. Planting one end in the
riverbed and the other against their shoulder, they walked a narrow deck
along both gunnels from bow to stern, pushing the boat forward. When
they got to the stern they yanked their pole from the water, jumped on
the roof of the cargo box at the center of the boat, and ran back to the
front of the line to repeat the process. In sections where the channel
dropped off quickly, the boatmen poled only on the gunwale facing the
river and returned to the front along the landward gunnel. Thus they
walked in circles—for months on end. In 1833 the legendary fur trader
William Sublette and a crew of thirty took his keelboat from St. Louis
two thousand miles up the Missouri to the Yellowstone River.

Poling and rowing were only two of the techniques available to a
keelboat, and much of the time the current was simply too strong to be
overcome by those means. As with the larger boats on the lower Mississippi, Sublette's men on the Missouri often used a thousand-foot-long

line known in the business as a cordelle. This was typically attached to the top of a thirty-foot mast near the center of the keelboat, which was supposed to keep the rope from dragging in the water or getting caught on the brush along the bank. If the bank was too broken, swampy, or steep for the men to walk along, they might fasten the line to a tree or an outcropping of rock. Then those still on the boat would haul the line in and the keelboat would be moored or held with poles, and the line walked ahead another thousand feet and tied off so the "warping" could be repeated.

If the water level brought the boat right up in the trees and brush along the bank, the crew might just grab any vegetation they could and walk from bow to stern. "We began to pull the boat up the stream, by a process, which, in the technics of the boatmen, is called 'bush-whacking,'" said Flint of this method, which was employed on one of his several trips up the Mississippi from the mouth of the Ohio. More than fatiguing, bushwhacking was regularly fatal. One slip could send a person overboard and downriver, perhaps under a mass of logs.

"I do not remember to have traversed this river in any considerable trip, without having heard of some fatal disaster to a boat, or having seen a dead body of some boatman, recognized by the red flannel shirt, which they generally wear," Flint went on. "The multitudes of carcasses of boats, lying at the points, or thrown up high and dry on the wreck-heaps, demonstrate most palpably, how many boats are lost on this wild, and, as the boatmen always denominate it, 'wicked river.'"

In all cases moving a boat upstream on the Mississippi without the benefit of steam power was backbreaking, soul-breaking, foot-rotting, snake-biting, fever-inducing, highly dangerous, low-paid work. Whereas floating downstream even a slow boat might expect to make ten or twelve miles an hour, going upstream a dozen miles was often all that could be expected out of long day's work.

By late September 1805 Pike and his men had made it to the Falls of St. Anthony [Minneapolis], which was the only major waterfall on the Mississippi River until it was replaced by locks and dams in the twentieth century. Albert Bierstadt's painting of the falls from the 1880s shows the six-hundred-yard-wide cascade as a panoramic shift in the crust of the earth, bathed in the painter's romantic evening light. With Bierstadt's familiar tiny human figures in the foreground beaching a canoe,

Owahmenah, as the Dakota called it, looks like a cataract to rival Niagara. Pike's first impression, however, was that it "did not strike me with that majestic appearance which I had been taught to expect from the descriptions of former travelers."

After portaging around the falls, Pike and his company pushed on up the river in progressively smaller boats to the vicinity of Painted Rock Rapids, or Little Falls. There, with the Mississippi starting to freeze, they built a winter fort. Some of the men stayed behind, but Pike and a smaller company of eleven men continued on foot with sleds of gear, living off the land with varying success. They feasted one day on elk, and made do with a porcupine or nothing on other days. The snow was three feet deep, and "the cold was so intense that some of the men had their noses, others their fingers, and others their toes frozen, before they felt the cold sensibly," he wrote in his journal on January 7. The cold may have tempted Pike to pitch his tent too close to the fire, and it went up in flames one night, burning up his leggings and moccasins. Even the booze almost froze: "Some spirits which I had in a small keg congealed to the consistency of honey." Meanwhile, his Sioux interpreters repeatedly told him the Chippewa up ahead would kill them all.

Finally, on February 1, the half-frozen travelers got up early, snowshoed across the bleak white prairie, and arrived at Lake La Sang Sue at half-past two o'clock. Another twelve miles of snowshoeing across the frozen lake found them banging on the door of the Northwest Company's trading post. By Pike's estimate they had come seven hundred miles from their winter camp.

"I will not attempt to describe my feelings on the accomplishment of my voyage, for this is the main source of the Mississippi," Pike wrote in his journal. The sense of accomplishment was made even better by getting served a "good dish of coffee, biscuit, butter, and cheese for supper" by the friendly factor of the post, Hugh M'Gillis.

Never mind that Leech Lake, as the lake is now known, is no longer considered the primary source of the river. (Lake Itasca was identified as such by Henry Schoolcraft in 1832.) Or that it wasn't really any kind of discovery, even by European standards, since the place was crawling with Canadian fur traders. Pike's ankles and legs were so swollen in recovery from the cold that he wasn't able to wear his own clothes and had to borrow some from M'Gillis. In the following days he traveled in a small sleigh dragged by dogs and visited Cass Lake, another thirty miles up. He eventually got, he believed, within about ten miles (two leagues) of the Hudson's Bay watershed. Cass Lake was far enough, and his men shot the Union Jack off of its flagpole and turned around.

Pike had accomplished all that General Wilkinson had asked him to do. He even brokered a temporary peace between the Chippewa and the Sioux, and told both them and the Canadians that the basin on both sides of the Mississippi was now a part of the United States. By the end of February he and his party were making their way back toward St. Louis, though not without more pain, which Pike's Indian guides attempted to alleviate by good cheer. "My young warriors were still in good heart, singing and showing every wish to keep me so. The pressure of my racket-strings [snowshoes] brought the blood through my socks and mockinsons, from which the pain I marched in may be imagined."

Zebulon Pike had been a soldier since he was fifteen years old, having joined his father's regiment in 1794 just in time to participate in the Battle of Fallen Timbers, which ended the Northwest Indian War. He was five feet eight inches tall, with blue eyes and light hair and a ruddy complexion. According to a fellow soldier who served with him on the Ohio River in 1800, shortly after Pike had been made a lieutenant, he was "very gentlemanly in his deportment—manners agreeable & polished." He didn't speak much, nor was he the type to joke around with the boys, having "less levity in his character than even many brother officers Senior to him in years and rank." His one affectation, if it can be called that, was that when on parade with troops he cocked his head to one side, "so that the tip of his Chapeau touched his right shoulder."

Whatever else he was, Pike was a decisive commander and disciplined explorer. He was brave, perhaps fearless, ready to walk until his feet bled and to die for his country if it came to that. He hoped one day to lead men into battle, but his journals do not leave one thinking that Zebulon Pike relished or reveled in exploration.

"I can only account for the gentlemen of the N. W. Company contenting themselves in this wilderness for 10, 15, and some of them for 20 years, by the attachment they contract for the Indian women," he wrote at Leech Lake. "The wealth of nations would not induce me to remain secluded from the society of civilized mankind, surrounded by a savage and unproductive wilderness, without books or other sources of intellectual enjoyment, or being blessed with the cultivated and feeling mind of a civilized fair [one]."

It wasn't just any civilized fair one that he was thinking about, but Clarissa Brown, whom he'd married in Cincinnati four years before. She was tall and well educated, particularly in French, the language in which she kept a journal, and whenever Pike had a chance to send letters back downriver on the Mississippi expedition, he wrote to her. Pike's personal letters and her journals were both lost in a fire, but it's safe to say that he and his men were looking forward to getting home.

"All hearts and hands were employed in preparing for our departure," he wrote in his journal about the day before they finally turned back south. "In the evening the men cleared out their room, danced to the violin, and sang songs until eleven o'clock, so rejoiced was every heart at leaving this savage wilderness."

Going downriver! They made great time, riding the spring freshet out of the interminable prairies and woods at a rate they couldn't have dreamed of when they were going up. Now they shot the rapids instead of hauling their heavy loads up them. "I have not been slow in my descent, leaving all the traders behind me," Pike wrote from Prairie du Chien, "nothing but the most insurmountable obstacles shall detain me one moment." Even the Falls of St. Anthony looked better when he was going with the flow. Writing to General Wilkinson he said, "in high water the appearance is much more sublime, as the great quantity of water then forms a spray, which in clear weather reflects from some positions the colors of the rainbow, and when the sky is overcast covers the falls in gloom and chaotic majesty."

One day they cruised nearly 150 miles by Pike's reckoning. "We embarked early and came from eight or ten leagues above the river Iowa to the establishment at the lower Sac Village [Nauvoo, Illinois] by sundown, a distance of nearly 48 leagues," Pike wrote cheerfully in his journal for Sunday, April 27. "At the establishment received two letters from Mrs Pike . . ."

Three days later they were back in St. Louis: "arrived about twelve o'clock at the town," Pike noted, "after an absence of eight months and 22 days." There were no doubt more letters from Clarissa waiting for him at

St. Louis. There was also, a month later, another letter, this one fr
General Wilkinson.

The country needed to know the origins of the Arkansas and the Red
Rivers, the letter read in part, and Pike was the man to do it. He should
begin to look for another keelboat immediately.

28

ALL ABOARD

Not everyone on the Mississippi preferred going downriver. Steamboats, when they showed up in the second decade of the nineteenth century, earned most of their keep going upriver. Black folks, who showed up with the first white folks in the sixteenth century, lost much of their hope going down.

The first commercially successful steam-powered vessel in the world began operation with Robert Fulton's service on the Hudson River between New York and Albany in 1807. Fulton's financial partner was Robert Livingston, who had negotiated the Louisiana Purchase, and the partnership's plan from the beginning was to expand steam navigation to the potentially far larger market of the Mississippi. Accordingly, in 1811 they built and launched the *New Orleans* at Pittsburgh. It took the 371-ton side-wheeler nearly two months to make the two-thousand-mile voyage down the river, but by early 1812 she was running regularly between her namesake city and Natchez, making good money for her owners, particularly on the upriver voyage.

Livingston and Fulton's business plan was based in part on a monopoly right to operate steam-powered vessels within Louisiana, which had become a state that year. It was a typical arrangement for that time: the partners had a similar grant from New York for their operation on the Hudson, and several other entrepreneurs had steam navigation monop-

olies from other eastern states. The grant from the Louisiana legislature, however, caused an uproar along the upper river and on the Ohio.
All over the watershed north of Louisiana, Livingston and Fulton's deal
was seen as an infringement on the right of commerce through New
Orleans.

"This monopolizing disposition of individuals will only arouse the
citizens of the West to insist on and obtain recognition of their rights,"
fumed a writer for the *Cincinnati Western Spy*. The suspicion that eastern moneyed interests, such as Livingston, were bent on controlling the
growth and commerce of the valley fed more than a few conspiracy
theories. Aaron Burr's alleged talk of breaking away from the United
States and setting up a new trans-Appalachian nation did not happen in
a vacuum: "The British government felt no jealousy against any portion
of the West, as is now felt by the mercantile states of the Atlantic and
particularly by New England," wrote an editorialist in Pittsburgh. "It
would have been much better for us that we had never separated from
Great Britain." Lawmakers in Ohio and Kentucky demanded that Washington undo the Livingston monopoly.

Farther up the river, on the Monongahela, a young river man named
Henry Shreve decided not to wait for action from the national government or anyone else. He and a partner had been building small steamboats in Brownsville, Pennsylvania, since 1813, and in 1815 Shreve took
the *Enterprise* from there to New Orleans in outright defiance of the law.
Enterprise was loaded with ammunition for the defenders of New Orleans
in the ongoing War of 1812, but that didn't stop the Livingston/Fulton
interests from demanding the boat be seized. Shreve simply paid the bail
for his boat, however, and steamed back north to something of a hero's
welcome. Not only had he defied the monopoly, the *Enterprise* was the
first steam-powered boat to ascend the rivers from New Orleans to Pittsburgh, something Fulton's boat was too deep-drafted and underpow-
ered to attempt.

The legal skirmishing over navigation rights continued for a few years,
but for all practical purposes the river was henceforward open to anyone
willing to risk their money (and lives) building a steamboat. There were
thirty-one vessels of various sizes and designs working the river by 1819.
They ran primarily on the profitable routes between New Orleans and
Pittsburgh in the early years, though the *Zebulon M. Pike* made the first

run up to St. Louis in 1817, and five years later the *Virginia* got all the way
to the Falls of St. Anthony. In 1822, the *Robert Thompson* steamed with a
load of military supplies up to Fort Smith, Arkansas, which at the time
was just a fort at the forks of the Arkansas and the Poteau Rivers.

After running the New Orleans gauntlet, Henry Shreve turned his
attention from the politics of the business to radically improving the
design of steamboats. Unlike his rival, Fulton, who was an outstanding
innovator but whose experience was more nautical than riverine, Shreve
grew up in keelboats and Kentucky flats.

He knew firsthand that the deep hull appropriate in the ocean or on
a lake only increased the chances of running aground on the ever-
changing river. The more boat that was underwater, the more the wood-
fired engine had to push against the current. The hulls of the first
steamboats—including Shreve's *Enterprise*—were like ships, with the
engine belowdecks in a relatively deep V-shaped hull. Shreve wondered
why one couldn't simply put a steam engine on a flatboat.

Even his own partners thought he had gone around the bend a little
bit, but Shreve went instead to Wheeling, West Virginia, and started
building his dream boat. Wheeling was a town with one foot in the coming industrial age, and one in the wilderness. "Considerable boat building is likewise carried on at this place," a traveler in 1810 said of the
town, "and, if I may judge from the stock of one man, bear raising must
be either an employment of profit or pleasure, as he has no less than five
of these monsters, all nearly full grown, chained to as many posts in the
front of his house."

When Shreve's new steamboat *Washington* slipped into the stream
for the first time, in 1816, it looked like it might tip over at any instant.
Instead of being tucked away in the depths of the hull, serving as ballast,
the steam engine was up on the deck above the water. The passenger
cabins, salons, and saloons were above that, with the smokestacks rising
even higher above those. The *Washington* looked like a layer cake, like
no other boat that anyone had ever seen before. It also looked in basic
form like virtually every steamboat that came after it, because as Shreve
had predicted, the *Washington* proved as stable as the Kentucky broad-
horn it was based on.

A close analysis of the evolution of western steamboats by Louis C.
Hunter suggests the evolution to a shallower riverine hull was the prod-

uct of many more innovators than simply Shreve, but the *Washington* was the boat that changed people's minds. It ran from New Orleans to Louisville in just twenty-five days, a trip that would have taken anywhere from three to four months by keelboat or barge, and that was just the beginning. By 1833 the fastest time for that trip was down to seven days and six hours; by 1853 it was down to four days and nine hours. The resulting decrease in freight rates was even more dramatic than the faster travel times. It cost $5 to move a hundred pounds by keelboat from New Orleans up to Louisville in 1815; it cost 37 cents by 1828.

The accelerating effect of steamboats on the economy and population of the watershed can hardly be overstated. In the decades before the Civil War the population west of the Appalachians grew at a rate three to four times that of the nation as a whole. There were a million people of all races in the watershed in 1810, a figure that grew sixfold by 1840. By the time the Civil War erupted, nearly half the population of the United States—fifteen million people—lived west of the Appalachians, many of them in the towns and cities that seemed to blossom out of nowhere along the rivers. In the forty years after 1810, St. Louis grew from fewer than 1,600 to more than 77,000. Cincinnati grew from 2,500 to more than 115,000. Louisville went from 1,300 to more than 43,000. Pittsburgh grew from 4,700 to nearly 47,000. New Orleans grew from 17,000 to 116,000. At the top of the river, Minneapolis went from a single army fort at the Falls of St. Anthony to a town of nearly 6,000 by 1860.

In addition to the stimulus of cheap fares, the business of constructing the boats—mostly on the upper Ohio and Monongahela Rivers— created an early demand for industrial products and skilled labor. The middle third of the 1800s transformed the Ohio in particular. Pittsburgh, Cincinnati, Wheeling, and Louisville all became centers of the iron industry, manufacturing boilers, nails, stoves, steam engines, and machinery of all sorts. Textiles, tobacco, and meatpacking were also large industries. The impact of cheaper access to markets reached inland from the new cities to the farms. Homesteaders who might have occasionally sent a bumper crop of apples or corn down the river on a homemade flatboat began to specialize their labors to suit distant markets.

More than simply economic, though, the steamboat traffic brought to every river town and city a sense that they were not, after all, so cut off from the world. "Natives of all sorts, and foreigners," is how Herman

"The Champions of the Mississippi," 1866.

Melville described the passengers on the steamboat *Fidèle* in his deeply strange 1857 novel *The Confidence Man*. In a fabulous passage that only he could have written, he went on:

> Men of business and men of pleasure; parlor men and backwoods-men; farm-hunters; heiress-hunters, gold-hunters, buffalo-hunters, bee-hunters, happiness-hunters, truth-hunters, and still keener hunters after all these hunters. Fine ladies in slippers, and moccasined squaws; Northern speculators and Eastern philosophers; English, Irish, German, Scotch, Danes; Santa Fé traders in striped blankets, and Broadway bucks in cravats of cloth of gold; fine-looking Kentucky boatmen, and Japanese-looking Mississippi cotton-planters; Quakers in full drab, and United States soldiers in full regimentals; slaves, black, mulatto, quadroon; modish young Spanish Creoles, and old-fashioned French Jews; Mormons and Papists, Dives and Lazarus; jesters and mourners, teetotalers and convivialists, deacons and blacklegs; hard-shell Baptists and clay-eaters; grinning negroes, and Sioux chiefs solemn as high-priests. In short, a piebald parliament, an Anacharsis Cloots congress of all kinds of that multiform pilgrim species, man.

The breathless editor of the Cincinnati-based *Western Monthly Review* raved in 1828 that "a steamboat, coming from New Orleans, brings to the remotest villages of our streams, and the very doors of the cabins, a little Paris, a section of Broadway, or a slice of Philadelphia . . . with pianos, and stocks of novels, and cards, and dice, and flirting, and love-making, and drinking, and champagne, and on the deck, perhaps, three hundred fellows, who have seen alligators, and neither fear whiskey, nor gunpowder."

What all passengers on the newfangled machines did have good reason to fear was the tendency of steamboats to explode. The phenomenon started early, when one of the boilers on Shreve's *Washington* exploded on the second day of its inaugural voyage in 1816. "Six or eight were nearly skinned from head to feet, and others slightly scalded to the number of 17," reported the *Philadelphia Weekly Aurora*. "In stripping off their clothes the skin peeled with them." Shreve himself was lucky not to be among the thirteen dead, and the boat was repaired.

Often when the boilers exploded on a steamboat, the initial mayhem was quickly overtaken by a devastating fire. Other times, the fire started first and the boilers exploded when their tenders fled their posts. Steamboats, after all, were great boxes of thin pine and fir surrounding as big a wood or coal furnace as the designers could fit aboard. Embers rained down continuously from the stacks, which was why they were built tall. Or sparks leapt out of the firebox doors, which were being fed with the best firewood available.

"Machinery, vast fragments of the boilers, huge beams of timber, furniture and human beings in every degree of mutilation were alike shot up perpendicularly many hundred fathoms in the air," a reporter for the *Louisiana Chronicle* wrote about the explosion of the *Clipper* in 1843:

> On reaching the greatest height, the various bodies diverged like the jets of a fountain in all directions—falling to earth, and upon roofs of houses, in some instances as much as two hundred and fifty yards from the scene of destruction. The hapless victims were scalded, crushed, torn, mangled and scattered in every possible direction—many into the river, some in the streets, some on the other side of the Bayou, nearly three hundred yards—some torn asunder by coming in contact with

pickets and posts, and others shot like cannon balls through the solid walls of houses at a great distance from the boat. . . . The watchman, a white man, was thrown alive, one hundred fifty yards through the solid wall of Baker's Hotel, into a bed. He retained his senses perfectly for some time after, but the poor fellow expired during the evening. The cabin boy was thrown about two hundred yards through the roof of a shed, and was picked up mangled.

Most disturbingly, perhaps, steamboat explosions were not an unusual event. Roughly twenty-five steamboats a year exploded between 1848 and 1852 on the "western rivers," as the Mississippi basin was called, killing more than eleven hundred passengers and crew. The carnage led to what some consider the earliest effort by the federal government to impose a modest standard of safety on an industry: the first steamboat acts, passed in 1838, achieved little, but the follow-up act of 1852 instituted boiler inspections and largely—though not entirely—succeeded in reducing the carnage.

If the thing didn't explode, however, one generally got what one paid for on a steamboat. Most often what was paid for was cargo space; even the best passenger accommodations were an afterthought to that business. On the earliest boats, there were only large dormitories; one for men and another for women. These early accommodations were often down in the hull, but by the mid-1820s most boats had a second story above the main deck devoted to passenger accommodations. As the nineteenth century progressed, staterooms, usually about six feet square or slightly larger, gradually replaced the dormitories. These were arranged around the periphery of the passenger deck, with doors both outward to the promenade that ran around the perimeter of the boat and inward, into a narrow "saloon" that ran down the middle of the vessel. This saloon, which could be as much as three hundred feet long in the largest vessels, was the showplace of the boat.

"Huge toppling steamers," said Melville, "bedizened and lacquered within like imperial junks."

Most important to the passengers, the saloon was where the bar was, dispensing mostly whiskey served four fingers deep and straight, unless it had been slightly diluted in the bottle by the bartender. "The bartender was also supposed to know how to manufacture a choice brand of French brandy," said the pilot Merrick, "by the judicious admixture of burnt peach stones, nitric acid, and cod-liver oil, superimposed upon a foundation of Kentucky whiskey three weeks from the still. He did it, too; but judicious drinkers again took theirs straight, and lived the longest."

A band, usually made up of African-American deckhands, played dances in the evenings in the saloon. It was here also that hustlers of all sorts worked the crowd, selling title to land in boomtowns that didn't exist, or lead mines that hadn't been found. The legendary riverboat gamblers—Melville's "Confidence Men"—did their work with cards that were marked by shaving, or cutting the sides of the face cards so that they were ever so slightly narrower than the rest of the deck. Professional sharks worked the same boats regularly, often with the cooperation of the bartender, who would supply a fresh deck of "stripped" cards if anyone grew suspicious.

A trip up the Mississippi became something of a tourist destination in the decades before the Civil War, and boat owners vied to create the most opulent feel, with columns, arches, vast murals and mirrors, gilt ceilings, stained glass, and candelabras. "The *Northern Light*, I remember, had in her forward cabin representations of Dayton Bluff, Saint Anthony Falls, Lover's Leap, or Maiden Rock, drawn from nature, for which the artist was said to have been paid a thousand dollars," said the steamboat pilot Merrick. "They were in truth fine paintings, being so adjudged by people who claimed to be competent critics."

Not everyone who traveled on Mississippi River steamboats was overwhelmed by the luxury of it all. "Oh! That carpet! I will not, I may not describe its condition," the British travel writer Frances Trollope sniffed in *Domestic Manners of the Americans* about her trip up the Mississippi in 1828 aboard the *Belvedere*. "Let no one who wishes to receive agreeable impressions of American manners, commence their travels in a Mississippi steam boat," she went on, "for myself, it is with all sincerity I declare, that I would infinitely prefer sharing the apartment of a party of well conditioned pigs to the being confined to its cabin." Charles Dickens added that "it is well for society that this Mississippi, the renowned father of waters, had no children who take after him. It is the beastliest river in the world." The river was "an enormous ditch," he said, "running liquid mud."

Audubon was equally unimpressed with his trip on the river in 1843.

Library of Congress Prints and Photographs Division

Memphis, circa 1906.

"The very filthiest of all filthy rat-traps I ever traveled in," he said of the steamboat *Gallant*. "And the fare worse, certainly much worse."

If he saw the way the fare was typically prepared, the great birdman would have thought twice about trying it in the first place. There was a standard joke among captains and boat owners that the best way to save money on food bills was to take the passengers through the kitchen on their way from the gangplank to their stateroom. In fairness to the cooks, it was something of a feat to produce three meals a day for several hundred passengers out of two small galleys, one for bread and pastries and the other for meat and potatoes. What's more, with no refrigeration the meat supplies were generally stored on board alive. At every stop, the steward went ashore and bought whatever provisions were available and they were improvised into the menu.

"Often, a dozen lambs could be picked up, or a dozen 'roaster' pigs, and these were killed and dressed on the boat by one of the assistant cooks," said Merrick. Failing that, there was always a supply of chickens as a backup:

A coop of chickens is placed near the master of ceremonies, and two or three assistants surround the barrel. The head dresser grasps a chicken by the head, gives it a swing from the coop to the barrel, bringing the chicken's neck on to the iron rim of the barrel. The body goes into hot water and the head goes overboard. Before the chicken is dead he is stripped of everything except a few pin feathers—with one sweep of the hand on each side of the body and a dozen pulls at the wing feathers. The yet jerking, featherless bodies are thrown to the pin feather man, who picks out the thickest of the feathers, singes the fowls over a charcoal grate-fire and tosses them to one of the under-cooks who cuts them open, cuts them up, and pots them, all inside of two minutes from the coop. A team of three or four expert drakes will dispose of one hundred and fifty chickens in an hour. Are they clean? I never stopped to inquire. If they were *dead* enough to stay on the platter when they got to the table that was all any reasonable steamboatman could ask.

Worldly and wealthy passengers such as Audubon and Trollope had tasted better food, and were inclined by dint of education and class to write down their memories for their relatives or publishers. There were plenty of people on the steamboats, however—most of them semiliterate men—who had been hungry at some point in their past and were unlikely to complain about the fare as long as the victuals were plentiful or at least frequent. People who had set out on flatboats from their hardscrabble farms and log cabins up in the tributaries with a load of produce to sell in New Orleans traveled back north on steamboats, usually sleeping on the decks below the main passenger level.

"We had about two hundred of these men on board," said Frances Trollope. "But the part of the vessel occupied by them is so distinct from the cabins that we never saw them, except to take in wood; and then they ran, or rather sprung and vaulted over each other's heads to the shore, whence they all assisted in carrying wood to supply the steam engine; the performance of this duty being a stipulated part of the payment of their passage."

Trollope, who was the mother of the novelist Anthony Trollope, did not hear good things from her butler about the character of these "Kain-tucks," as they were called. "From the account given by a man servant we had on board, who shared their quarters, they are a most disorderly set of persons," she said, "constantly gambling and wrangling, very seldom sober, and never suffering a night to pass without giving practical proof of the respect in which they hold the doctrines of equality and community of property."

She watched her purse, therefore, but she liked what she saw. "These Kentuckians are a very noble-looking race of men; their average height considerably exceeds that of Europeans, and their countenances, excepting when disfigured by red hair, which is not unfrequent, extremely handsome."

Audubon, on the other hand, clearly preferred the company of Common Grebes to the common man. "Our *compagnons de voyage*, about one hundred and fifty, were composed of Buckeyes, Wolverines, Suckers, Hoosiers, and gamblers, with drunkards of each and every denomination, their ladies and babies of the same nature, and specially the dirtiest of the dirty. We had to dip the water for washing from the river in tin basins, soap ourselves all from the same cake, and wipe the one hundred and fifty with the same solitary one towel rolling over a pin, until it would have been difficult to say, even with your keen eyes, whether it was manufactured of hemp, tow, flax, or cotton."

29

DOWN BELOW

On steamboat voyages down the Ohio and Mississippi, as opposed to up, there was often still another class of passengers belowdecks. These were people Audubon and Trollope might not have seen at all, for they did not even have the privilege of sharing the communal towel.

"When I was about twelve years of age my mistress's brother stole me from my mistress and took me to New Orleans and sold me from the Slave Block," the self-proclaimed "river rat" George Taylor Burns recalled. Celia Henderson, who was born enslaved in Harden County, Kentucky, around 1849, told a similar story. "Mah mammy were name Julia Dittoe, an' pappy, he were name Willie Dittoe. Dey lives at Louisville, 'til mammy were sold fo' her marsters debt," she told an oral historian from the Works Progress Administration.

"She tuk us four chillen 'long wid her, and pappy an th' others staid in Louisville. Dey tuk us all on a boat down de big rivah—evah see de big river? Mississippi its name—but we all calls it De Big River. Natchez on de hill, data weah de tuk us to—Natchez on de hill, dis side of N'Orleans. . . . Mammy she have eleven chillen. No'em don't 'member all dem names no mo'. . . . No'em, nevah see pappy no moah."

There were always slave traders on the river. Some of these "soul drivers," as they were known, had their own flatboats, but by midcentury it wasn't unusual for slavers to hire space on a steamboat. "Surplus" slaves

bought or stolen from Kentucky and Tennessee were such regular passengers south that the abolitionists came to call the a trip down the Ohio
and Mississippi the "American Middle Passage." Burns's home state of
Missouri, in particular, had a reputation among soul drivers as a place
where slaves were "bred" for sale down the river.

"As far as I have any knowledge of the state," said William Brown, also
of Missouri, "those who raise slaves for the market are to be found among
all the classes, from Thomas H. Benton down to the lowest political dema-
gogue who may be able to purchase a woman for the purpose of raising
stock, and from the doctor of divinity down to the most humble lay member in the church." Brown knew the soul-drivers' business from the inside,
having been enslaved for years to a man who hired him out to work for a
slave trader who made regular runs from St. Louis down to New Orleans.

"There was a large room on the lower deck, in which the slaves were
kept, men and women, promiscuously—all chained two and two and a
strict watch was kept that they did not get loose," he said. Here, out of
sight of the passengers, it was Brown's duty as they neared market towns
to pluck out any gray hairs or, if a prisoner had too much gray to pluck,
to blacken beards and heads to make the property for sale look younger.
Some of these unfortunate people were sold at Natchez, but the main
market was in New Orleans.

"Before the slaves were exhibited for sale, they were dressed and
driven out into the yard. Some were set to dancing, some to jumping,
some to singing, and some to playing cards. This was done to make them
appear cheerful and happy," said Brown, who later escaped to Canada
and published a well-known narrative of his life as a slave on the river.
"My business was to see that they were placed in those situations before
the arrival of the purchasers, and I have often set them to dancing when
their cheeks were wet with tears."

The abolitionist Henry Brewster Stanton wrote to the editor of the
New York Emancipator from Cincinnati in 1834 that "those who are
transported down the Mississippi River receive treatment necessarily
different [from seafaring ships] but in the aggregate no less cruel."

They are stowed away on the decks of steamboats (our boats are constructed differently than yours), males and females, old and young,
usually chained, subject to the jeers and taunts of the passengers and

navigators, and often, by bribes, or threats, or the lash, made subject to abominations not to be named. On the same deck you may see horses and human beings, tenants of the same apartments, and going to sup-ply the same market. The *dumb* beasts, being less manageable, are allowed the first place, while the *human* are forced into spare corners and vacant places. Many interesting and intelligent females were of the number. And if I were satisfied that the columns of a newspaper was the proper place to publish it, I could tell facts concerning the brutal treat-ment exercised towards these defenseless females while on the down-ward passage, which ought to kindle up the hot indignation of every mother, and daughter, and sister in the land.

The heat of indignation was rising on both sides of the Mason-Dixon Line, but even where the river flowed between free banks or along the border between the two sides, the slave power was rarely contested. As the century progressed toward the Civil War, the lines on land between slave and free hardened, but the Mississippi and its tributaries were like a slaveholding state unto themselves.

"On the river there was no other side to the question," recalled the upper Mississippi pilot Merrick. "A black man was a 'nigger' and noth-ing more. If he were the personal property of a white man in St. Louis, or below, he was worth from eight hundred to fifteen hundred dollars, and was therefore too valuable to be utilized in the make-up of a boat's crew running north. The inclemency of the weather, or the strenuousness of the mate, might result in serious physical deterioration that would greatly depreciate him as chattel, to say nothing of the opportunities offered him by the northern trip to escape to Canada, and thus prove a total loss." With slaves too valuable to use, and free blacks too rare—and no doubt leery of a job that took them repeatedly downriver—Merrick estimated that nine-tenths of the deck crew were Irish.

When the enslaved river rat George Burns was sold down the river, his missing toes once more saved him from a life of hard labor. The planter who bought him demanded a refund from the soul driver as soon as Burns's infirmity was discovered. Unfit for plantation work, he was soon indentured to another boat captain and he spent the rest of his career—both enslaved and, after the defeat of the Confederacy, a free American—working on the river.

Placard advertising the execution of the Madison Henderson Gang, which
included the abolitionist Charles Brown.

Near the end of his long life, Burns was asked by the interviewer
from the Works Progress Administration if he remembered any songs
from his days on the Mississippi and Ohio. He told Lauana Creel that of
course he remembered many songs, as there was always music on the
river. Many of the best tunes, he said, were variations on familiar songs
that were personalized with the names of the current boat and captain.
Burns may have sung more than one number, but the one Creel wrote

down in her notes is not today considered to be a bona fide homespun tune, of the sort that was written by no one and everyone. The song he sang was written by Daniel Decatur Emmett, an Irish-American song-writer from Ohio who founded the first troupe of white entertainers to "black up" their faces and perform their entire minstrel show as caricatures of African-Americans.

Emmett wrote what is probably the most famous song about the life of boatmen on the river. Whether he borrowed parts or all of it from actual songs he heard real boatmen sing during his youth in a traveling circus is unknown.

De boatman dance, de boatman sing,
de boatman up to eb'rything.
And when de boatman get on shore,
he spends his cash and works for more.

(chorus)
Dance, de boatman dance! O dance, de boatman dance.
O dance all night till broad daylight
And go home wid de gals in de morning.
Hi ho de boatman row, Floatin' down de ribber on de Ohio!
Hi ho, de boat man row, up an' down de ribber on de Ohio!

De boatman is a thrifty man
Da is none can do as de boatman can;
I neber see a pretty girl in all my life
But dat she be some boatman's wife.

De oyster boat should keep to de shore,
De fishin' smack should venture more.
De schooner sails before de wind,
De steamboat leaves a streak behind.

I went on board de odder day
To see what de boatman had to say;
An dar I let my passion loose
An' dey cram me in de calaboose.

I've come dis time, I'll come no more,
Let me loose, I'll go ashore;
For dey whole hoss, an' dey a bully crew
Wid a hoosier mate an' a captain too.

When you go to de boatman's ball,
Dance wid my wife or not at all;
Sky-blue jacket an' tarpaulin hat,
Look out, my boys, for de nine tail cat.

When de boatman blows his horn,
Look out, old man, your hog is gone;
He steal my sheep, he cotch my shoat,
Den put 'em in bag and tote 'em to boat.

Nowadays "The Boatman's Song," usually scrubbed of its original ersatz slave dialect, is considered one of those great classics that most people assume is a folk creation. But it wasn't "The Boatman's Song" that the ex-slave George Burns wanted to sing to the white woman from the WPA. He wanted to sing an even more famous song by D. D. Emmett called "Dixie," albeit with the lyrics that he and other blacks on the riverboats preferred to the ones that had become the theme song of the Confederacy.

Oh, I was a slave in the land of Dixie
But Captain Daniels saw I was Pert and frisky,
Now I . . .
Am glad . . .
I'm a steamboat man.

Old missus called me fat and lazy
But after I left her, she went plum crazy
She missed . . .
Me so . . .
From Dixie Land.

Now a boatman's life is a life of pleasure
Plenty to eat and money to treasure

Oh, who . . .
Would go . . .
Back to Dixie Land?

The rousters are always dancin' and singin'
Boat horns a blowin' and bells a ringin'
Oh, who . . .
Would go . . .
Back to Dixie Land?

Pretty gals come crowdin' where boats are landin'
Smile at de Cap'n where he is standin'
And smile . . .
At de darkey . . .
From Dixie Land.

Some time its stormy winds keep blowin'
Then it's hard to keep de steamboat goin'
Still I wouldn't . . .
Go back . . .
To Dixie Land.

White-painted steamboats and black slaves are the cultural levees that hold the popular image of the Mississippi in place in the decades before the great flood that was the Civil War. Close your eyes, and you can see Paul Robeson sitting on a cotton bale on the dock, and hear him singing as a big bric-a-brac paddle wheeler passes, heading north toward freedom. "Tired of living . . . and skeered of dyin . . . But Old Man River . . . he just keeps rolling along."

By 1860, however, those cultural levees could no longer hold back the tide of blood.

BOOK SIX

RIVER OF BLOOD

. . .

Lincoln and Davis, New Orleans and Vicksburg,
Victory and Defeat

The Country is in ruins, but the river remains.

—JAPANESE PROVERB

30

BLOOD ON THE TRACKS

Six years before he became president of the Confederate States of America, Jefferson Davis sent a letter to a construction site in Rock Island, Illinois. This was the spring of 1854, and the first bridge across the Mississippi River was slowly creeping out from the banks of the river. The Rock Island Bridge was an ambitious piece of engineering, with three trestles on the Illinois side, one of them a swiveling drawbridge section over the customary navigation channel, and then three more trestles to get across the river to Davenport, Iowa. When completed, the single railroad track that ran along the nearly sixteen-hundred-foot length of the bridge would connect the Chicago and Rock Island Railroad with the Mississippi and Missouri Railroad. The M&M began in Davenport, Iowa, and was still under construction, but it was headed toward Council Bluffs on the Missouri River. This first bridge across the Mississippi River was to be a major milestone in the history of railroads and in the development of the American West, but Davis, who was at that point the secretary of war of the United States, wanted it stopped in its tracks.

Davis's reasons had nothing to do with national security. Fort Armstrong, which was built on Rock Island after the War of 1812 and served as the army's headquarters during Black Hawk's War, had been abandoned a decade before. With Black Hawk's Sauk, who considered the island at the foot of the rapids sacred, having been banished from the river, there was no conceivable threat to the United States on the Illinois-Iowa border. Nor was Franklin Pierce's secretary of war concerned that the location was unsafe for a railroad bridge: an 1837 topographical survey by a young lieutenant Robert E. Lee had concluded Rock Island was the perfect location for construction. Davis was also unfazed by the concerns of the city fathers of St. Louis and the owners of steamboats, all of whom were alarmed about the impact railroads were having on their business.

With the 1849 California gold rush under way, the country was obsessed with creating a transcontinental railroad and Jeff Davis wanted a railroad bridge across the Mississippi River as much as anyone else did. He just wanted the first bridge to the West to be in the South.

Davis was from Natchez, Mississippi, but there was more than mere parochialism at play. By the time the Rock Island Bridge Company began grading its access to the river, the United States was hurtling toward a civil war that was less about slavery, per se, than it was about whether slavery would be extended indefinitely into the western half of the Mississippi basin. The Missouri Compromise of 1820, which admitted Missouri as a new slave state and carved Maine out of Massachusetts as a counterbalancing free state, had created a truce of sorts. Yet even at the time it was passed, many knew it couldn't hold forever. Thomas Jefferson, who had purchased the west and for whom Jefferson Davis was named, knew trouble when he smelled it.

"This momentous question, like a fire bell in the night, awakened and filled me with terror," he said of the Missouri Compromise and the underlying question of slavery west of the Mississippi. "I considered it at once as the knell of the Union. It is hushed indeed for the moment, but this is a reprieve only, not a final sentence."

The first tones of Thomas Jefferson's knell for the Union were beginning to toll by the time the Illinois State Legislature chartered the Rock Island Bridge Company in 1853. The white population of the South at that time was the richest segment of the country, thanks to slave labor and a booming export market for the cotton and sugar that were grown primarily in the fertile Mississippi delta lands that had been opened a few decades earlier. With immigrants and industry flooding disproportionately to the fertile and free-market territories north of the Ohio, however, some 70 percent of the free population of the United States and 80 percent of its industry were in the North. Texas had been admitted as a slave state in 1845, but in a bitter series of compromises in 1850, California had been brought into the Union as a free state and the status of Utah and New Mexico was left undetermined. With intensive cotton cultivation rapidly exhausting the soil in the older parts of the South, the survival of the old slaveholding regime appeared to depend on the possibility of slavery being extended.

Davis and other expansionist Southerners were interested in spreading slavery not just into the new western territories below the line at the 36'30" parallel that the Missouri Compromise stipulated. Fresh off the American conquests in the Mexican War, they had their eye on Cuba and the Yucatan Peninsula as potential new slave states. Closer to home, when Senator Stephen A. Douglas of Illinois proposed in 1854 the opening of Kansas and Nebraska to homesteaders as a way of encouraging the development of a transcontinental railroad, the slave power states announced that the price for their support was the repeal of the existing prohibition of slavery north of the line. Though a Free-Soiler himself, Douglas took the bait in order to get the Southern votes, and the Kansas-Nebraska Act was passed with a provision allowing "popular sovereignty" to determine whether the new states would be free or enslaved.

The North, already primed by the passage of the Fugitive Slave Act of 1850, which made it a crime not to assist bounty hunters in search of runaway slaves even in free states, erupted in protest. Even to non-abolitionists in the North, the Kansas-Nebraska Act raised the specter of slavery spreading everywhere. In *Midnight Rising*, his remarkable biography of John Brown, Tony Horowitz summarized the effect of the act:

> In the wake of the Kansas-Nebraska debate, opponents of slavery's extension formed a new political coalition: the Republican Party. Societies also sprang up to recruit and assist emigrants to Kansas. Since the territory's status would be determined by popular vote, antislavery activists—and their proslavery counterparts—sought to fill Kansas with settlers sympathetic to their cause. In doing so, partisans on both sides resorted to scare tactics and crude stereotypes. Southerners conjured a tide of "grasping, skin-flint nigger stealing Yankees" washing over Kansas, while Northerners caricatured southern pioneers as "Pukes"— illiterate backwoodsmen with whiskey-red eyes, tobacco-stained teeth, and bowie knives.

With the passage of the Kansas-Nebraska Act, the prospect of an unbroken rail line from New York, Boston, Philadelphia, and Chicago across the Mississippi into the heart of the new territory was suddenly a matter of great importance to Jefferson Davis. The trains would almost certainly bring a flood of Free-Soilers into the territory, potentially swinging any local votes over slavery toward freedom. Citing the fact that the army had previously maintained Fort Armstrong on Rock Island, over which the bridge was to cross, he used his authority as secretary of war to order that construction be halted.

His letter arrived in April 1854, but the Rock Island Bridge Company, presumably after consulting its lawyers and taking stock of the political winds in Illinois, simply ignored the orders and carried on working. Davis then sent a US marshal to enforce his order, but the marshal didn't evict the work crews for reasons that are unclear. Davis then took the matter to court, where, in the case of *United States v. the Railroad Bridge Company*, the Circuit Court judge for Northern Illinois ruled that the army had abandoned the island and therefore had no standing to sue.

With that ruling, Jefferson Davis was effectively vanquished, and crowds in both Rock Island, Illinois, and Davenport, Iowa, gathered by the tracks and cheered on April 22, 1856, as the first train crossed the Mississippi carrying eight cars full of passengers. A new era seemed to have arrived, but two weeks later, the steamboat *Effie Afton* crashed into one of the pylons and burst into flames, destroying a section of the bridge.

The resulting lawsuit by the boat's owners was potentially an even bigger threat to the bridge and the railroads than Jefferson Davis's attempts at obstruction. What the powerful steamboat industry was after in *Hurd v. Rock Island Railroad* was not just removing the Rock Island Bridge, but stopping all bridges across the Mississippi as a way of protecting their business from the burgeoning railroad industry. The case pitted the power of St. Louis and New Orleans against that of Chicago and New York: riverboats against railroads. Under the circumstances the Rock Island Railroad Company hired the best railroad lawyer in Illinois, a gangly former congressman with a homespun style named Abraham Lincoln.

Lincoln was the corporate lawyer of choice for railroads in Illinois, and counted the Illinois Central—then the longest railroad in the

world—and the Alton and Sangamon Railroads among his most important clients. Even before his single term in Congress, he lobbied for the
subsidies and vast land grants that built the great private railroads, writing that the federal government should give 2.5 million acres to the state
of Illinois so they could in turn give it to the Illinois Central. Before taking
on the Rock Island Bridge case, Lincoln defended the Illinois Central in a
lawsuit brought by a shareholder, and won. He also succeeded in getting
an exemption from county taxes for the same railroad, saving it millions.
When the Illinois Central balked at one of his legal bills, telling Lincoln,
"This is as much as Daniel Webster himself would have charged," he
revised the bill upward from $2,000 to $5,000, sued the railroad, and won.

Lincoln won the case for the Rock Island Bridge Company as well,
displaying a complete command of all the obtainable facts about the
river current and topography of the site, including those collected two
decades earlier by Robert E. Lee. He dissected for the jury the bizarre
behavior of the *Effie Afton*, which had passed successfully under the
bridge heading upstream before seemingly turning on purpose and losing power, planting the justifiable seed of suspicion that the collision and
resulting fire had not been accidental. Then, in his own particular style,
he reframed the entire question in the grandest terms, asserting that the
rights of people to travel from east to west in trains were equal to the
rights of boat passengers to travel south to north.

Lincoln's summation lasted two full days and produced a hung jury,
after which the judge threw the case out. The Mississippi was bridged,
and the brief gilded wooden age of steamboats began to give way to the
black-iron era of trains. "Had Lincoln never done another thing for the
railroads, he had earned their gratitude on this one," wrote Stephen
Ambrose in *Nothing Like It in the World*, his history of the building of
the first transcontinental railroad.

Lincoln went on to win the presidency in 1860, of course, and before
he was even inaugurated seven states seceded from the Union and chose
Jefferson Davis as their own president. Lincoln didn't say much publicly
about the secession before his inauguration, but he did write to his
allies in Congress, saying, "let there be no compromise on the question
of *extending* slavery. . . . The tug has to come & better now, than any time
hereafter."

31

ANACONDA

Both sides expected the coming "tug" to be brief, but for two years the war lurched along in a series of grim and inconclusive battles. In the eastern theater in particular, Lincoln could not find a general who would follow up on victories and chase Robert E. Lee and his army down and finish them off. Davis and Lee, on the other hand, couldn't score a game-changing victory in enemy territory and couldn't convince England or any other foreign country to side with them in the fight.

Across the Appalachians in the Mississippi basin, on the other hand, after a shaky first year of war the Union fared somewhat better. This no doubt comforted Lincoln, who said, "the Mississippi is the backbone of the Rebellion." The Confederacy depended on exports of cotton and, to a lesser extent, tobacco. If the Union could use its naval superiority to stop that trade, the rebellion would starve. Furthermore, if the North could control the Mississippi, Lincoln's "backbone," the Confederacy would be split and presumably starve even faster. "A house divided," Lincoln had warned in another context in 1858, "cannot stand."

The Northern strategy was not news to Jefferson Davis and Robert E. Lee, as it was widely publicized—and derided by some—as the Anaconda Plan because it envisioned a slow suffocation of the rebellion. Nonetheless, Lee and Davis's strategy appeared to focus not on defending the river but on capturing Washington. This perceived lack of Confederate attention to the central artery of the South was often noticed by later writers from the region.

"Jefferson Davis, the unapproachable, stubborn aristocrat of Natchez, failed strangely to understand that his river was more important than Richmond," the Mississippian Hodding Carter wrote in a typical iteration of the theory in his classic *Lower Mississippi*. "The Confederacy could have lost its capital, a dozen Virginia battles, and the state itself with less disaster than it suffered from weakly defending the Mississippi."

Carter's complaint, while perhaps not entirely unfounded in hindsight, should not overshadow the fact that the South did in fact fight hard for the river. Even before Lincoln was inaugurated, before Fort Sumter fell, Louisiana troops took over the United States arsenal and barracks at Baton Rouge and Forts Jackson and St. Philip, which guarded the river below New Orleans. Likewise, Mississippi sent artillery to Vicksburg. At the northern end of the enslaved states, rebels early on occupied and fortified New Madrid, Missouri, and the strategically placed Island Number Ten not far upstream. There were batteries overlooking the Mississippi on Iron Bluffs, near Columbus, Kentucky, and elsewhere. The Confederate States of America built and bought as good an inland navy as they could afford and were racing to finish the most powerful gunboats in the war up to the day New Orleans fell. They sent an army to defend Vicksburg.

When the fight came, however, the Confederacy was beaten. The North won the river by a combination of better boats, better officers, and more than a little audacity on the part of a few naval crews. Whatever the cause of the ultimate Union success on the western rivers, the effect was the same. As Carter put it, "The confederacy's back and much of its spirit was broken on the Mississippi."

In general terms, the Northern strategy called for the army to work its way south from Pennsylvania, securing first the Ohio River and then the Mississippi River. The navy, meanwhile, would attempt to move north from the Gulf of Mexico. The fighting began only weeks after the firing on Fort Sumter officially opened hostilities. In May 1861, St. Louis erupted in mob violence between pro-Union (and heavily German) groups and secessionist groups encouraged by the governor, Claiborne

Jackson. By June, however, Jackson and a remnant of his militia were on the run and the Missouri River and upper Mississippi were firmly in the control of the Union. By the following summer, the rest of Missouri and northern Arkansas were secured by the Union, though not without a fight. There were dozens of skirmishes and small engagements in Missouri, which were deadly enough to the limited companies of soldiers who participated in them. And there were larger battles as well. More than one thousand were dead, wounded, or missing after the Battle of Pea Ridge, when the 10,500-member Union army of the Southwest defeated the 16,500-member Confederate army of the West over the course of March 6–8, 1862.

"Our loss is heavy," wrote the Union commander, General Curtis, in his official report of the battle. "The enemy's can never be ascertained, for their dead are scattered over a large field. Their wounded, too, may many of them be lost and perish."

Less than a week after Pea Ridge, Confederate troops abandoned the town and fortifications at New Madrid following a single day of heavy bombardment from Union cannons under General Pope. This was only a partial victory, however, because most of the rebel forces retreated to Island Number Ten, the old pirate redoubt at the bottom of the hairpin turn in the river just upstream from New Madrid. Even more than the batteries at New Madrid, Island Number Ten was the bottleneck preventing passage by Union vessels to the heart of the Confederacy below. The double oxbow called the New Madrid Bend is treacherous enough under normal circumstances, and the rebels had some 140 heavy guns in place on both the island and the eastern bank of the river. Any hope by the Union to retake the great S-curve, therefore, lay in getting troops and heavy arms around behind the island on the Tennessee side.

This was not a simple proposition, as the land was too swampy above the island on the eastern bank to attempt to march an army. Nor did the Union forces on the Missouri side below Island Number Ten at New Madrid have adequate boats with which to cross the river. Over the course of a month, Pope's troops in New Madrid dug a narrow canal through the swamps above the town, across the neck of the upper oxbow. Through this they were able to move some transport ships and supplies past the island to the troops below. But the gunships they needed in order to prevent any attempt to cross those troops over were too big for the

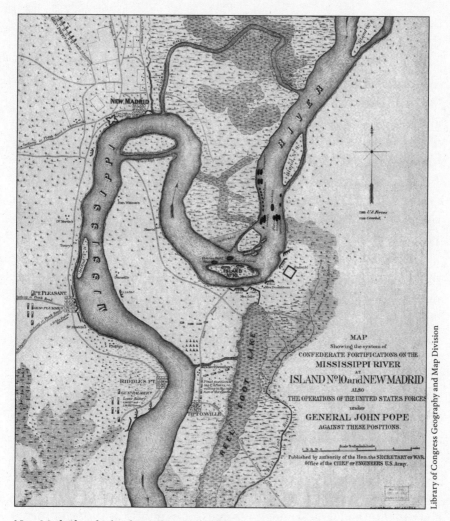

New Madrid and Island Number Ten, 1862.

canal. There was no choice, therefore, but to run the gauntlet, and during a heavy midnight thunderstorm on April 4, 1862, the ironclad gunboat *Carondelet* made a daring dash around the oxbows.

The *Carondelet* was one of eight gunboats built for the Union by James Eads at St. Louis and elsewhere over the course of one hundred days. Eads, who went on to become the most famous of American engineers, made a fortune before the war salvaging steamboat wrecks using a diving bell that he largely invented. He was an early advocate of the Union strategy of controlling the river, and paid for the construction of the warships in part out of his own funds. Like her sister "turtles," the *Carondelet* was an ugly thing. She sat low in the water, like a pup tent on a barge with side-by-side smokestacks and flags fore and aft. But she was tough and river-worthy. Whenever the lightning lit up the water, rebel forces on Island Number Ten and the Tennessee shore could see her gliding past and fired their big guns furiously, but it was too late, too dark, and too stormy. The daring of the *Carondelet* paid off and she was soon past the island to the safety of New Madrid.

Now with a gunboat below Island Number Ten, a flotilla above, and an army ready to cross from New Madrid to Tiptonville, on the Tennessee side, Pope laid his plans in earnest. The action began on April 6, 1862.

That same day, up on the Tennessee River, more than a hundred thousand soldiers were battling near a church called Shiloh. During the months that Pope and others had been securing Missouri, Ulysses S. Grant, headquartered at Cairo, Illinois, was rapidly gaining confidence as a commander in a series of operations on the rivers that led from Virginia and Tennessee to the Mississippi. In February 1862 he took control of Fort Henry guarding the Tennessee River. A week later, on the Cumberland River, Grant told the Confederate defenders of Fort Donelson, "No terms except unconditional and immediate surrender can be accepted," and took some twelve thousand Confederate prisoners.

This was the first major victory in the war for the North and it earned U. S. Grant the nickname "Unconditional Surrender Grant," and a promotion to major general of volunteers. More to the point, the fall of the two forts had large strategic repercussions in the battle for control of the rivers, leading to the Federal retaking of Nashville without a fight. On the Mississippi, the Confederate stronghold overlooking the river at Columbus, Kentucky, suddenly found itself with no Confederate troops left in the region to support it. It, too, was abandoned and its troops and hundred heavy guns joined the force at Island Number Ten.

Despite the importance of Grant's successes at Forts Henry and Donelson, Shiloh was a different order of magnitude. It is a telling reminder of how rudimentary the state of warfare communications was in 1861 that an army of forty-two thousand rebels under Generals Beauregard and Johnston was able to catch an army of sixty-two thousand soldiers under Grant largely unawares. Today the Battle of Shiloh is more often remembered than the Battle of Island Number Ten, and rightfully so given the terrible toll in lives on both sides and the slimness of the margin of the victory that the Union forces managed to eke out of a horrendous start. At the Bloody Pond, the Peach Orchard, the Hornet's Nest, and the Sunken Road, Shiloh was the Civil War at its most horrific. In two days, nearly twenty-four thousand people were killed, wounded, or missing. Yet Grant had taken the hit and turned back the enemy. One of his principal subordinates, William T. Sherman, had also shown his mettle in combat, which Grant noticed and remembered.

The Confederates at Shiloh had not surrendered, however, which made the outright capitulation of Island Number Ten on the same day as Shiloh an even better news story back East. General Pope, not Grant, became the hero of the moment in the Union. When Island Number Ten surrendered, he took thousands of rebel soldiers prisoner and extended Union control of the Mississippi River further south.

"Where is BEAUREGARD'S army?" crowed the *New York Times* in an editorial after the news of Pope's victory on the Mississippi. (Never mind that Beauregard was at Shiloh, not Island Number Ten, and that the number of prisoners taken was exaggerated in the newspapers.)

Gen. POPE, by one of those brilliant Napoleonic movements which have placed his name first and foremost on the roll of Western Commanders, has taken prisoner ten thousand of its number, has captured fifteen thousand stand of arms, and is still in pursuit of, and scattering to the winds, that fraction of it which holds together. This is the glorious news which will make the eyes of the nation glisten this morning, and which will strike terror and dismay to the hearts of the infernal Southern traitors. The vaunting and insolent chivalry of the Cotton States is routed and disgraced. The General in whom the rebels most trusted is discomfited. An army of men who swore that they would contest every inch of Southern soil till they reached the last ditch, and then and there would fight till the last of them had been hacked to pieces, has ignominiously thrown down its arms, and resigned itself to the clemency of its captors. A General whose bluster has only been equaled by his falsehoods—who, in his efforts to fire the Southern heart, has stopped at no perfidy, scrupled at no means, however atrocious—has now fled frantically before the National army, anxious only to save his worthless life, and shouting to his deluded followers as he flees "to save themselves the best way they could."

After Island Number Ten, the rebel dominoes downstream began falling to the ironclad riverboats. The Confederate "River Defense Fleet" had a small success when it surprised the Union's Western Flotilla and ran two Union ironclads aground at Plum Point Bend, about forty miles above Memphis. That was small consolation, however, for the fact that rebel forces abandoned Fort Pillow at the beginning of June without a fight. On the Tennessee side of the river just below Osceola, Arkansas, Fort Pillow was the last Confederate stronghold above Memphis.

Memphis capitulated to the Union in spectacular fashion early in the morning on June 6, 1862. The residents of the city thronged the bluffs overlooking the river to watch in tears as the last and most important battle between ships on the Mississippi unfolded on the river below. It was not a well-choreographed naval affair, but it was dramatic and decisive. Seventeen vessels of various sizes, all spewing steam and black smoke, wheeled and turned in the current in a deadly game of bumper cars out in the river's swirling currents. When as much damage as possible by that method was done, the bigger guns of the Federal boats destroyed all but one Confederate gunboat, the *Van Dorn*, which escaped.

During the same months that the Federal ironclads were pushing their way down the river from Cairo, a United States Navy fleet under Captain David Farragut was making similar progress working up the river from the Gulf of Mexico. Farragut, who later became famous for saying, "Damn the torpedoes, full speed ahead," and who would become the first admiral in the United States Navy, had been given the mission of taking New Orleans. It was an enormously important assignment, especially for an officer who had been in the navy for decades but had not yet distinguished himself. What's more, Farragut was almost passed over for any Civil War duties because of his Southern roots: he had lived in New Orleans as a child before joining the navy at age nine, was married to a woman from the South, and until the war broke out lived in Norfolk, Virginia.

This wasn't just any assignment, either. New Orleans—the former Chitimacha village that had been governed by the French, by the Spanish, by the French again, and then by the Americans, who almost lost it to the British in 1812—was now the largest city in the Confederate States of America. Its population of 170,000 was nearly 100,000 more than Washington, D.C., at the time and roughly the same size as that of Boston. Most important, of course, New Orleans is the last port at the bottom of the Mississippi River.

The Union bottled up the mouth of the river almost immediately after hostilities began, staking out the Head of Passes, which is some ninety miles downriver from New Orleans. The effect of the navy's success in the Gulf of Mexico on the economy of the Confederacy cannot be over-stated: the year before the blockade, New Orleans exported some two million bales of cotton; in the eight months after the blockade started, the figure was fewer than thirty-five thousand bales.

A few Southern ships did manage to slip past Farragut's fleet to open water, most notably the CSS *Sumter*, which captured eighteen Northern commercial vessels before being trapped in Gibraltar by the United States Navy. More alarming, on October 12, 1861, a 128-foot-long iron cigar with one gun pointing forward and one smokestack sticking out of her rounded deck steamed down from New Orleans and rammed the United States ships *Richmond* and *Vincennes*. Though she had been built in Massachusetts as the icebreaker *Enoch Train*, the CSS *Manassas* was the first ironclad ship employed during the Civil War. Through pluck, dar-ing, and whatever else it takes to sail a single newfangled ship into a large fleet of the enemy, her crew succeeded in dispersing the Union blockade for a short time. She was hopelessly outnumbered, however, and eventu-ally limped back upstream to the Confederate strongholds of Forts Jack-son and St. Philip, which guarded the approach to New Orleans.

When Captain Farragut and his fleet showed up six months later in full force below those forts, they discovered that the rebel defenders had sunk a line of wrecks across the river and had strung great chains between them to further hinder navigation. Traveling with Farragut's fleet was a squadron of schooners fitted out with heavy mortars under the separate command of his adoptive brother David Foster. On April 18, 1862, these began bombarding the twin forts. Foster and Farragut had no real expectation that the shelling would destroy Fort Jackson or Fort St. Philip, but they hoped to soften them up a bit before their big ships attempted to run past them toward the otherwise lightly defended city of New Orleans. In some ways, the attack on the forts was a diversion from the primary goal: in a harrowing late-night operation two Union ships managed to blow a navigable hole in the line of wrecks and chains blocking passage up the river.

For six days the ships and forts traded cannon fire, without causing much damage to either side. With no sign of progress through bombardment, and no realistic hope of a land operation against the fortifications due to the swampy terrain, Farragut decided to make a run for it. Dividing his force into three flotillas, at three in the morning on April 24 his first eight ships slipped through the slot in the wreckage and past the forts without being noticed. Farragut himself was with the second group, which was seen by the light of the rising moon and fired upon from both forts.

It was a fierce scene. Shells and balls flew in all directions, mostly sending up waterspouts when they missed the ships. To create more light, and potentially cause more damage, the Confederate forces sent flaming barges down the river. Farragut didn't pause to fight, however, but steamed on at full speed. Three ships were badly damaged, but the fleet got past

Farragut's fleet passing Forts Jackson and St. Philip on its way to New Orleans.

the forts. The repaired *Manassas* and whatever other fighting ships the rebels were able to cobble together were waiting for them upstream but proved to be no great challenge. Without pausing to secure the forts, Farragut steamed ahead for New Orleans.

When word came to the commander of the Louisiana militia in New Orleans that Farragut was past the forts, he knew that his city was doomed. "I was well aware that my batteries of 32 pounders at the lower levees, manned by inexperienced troops, could not detain for any length of time the heavy ships of war of the enemy armed with 9 and 11 inch guns," General Lovell wrote in his report explaining why he ordered his forces to take their supplies and get out of town while they still could.

In New Orleans, word spread to the general population that the United States Navy was above the forts and general panic ensued. People raced to banks to try and trade in their worthless CSS currency and remove their safe-deposit holdings. Others buried silverware and guns. Late into the night on April 24 mobs—both white and black—raged on the waterfront, looting warehouses for supplies and setting fires. Anyone with a ship or boat took it upriver, hoping to find sanctuary in the shrinking portion of the Mississippi that was still in rebel hands. Two huge ironclad warships under construction, *Mississippi* and *Louisiana*, were torched and set adrift.

The potential havoc that these two vessels could have wreaked to the Union blockade had they been completed may well have encouraged the timing of Farragut's daring run. The *Mississippi*, he said in his report, "was to be the terror of the seas, and no doubt would have." Farragut's adoptive brother David Dixon Porter, in command of the mortar boats in the action, thought the window for their great success had been a single day.

"I shake a little now when I think how near we came to being defeated," he wrote in a letter to the assistant secretary of the navy. "One day's more delay and the game would have been blocked on us. They would have put the *Louisiana* in the only narrow channel where the ships had to pass, and she would have sunk everything that came up unless we could have put some bombs through her."

The burning hulks of Confederate naval hopes twisting away in the current devastated the crowd on the waterfront. "It was a terribly magnificent spectacle," said Loreta Janeta Velazquez. "And it impressed upon me more strongly with the idea of warfare than all the fighting and slaughter I had ever seen."

On the morning of April 25, eleven United States warships were anchored off of New Orleans. The waterfront blazed with burning cotton bales. The crowd onshore was angry and hostile, but also disorganized and drunk. Some cheered when the Union flag went up, but were immediately beaten by the defiant majority. The Confederate army, under General Lovell, had abandoned the city, leaving it in the hands of Mayor Monroe and his city council. Monroe refused to lower the rebel flags but did not overtly propose to stop Farragut's forces from doing it themselves.

The mob, on the other hand, tore down the American flag that was raised over the mint and dragged it through the streets. Farragut was a better naval commander than he was an occupier, and while he waited for the mayor to surrender, the rebel forces had plenty of time to remove any matériel worth taking out. Finally on the twenty-eighth, however, even Farragut had had enough. Emboldened by the fact that the two forts below the river had fallen and were now under Union control, he gave the city an ultimatum: if the rebel flags did not come down, his ships would bombard New Orleans. He would hold off for forty-eight hours, if they wished to leave the flags up and evacuate women and children, but after that he would not hold back.

When news of the situation reached Confederate President Jefferson Davis, he sent the mayor a telegram, saying, among other things: "My prayers are with you. There is no personal sacrifice I would not willingly make for your defense."

But a telegram and a prayer was all the Confederacy could muster, and on the twenty-ninth of April, 1862, the United States Marines came ashore and removed the secessionist flags from the US Custom House and the city hall. New Orleans was lost to the CSA and, according to the *New York Times*, Washington, DC, went "wild with rejoicing."

In London, Henry Adams came home from a walk and found his father, Lincoln's ambassador to the Court of St. James's, dancing across the room. "We've got New Orleans!" he sang. Among other things, the loss of the city doomed Confederate efforts to get Britain involved in the war. The English public up to that point had been largely pro-Confederacy, if only to humble the rising power of the United States and lower the price of cotton. The news of the fall of New Orleans went through London "like a violent blow in the face on a drunken man," said Adams. "The whole town was in immense excitement as though it were an English defeat."

It was the same story in Paris, where the French foreign minister had a meeting with the Confederate commissioner John Slidell after the news of Farragut's victory reached Europe. "Although he did not directly say so," Slidell said later, "it left me fairly to infer, that if New Orleans had not been taken and we suffered no very serious reverses in Virginia and Tennessee, our recognition would very soon have been declared." The CSA was never recognized by any foreign country.

After New Orleans, there were other battles along the Mississippi. None of them were inconsequential to the people who died in them. At none of them, however, did the rebels put up much resistance to the Union. The wooden ships of Farragut's fleet advanced northward, and the ironclad riverboats of Grant and his subordinates made their way south from Memphis.

Until they got to Vicksburg, Mississippi. Some 250 miles upriver from New Orleans, by the summer of 1862, the town perched on terraced bluffs rising more than two hundred feet above the river was the last strategic toehold of the Confederacy on the river. Vicksburg was far more than symbolic in importance. Not only was it near the mouth of the Yazoo River, but the railroad from Jackson, Mississippi, and points south and east also terminated at Vicksburg. Directly opposite, on the western side of the Mississippi, began the Vicksburg, Shreveport, and Texas Railroad. This was the rebel lifeline west to Shreveport, Louisiana, through which came desperately needed Texas beef and a trickle of European manufactures via Matamoros, Mexico. For a time these could be floated down the Red River, and then up the Mississippi to Vicksburg, but the fall of Natchez and Baton Rouge to loyal forces closed the mouth of the Red River to rebel vessels and made Vicksburg even more vital. Ferries crossed the river every half hour to De Soto Point on the opposite shore. By 1863 it was the only remaining point of communication between slave states on either side of the river.

The importance of Vicksburg was a singular point of agreement between Abraham Lincoln and Jefferson Davis. "Vicksburg is the nail head that holds the South's two halves together," said Davis.

"Vicksburg is the key," echoed Lincoln. "The war can never be brought to a close until that key is in our pocket."

32

UP IN FLAMES

It took nearly another year to put the key firmly in Lincoln's pocket. Farragut arrived at Vicksburg first, largely because the Confederacy wagered so heavily that the forts below New Orleans would block passage upstream that the river above was left relatively undefended. Baton Rouge and Natchez both fell without a fight, and Farragut's oceangoing vessels moved upriver in a haze of thick smoke. On both sides of the Mississippi as the fleet steamed past, the locals carried on where the waterfront throngs in New Orleans had left off, destroying the cotton crop rather than let it fall into enemy hands.

"They seem to think they are doing us a great injury by destroying their own property," said William H. Smith, a sailor onboard the Union ship *Winona*. "As we came up the river it was for two hundred miles covered with cotton which had been thrown into it. Along the banks was one continuous bonfire."

It made for an eerie voyage, but three weeks after the fall of New Orleans, on May 18, 1862, Farragut's fleet took up position just below Vicksburg, but out of range of the artillery emplacements on the bluffs. Any hopes the sixty-one-year-old admiral may have held that the town would follow the meek lead of Natchez and Baton Rouge, and surrender quietly, were quickly dashed when his messenger returned from town with a reply from the local commanders.

"Having been ordered here to hold these defenses, my intention is to do so as long as it is in my power," the Northern-born Confederate general Martin Luther Smith responded in the genteel military style of the West Point graduate that he was.

"Mississippians don't know, and refuse to learn, how to surrender to an enemy," added the local militia commander. "If Commodore Farragut or Brigadier General Butler can teach them, let them come and try."

Farragut sized up the situation and decided to save his lesson plans for Vicksburg for another time. In a Northern variation on the Southern historian's theme of blaming the generals, some have suggested that Farragut's "damn the torpedoes" instincts failed him and that he should have stormed the city. Vicksburg was still waiting for the reinforcements that were on the way from points east. From Farragut's point of view, however, his fleet was at the end of an immensely long supply chain that ran through barely subdued territory. Furthermore his tall, oceangoing wooden ships were vulnerable to the guns that the enslaved blacks of Vicksburg had been busily implanting into various locations along the waterfront and up on the bluffs of town. Better, he reasoned, to wait at least until Porter and his flotilla of mortar barges could be brought up from New Orleans to soften the defenses. Even better still to wait for confirmation that the ironclad riverboats from the north had passed Memphis and that a coordinated attack from both sides could take place. Farragut returned downriver.

A month later he was again below Vicksburg, with Porter and his mortars in tow, and the daily bombardment of the town began. Less than a week later, the low ironclads from the northern force began to arrive at the bend in the river just above Vicksburg. The stretch of river still controlled by the Confederacy had now shrunk to less than five miles, and even that stretch was passable by Union ships. Farragut proved this a few days later when, leaving Porter's flotilla behind to continue the relentless bombardment of the town, he took most of his fleet and ran the gauntlet of guns at Vicksburg without losing a ship. The two very different squadrons of ships that between them had conquered the river met for the first time. Even without their topmasts and rigging, Farragut's naval vessels towered over the half-submerged "turtles" of Flag Officer Charles Davis's Western Flotilla, which were mostly crewed not by sailors, but by midwestern-born soldiers who had never seen an oceangoing vessel before.

Farragut's willingness and ability to race the fleet past Vicksburg's guns with minimal damage was impressive but did little to change the situation. Neither, it seemed, was the constant barrage from Porter's mortars inflicting any serious damage on the defenders of the place. The guns weren't accurate enough to take out the Confederates' own defensive weapons, and though the shuddering blasts were unnerving, they did not shake the will of the townspeople to resist. What's more, Vicksburg was swelling with reinforcements, now under the overall command of General Van Dorn, who had been the loser at the Battle of Pea Ridge. By July it was obvious that Vicksburg could not be taken quickly through naval action alone, but would require a drawn-out ground offensive.

Any such effort required a more reliable way of moving supplies and forces past the town than running the gauntlet in ships and boats. Like New Madrid upstream, Vicksburg was seated in a sinuous stretch of the river, near a hairpin turn, and troops were put to work digging a canal across the neck of De Soto Point. The tactic had worked reasonably well at Island Number Ten, after all. Wouldn't it be something, the officers said, if they could induce the entire river to jump into the new channel, leaving Vicksburg on a useless backwater? It didn't work out that way, however. As usual in midsummer, the river level was falling fast—faster than the shovels could dig through the oozy soil. The air was thick and hot, and black with clouds of mosquitoes. Men fell ill with dysentery and malaria and began to die. Yellow fever and measles also claimed victims. Even the addition of a thousand slaves rounded up from the surrounding plantations did little to speed the progress, for the engineers had misread the river and were working at cross-purposes to the current. The Union forces succeeded in destroying the railroad terminus on the Louisiana side of the river, hampering the movement of supplies from the western Confederacy to the main armies in the east. Ultimately, however, with half of their force dead or debilitated by disease, they gave up on the canal effort. (Ironically, during one flood in 1876, the river did the work on its own, eliminating the oxbow and leaving the city without a decent port until the Army Corps of Engineers diverted the Yazoo through town in 1903.)

Making matters worse from the Union perspective, on July 15 three boats from the Western Flotilla were patrolling the Yazoo River, which entered the Mississippi upstream of Vicksburg, and rounded a corner to find a new Confederate ironclad steaming down at them with guns blazing. The *Arkansas* wasn't much to look at, a cobbled-together effort armored with railroad rails instead of iron plating. But she promptly drove the smaller *Carondelet*—the hero of Island Number Ten—aground and chased the other two Union boats back into the Mississippi River. Firing madly with a stern gun, the Union's *Tyler* managed to blow the smokestack and pilothouse off the *Arkansas*, but all that the Union's undergunned boats could hope for was that they would beat their pursuer back to the rest of the fleet.

There was no radio, of course, which meant no way for Farragut's fleet anchored above Vicksburg to know what was happening upstream until they heard the guns booming and suddenly the three boats rounded the corner and were in their midst. By now, with the loss of her pilothouse and stacks, the *Arkansas* was not moving fast, but she had the advantage of being under way and moving downstream. The Union fleet, by contrast, was not up to steam and lay anchored on both sides of the river, which made it difficult for them to fire indiscriminately for fear of hitting their own forces on the opposite bank. Guns blazing out of both sides, the *Arkansas* gamely plowed straight down the channel. She took a few nonlethal hits, scored a few hits, and won the day just by making it in one piece to the waterfront below Vicksburg. Crowds of residents, who had watched the fight from the bluffs and from rooftops, cheered wildly. It was only one ship, and an ugly and wounded one at that, but it was their ship and it had shamed the enemy at the gates.

Farragut was livid, and he determined to destroy the *Arkansas* that same evening, while she was still wounded. Equally important to his thinking, Porter's convoy of mortar boats could not be left unprotected below Vicksburg now that the enemy had an ironclad of their own. The fleet got a late start, however, and instead of the setting sun lighting up their prey and blinding their adversaries, it was dark by the time the ships passed Vicksburg. There was a fierce firefight, but neither side scored any significant hits.

"We could see nothing but the flash of the enemy's guns to fire at," Farragut later complained. "I looked with all the eyes in my head to no purpose."

A few days later, the Union ram *Queen of the West* and the ironclad

Essex made another attempt to destroy the *Arkansas* while she lay at the wharf. In a daring run they survived a barrage of cannon fire from shore and managed to land a few glancing blows. The *Arkansas* by now was beaten to hell, but she lived to fight a few more days.

At the end of July, on orders from the secretary of the navy, Farragut's fleet withdrew to New Orleans. It was clear the battle for Vicksburg would be a long one, and no one, least of all Farragut, wanted to keep his deepwater fleet up above Natchez through the low-water months of summer. Even though this effectively reopened the Red River for the rebels, the way Farragut and his superiors in Washington saw it, there was no chance of defeating Vicksburg while the town maintained its supply lines eastward to the heart of the Confederacy. Cutting that connection would have to be done, if it could be done, by land forces under Ulysses S. Grant, who that same week had been given command of "all troops in the Army of the Tennessee and Army of the Mississippi, and in the District of the Mississippi and Cairo."

Grant, however, was not ready to attack Vicksburg. All through the summer and fall of 1862, he and his armies were fully engaged in trying to hold on to their earlier gains. These had been impressive, but stretched Union forces dangerously thin. The rebel general Van Dorn, from his base at Vicksburg, was a constant threat, but it wasn't clear what target he was likely to strike first. For a time Grant worried that Van Dorn was aiming for Memphis. Or was he aiming for Corinth, Mississippi, where the Mobile and Ohio Railroad crossed the Memphis and Charleston Railroad? They were critical months, for despite the progress on the Mississippi River, the war was not going well for the Union in the East at this time. Lincoln was so frustrated with McClellan's inaction by this point that he said when reviewing the camps of the massive Army of the Potomac, "This is General McClellan's bodyguard."

For his part, Grant knew that more than just the military situation on the ground was at stake in the West:

"If I, too, should be driven back, the Ohio River would become the line dividing the belligerents west of the Alleghenies, while at the East the line was already farther north than when the hostilities commenced at the opening of the war," he later wrote in his memoir. "To say at the end of the second year of the war the line dividing the contestants at the

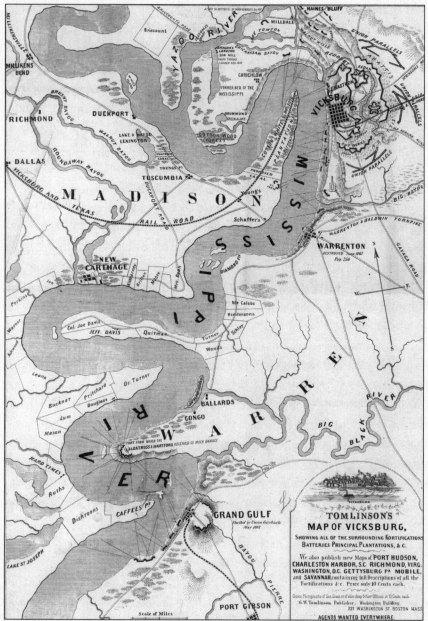

Map of Vicksburg, circa 1862.

East was pushed north of Maryland, a State that had not seceded, and at the West beyond Kentucky, another State which had always been loyal, would have been discouraging indeed. As it was, many loyal people despaired in the fall of 1862 of ever saving the Union."

Finally, on October 4, Van Dorn made what Grant called "a dashing attack" on Corinth. Grant was not caught unawares and had sent reinforcements to General Rosencrans at Corinth. It was nonetheless touch and go for a time. The Federals were driven back in Van Dorn's fierce initial attack but held their ground in defensive positions that had been constructed for that purpose in the previous months.

"The enemy was finally driven back with great slaughter: all their charges, made with great gallantry, were repulsed," said Grant, who privately wished he was commanding a single cavalry unit on the Potomac rather than running the entire war in the west. But the victory gave him the confidence to go on the offensive.

"The battle relieved me from any further anxiety for the safety of the territory within my jurisdiction, and soon after receiving reinforcements I suggested to the general-in-chief a forward movement against Vicksburg."

The operation began on November 2 and for the next two months Grant and his army of about thirty thousand made steady progress from various points toward Vicksburg. On December 20, however, Van Dorn got his revenge for the defeat at Corinth when he swept in from Grenada, Mississippi, and overran Grant's supply post at Holly Springs. The commander of the Union garrison had been specifically forewarned of the threat but failed to act on his orders. As a result, Van Dorn's forces easily took fifteen hundred Union prisoners and destroyed a huge stockpile of supplies. Grant was understandably furious. "The surrender of Holly Springs," he later wrote, "showed either the disloyalty of Colonel Murphy to the cause which he professed to serve, or gross cowardice."

Even though the loss was due to Murphy's incompetence rather than a flaw in the overall plan, the incident caused Grant to rethink his strategy of fighting his way overland to Vicksburg. Rather than put his attacking forces at the end of an immense and vulnerable supply chain, which the rebels could harass at will, he decided instead to move his headquarters to Memphis and use the Mississippi River as his supply line.

The new plan presented its own challenges, not the least of which was finding forty thousand campsites along the river. The land on either side of the river between the bluffs of Memphis and those of Vicksburg is almost uniformly low, crisscrossed with bayous and old river channels, and the Mississippi in the winter of 1862–63 was unusually high. Just about the only dry ground was on the levees, and the Union camps eventually spread to seventy miles above Vicksburg. All through January it seemed to rain constantly, making it impossible to even consider an assault through the marshy land on the town.

"Then commenced a series of experiments to consume time, and to divert the attention of the enemy, of my troops, and of the public generally," Grant wrote later. "I, myself, never felt great confidence that any of the experiments resorted to would prove successful. Nevertheless I was always prepared to take advantage of them in case they did."

The key to an attack on Vicksburg, whenever the time came, was going to be finding a dry enough place on the east side of the river to land an assault force. It was also crucial that a way be found to move men and supplies past the town without having to run the gauntlet of guns on the bluffs, which had been increased significantly over the past six months. Four thousand men were therefore put to work on the partially completed canal across the neck, which the troops with Farragut had abandoned the previous summer. The new forces made some progress until the levee at the top end broke and the whole thing flooded prematurely.

An even more ambitious attempt to create a new channel through the bottomlands began seventy miles upriver at Lake Providence. Teams cut trees out of the swamp, as low as they could reach under the cold two-foot-deep water. Grant knew from the moment he inspected the progress that this project would have no better success than the canal opposite Vicksburg, but he "let the work go on, believing employment was better than idleness for the men."

Forces also cut a hole in the levee across the river from Helena, Arkansas, more than two hundred river miles above Vicksburg. There, a formerly navigable bayou leading from the Mississippi to the Tallahatchie River had existed within memory but had been cut off by artificial levees to protect the nearby plantations. If Union boats could get on the Tallahatchie via the old bayou, they could take it to Greenwood, Mississippi, where it joins the Yalobusha River to form the Yazoo. The Confederate Fort Pemberton was located at the juncture of the rivers in

Greenwood, but if the Union boats could manage to get past that, the Yazoo would take them some 190 miles down to the back door of Vicksburg.

In this case the high water was a blessing. Grant's men breached the levee and a torrent of muddy water poured into the old bayou. Soon the water level was sufficiently raised to allow troop transports to float down, and on February 24, some forty-five hundred troops started down the new waterway. There were hundreds of trees to be cleared away, which their counterparts in the Confederate forces had felled into the bayous to slow their progress. It was slow work, but steady, until they reached the rebel guns of Fort Pemberton. Try as they might, the Union Forces could not push their way past the rebel defenders. Stymied, they turned back.

The fourth attempt to get behind Vicksburg via a bottomland water- way came the closest of all at succeeding, and the closest of all to failing disastrously. This time the route was through a series of bayous and the Big Sunflower River to enter the Yazoo River below Fort Pemberton, thus avoiding the necessity of taking the fort. On March 15, five gunboats and four mortar boats under the command of Porter made their way through the snaking stream, cutting away overhanging timber as they went. It was torturously slow going, particularly for the wider mortar boats. The gunboats in the lead made somewhat better progress and were soon far ahead of the rest of the growing line of transports and troop ships. This was a tactical error that left no troops to defend the vanguard when, only a few hundred yards from the open water of the Big Sunflower River, Confederate sharpshooters opened fire. Unable to clear the obstruc- tions in front of them, and unable to work their own decks and back out without some cover against the four thousand enemy soldiers around them, Porter decided to blow up the boats rather than let them fall to the enemy.

What he didn't know was that word of the impending disaster had gotten back, and General Sherman and a company of men were carrying candles to light their way through the pitch-black night along a narrow lane of high ground. They arrived at noon the following day, just in time to prevent Porter from scuttling his ships.

"More welcome visitors he probably never met than the 'boys in blue' on this occasion," Grant said of Porter. Sherman and his men were not able to drive the Confederates off completely but were able to provide enough cover for the boats to retreat. "Thus ended in failure the fourth attempt to get in rear of Vicksburg," said Grant.

So it went, with the river at flood stage all the way from Christmas of 1862 to the following April. Between the cuts made in the levees by the various Union experiments and lapsed maintenance of the levees due to the war, most of the bottomlands around Vicksburg were flooded. For Grant and his troops it was a winter of malaria, smallpox, and measles, along with complaints and second-guessing by junior officers and the press. In the town itself, meanwhile, the spring of 1863 was a time of anxious optimism as news of each failed effort by Grant and his army came in. The rumor mill was working inside Vicksburg, too, however, as some grumbled that the Northern-born general in charge of the Confederate defenses, John Clifford Pemberton, was not to be trusted. And where in God's name were the reinforcements from Jefferson Davis?

When finally the waters receded to the point that the roads behind the levees began to reemerge, Grant, who had kept his plans for the spring to himself, called a meeting with Admiral Porter. Could Porter and his fleet of gunboats manage to run the fourteen miles of rebel batteries and escort a collection of steamboats to be used as ferries past Vicksburg? Advance troops were already on the march down the west side of the river and would need to be moved over to the east side of the Mississippi once they were below Vicksburg. Porter believed it could be done and ordered his sailors to pile hay and cotton bales as high as they could around the decks of the steamboats to protect their boilers and hide the light of their fires. On the dark night of April 16 they set out, with men stationed belowdecks with supplies of cotton to try to stop up any holes should they be hit by gunfire.

As soon as the first ship, the *Benton*, was spotted from the artillery emplacements, the cannons roared and huge bonfires were lit all along the waterfront to throw light on the river. "The sight was magnificent," said Grant, who was watching from midriver just out of range, "but terrible."

Every ship was hit more than once, and some were only useful as barges after losing their machinery, but only the steamboat *Henry Clay* was lost entirely. With a fleet of ferries now safely below Vicksburg, Grant ordered the bulk of his forces to follow the advance troops on the sloggy march down the western side of the river to a place called Hard Times, Louisiana. Sherman was sent with a small army to run a diver-

sionary feint north of Vicksburg, in the hope of distracting the defenders of the town from Grant's real aim, which was to secure a beachhead
across from Hard Times on the eastern side of the river below Vicksburg. It worked, and at dawn on the last day of April 1863, twenty thousand Union soldiers were landed below Grand Gulf.

"When this was effected I felt a degree of relief scarcely ever equalled
since," Grant later recalled. "Vicksburg was not yet taken it is true, nor
were its defenders demoralized by any of our previous moves. I was now
in the enemy's country, with a vast river and the stronghold of Vicksburg between me and my base of supplies. But I was on dry ground on
the same side of river with the enemy. All the campaigns, labors, hard-
ships and exposures from the month of December previous to this time
that had been made and endured, were for the accomplishment of this
one object."

The weeks that followed were filled with feints and probings, skirmishes and fearsome battles, spies and intrigues, jealousies between
generals and forgotten acts of valor. Within a week, Sherman arrived as
well, having pulled back from his ruse upriver and hurried south. This
brought the total Union forces below Vicksburg to thirty-three thousand, and it eventually grew to some forty-two thousand. The Confederates, according to Grant's own estimates, had sixty thousand soldiers
within fifty miles, which were divided between those at Vicksburg,
under General Pemberton, and a smaller force in Jackson, Mississippi,
under Johnston.

Instead of slowly building supply lines and waiting for reinforcements Grant, who was beginning to trust his ability to find food in the
surrounding countryside, ordered his army to race forward with only
several days' rations and as much ammunition as could be hustled forward on all manner of wagons and carriages. They drove off the enemy
at Grand Gulf and plunged toward Jackson, the capital of Mississippi,
which lies due east of Vicksburg and through which ran all the important rail lines supplying the town. The defenders of Jackson retreated so
quickly that workers in the factories—most of them young girls—were
still at the machines when Grant and Sherman walked in.

"We looked on for a while to see the tent cloth which they were making roll out of the looms, with 'C.S.A.' woven in each bolt," said Grant.
"Finally I told Sherman I thought they had done work enough. The

operatives were told they could leave and take with them what cloth they could carry. In a few minutes cotton and factory were in a blaze."

There were sizable battles with Pemberton at Champion's Hill and at a bridge across the Big Black River, but in both cases the Union forces prevailed and by mid-May Vicksburg was encircled. Every attempt to storm the city ramparts produced nothing but casualties, however, and Grant "determined upon a regular siege—to 'out-camp the enemy,' as it were, and to incur no more losses."

Reinforcements continued to pour in until Grant had seventy-one thousand men, roughly half of them facing the city where General Pemberton commanded the Confederate forces, and half facing outward to where the Confederate general Johnston was also gathering what reinforcements he could. For weeks all three armies were largely stationary, with Pemberton bottled up within Vicksburg, Johnston not strong enough to break through Grant's lines to relieve the city, and Grant unwilling to loosen his grip on Pemberton long enough to go attack Johnston outright. This isn't to say it was all quiet: sharpshooters were ever vigilant for anyone who showed their head to the enemy, and both sides regularly lobbed grenades and shells into each other's positions, sometimes with devastating results.

"They throw shells all around [our] breastworks—& they burst with fury in the midst of our brave troops—mangling their exposed bodies—& sending many of them to their long home," a Confederate chaplain named William Lovelace Foster wrote to his wife in a letter he had no way of mailing. "Yet there is no help. There they lie exposed to this galling fire calmly viewing their dangerous situation & in awful suspense listening to the whizzing balls and rushing shells—& to the more screams of the[ir] wounded and dying companions. Nothing is more painful—nothing is more demoralizing than to lie under a galling fire without the power of replying."

From the river, the United States Navy also fired shells into the city day and night, though these were usually less effective, and people sat out sometimes and watched them like fireworks. "I sat on the front porch of our house last night, & observed the broad flash of the mortars as they banished forth their dreadful progeny, which rose and burned through the air like a firefly until a more vivid flash & a louder report told that the fuse had communicated with the powder inside the shell, & notice was given to

'stand from under,'" one soldier wrote home. "Then I sat on the back gal-
lery & observed the flashes all round the horizon; sometimes a shell
whizzed past looking like a meteor. Truly we are surrounded by a wall of
fire; the atmosphere is smoky and filled with the sulphureous smell of gunpowder. They are plowing up the land with their deadly missiles and sow-
ing it with gunpowder. Sometimes the powder falls around us, & sounds
like a shower of rain among the trees. We are lulled to sleep by a lullaby of
roaring cannon & bursting shells, & in the morning the same sounds take
the place to our ears of birds' singing and chanticleer's clear ring."

In some ways the siege of Vicksburg was medieval, with townspeople
locked into a walled-off city watching their supplies of food and ammunition dwindle. By the end of June flour sold for $600 a barrel, and bis-
cuits were eight dollars a dozen. Most people moved out of their homes
into caves dug into the clay bluff. Some of these caverns were quite well
appointed, with multiple rooms and rugs and furniture from the houses
on the street. When paper ran out, the newspaper was printed on the
back of unused wallpaper, with gallows humor stories of people passing
off their house cats as roasted rabbit.

The "caves" of Vicksburg.

Library of Congress Prints and Photographs Division

There was no escaping that it was war, however. After one of the early attempts to storm the ramparts, Grant asked Pemberton for a truce long enough to go collect the dead and wounded Union soldiers lying in the sun between the two positions. Pemberton refused.

"Afterward the effluvia from the dead bodies became so intolerable that he was obliged in his turn to ask a truce and request the Federal officers to bury their dead," said Mary Ann Loughborough in her memoir of the siege, *My Cave in Vicksburg*. "I was distressed to hear of a young Federal lieutenant who had been severely wounded and left on the field by his comrades. He had lived in this condition from Saturday until Monday, lying in the burning sun without water or food; and the men on both sides could witness the agony of the life thus prolonged, without the power to assist him in any way. I was glad, indeed, when I heard the poor man had expired on Monday."

At other times the operation seems less a throwback to the Middle Ages and more like a foreshadowing of World War I, with men in trenches facing off for weeks on end over short distances. At times during the siege the combatants were close enough to be able to speak to one another. "Sometimes they exchanged the bread of the Union soldiers for the tobacco of the Confederates," said Grant.

"Hey Yank," a Confederate would call.

"Yeah Johnny," a Union boy would call back, both sides invariably using the traditional salutations for one another.

"When you coming to town?" Johnny Reb would yell, in what was becoming a running joke between the two lines.

"Seems like a good place to celebrate the Fourth of July," Yank would holler back.

By the end of June, after six weeks of siege, the approaching Fourth of July began to assume a kind of mythic status on both sides. It was painfully obvious to the defenders of Vicksburg that despite the constant words of courage from their comrades elsewhere in the Confederacy, there wasn't much chance of Vicksburg being liberated by Johnston or any other rebel force.

What news did creep into Vicksburg was all of offensives in the east, into Pennsylvania, and none of rescuing the last Confederate stronghold on the Mississippi.

"I am almost sorry to hear of Lee's progress Northward," wrote one

rebel soldier from Vicksburg on June 28, "for it looks as if the importance of Vicksburg were not understood. What is [Philadelphia] to us if
the Mississippi be lost. Our existence, almost, as a nation, depends on
holding this place. Why not then remain on the defensive & send troops
hither, instead of employing them on useless expeditions, which are only
raids on a grand scale, having no decisive results. Our rulers seem to
have gone clean daft. Even if we are finally relieved, I shall not excuse
them, for it is only owing to the total inefficiency of the enemy that we are
not already captured, & no good general ever counts on such mistakes."

By that point the Union forces were starting to blow holes in the
walls defending Vicksburg. On the twenty-fifth of June, Grant's sappers
loaded explosives into the first of a series of tunnels that extended from
their own lines to points beneath the city parapets. Those inside the
town knew of the operation and had frantically dug their own tunnels to
try to find and destroy the effort, to no avail. They set up another line of
defense behind the first one and waited. At three o'clock the bomb went
off, sending those few people still on the ramparts or in the Confederate
tunnels flying.

"All that were there were thrown into the air, some of them coming
down on our side, still alive," said Grant. "I remember one colored man,
who had been under ground at work when the explosion took place, who
was thrown to our side. He was not much hurt, but terribly frightened.
Some one asked him how high he had gone up. "Dun no, massa, but t'ink
'bout t'ree mile," was his reply. General Logan commanded at this point
and took this colored man to his quarters, where he did service to the
end of the siege."

By the first of July, Grant's forces had ten places where they could get
within a few hundred yards of the enemy lines without exposing themselves to enemy fire. They were also in a position with their various tunnels and mines to blow several holes in the town's defenses at any time.
With the progress of the sappers and the holes in the city walls, the constant quips from Union soldiers about being there on Independence Day
began to seem like more than mere jokes. Maybe Grant really was plan-
ning his final assault on the fourth. Inside the walls, General Pemberton
consulted his division commanders. On the third of July, at ten in the
morning, white flags rose over a portion of the walls. A messenger came
out from Pemberton asking for a meeting to discuss terms.

True to his nickname from the battles along the Tennessee River, Grant replied that there was no need to talk because, as he put it, "the useless effusion of blood you propose stopping by this course can be ended at any time you may choose, by the unconditional surrender of the city and garrison." He added at the end of his note, "I have no terms other than those."

In the end, largely because he didn't have the resources to transport thirty thousand prisoners of war to Cairo, Grant agreed to immediately parole the rebel forces and allow the officers among them to retain their sidearms and one horse. When the exhausted and half-starved rebels marched out to lay down their arms within firing distance of the Union troops, there was no jeering or cheering from the victors, only silent respect, perhaps mixed with a sense of disbelief that the long siege of Vicksburg was at last over.

The larger war, of course, was far from over, though on that same Fourth of July the Union armies finally turned back Lee's advance at Gettysburg. The twin victories of Gettysburg and Vicksburg "lifted a great load of anxiety from the minds of the President, his Cabinet, and the loyal people all over the North," said Grant. "The fate of the Confederacy was sealed when Vicksburg fell. Much hard fighting was to be done afterwards and many precious lives were to be sacrificed; but the *morale* was with the supporters of the Union ever after."

For the remainder of the war, the United States controlled the river. There was mopping up to do, along the Bayou Teche in Louisiana and on the Red River. There were periodic raids by ragged rebel outfits. But the great serpent of the Anaconda plan was firmly in place, dividing the Confederacy in two. Sherman was soon on his way toward Atlanta, and Grant on his way toward Washington and, eventually, Appomattox, where Lee surrendered unconditionally in April 1865.

A few weeks after Appomattox, the steamboat *Sultana* arrived at Vicksburg from New Orleans. On her voyage down the river a week before, *Sultana* had brought the grim news of Lincoln's assassination. Now on her way back north, Captain J. Cass Mason took on board twenty-four hundred recently released Union soldiers who had been prisoners of war at Andersonville. With the war over, the men and boys were at last heading home, mostly up the river to Ohio and Illinois. Never mind, therefore, that the 260-feet-long *Sultana* was only licensed to carry 376 passengers. Never mind either that mechanics were attempting to fix a faulty boiler on the *Sultana* even as the veterans were being transferred from trains to the ship. At the rate the army was paying, Mason figured to make an extra $6,000 profit on a run upriver.

When the *Sultana* pulled away from the dock after midnight there were nearly twenty-six hundred people crammed into every available inch of space on the vessel. Nonetheless, the mood was jolly. "A happier lot of men I think I never saw than those poor fellows were," one of the passengers later wrote.

At two in the morning, about eight miles above Memphis, the boilers exploded. The first mate, William Rowberry, was standing in the pilot-house one moment and the next was in the middle of the river surrounded by hundreds of others, some scalded by the steam, some with broken or severed limbs. Another survivor went side to side on deck, stepping over the bodies of passengers who had been crushed in the frenzy, trying to find a place to jump into the water where it wasn't "a sea of heads, so close together that it was impossible to leap without killing one or more."

The whole scene was lit by the floating bonfire that the *Sultana* had become, drifting now out of control in the middle of the river, which was at flood stage and nearly five miles wide at that point.

"In twenty minutes after the explosion the whole boat was in a sheet of fire," wrote a reporter who interviewed Rowberry and other survivors. "A dense mass of people, estimated at 500, took refuge on the bow of the boat while the flames were driven aft by the wind; but the boat soon turned stern down the stream, reversing the flame, when the entire mass perished together, many roasted while clinging to the boat."

With the horrific coda of the *Sultana*—with some sixteen hundred victims, the deadliest shipwreck in American history—the war was really over, as was the golden age of river travel. The disaster was a ghoulish bookend of sorts; the worst steamboat disaster on the river prior to the war was the 1837 wreck of the *Monmouth*, which was similarly overfilled by profiteers on a government mission, though this time the victims were Native Americans in the process of being "removed" across the river to Oklahoma.

In many ways the Civil War can be seen as the final great conflagration of the long line of wars for control of the basin that began with de

Soto's fleeing army centuries before. In three hundred years the river had been Native American, Spanish, French, English, American, and Confederate. Now it belonged undisputedly to the free men and women of the United States.

The American war *against* the river, however, had only just begun.

BOOK SEVEN

ON THE LAKE OF THE ENGINEERS

· · ·

*Floods rise, levees rise, dams rise, while
mountains fall and grasses sink*

To spend an entire day on the bank of a river without
feeling guilty about it; such is the mark of a successful
person.

—CHINESE PROVERB

33

THE MOUTH

Early on in my travels I wanted to go to the mouth of the Mississippi, a place I had never seen and that you cannot get to on foot as there is no road to it and very little firm ground once you arrive. So I booked a room in the last hotel at the bottom of the river and made my plans. A friendly voice at the front desk of the Cypress Cove Lodge in Venice, Louisiana, assured me that it would be no problem finding a boat to take me where I wanted to go: fishing was slow and hunting hadn't started. Slow fishing aside, that sounded perfect.

Then, three weeks before I was set to go, British Petroleum punctured the bottom of the Gulf of Mexico and the worst oil spill in American history began. By the time I arrived in Venice everything about the mouth of the river was at the center of a sea of unknowns. Sweet light crude was gushing into the Gulf of Mexico at a rate of five thousand barrels a day, unless it was ten thousand barrels a day, or twenty-five thousand barrels. Exotic detergents were being pumped into the bottom of the sea near the gusher, which were going to lessen the damage to the Gulf unless they were going to compound the problem. British Petroleum and the federal government were doing everything they could, unless they weren't. The Gulf was going to die, unless it was not.

Under the circumstances, my otherwise unremarkable reservation at the last hotel on the Mississippi River was a hot commodity. Journalists from around the world were double bunked in the dorm-like rooms of the Cypress Cove Lodge. The antenna-sprouting vans of broadcast crews nearly filled the parking lot behind the uninspired, three-story building, taking spaces that in more normal times along the river were filled with pickup trucks and boat trailers. Well-groomed telecasters took the place of the usual good old boys and girls, come down from points north for some of the finest sport fishing in the world: redfish, snook, drum, catfish; and farther offshore, bluefin, yellowfin, jack, and marlin.

When I got there, the broadcasters and their technical crews were schooled up around a microphone-festooned makeshift podium on the waterfront. The governor of Louisiana arrived in a dark SUV to deliver a grim update on the progress of the spill, to report on the progress of the cleanup, and to reiterate his unwavering commitment to the future of the oil business in the Gulf.

"Governor, what if you had a machine that could suck up twice as much oil as the well is pumping out every hour?" asked a tall fellow with the regal bearing of a retired navy admiral and submarine captain, which he was. "That would be great," the governor responded, but moved on quickly to the next question, sensing—as everyone else in the crowd did—that the admiral's follow-up was surely going to be some version of "I have just such a machine."

"Is it true some brown pelicans were flown in a helicopter back to Florida?" someone else asked. "Yes . . ."

Behind the podium an endless relay of military helicopters thwapped to and fro, swinging beneath them sandbags the size of Volkswagen buses. The big choppers were on their way to the barrier islands where they dumped the sand in the hope that they could extend and fortify that last line between the approaching oil and the famous marshes and bayous of the Mississippi delta. Few ecosystems on the planet are as full of life as the places where big, continental rivers meet the sea, and the Father of Waters has not surprisingly produced the Mother of all North American estuaries. By some measures 40 percent of the salt marsh in the lower forty-eight states was created by the Mississippi River, forming the nurseries for all the shrimp, crab, crayfish, and Cajun whatnot at the bottom of the Gulf of Mexico food chain.

There is no view of the river proper, or the Gulf of Mexico, from the harbor side at the Cypress Cove Lodge. Surrounded by low green land

and wetland, there is little to suggest the geographical importance of the place. Still, in spite of the din of the helicopters and the clicking of the cameras between the squinting governor's answers, it was an exquisite spring day at the bottom of America's greatest river. The faint whiff of oil in the air was from the nearby refineries, not from the spill. The sportfishing boats nodded at their berths in the harbor. Birds wheeled and cell phones chirped.

Given all the hubbub surrounding "the greatest environmental disaster in American history," I was surprised at how easy it turned out to be to get my ride out to the mouth of the Mississippi and beyond. After the press conference I wandered up to the fellow who had asked about a hypothetical oil-sucking machine and he, in turn, introduced me to Al Andry, one of four young men who were out tuna fishing under the *Deepwater Horizon* rig the night it blew up. A few days later the five of us went out to the Gulf in Andry's twenty-one-foot Mako.

The wind was kicking up from the south as we rounded the corner out of Venice and got in line behind a convoy of half a dozen or more commercial fishing boats. They were not headed out for their usual harvest of shrimp but were loaded down instead with bales of absorbent booms meant to sop up the incoming oil. It was an earnest effort, the citizens in their forty-foot boats piled high with bandages and tourniquets and, I imagined, donated hair from eco-salons. It felt distinctly Lilliputian, however, as if ants were being marshaled out to tend to the aftermath of the Battle of Gettysburg. The Mississippi River below Venice is so wide and wind driven on the surface, and so populated by titanic oceangoing vessels, that there is little to suggest to the eye that it is a river and not a bay. Except, that is, for the color of the water, which is the color of a coffee milk shake.

Pilot Town, which really is the last human outpost on the river and is accessible only by boat, perches on the east bank of the river just above the Head of Passes. Incoming ships from the sea stop there to hire a river pilot, and the Coast Guard had moored a giant cleaning station in midstream nearby so that all vessels coming with signs of oil on their hull could be washed with chemical dispersants.

It made perfect sense to swab the incoming ships, though from the perspective of the wounded sea it was an ironic twist. It is the Mississippi River, after all, that year in and year out dumps an ungodly soup into the

Gulf of Mexico: pesticides, fertilizers, industrial chemicals, and the toxic runoff of a million parking lots, streets, storm sewers. Not to mention measurable levels of caffeine, which peak in the Mississippi at its confluence with the Ohio and then decline. Every second of every day, someone somewhere dribbles something that winds up in the river—at the gas pump, at the boatyard, out behind the woodshed.

Nor is it only the deadly drip of runoff that flows past Head of Passes. Every few years barges collide or pipelines break. Or trains go off their rails and leak their noxious contents somewhere in the vast drainage basin of the Mississippi River. Only a year after the BP disaster in the Gulf of Mexico, ExxonMobil failed to prevent a pipeline in Montana from sending a massive slick into the Yellowstone River way up in the northern reaches of the basin. At least once a decade there are notable spills: 420,000 gallons of heavy fuel oil went into the river after a barge collision in 2009; 400,000 gallons of toluene and benzene went in at Baton Rouge in 1997; 210,000 gallons of styrene in 1988; 64,000 gallons of chloroform in 1973.

The good news is that the Mississippi River and almost all of its major tributaries are remarkably cleaner today than they were in the 1970s. This is thanks entirely to the United States Congress, which functioned long enough in 1972 to override Richard Nixon's veto of the Clean Water Act. It's difficult today to imagine how bad the bad old days really were, when it was not just acceptable but expected that every factory beside every stream in the basin simply ran a pipe out the back to discharge its waste into the great river. Towns and municipalities were no better. Most simply flushed their waste into the nearby river and figured it was no longer their problem. The solution to pollution was dilution, as the old thinking went, and folks downriver were simply not as lucky or smart as people upstream.

Most notoriously of all, in 1900 Chicagoans decided they didn't want to continue dumping their sewage into the lake in front of their city, from which they drew their drinking water. By removing a short section of the terminal moraine left by the receding glaciers, they were able to reverse the flow of the Chicago River and send their effluent instead out their backyard toward their historic rival, St. Louis, and beyond. The Chicago Sanitary and Ship Canal, as it was rather disingenuously named, made the Great Lakes a part of the Mississippi basin.

Today, thanks to the Clean Water Act and the Environmental Protection Agency, almost every obvious source of industrial and municipal pollution has been brought under control. As a result, the river from top to bottom is full of fish, insects, birds, amphibians, reptiles, and aquatic mammals. There are some 260 species of fish alone, including at least ten varieties of catfish, a dozen kinds of perch, thirty different minnows, three pikes, three sturgeons, a dozen suckers, miscellaneous cods, drums, eels, and herring. There are alligator gar that grow to nearly ten feet long and weigh as much as three hundred pounds, and seven-foot-long paddlefish that weigh more than two hundred pounds. Bullhead sharks have been caught as far up the river as St. Louis, and pallid sturgeon have been pulled out of the Yellowstone River in the foothills of the Rockies.

There are also dozens of invasive species, most notably several varieties of Asian carp, voracious feeders on algae and plankton that escaped from landlocked fish farms during floods. The variety known as silver carp can grow to one hundred pounds, and in addition to their capacity to virtually eliminate the bottom of the food chain, they are known for jumping as high as eight to ten feet when alarmed by a passing boat. The reemergence of pleasure boats of all kinds on the upper stretches of the river, as well as swimmers, is another sign that the waters of the Mississippi basin are cleaner, but running into a fifty-pound fish at head high while waterskiing is a new hazard.

None of this is to say that pollution has been entirely eliminated from the river, particularly when heavy rains overwhelm aging city sewers and cause untreated discharges. The main sources of filth in the river now are much harder to find and fix than the rusty pipes of a half century ago. The culprit today is "non-point" runoff pollution, primarily from cornfields and livestock operations, but also from almost every paved surface between the Rockies and the Appalachians. The upshot is that cleaner is by no means clean, and marine biologists fear that the Gulf of Mexico is being converted into a semi-toxic algae pool by runoff from the river of fertilizer flowing into it. Most years, the hypoxic dead zone in the northern Gulf is about the size of Lake Ontario.

The scene off Pilot Town when we arrived in Andry's twin-V was suitably dramatic, with the stainless steel Coast Guard boats, sirens flashing, the grim convoys of shrimpers turned oil-daubers, and the incessant helicopters overhead. Nature, too, was active, sending a squall through, complete with towering thunderheads and a waterspout that touched down behind us at one point, weaving like a dervish back and forth across the river and leaving Al and his buddies whooping and hollering.

"Did you see that thing?!"

"That was close!"

"Damn."

We diverged from the rest of the boat traffic at Head of Passes, where the river divides into three main distributaries, each one as big as any other river in North America. In what is called the birdfoot delta, these three toes of the river then flow through what appear to be endless grasses, but are not. The cleanup convoy bore off to the left, into the North Pass, while the oceangoing vessels used the jettied Southwest Pass. This left the route in the middle, the South Pass, pretty much to us. By the time we reached the open sea the weather had lifted and we seemingly had the coast of America to ourselves.

Arriving at the edge of the ocean was exhilarating, as it always is under any circumstances, and after a surprisingly brief stretch of steep, standing waves at the border between river, land, and sea, we were out under scudding clouds banging our way up and down four-foot seas toward a nearby oil-drilling platform. The boys in the boat wanted to try to jig up some tuna, which was what they were doing the night the *Deep-water Horizon* nearly exploded right over them. That night they were almost underneath the five-story behemoth, casting to breaking fish around the base of the floating tower.

"I wasn't paying much attention, to tell you the truth," Dustin King told me. He's a good-humored twenty-two-year-old who, when he is not fishing with his buddies, is looking for a job as a firefighter. "I was hooked up on a good fish and I was having fun."

When mud started pouring off the sides of the rig, his buddy Wesley Bourg, who was the only one of the four who had ever worked on an oil platform before, looked up and could see that the rig was shrouded in an ethereal mist of gas. He could also hear the rising howl of the out-of-control well—a hissing of gas loud enough to drown out the revving engines of the *Horizon*'s generators, which were now sucking in natural gas instead of air. It sounded like a couple of 747s coming up out of the ground a few miles below them.

"Once you've heard that sound you don't forget it," he says. "I said to Al, 'Guys, it is time to LEAVE. GO GO GO GO GO!'" And Al, who as a teenager lost half an arm when the end of a long brush with which he was cleaning a swimming pool touched an overhead power line, didn't need to be told twice.

"I just pinned it," he said to me, pantomiming the way he threw the boat's throttle forward. On the glass-flat waters of the Gulf that night they shot away and when they were about fifty yards away the rig blew.

"Oh, it was awful," said Al, who had ducked down behind the boat's console expecting to be hit by debris. "It was fucking terrible and sad. You just knew immediately that people were dead up there. I didn't think anyone could survive that."

By the time I was out there bouncing fishing plugs off the metal legs of drilling platforms with Al and his friends, the *Deepwater Horizon* was at the bottom of the sea and the oil was pouring out unabated. There were plenty of other rigs and platforms to fish under, however. Due to the way the Mississippi's delta protrudes sixty or seventy miles out into the Gulf of Mexico, we were almost immediately out of sight of land, but we were never out of sight of the thousands of drilling platforms, production platforms, and pumping stations that make the Gulf Coast of Louisiana, Alabama, and Texas seem less like an ocean than an eerie Mad Max industrial park. It reminded me of evenings I used to spend fly-fishing around Manhattan, bouncing Clouser minnows off the trash cans below the Statue of Liberty's feet. Strange and fun, and a hopeful sign that there were wild fish in our urban midst, but not nearly as restorative as an hour casting out toward an unbroken horizon or paddling a free-flowing stream.

There were no tuna for us that afternoon out in the Gulf of Mexico. We jigged up a few skipjacks beneath a platform that hissed and clanked like a steamboat engine. For a while a burly roughneck watched us from a steel staircase four stories above. He looked lonely, or at least I imagined he must be, out there watching the sun come up and go down on his Tinkertoy platform in the middle of nowhere. Perhaps he was thinking about his colleagues whose tower had recently blown up under them, or about his family onshore, or about potential terrorists pretending to be tuna fishing beneath his rig.

We waved up at him, but his orange hard hat didn't move perceptibly and eventually he resumed climbing the stairs. He was on his way, no doubt, to turn some gargantuan valve slightly to the left. Or to check a pressure gauge, keeping tabs on that other ocean lying a mile below the floor of this one on which we floated; the liquid fossilized remains of a dozen extinct eons, a sea of oil and gas that had been sitting there for a hundred million years, held down by the weight of the world.

We went rig to rig like that for a couple of hours, until we were about fifteen miles offshore, and then turned back north, toward the now-invisible mouth of the North American continent. We were still, in some very real way, floating on the Mississippi—the current of freshwater does not fully dissipate into the ocean until it is around the southern tip of Florida and halfway up the Gulf Stream to Bermuda. But I had seen what I came to see. To say that a person in a small boat on the Gulf of Mexico is still on the Mississippi is as true as saying that a child in the rain in Minnesota is really feeling the distilled spray from the North Atlantic. I had seen Old Man River keep on rolling until he was completely out of sight under the deep blue sea, and I would be lying if I didn't say I *Loved It.*

Rivers are metaphorically linked to the passage of time, and to human blood and empires, while the seas into which they dissipate embody the timeless, the eternal despond and fallen sandcastles. The old metaphors for rivers and oceans still hold, of course, but as the flat green shoreline of America reappeared ahead of our bow and we made our way back through the mouth of the river and up between the waving walls of saw-grass toward Head of Passes, the metaphor that I couldn't shake was not of time or eternity.

The whole thing, it seemed to me, was a Rube Goldberg contraption: the Gulf full of derricks and spills; the bandaged-up coastline of the dis-appearing marshlands; the helicopters flying overhead carrying tarps full of sand; the Coast Guard boats waiting to wash down incoming ves-sels; the levees and dams all up and down the watershed that keep good floods from replenishing the land and seem to do little to prevent bad floods; the pavement and storm drains in a million parking lots in mid-dle America; the pesticides and the corn barges. The whole thing was a vast, if deeply malfunctioning, machine. A rickety empire without an emperor that might last another hundred years, or a thousand years, but that was also, quite possibly, already halfway washed to the sea.

The trip to the bottom had produced what I hoped. I had seen the end of the Mississippi. Only I wasn't writing a book about a broken machine. I was looking for a river.

34

ALL THE LISTS OF CLAY

The Mississippi River delta was locked in a losing battle long before the BP oil spill of 2009. Every forty-five minutes an area of Louisiana marsh roughly the size of a football field disappears under the waves of the Gulf of Mexico. This works out to roughly twenty-four square miles a year, or more than two thousand square miles of Louisiana gone since 1932. (Think one Manhattan a year, one Delaware a century.) Hurricanes occasionally take enormous gulps of marsh in a few hours, but most of the loss is more gradual: first the plants die, usually from saltwater intrusion, then the muck they were holding in place washes away, and what was once a nursery for shrimp and other creatures is now open water. There are numerous causes for the disappearance of southern Louisiana, but the oldest and most curious of them may be the astonishing fact that the planet hasn't quite recovered its equilibrium from the end of the last ice age.

Continental ice sheets are not static beings but are constantly flowing and ebbing. They ooze outward from the higher latitudes, where more snow falls each year than melts, toward some equilibrium in a warmer latitude, where their leading edge melts at the same rate that their icy heart is growing. In warmer millennia, therefore, the ice sheets fall back; in colder times they advance. Beginning roughly ninety-five thousand years ago, the mile-high ice of the Laurentide Ice Sheet periodically advanced and retreated over most of Canada, New England, New York, and the Upper Midwest. It was a frozen ocean that came and went from the North Pole on a tidelike cycle measured in tens of thousands of years and driven, most scientists believe, by wobbles in the earth's rotation.

The most recent great ice age in North America, known as the Wisconsin Glaciation, began its final retreat north some twenty thousand years ago when the climate started to warm. Why the climate slowly warmed is still being debated, but what happens when a mile-thick ice cube the size of Canada melts is not in doubt. The rivers coming off of that continent of ice dwarfed even the Mississippi at the highest of high water, and they were muddier too, the ice having scraped up anything that could be pried free of the bedrock during its advance. In relatively short order geologically speaking, this deluge of meltwater deposited a layer of silt up to hundreds of feet thick in places over the entire delta area. In winters, when the flow of meltwater diminished to a relative trickle, the howling winds picked up the lighter silt and spread it over a broad area. This blanket of loess, as the soil is called by geologists, is so heavy that the crust of the earth beneath its thickest concentrations continues to buckle and sink into the magma below, taking the marshes above with it.

It isn't just the sediment that is weighing down the Mississippi River delta, either. The globe has a finite amount of total water, whether fresh or salt, liquid or solid, belowground or in the clouds above it. The more of that global supply of water that is piled up as freshwater ice over the high latitudes, the less there necessarily is in the oceans of the world. At the peak of the Wisconsin Glaciation some twenty-one thousand years ago, when the ice extended from Nantucket Island off the coast of Massachusetts to Long Island, New York, and on across the heartland to the banks of the Missouri, there was so much water locked in ice piled on land that sea levels were four hundred feet lower than they are today. As the ice melted, the ocean advanced, adding its weight to the downward pressure on the coastline.

Geology is a slow-motion business. The melting of the ice and the resulting filling of the oceans stabilized some eight thousand years ago, but scientists at NASA's Jet Propulsion Laboratory calculate that the crust beneath the Mississippi River delta is still sinking under the weight of mud and saltwater at a rate of about a centimeter a decade. Part of the problem for the mouth of the Mississippi, in other words, is that the entire spinning planet appears to be still gravitationally adjusting itself to a ten-thousand-year-old change in the weather.

If one measure of human success is the ability to spend an entire day on the bank of a river without feeling guilty, as the ancient Chinese proverb prescribes, it would be considerably easier to achieve such serenity beside the Mississippi if the only explanation for the disappearing delta was a flip-flop in the climate during the heyday of giant sloths and saber-toothed tigers. The reality, however, is that over the course of the past few centuries, we the people of the United States have expended trillions of tax dollars and more than a few lives doing everything possible to hasten the demise of the delta and its ecosystems. It's not just the pollution, already mentioned. The delta is disappearing into the sea because the Army Corps of Engineers has spent two centuries attempting to prevent the Mississippi from being a river.

Spreading mud around is what deltaic rivers do, and from the end of the ice age to the dawn of the twentieth century, the Mississippi more than replenished the sinking bottomlands of Louisiana with new layers of silt. Quartz from the Rockies, feldspar from the Appalachians, limestone from the Ozarks, and mud from all over. The river brought whatever detritus its countless tributaries could pry loose from the plains and mountains. "Too thick to drink," as the boatmen used to say about the water of the Mississippi River, "too thin to walk on."

Before the nineteenth century, much of this wealth of sediment was distributed into the surrounding countryside. Most dramatically, this happened during the fairly regular occurrence of spring floods when the river or one of its tributaries jumped its banks. As soon as a river spreads out into its floodplain, its current slows, and slow water drops its load of sediment the way undissolved sugar falls to the bottom of a glass of iced tea when you stop stirring. The aftermath of a flood invariably is mud.

There have always been floods on the Mississippi, of course. While de Soto's remnant forces were building their makeshift fleet in 1543, the river suddenly rose. "In the month of March, although it had not rained in that land for over a month, the river rose in such manner that it stretched clear to Nilco, nine leagues away; and the Indians said it spread over another nine leagues of land on the other side," said the survivor known as the Gentleman of Elvas. The town where they were encamped

Special Collections Research Center, University of Chicago Library

Flood victims in Hamburg, Louisiana, 1927.

was somewhat elevated, but even there, he said, "the water rose to the stirrups. Wood was piled up in heaps, and many branches laid on top, and there they fastened the horses; and in the houses they did likewise." The flood lasted for two months, but the locals did not appear surprised. High water came every fourteen years, they told the Spaniards.

No one kept much of an account of the floods during the next centuries: New Orleans was underwater for several months in 1734, and the Cajun country was flooded in 1788. There were thirteen notable floods on the lower Mississippi River in the nineteenth century: in 1809, 1825, 1849, 1851, 1858, 1859, 1874, 1882, 1883, 1884, 1890, 1893, and 1897. In that same period there were hundreds, or perhaps thousands, of other high-water events elsewhere in the basin, each attended with its own particular mix of death, destruction, inconvenience, and mayhem. George Burns, the once-enslaved river man, remembered a flood on the Arkansas River in the 1870s that washed out the Perkins graveyard below Little Rock.

"Five hundred dead bodies were discharged into the water," he recalled. "Mr. Jasper Pillow, a white man living at Little Rock, told me that the body of his cousin, Seely Pillow, who had only been dead about six weeks, was recovered from the river. He said about forty-five bodies were recovered on Sunday near the graveyard. Bodies were picked up at

Little Rock for several days. The stream was swollen and caskets floated about like small boats."

Even in years without floods, the river managed to leave much of its sediment load behind. Whatever didn't go over the banks in spring floods, into fields and bottomland hardwood forests, spread into delta lands via dozens of distributary streams, large and small. We are accustomed to envisioning rivers as a gathering together of many mountain sources into one outlet, but that is not the case with deltaic rivers such as the Mississippi, which divide as they near the sea into a web of myriad outlets. These bayous in turn split and spread further into countless nameless swamps and quiet backwaters, places where even the finest silts find time to settle out. Before people began piling up artificial levees, distributary streams branched off of the main stem of the Mississippi starting hundreds of miles north of New Orleans. Many of these only received water when the main river was high or flooding, and many found their way back to the main stream before reaching the Gulf. Others, such as the Atchafalaya, were major rivers in their own right. All of the distributary flows, however, served to slow down the fall of water off the continent, allowing the sediment to settle to the bottom.

Where it meets the sea, in particular, the dissipating Mississippi built extensive marshes and sandbars on either side of itself. Take out your map and look at it: below New Orleans the Mississippi flows between an ever narrower and soggier conduit, poking its way out into the Gulf like a serpent emerging from a basket. From the Algiers Point in New Orleans it is eighty-five miles to Venice, and then ten miles farther to Pilot Town, which is accessible only by water. Below Pilot Town is Head of the Passes, where the three-toed birdfoot delta begins. The Southwest Pass, through which all large oceangoing vessels enter the river, is another twenty miles long, though there is very little you would call dry land on either side of it. Left to its own devices, the river doesn't so much flow through the delta lands, it builds the delta lands around itself. Estimates are that in the five thousand years before the twentieth century and the beginning of decline, the coast of Louisiana advanced into the Gulf by as much as fifty miles.

Beginning in the 1700s but accelerating in the centuries that followed, Americans attempted to protect themselves from local flooding by building ever higher levees, until today the river lives between twin walls some fifteen hundred miles long. Before the Civil War, planters in the delta forced their enslaved workers to pile the dirt up, and after emancipation folks along the river north and south forced their state and national government to hire immigrants to pile it higher still. One by one, the various bayous were artificially closed, funneling ever more water through the main stem and allowing ever less sediment onto the land. It was via these formerly navigable streams that Ulysses S. Grant and company tried and failed to work their way around behind Vicksburg in the months before the successful assault on the town.

By eliminating outlets to the wetlands that had previously moderated floods through their capacity to hold and dissipate high water, the ever-rising levees had the perverse and unintended effect of exacerbating big floods. Bigger floods inevitably led to more political pressure for still higher walls. In 1849, in response to a flood in the lower Mississippi valley, the federal government gave away nearly twenty-five million acres of public lands in the floodplain to the states of Louisiana, Arkansas, Missouri, and Mississippi with the idea that the states would sell the land and use the money raised to build higher levees. No one seemed to notice that twenty-five million more developed acres in the floodplain meant twenty-five million more acres to protect from flooding. Or that an end to periodic flooding meant no mud to replenish subsiding fields and sidewalks. The eternal refrain from the people who live by the river has always been for their government to ensure that there will be no water in the streets, no muddy living rooms. And no taxes, either.

Meanwhile, what the farmers and townsfolk didn't want in their living rooms, the steamboat pilots and owners didn't want in their navigation channel. Like their fellow citizens, they too turned increasingly to the federal government for subsidies and technical assistance. For the good of the nation, Congress almost invariably came through. Federal navigation efforts officially began in 1820, when Congress appropriated $5,000 to survey the Ohio and Mississippi in search of "the most practicable mode of improving the navigation of these rivers." Four years later, Congress appropriated $75,000 to improve navigation on the Ohio and Mississippi, and over the next two decades spent another $2.5 million on various projects, including canals around the rapids at Louisville and Des Moines.

Much of the initial effort was directed by Henry Shreve, whose shallow-draft steamboat *Washington* had ushered in the golden age of power navigation on the river. Under the auspices of the Department of the Army, he turned his considerable engineering talents to removing snags and other obstructions. He built a series of twin-hulled boats equipped with steam-powered derricks that could pull the most recalcitrant logs from the riverbed. They were known as "Uncle Sam's Toothpullers," and in the 1830s even the Great Raft of the Red River was removed as far as Shreveport, which was accordingly named for Shreve. Perhaps inevitably, the snag teams moved on to preemptively clearcutting any standing trees that looked as if they were in danger of eroding into the stream. In less than three years during the 1840s, they removed 21,681 "snags, rigidly speaking," 36,840 "roots, logs, and stumps," and nearly seventy-five thousand "impending trees."

As superintendent of the western rivers, Shreve was also an early advocate of the use of wing dams to control sandbars. Initially constructed of brush and stones, but now mostly substantial creations of rock, these protrude from the bank less than halfway across the river and are designed to constrict the flow of water so that it scours out a deeper navigation channel. The first experimental wing dam was built in the 1830s and succeeded in scouring a channel across the bar below it. Shreve, ecstatic, predicted that eventually sixty-one wing dams would be sufficient to maintain the navigation channel for the entire Mississippi River system.

In a river of mud, however, one tweak invariably leads to another. Eighty years after Shreve's prediction, there are more than that many dikes and weirs (wing dams) in the first fifty river miles of the Mississippi below Cairo, Illinois, alone. In that same stretch, the corps has also hardened the shoreline of more than fifty miles of banks on one side of the river or another. This is typically done with stone riprap or a lattice of concrete pavers. From a distance, when traveling in a boat, the pavers can look like symmetrically cracked mud; up close they look like a five-mile-long bad patio job. A trip down the river—or, for that matter, a brief glance through the Army Corps' navigation charts for the lower Mississippi—reveals that the first fifty miles of the river below the mouth of the Ohio are not atypical of the remaining nine hundred miles to the Gulf of Mexico in terms of the density of engineering experiments. There are not as many dikes and weirs upriver from Cairo, but only because on all the major tributaries to the lower Mississippi the corps

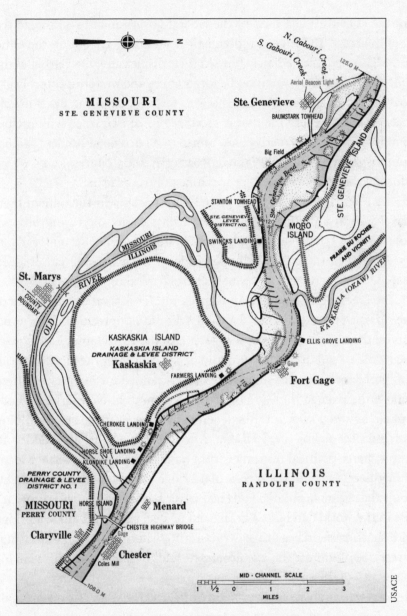

Nautical chart showing "improvements" below Cairo, Illinois.

has built locks and dams—converting free-flowing rivers into a series of slack water "navigation pools."

From the beginning there were dissenters to the public works gravy train in the Mississippi basin. Most notably, perhaps, President James Polk used his veto pen in the 1840s to back up his argument that it was not the constitutional duty of the federal government to subsidize the river interests. The rugged individualists and pioneers out on the Ohio and Mississippi immediately howled their displeasure: the veto, said the *Cincinnati Gazette*, "can never be forgotten by the western people. Every boat that is snagged, every one that gets fast on a sand bar, every article that is lost, and every life that is sacrificed in consequence will forcibly remind us of this destructive blow aimed by a Locofoco President against our prosperity." The Civil War temporarily slowed Congress's civil works effort on the rivers, but with peace came politics as usual.

"In 1866 rivers were again linked with harbors in the annual pork barrel which, unfailingly refilled, took on steadily increasing proportions," wrote Louis Hunter in his classic study *Steamboats on the Western Rivers*. "In these post-bellum decades it was a sorry stream indeed that did not receive at least a small slice of federal funds."

The creeping of concrete and riprap into ever smaller tributaries of the Mississippi system after the Civil War did not preclude major projects on the main branches of the system. In the 1870s James Eads solved the riddle of sandbars and silting in at the mouth of the river. It was a real problem; dozens of ships were often stranded for months at a time outside the river in the Gulf, or above the mouth in New Orleans. Eads was already well known to the federal government for his role building the river fleet during the Civil War. After the war, against great odds and despite fierce political resistance from none other than the Army Corps of Engineers, he built the spectacular bridge across the Mississippi in St. Louis that bears his name. Eads had never built a bridge before, and no one in the world had built a bridge out of steel before, let alone a bridge with the longest arches of any structure anywhere. It was a monumental success, and before it was even complete Eads began pushing his plan for the mouth of the river.

Eads was almost a force of nature himself. The Army Corps of Engineers by then had given up on trying to remove the sandbars. Led by another legendary nineteenth-century engineer, Andrew Humphreys, the corps proposed to build a canal from New Orleans to the sea and had lined up the congressional votes needed to move that scheme forward. Humphreys was not pleased, therefore, when Eads announced that he was so confident that a pair of gigantic jetties constricting the mouth of the river would scour out a year-round navigational channel, that he

Library of Congress Prints and Photographs Division

Eads Bridge, St. Louis, 1872–1873.

offered to build it with his own money and take payment from the government only after the channel was open. The story of the clash of wills and egos among Eads, Humphreys, and a third legendary American engineer, Charles Ellet, was almost as outsize as the river itself, and is particularly well told in *Rising Tide*, John Barry's fascinating book on the Great Mississippi Flood of 1927. Suffice it to say here that Congress took Eads's bait, the jetties were built, and by July 1879 the channel through the sandbars at the mouth of the river was open.

Even before the jetties were fully complete, oceangoing commerce through the Port of New Orleans began to grow exponentially as the channel deepened. Today, the Port of South Louisiana, which stretches essentially unbroken from New Orleans to Baton Rouge, is the largest in the Western Hemisphere. The jetties have done exactly what Eads claimed they would do for the shipping industry, and the sediment coming down the Mississippi from all over the middle of the continent no longer piles up at the mouth. Nor does it get dispersed from the mouth alongshore to the disappearing barrier beaches, the sinking marshlands, and the dying shrimp nurseries. By design, the jetties spew as much sediment as possible far out into the deep water of the Gulf of Mexico.

The strategy of containing the river between levees abjectly failed at its primary goal of preventing the largest floods. There is evidence as well that the thousands of navigational improvements and flood control efforts perversely increased the frequency and depth of major floods. The floods of the twentieth century were more frequent and devastating than those recorded in the nineteenth century, and only in part because there were more people and infrastructure in the valley to dislocate and destroy. There were notable deluges in 1903, 1908, 1912, 1913, 1916, 1922, 1927, 1928, 1929, 1931, 1932, 1935, 1937, 1944, 1945, 1950, 1973, 1975, 1979, 1983, and 1997. During the most destructive flood on record, that of 1927, the river was eighty miles wide at Vicksburg. Some five hundred people were killed and more than half a million were left homeless.

After that flood, the army engineers modified their strategy some-what from the old plan of keeping all the water in a single channel. In extreme events the corps now blasts a hole in the levee and opens a "floodway" at Birds Point, Missouri. By thus allowing the river to send half a million cubic feet per second onto roughly three hundred square miles of Missouri lowlands, the pressure on upstream levees is relieved at the expense of the floodplain farmers between Birds Point and New Madrid, where the water returns to the main channel. Downstream two mechanical "spillways," at Morganza and at Bonnet Carré, similarly divert floodwaters into alternative outlets. These small concessions to the power of the river should not be confused with a wholesale change of strategy regarding containing and controlling the river, however: the Birds Point floodway has been used twice, in 1937 and 2011. Morganza has likewise been opened twice, in 1973 and 2011. Bonnet Carré, which is thirty miles above New Orleans and diverts water into Lake Pontchartrain behind the city, has been used eight times, including in 2011. (Ironically, perhaps, the devastating floods of Hurricane Katrina came principally via canals and waterways leading from Lakes Pontchartrain and Borgne. The Mississippi levees were not breached.)

As spotty as the record is on preventing catastrophic Mississippi River floods, the effect of two centuries of levees and bayou closings on

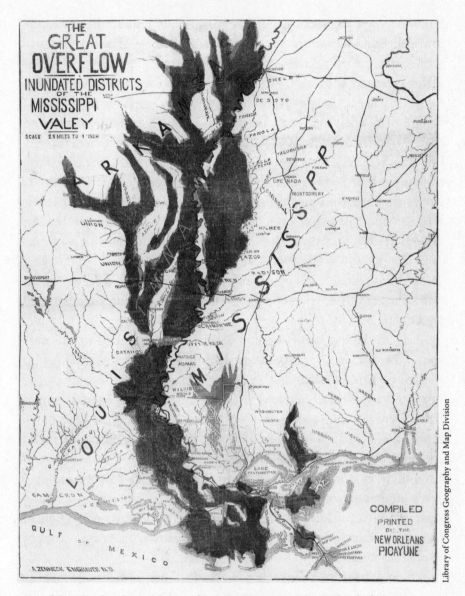

Map of the inundated areas during the Great Mississippi River Flood of 1927.

small and local riverine ecosystems is a different story. The walls that line the Mississippi and its tributaries have thoroughly ended the semi-regular high-water events that once resulted in a continual supply of mud and nutrients (and, more recently, pollution) being spread around the floodplain. To the degree that a century and a half of engineering has succeeded in keeping the river within its banks, therefore, the lowlands up and down the watershed have been starved of sediment.

It's intuitive and comforting to imagine that all rivers carve themselves a channel through the landscape, so that except in times of flood their water level is below that of the surrounding countryside. A curious feature of deltaic rivers such as the Mississippi, however, is that left to their own devices they slowly raise themselves above the level of the surrounding countryside in a twofold process that takes place over the course of thousands of flood and low-water cycles. Whenever a river crests its banks in a flood, the water immediately loses velocity and drops its heaviest sediment. This sediment slowly builds up a series of natural levees. In periods of low water, on the other hand, the lazy summer current drops sediment into the riverbed itself, thus slowly raising the floor of the river. The result is that over the centuries a deltaic river rises like an aqueduct, until it is literally flowing above the surrounding countryside between levees of its own making.

Prior to the twentieth century, whenever the elevation of the river above the surrounding landscape became unstable, the Mississippi jumped its banks and cut itself a shorter path to a lower elevation. The vast majority of these course changes were minor—the river cut off an oxbow here or commandeered a chute there. Every thousand years or so, however, during an epic flood or an earthquake, the river made a major course change somewhere below Natchez and redirected its main flow to an entirely new mouth somewhere to the east or west of the old one. There it began the process of accretion anew. Like a garden hose pushing itself around a yard (though not for the same reasons), the river spread its bounty of sediment to and fro over an area of coast some two hundred miles wide.

When the Army Corps of Engineers concluded in the 1940s that the river was overdue for a major course correction, Congress became understandably alarmed. The Atchafalaya River, as the last major distributary of the Mississippi that had not been closed off by the levee builders, was in the process of abducting the main stream. Every decade the Atchafalaya took a greater share of the water from the big river down its 150-mile shorter and steeper route to the sea. In a geological time frame, the Atchafalaya is almost certainly the inevitable future route of the river. In the human lifetimes of engineers and politicians, on the other hand, the

Mississippi cutting a right turn at Simmesport, Louisiana, and heading down the Atchafalaya is unthinkable. In such a scenario New Orleans and Baton Rouge would be left to figure out a future for themselves on silting-in backwaters, or at best on a canal built and maintained by the corps. At the mouth of the Atchafalaya, on the other hand, Morgan City would be washed away into the Gulf of Mexico.

After the great flood of 1927, the federal government essentially declared all-out war on the natural processes of the Mississippi River and by midcentury there was no question that the government would act boldly to keep the river from changing its course so dramatically. Congress told the corps to build a tremendous public works project, known as the Old River Control Structure, to ensure that at least 70 percent of the Mississippi River's water continued to travel down the current channel to New Orleans and beyond. As John McPhee so elegantly detailed in *The Control of Nature*, the river almost took the whole contraption out during the floods of the 1970s, and Congress ordered up another, even larger structure to supplement the earlier effort.

Four decades later these two engineering marvels still stand guard over Old Man River's wandering ways. The floods of 2011 may have qualified as a "hundred-year flood." All-time records were broken at a few gauges. The control structures have not, however, faced a five-hundred-year flood or, God forbid, a thousand-year flood. One of the predicted effects of human-caused climate change is that floods like the one in 2011 are likely to come to the Mississippi more often than once a century. At the other end of the spectrum, catastrophic droughts are also predicted to be more common and more sustained. The year after the great floods of 2011 found the corps struggling and improvising to keep barge navigation on the river between St. Louis and Cairo open.

The engineers, in other words, will never be finished tinkering with the river as long as there are industry lobbyists and willing taxpayers. Gone altogether are the grand predictions of a finished product that their nineteenth-century predecessors, such as Eads, were fond of making. "There's nothing that man can do that nature can't overcome," Maj. Gen. John W. Peabody, commander of the Mississippi Valley Division of the corps, told the *New York Times* in the aftermath of the great drought of 2012. "We'll continue to respond to what nature throws at us."

The great valves of Old River Control that stand guard where gravity

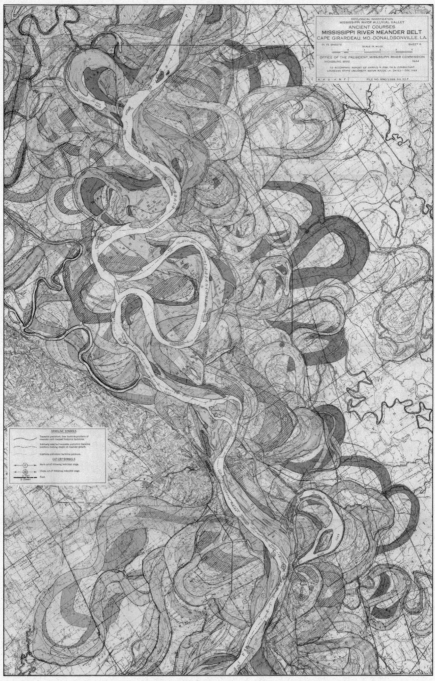

"The Meander Belt" below Cape Girardeau.

calls the Mississippi River to jump into the Atchafalaya are only the most dramatic of the tens of thousands of structures large and small up and down the entire watershed. Almost all of them have unintentionally and adversely affected the mouth of the river by reducing the flow of sediment to the lowlands. From the point of view of a mote of mud on its way from Pikes Peak to Bayou Lafourche or some other new home in Louisiana, the structures fall into two broad categories: those that speed the current up by constricting it and the dams that virtually stop the current altogether.

The contrivances that speed up the current include the levees that line the banks and the thousands of groins, wing dams, riprap banks, and other navigational "improvements" within the stream itself. By funneling the current here and there to prevent the formation of the sandbars, the engineers have undeniably made it far easier to move large barges of cargo up and down the watershed. They have also made it far more likely that a traveling particle from the short-grass prairie or the Cumberland Gap will end up at the bottom of the Gulf of Mexico, way too far offshore to help the delta. It all makes for cheap corn and other pleasures, but meanwhile Louisiana disappears into the sea.

As bad as the groins and levees are for the health of the delta, the dams up in the tributaries are arguably worse. Dams stop the flow, which stops the sediment from ever even getting into the lower river. Tearing down mountains and moving them to the sea is "the work, and the law, of rivers," Paul Horgan once wrote. Dams, however, turn rivers into lakes, which operate under another code of conduct and are more the type to let the dust settle. A century ago the lower Mississippi River carried four hundred million metric tons of sediment to the lowlands and Gulf Coast every year—enough to cover the entire state of Louisiana in almost an inch of mud, more than enough mud, in other words, to build marsh out into the Gulf. The figure today is only about a third of that.

It is not a matter of a few dams, here and there. There are forty dams on the upper Mississippi itself above St. Louis. There are fifteen dams on the Missouri above Yankton, South Dakota, and twenty-one dams on the Ohio. It's when you start looking at the tributaries to the tributaries, however, that the real picture begins to come into focus. There are more than 500 dams on the various forks of the Platte River. In the state of Kansas alone, there are 6,087 dams on tributaries to the Mississippi

River, while Missouri has another 5,099 and Oklahoma has 4,758; in Iowa there are 3,374 while Montana has 2,917. It is the same all over the watershed: in just the eleven states that lie entirely within the watershed there are more than 30,000 dams. It is harder to parse the data for Canada and the big Ohio valley states that are only partially in the Mississippi's basin, but the total number of dams that alter the Mississippi River watershed is in excess of 50,000. On the corps' dam inventory Web site you can zoom in and the icons representing dams look like beads strung along all the streams and rivers between the Appalachians and the Rockies; zoom out and they merge to bury the watershed in a cloak of blue.

Every one of the dams and levees has a story behind it: an astonishing engineering feat, an epic political battle, an abrogated Indian treaty, a dubious economic study, a broken back, a drowned coolie, a blown-up rig, a lost homestead, an irrigated field, a picnic by the reservoir, maybe some skinny-dipping. Some of the stories are very good, and some are sad. But none of the stories are much solace to a homeless shrimp or a hungry Cajun at the bottom of the river. Or a flooded city.

There are some hopeful signs of change: in June 2012 Congress passed the Restore Act, which directs that all the Clean Water Act fines eventually paid by British Petroleum be used in efforts to restore the Gulf. Also, the Army Corps' 2013 budget included a request for $26 million for "Louisiana Coastal Area Ecosystem Restoration" and $18 million for "Upper Mississippi River Restoration." It's worth noting, however, that the same Army Corps budget requested $46 million for new "channel improvements," another $45 million for levee construction in the same states, and $144 million to continue building a new multibillion-dollar dam across the Ohio.

So Louisiana continues to sink into the sea under the weight of its load of ice-age mud, while the only thing that can save it—the river of mud that made it in the first place—is shackled from top to bottom. The bayou, in other words, has been sold down the river.

35

OLD MAN RIVER

"You can never step into the same river twice," goes another of the countless proverbs. Stand waist-deep in the Big Muddy anywhere it flows, and your knees and ankles will alert you instantly that you are not even in the same river for consecutive moments. Stand in a lake and you are part of the lake. Wade into the Mississippi, and as long as your soles are on the ground you remain what you were, a part of the rest of the continent—the Rockies and the Appalachians, the prairies and the woodlands. You remain, in other words, the object upon which the strong brown god is applying its relentless and patient will.

Sand and silt scour around your feet. At one moment the Mississippi sucks you into the mud, planting you in place like a snag. Another instant the river undermines your balance. It takes the ground out from under you, in order to tip you in and take you along with the flow. It pulls you closer to the sea, which is where you are going whether you know it or not. The Mississippi is as patient as gravity, as relentless as water. When the core of the earth at last has cooled to the point that the crust can no longer drift and new mountains can no longer rise, rivers will still flow until they have torn down the last of the hills and put them under the sea.

Both outcomes are equally horrifying: to be a zombie snag half buried in the river bottom or a mote of human driftwood carried away. But when you are gut-deep in the river, desire sings to you to lie back and let the water take you with it wherever it wants. "Dive in if you are brave," murmurs the eddy that forms before you as you face downstream. "Come drift, loosed from the land, subject to the flow. Become the river. Rest."

I did it once. I puffed up my chest and floated on my back somewhere above Memphis and below New Madrid for a few dozen seconds until abject terror drove me back to shore. Far better to be in a boat. Any boat. Regaining the banks, I returned to my skiff and shoved it back in, climbed aboard. Breathing hard, I lay back on the plywood deck and let the hot sun of the morning evaporate the remains of such momentary foolishness off my skin.

In Pittsburgh, at the top of the Ohio River, I had forgone my customary plastic kayak and wooden paddle and put in on the river in a fourteen-foot aluminum boat with a small outboard motor. The reason was only partly laziness, though the prospect of paddling the nearly still waters of the Army Corps' Ohio River navigation pools did not flood me with wanderlust. More important in the decision to change ships was the knowledge that as it is with people and rivers, so it is with boats. No two boats ever travel the same river twice, and I knew from experience that a river traveled in a kayak is not the same as a river traveled in a different species of vessel. I was heading down through the main stem of the industrialized river, and I wanted some horsepower of my own.

For a perilous moment I considered buying a fifty-year-old houseboat listed for sale in Wheeling, West Virginia. It was called *Prince of Tides*, a name I detested but thought I might easily convert with a little white paint and a bottle of cheap bubbly to the *Prince of id*. The prospect of tooling up and down the arteries of the heartland in the *Prince of id* amused me greatly, and the boat was priced to sell. Down the Ohio; up the Arkansas or the Red; up the Missouri and over to the Platte; to the Falls of St. Anthony, or to Great Falls, Montana. Who could say where my id and I might go? Ten thousand miles, maybe more.

"How many miles to the gallon do you figure it gets?" I asked over the phone from Massachusetts.

"Depends on conditions," replied the current captain of the *Prince*, "but usually about one."

"One mile to the gallon?"

"Yeah," he said with the kind of resignation in his voice that comes to everyone the moment they realize a fish they thought they might be reeling in has slipped the hook and is loose in the water again.

With the money I saved from not buying the *Prince of id,* I bought a piece of plywood and built a new deck for the fourteen-foot aluminum boat I already owned. It's a good boat, known to my friends as the *Colander* because its predecessor of the same name leaked like a sieve. The new deck did not make the *Colander* into a houseboat by any means, but it did allow me to convert it at night into a pup-tent boat. I loaded the holds with the usual power bars and instant oatmeal and trailered the *Colander* over the Appalachians to Pittsburgh, where I got on the water.

Since then I'd been one thousand miles through the heart of the Rust Belt. I'd passed through the locks of a dozen corps dams and heard their gates creaking and machinery singing a song that sounded like whales in the ocean. I saw coal out of the mountains poured into barges, and barges of coal being sucked into the burners of goliath plants. For the first few hundred miles, it seemed as if every flat corner that once was a farm or a Mingo encampment is now an electric plant.

I saw new barges emerging from gleaming shipyards and old barges aground filled with mud and young trees. There were barges of corn with an odor like muffins and mountains of salt that had been painted blue, mountains of steel scrap and mountains of chrome.

I was awed and surprised at the magnificence of industry, which was neither as rusty or as ugly as I'd imagined it might be. It was instead fearsome and giant. It clanged and huffed and belched and filled me with fear for the planet. The price of cheap coal-fired power must be paid in climate-change and acid rain. We know this. And the price of cheap corn includes a dead zone in the Gulf of Mexico the size of Lake Ontario. Yet the works of the people by the river, and the work going on night and day, was also astounding in scale. It was beautiful in both form and function, and in headlong optimism. Worthy of Walt Whitman singing, I thought, without really knowing enough about Walt Whitman to know why I thought that.

As for the river, it didn't appear to mind the buzz of activity at all. Tearing down mountains and sending them to the sea is the work of rivers, after all, so why should the Mississippi and its tributaries care if the black petrified heart of the Appalachians gets sent to the Atlantic a little bit faster as air pollution? The people in the mines and barges were allies in the river's long-term project, it seemed to me.

And why should a river that remembers the mile-high ice and the rising of the Rockies worry itself with the pathetic concrete fiddlings of the Army Corps of Engineers? Why shouldn't a river that once bathed mammoths and pterodactyls welcome a batch of strange jumping fish from China? The Mississippi has lost enough friends over the eons to know how to deal with the potential extinction of the pallid sturgeon, doesn't it?

I know very well why I care about all of these things, and more. I know why I hope others care about them, too. But the Mississippi itself? During the long, lovely days on the water as the wooded hills and industry of the upper Ohio slowly gave way first to Illinois farmland and then to the semi-paved illusion of wilderness on the lower Mississippi, I wondered about what the river would say. Sure, the occupation of all rivers is to tear down mountains, but their great talent and art is to provide a home for all manner of riverine creatures, native and volunteer alike.

I met a man with no legs who was paddling from Minnesota, doing it for his brothers who were wounded in warfare. I met three women from Nashville headed for New Orleans, who said that floating was more fun than waiting tables. I met two guys in canoes who were suffering in the sun, who had left their home in the hills and were heading for the ocean. I met a woman with a houseboat who had come down the Missouri. I heard about a boat made from a Volkswagen that had passed by Memphis, and another powered by bicycles that the Coast Guard had vanquished. I saw a nude wading in the middle of nowhere, and it was a mile or two on from there that I went for my own nervous swim.

I believe that my river madness may be in remission for the time being, though sometimes when I wake up early in the morning and can't fall back asleep, I catch myself wondering about the confluence of the Purgatoire and the Arkansas up in Oklahoma. Or about the passage between the Fox River and the Wisconsin. Or the stretch of the Yazoo that hides the remains of twenty-nine sunken Civil War ships. Or whether there might truly be one last bear mound in Minnesota that has escaped the plow. I want to see where the Dry Cimarron River becomes wet.

At night though, drifting off, I'm more likely to slip back to the places I've already floated. Stretches of the Mississippi that I will not see ever again. Not even if I do go back to where I met them first time around.

ACKNOWLEDGMENTS

All of my previous books are dedicated to Nina Bramhall, and though her name is not at the front of this book, she is still foremost among those who deserve my gratitude. Jack Macrae at Henry Holt also bears much responsibility for this book emerging from the low fog of its morning hours. My various traveling companions in the watershed, both those who came along by plan and those I met here and there along the way, deserve my thanks. There are too many of these to name, but Natty Schneider, Loren Demerath, Clayton Omer, Al Andry, and Pat Schneider come to mind. The guys at Boyden and Perrin who fixed my outboard motor on short notice are remembered, as is the fellow in Louisville who had a replacement propeller for me. Thanks too to the Schwabs of Tidiute, Pennsylvania; the Omers of Louisville, Kentucky; the McCraws of Memphis, Tennessee; Cory Werk on the Bayou Teche; Hoppie of Hoppie's Marina in Imperial, Missouri; Lionel Sutton; Will Dana and Brad Weiners at *Men's Journal*; Barbara Ireland and especially Wendy and Boatner and the rest of the Riley clan of New Orleans. Thanks as well to all the friendly lock operators of the Army Corps, the dock personnel, and the many historians, archaeologists, and writers whose work is mentioned in the source notes. Thanks also to my agent, David Kuhn, to Courtney Reed, Muriel Jorgensen, Kelly Too, and the rest of the folks at Henry Holt. Early readers of parts or all of the manuscript include various Schneiders and Bremhalls, Bee Ridgway, Ward Just, and Loren Demerath. Thanks Quinn Brady for the marvelous maps and Mark Godfrey of the Nature Conservatory for the beautiful photo on the title page.

Last, I am grateful to the United States Congress, which in 1971 functioned long enough to override Richard Nixon's veto of the Clean Water Act by a wide, bipartisan margin.

SOURCE NOTES

Most history is retelling. I am deeply indebted to all of the sources listed in the Bibliography, even those that are not quoted directly in this book. That said, I've tried to point out the most important general sources for each chapter, followed by specific citations for direct quotes. While I almost invariably found my way to the original sources myself, in cases where I have quoted primary documents that I found first quoted by other authors, I have noted the primary source first, and the source in which I found it second. In general, I have listed only the author's last name, except in cases where there is more than one work by the same scholar in the Bibliography.

1: ICE ON THE ROCKS

The best book on deep geological history is McPhee's masterpiece, *Annals of the Former World*. Also see Fremling's *Immortal River*, particularly for his discussion of the glacial origins of the upper river, and Meltzer's *First Peoples in a New World*, for the end of the ice age generally. There are also a plethora of resources online about climate change and geography, including several at the National Oceanographic and Atmospheric Administration.

2: THE MISSOURI LEVIATHAN

Most of the material on Albert Koch comes from his own writings and from the elegant introduction to his journals by Ernst A. Stradler in the edition I used. The best general discussions of the emergence of the idea of prehistory from the bones of mammoths are found in Stanley Hedeen's *Big Bone Lick* and Paul Semonin's *American Monster*. Also see articles by Levin, Eiseley, and Montagu.

14	"tooth of a giant": Semonin, 15.
14	"an admirable obturation": Levin, 762.
15	"that in ancient times": Jefferson, *Notes*, 165.
16	"The GREAT PERSIAN KOULAH..." and related promotional quotes: Koch, *Journey*, xxii.
16	"I was still lying on my sofa": Koch, *Journey*, xxiv.
17	"These arrow-heads": Koch, *Description*, 20.
17	"Citizens of Missouri": Koch, *Journey*, xxv.

3: BONES AND STONES

See books by Meltzer and Gibbon, and various articles in the Bibliography on paleontological subjects for more detailed treatments of the discovery of Folsom, Clovis, and pre-Clovis sites in the Mississippi River basin.

20	"the heaviest rain": "Cloudburst Drowns 15 in New Mexico."
22	"The population of America": "New Evidence on Man in America."
22	"Only if they spoke": Meltzer, *First Peoples*, 81.
22	"The body proportions": "Sees American Man Superior of Woman."
23	"excellent, healthy white stock": "Finds Hope in Boston for 'American Race.'"
25	"best men in the country": Meltzer, 87.
25	"cannot be linked": "New Evidence on Man in America."
27	"True hunters would be offended" and related quotes: Frison, 767.

4: BROKEN ARROWS

Most of the family history section of this chapter has been passed along to me orally by members of my family. Some of the stories have been told before in my mother Pat Schneider's book *Wake Up Laughing*, and also in my grandmother Lelah Ridgway's genealogy of the Ridgway-Ridgeway family of Missouri.

31   "here is one": Collyer, 307.
31   "broke forth into an extravagant eulogy": Thoreau, *The Journal*, October 29, 1837.
34   "As sportsmen go in search": Ibid., March 28, 1859.

5: MAMMOTH SEASON

The general sources for this chapter are the same as those for chapter 3. See also Fox et al. and various scholarly articles on extinctions. The material on Black Jack Ketchum comes largely from newspaper accounts of his capture and death.

36   "I smuggled a letter out" and related quotes: "'Black Jack' Executed."
40   "time is a sort of river": Aurelius, 76.

6: AMONG THE EFFIGIES

There are several good overview studies of the various mound building cultures that were helpful to me during the writing of chapters 6 through 10: Milner, Woodward and McDonald, Gibbon, and Squier and Davis. The baseline study of global bear ceremonialism is Hallowell. Also, see various scholarly articles on ancient cultures of North America listed in the Bibliography, as well as the Institute for Minnesota Archaeology resources.

43   "it is a remarkable river": Twain, *Life on the Mississippi*, 39.
43   "The high hills are perceptible": Coues, vol. 1, 294.
44   "Black loam energy": Peter Schneider, 30.
45   "To a certain extent in Michigan": Squier and Davis, 2.
46   "The little town of Alexandersville": Ibid., 83.

46   "It is hardly possible": Garvey, Heritage Plowed Under Web site.

46   "the son of the original owner" and related quotes: Evans, 2.

48   "A bear is wiser": Hallowell, 27.

7: POVERTY POINT

54   "In short, they occupy the entire basin": Squier and Davis, 1.

54   "Middle Archaic hunter-foragers": Saunders et al., 632.

56   "a cosmopolitan society": Sassaman, 336.

8: 60,000 PEARLS

60   "The mounds in that valley": "Our Ancient Peoples."

9: THE MISSISSIPPIAN MOMENT

In addition to the references previously listed at the beginning of the notes for chapter 6, I am indebted to the work of Pauketat, Milner, Birmingham, Hudson and Tesser, Clayton et al., and Swanton.

64   "the son of the sun" and related quotes regarding de Soto and Quigaltam: from the account of the de Soto survivor known as the Gentleman of Elvas. I used the translation in Clayton et al., vol. 1, 134ff.

66   "At each public event": Pauketat, 85.

67   "it is useless for me": Swanton, *The Indians of the Southeastern United States*, 358.

69   "Under Mississippian influence": Birmingham, 84.

71   "some of which held sixty" and related quotes: Clayton et al., vol. 1, 156–57.

10: THE GREAT SERPENT

74   "There are several ancient remains in Kentucke": Filson, 74.

75   "The most prominent of these": Thomas Emerson, 141.

11: BONJOUR GREAT KHAN

Whatever you may think of the Jesuit "black robes," residents of North America have them to thank above all others for what we know about the arrival of Europeans in the Mississippi basin. Having worked with the paper and leather *Relations* twenty years ago while writing *The Adirondacks*, I was overjoyed to find the magnificent, searchable online facsimile hosted at Omaha's Creighton University. In addition to the *Jesuit Relations* and other primary sources noted below and in the Bibliography, chapters 11 through 19 could not have been written without consulting the previous work of Parkman, Morison, Morgan, Howe, Severin, and Ekberg.

82   "He tarried with them two years": Thwaites, *Jesuits Relations*, vol. 23, 274.

83   "I rested my musket": Jameson and Grant, 165.

83   "My pen can no longer express": Thwaites, *Jesuit Relations*, vol. 35, 187.

83   "The people of the Countrie": Jameson, 22.

85   "he passed for one of that nation": Thwaites, *Jesuit Relations*, vol. 23, 275.

85   "go in troops": Jameson and Grant, 303.

85   "some of the French call them the 'Nation of Stinkards'": Thwaites, *Jesuit Relations*, vol. 18, 231.

86   "embarked in the Huron country" and related quotes: Ibid., vol. 23, 277.

12: IN THE IROQUOIS LONGHOUSE

88   "The Father was stripped quite naked" and related quotes: Thwaites, *Jesuit Relations*, vol. 26, 41.

90   "they commenced to treat him": Ibid., 55.

90   "It was quite true": Ibid.

91   "Bay of Stinkards": Ibid., vol. 54, 195.

91   "When all were seated": Ibid., 229.

92   "It is a country which has none" and related quotes: Ibid., vol. 47, 145.

93   "numerous gold mines": Ibid., vol. 59, 117.

93   "to discover the sea of the South": Frontenac to Colbert, November 2, 1672, as quoted in Jaenen, 304.

94   "to diminish quietly": Colbert to Duchesneau, April 15, 1676, as quoted in Jaenen, 301.

95   "The life of the coureurs": 1 Archives des Colonies, Series CHJA, vol. 22, ff. 362–364, MG 1, PAC., as quoted in Jaenen, 305.

13: THE AMERICAN BOTTOM

99   "I am alarmed when it happens": Thoreau, "Walking," 211.

14: THE ILLINOIS COUNTRY

All the quotes of Father Marquette in this chapter are from Thwaites, *Jesuit Relations*, vol. 59.

15: ADRIFT

111   "One cannot see too many summer sunrises": Twain, *Life on the Mississippi*, 228.

113   "Some months ago I went to see a panorama": Thoreau, "Walking," 225.

115   "an accumulation of large and entire trees": Thwaites, *Jesuit Relations*, vol. 59, 140.

115   "the graveyard": Hunter, 234.

117   "Above all": Thoreau, "Walking," 245.

117   "The finest country in the world": Cox, vol. 1, 156.

118   "This Fort is situated on a plain": Babson, 24.

16: THE INCOMPARABLE LA SALLE

As with the previous several chapters, the various volumes of the *Jesuit Relations* were invaluable in the process of researching the story of La Salle and his friends and enemies. His story begins in earnest in volume 60. Also of great help were the original narratives of the La Salle expedition that appear in La Salle, Cox, Kellogg, and the Ontario Historical Society papers.

120   "They have guns" and related quotes from Marquette: Thwaites, *Jesuit Relations*, vol. 59, 147.

120   "animated our courage": Ibid., 89.

121   "on account of the continual forays": Ibid., 153.

121   "Beyond a doubt": Ibid., 167.

123   "This river is called" and related quotes from Galinée: Kellogg, *Early Narratives*, 168.

124   "labor for the salvation of the Indians" and remaining quotes from Galinée: From the translation in Ontario Historical Society, vol. 1, 3ff. They can also be found, in a slightly different translation, in Kellogg, *Early Narratives*, 168ff.

125   "The Senators of Venice": Cox, 69.

127   "the seignory of the government": Ibid., 189.

127   "finding a port where the French": Ibid., 171.

127   three hundred thousand North American beaver pelts: This figure is from Fremling, 143.

17: NOUS SOMMES TOUS SAUVAGES

As with the previous chapter, most of the material in this chapter comes from the various narratives of La Salle as translated in Cox.

129   "After having been eight years": Cox, 1.

130   "He undertook this journey" and related Hennepin quotes: Ibid., 73.

130   "No vessels had yet been seen": Ibid., 98.

131   "It was never known what course": Ibid., 76.

131   "the rudest of our men": Ibid., 100.

132   "As soon as I arrived": Ibid., 5.

132   "The Sieur de la Salle had a calumet" and related quotes from Father Membre: Ibid., 101ff.

133   "It was easy for me": La Salle, "Memoir of La Salle to Frontenac," 198.

133   "on account of the many disappointments": Cox, 104.

133   "because the desertion": Ibid., 84.

134   "*Nous sommes tous sauvages*": La Salle, *Relation*, 233.

18: THE WRATH

136   "They immediately surrounded him": Cox, 119.

137   "There was a man": Ibid., 9.

137 "We supported this remnant": Ibid., 122.

137 "We followed the shore of Lake Erie": La Salle, *"Letter,"* 62.

138 "Upon most of these stakes" and the quotes that follow from La Salle's official report: La Salle, *Relation*, 225ff.

140 "He was very glad to see us again": Cox, 16.

140 "pointed out to them the fertility" and related quotes: La Salle, *Relation*, 271.

141 "These Indians do not resemble" and remaining quotes from Membre: Cox, 137ff.

19: IF THE RIVER DON'T RISE

In addition to the various primary sources mentioned in previous chapters and miscellaneous scholarly articles listed in the Bibliography, the books of Ekberg and Severin were of particular use in this chapter.

147 "having pluged into every kind of debauchery": Cox, 211.

147 "I saw him fall a step from me": Ibid., 244.

149 "They do not immediately merge": Abbey, 303.

20: THE SCRAMBLE FOR THE FORKS

In addition to the various primary sources and scholarly articles listed in the Bibliography, I am particularly indebted in chapters 20–23 to Fred Anderson's massive and spectacular study of the Seven Years' War in North America. Parkman, to whom Anderson's work has justifiably been compared, endures. Also, Michael McConnell's studies of the Ohio Valley, Barr's work on the Western Delaware, and the University of Toronto's *Dictionary of Canadian Biography* online: www.biographi.ca.

154 "We found the French colours" and related quotes: Washington, 13ff.

154 "The lands upon the Ohio": Ibid., 25.

21: THE HALF KING

159 "they ate my father": This story about the origin of Tanaghrisson's animosity toward the French is repeated in many sources, especially

online, but I have not yet found a primary or contemporary source for the reference. Hence my use of "reputed to have said."

161   "the Air of a Warrior" and related quotes: Pa. Council Minutes, 5: 535–36, as quoted in McConnell, 93.

162   "At this time the Delawars": "The Treaty of Logg's Town," 155.

162   "The Indians take a great deal of pains": Filson, 76.

164   "When they came near" and related quotes from the treaty negotiation: "The Treaty of Logg's Town," 154ff.

167   "Although it is quite clear that Canastego": Fred Anderson, 23.

22: ADIEU NEW FRANCE

172   "We don't know what you Christian French and English": McConnell, 106.

172   "should any French priests now dare": Answer of the Six Nations to His Excellency the Governor at Albany, August, 23 1746, as quoted in Parkman, *Half-Century*, vol. 1, 212.

174   "If they should prove equally strong" and related quotes from Washington's journal: Washington, 11.

177   "Tu n'es pas encore mort, mon père" and "He then took out his brains": As quoted in Fred Anderson, 55.

178   "for the future": The Treaty of Paris.

23: THE AMERICAN WATERSHED

In addition to books previously mentioned, Utley and Washburn's *Indian Wars* was helpful in researching this section, as was Adams.

180   "From this period it remained concealed": Filson, 7.

180   "the regiments were being stationed": Anderson, 563.

181   "It is just and reasonable": George III.

182   "I sold my farm on the Yadkin": Filson, 44.

183   "In October following, a party" Ibid., 61.

184   "The inhabitants, at present": Ibid., 23.

186   "Where today are the Pequot?": Utley and Washburn, 117.

187   "The cession of Louisiana and the Floridas": Lipscomb and Bergh, vol. 10, 315.

188   "They ask of me only one town" and related quotes of Napoléon: Henry Adams, *History*, 27ff.

189   "We have lived long": Ibid., 67.

189   "on the Joyfull event of the cession": Jackson, 354.

190   "perceptibly tinged with the blood": Limerick, 35.

190   "he believed it to be right and honorable" and related quotes: Utley and Washburn, 206.

191   "We had just reached the edge of a shallow ravine": Ibid., 223.

24: ALLEGHENY MORNINGS

195   "There is an old agreement that no white men": Congdon, 14.

196   "A man's ignorance sometimes is not only useful": Thoreau, "Walking," 240.

198   "Few rivers and perhaps none": Cramer, 18.

25: DOWN A LAZY RIVER

Several books were particularly helpful in researching this chapter and those that follow: Flint, Thomas Ruys Smith, Cramer, Rawick, Mathews, Merrick, and Sandlin.

205   "Yes Ma'am I know a lot about boats" and other quotes from George Taylor Burns: Rawick, vol. 5, 33ff.

207   "No country perhaps in the world": Cramer, 13.

207   "The first thing that strikes a stranger" and related quotes: Flint, 13ff.

210   "You, Abraham Whipple": Mathews, 177.

210   "The ship 'Pittsburg' and the schooner 'Amity'": Hulbert, 246.

212   "a singular aquatic race": Irving, 106.

212   "I am a man; I am a horse": Henry Adams, *History*, 54.

212   "Fink was a manifestation of Seek": Thomas Ruys Smith, *River of Dreams*, 66.

213   "Fifty steps from there we found": Bossu, 160, as quoted in Prentice, 256.

213   "Hoop-poles and punkins": Merrick, 185.

213 "cotton, furs, swan skins": Thomas Ruys, Smith, *River of Dreams*, 47.

213 "Some of them, that are called family-boats" and related quotes: Flint, 103ff.

215 "They give it a certain turn": Thwaites, *Jesuit Relations*, vol. 59, 135.

216 "Upwards of two hundred torches": Le Page du Pratz, 192.

216 "In all canoe journeys undertaken" and related quotes about singing voyageurs: Barbeau, 148ff.

217 "mask and mix in bands": Baron, 287.

218 "It was impossible not to stare" and related quotes: Latrobe, 21ff.

219 "I went to the spot": Ibid., 49.

220 "In one place": Flint, 103.

222 "more than any other holds in it the brooding rhythm of the sea": Walton, 157.

26: I LONG TO SEE YOU

See in particular: Hunter, Dow and Dow, and Sandlin.

224 "At first the Mississippi seemed" and related quotes from Bryan: Dow and Dow, 344–46.

225 "The shaking would knock you loose" and related quotes from Crist: Crist (online).

227 "went up through the starboard guard": *Louisville Courier*, January 7, 1852, cited in Hunter, 273.

227 "As she struck a sawyer": Audubon, vol. 1, 450.

227 "The night of the 18th": Koch, *Journey through Part of the United States . . .* , 79.

228 "I met a slave who was a cousin to my own mother" and related quotes: Rawick, 40.

228 "These decoys pleaded" and related quotes: Rothert, 43ff.

230 "I want to preserve that for a trophy": Ibid., 127.

230 "his depredations became the talk": Audubon, vol. 2, 232.

231 "I have received information" and related quotes surrounding the trial of Mason: Rothert, 196ff.

234 "Instead of coming from the stomach": "The New-Orleans Plague."

234 "Its victims were mainly among the poor": Jones, 1.

27: UP THE WICKED RIVER

236   "From the cabins and houses": Flint, 27.

238   "I have seen them day after day": Ibid., 107.

239   "We passed a very bad part of the River": De Voto, *Journals of Lewis and Clark*, 3.

239   "sailed from my encampment": Coues, vol. 1, 1.

239   "the most consummate artist": This quote is attributed to Frederick Jackson Turner in many places, including Linklater, 3, but I was unable to find the original source of the quote.

239   "a general who never won a battle or lost": Leckie, 318.

239   "Soon after the purchase of Louisiana": Coues, vol. 1, i.

240   "spare no pains to conciliate the Indians": Ibid., vol. 2, 843.

240   "I arrived here [at the Des Moines Rapids] this day": Ibid., vol. 1, 221.

241   "I do not remember to have traversed": Flint, 93.

242   "did not strike me with that majestic": Coues, vol. 1, 311.

242   "the cold was so intense": Ibid., 138.

242   "Some spirits": Ibid., 151.

242   "I will not attempt to describe": Ibid., 152.

243   "My young warriors": Ibid., 176.

243   "very gentlemanly in his deportment" and related quotes: Ibid., xxiv.

243   "I can only account for the gentlemen": Ibid., 279.

244   "All hearts and hands": Ibid., 193.

244   "I have not been slow in my descent": Ibid., 264.

244   "in high water the appearance is much more sublime": Ibid., 311.

244   "We embarked early": Ibid., 211.

244   "arrived about twelve": Ibid., 215.

28: ALL ABOARD

The classic study of the western steamboats remains Hunter, but also see Sutcliff.

247   "This monopolizing disposition of individuals": *Cincinnati Spy*, November 15, 1816, as quoted in Hunter, 10.

247   "The British government": Hunter, 21.

248   "Considerable boat building is likewise carried on": Schultz, 137.

250   "Men of business and men of pleasure": Melville, 10.

251   "a steamboat, coming from New Orleans": Turner, 104.

251   "Machinery, vast fragments of the boilers": *Boston Advertiser*, October 4, 1843, as quoted in Hunter, 288.

252   "Huge toppling steamers": Melville, 8.

252   "The bartender was also supposed to know": Merrick, 135.

253   "Oh! That carpet!": Trollope, 16.

253   "it is well for society": Dickens, 194.

254   "The very filthiest of all filthy": Audubon, 450.

254   "Often, a dozen lambs" and related quotes: Merrick, 128.

255   "We had about two hundred of these" and related quotes: Trollope, 19.

256   "Our *compagnons de voyage*": Audubon, 451.

29: DOWN BELOW

257   "When I was about twelve years of age": Rawick, 40.

257   "Mah mammy were name Julia Dittoe": Ibid., 373.

258   "As far as I have any knowledge of the state" and related quotes: William Wells Brown, 38.

258   "those who are transported down the Mississippi": *Proceedings of the New England Anti-Slavery Convention*, 34.

259   "On the river there was no other side": Merrick, 65.

262   "Oh I was a slave in the land of Dixie": Rawick, 29.

30: BLOOD ON THE TRACKS

See especially: Grant, Ambrose, Horowitz, Hunter, Long and Long, and Shea and Winschel.

268   "This momentous question": Jefferson, "Letter to John Holmes."

269   "In the wake of the Kansas-Nebraska": Horowitz, 40.

271   "This is as much as Daniel Webster himself would have charged": Ambrose, *Nothing Like It in the World*, 29.

271   "Had Lincoln never done another": Ibid., 30.

271   "let there be no compromise": Long and Long, 10.

31: ANACONDA

272   "the Mississippi is the backbone": Shea and Winschel, 1.

273   "Jefferson Davis, the unapproachable, stubborn" and related quote: Carter, 263.

274   "Our loss is heavy": "Battle of Pea Ridge."

276   "No terms except unconditional and immediate surrender": Long and Long, 172.

277   "Where is BEAUREGARD'S army?": "Rout of Beauregard's Army."

281   "I was well aware that my batteries": Lang, 282.

281   "was to be the terror of the seas": Dufour, 163.

281   "I shake a little now when I think": Thompson and Wainwright, 106.

281   "It was a terribly magnificent": Lang, 287.

282   "My prayers are with you": Ibid., 296.

282   "wild with rejoicing": "The News in Washington."

282   "We've got New Orleans!": Worthington, 145ff.

283   "Although he did not directly say so": Dufour, 160.

284   "Vicksburg is the nail head": Winschel, 14.

284   "Vicksburg is the key": Shea and Winschel, frontispiece.

32: UP IN FLAMES

285   "They seem to think" and quotes following: Shea and Winschel, 15ff.

288   "We could see nothing but the flash of the enemy's guns to fire at": Charles Lewis, 114.

289   "all troops in the Army of the Tennessee": Long and Long, 241.

289   "This is General McClellan's bodyguard": Ibid., 274.

289   "If I, too, should be driven back" and related quotes regarding the siege of Vicksburg: Grant, *Personal Memoirs*, 214ff.

296   "They throw shells all around": John David Smith, 106.

296   "I sat on the front porch of our house": Ginder and Simms, 373.

298   "Afterward the effluvia from the dead": Loughborough, 102.

298   "Sometimes they exchanged" and related quotes: Grant, *Personal Memoir*, 293ff.

298   "I am almost sorry to hear of Lee's progress": Ginder and Simms, 377.

301   "A happier lot of men": Huffman, 186.

301   "a sea of heads, so close together" and related quotes: "The Late Ter-
         rible Explosion."

33: THE MOUTH

Most of this chapter reflects the reporting and interviews I did during my
travels in the basin. Also see Adler et al., Fremling, Sandlin, and the online
resources at the Environmental Protection Agency.

34: ALL THE LISTS OF CLAY

See: McPhee, Hunter, Barry, Fremling, and miscellaneous scholarly articles on
loess, subsidence, and related issues in the Bibliography.

316   "In the month of March, although it had not rained": Clayton, vol. 1,
         153.

317   "Five hundred dead bodies were discharged": Rawick, 35.

319   "most practicable mode of improving": Hunter, 191.

320   "snags, rigidly speaking" and related quotes: Ibid., 199ff.

327   "There's nothing that man can do": "Keeping the Boats Moving Along
         a Mississippi Dwindled by Drought."

329   "the work, and the law, of rivers": Horgan, 2.

330   "Louisiana Coastal Area Ecosystem" and related figures: Department
         of the Army Office, 3ff.

BIBLIOGRAPHY

Abbey, Edward. *The Best of Edward Abbey*. San Francisco: Sierra Club Books, 1984.

Adams, Henry. *History of the United States of America during the Administration of Thomas Jefferson*. New York: Albert & Charles Boni, 1930.

Adams, Henry. "A New Interpretation of Bingham's Fur Traders Descending the Missouri." *Art Bulletin* 65, no. 4 (Dec. 1983): 675–80.

Adams, Robert McCormick. "Diagnostic Flint Points." *American Antiquity* 6, no. 1 (July 1940): 72–75.

Adler, Robert W., Jessica C. Landman, and Diane M. Cameron. *The Clean Water Act 20 Years Later*. Washington, D.C.: Island Press, 1993.

Adney, Edwin Tappan, and Howard I. Chapelle. *The Bark Canoes and Skin Boats of North America*. Washington, D.C.: Smithsonian Institution, 1964.

Albrecht, Andrew C. "Indian-French Relations at Natchez." *American Anthropologist*, New Series, 48, no. 3 (July–Sept. 1946): 321–54.

Allen, Michael. "The Riverman as Jacksonian Man." *Western Historical Quarterly* 21, no. 3 (Aug. 1990): 305–20.

———. "'Sired by a Hurricane': Mike Fink, Western Boatmen and the Myth of the Alligator Horse." *Arizona and the West* 27, no. 3 (Autumn 1985): 237–52.

Ambrose, Stephen E. *Nothing Like It in the World: The Men Who Built the Transcontinental Railroad*. New York: Touchstone, 2000.

——. *Undaunted Courage: Meriwether Lewis, Thomas Jefferson, and the Opening of the American West*. New York: Simon and Schuster, 1996.

Amick, Daniel S. "Regional Patterns of Folsom Mobility and Land Use in the American Southwest." *World Archaeology* 27, no. 3, Hunter-Gatherer Land Use (Feb. 1996): 411–26.

Anderson, David G., and J. Christopher Gillam. "Paleoindian Colonization of the Americas: Implications from an Examination of Physiography, Demography, and Artifact Distribution." *American Antiquity* 65, no. 1 (Jan. 2000): 43–66.

Anderson, Fred. *Crucible of War: The Seven Years' War and the Fate of Empire in British North America, 1754–1766*. New York: Vintage, 2000.

Andrews, Brian N., Jason M. LaBelle, and John D. Seebach. "Spatial Variability in the Folsom Archaeological Record: A Multi-Scalar Approach." *American Antiquity* 73, no. 3 (July 2008): 464–90.

Andrews, George Gordon. *Napoleon in Review*. New York: Alfred A. Knopf, 1939.

"Another Serpent Mound." *New York Times*, July 5, 1890.

"Another Serpent Mound Discovered." *New York Times*, July 31, 1892.

"Argument in the Rock Island Bridge Case." *Daily Press* (of Chicago), September 24, 1857.

Arrington, Joseph Earl. "Henry Lewis' Moving Panorama of the Mississippi River." *Louisiana History: The Journal of the Louisiana Historical Association* 6, no. 3 (Summer 1965): 239–72.

Audubon, Maria R. *Audubon and His Journals*, vol. 1. New York: Dover Publications, 1986.

Aurelius, Marcus. *Selections from the Meditations of Marcus Aurelius*. Translated by Benjamin E. Smith. New York: Century, 1899.

Babson, Jane F. "The Architecture of Early Illinois Forts." *Journal of the Illinois State Historical Society* (1908–1984), 61, no. 1 (Spring 1968): 9–40.

Bailey, Ben E. "Music in the Life of a Free Black Man of Natchez." *Black Perspective in Music* 13, no. 1 (Spring 1985): 3–12.

Ballard, Michael B. *Vicksburg: The Campaign That Opened the Mississippi*. Chapel Hill: University of North Carolina Press, 2004.

Bannon, John Francis. "The Spaniards and the Illinois Country, 1762–1800." *Journal of the Illinois State Historical Society* (1908–1984), 69, no. 2 (May 1976): 110–18.

Banta, R. E. *Rivers of America: The Ohio*. New York: Farrar and Rinehart, 1949.

Barbeau, Marius. "The Ermatinger Collection of Voyageur Songs (ca. 1830)." *Journal of American Folklore* 67, no. 264, Canadian Number (Apr.–June 1954): 147–61.

Barce, Elmore. "Tecumseh's Confederacy." *Indiana Magazine of History* 12, no. 2 (June 1916): 161–74.

Baron, John H. "Music in New Orleans, 1718–1792." *American Music* 5, no. 3 (Autumn 1987): 282–90. Published by University of Illinois Press.

Barr, Daniel P. "A Road for Warriors: The Western Delawares and the Seven Years War." *Pennsylvania History* 73, no. 1 (Winter 2006): 1–36.

———. "Victory at Kittanning?: Reevaluating the Impact of Armstrong's Raid on the Seven Years' War in Pennsylvania." *Pennsylvania Magazine of History and Biography* 131, no. 1 (Jan. 2007): 5–32.

Barry, John M. *Rising Tide: The Great Mississippi Flood of 1927 and How It Changed America*. New York: Touchstone, 1998.

Bartlett, Richard A. *Rolling Rivers: An Encyclopedia of America's Rivers*. New York: McGraw-Hill, 1984.

"Battle of Pea Ridge." *New York Times*, March 12, 1862.

Beard, William D. "Dalby Revisited: A New Look at Lincoln's 'Most Far-Reaching Case' in the Illinois Supreme Court." *Journal of the Abraham Lincoln Association* 20, no. 2 (Summer 1999): 1–16.

Bearss, Edwin C. "The Battle of Baton Rouge." *Louisiana History: The Journal of the Louisiana Historical Association* 3, no. 2 (Spring 1962): 77–128.

———. "The First Day at Pea Ridge, March 7, 1862." *Arkansas Historical Quarterly* 17, no. 2 (Summer 1958): 132–54.

Beers, Henry P. "The Papers of the British Commanders in Chief in North America, 1754–1783." *Military Affairs* 13, no. 2 (Summer 1949): 79–94.

Beidleman, Richard G. "The 1820 Long Expedition." *American Zoologist* 26, no. 2 (1986): 307–13. Published by Oxford University Press.

Berres, Thomas E., et al. "Bear Imagery in Northeast North America: An Update and Assessment of A. Irving Hallowell's Work." *Midcontinental Journal of Archaeology* 29, no. 1 (Spring 2004): 5–42.

Berry, Trey. "The Expedition of William Dunbar and George Hunter along the Ouachita River, 1804–1805." *Arkansas Historical Quarterly* 62, no. 4, The Louisiana Purchase: Empires, Nations, Communities (Winter 2003): 386–403.

Bets, Colin M. "Pots and Pox: The Identification of Protohistoric Epidemics in the Upper Mississippi Valley." *American Antiquity* 71, no. 2 (Apr. 2006): 233–59.

Bevan, Elinor. "The Goddess Artemis, and the Dedication of Bears in Sanctuaries." *Annual of the British School at Athens* 82 (1987): 17–21.

"Big, Broad Skulls Mark 'Best Minds.'" *New York Times*, January 23, 1941.

"Big-Game Hunt Adds to Evidence of Early North American Settlement." *New York Times*, October 20, 2011.

Birmingham, Robert A. *Spirits of Earth: The Effigy Mound Landscape of Madison and the Four Lakes.* Madison: University of Wisconsin Press, 2010.

"'Black Jack' Executed." *New York Times*, April 27, 1901.

Blasingham, Emily J. "The Depopulation of the Illinois Indians, Part 1." *Ethnohistory* 3, no. 3 (Summer 1956): 193–224.

Bosse, David. "'The Enemy Were Falling Like Autumn Leaves': Fraudulent Newspaper Reports of the Battle of Pea Ridge." *Arkansas Historical Quarterly* 54, no. 3 (Autumn 1995): 359–75.

Bossu, Jean-Bernard. *Travels in the Interior of North America 1751–1762.* Translated by Seymour Feiler. Norman: University of Oklahoma Press, 1962.

Botkin, Daniel B. *Passage of Discovery: The American Rivers Guide to the Missouri River of Lewis and Clark.* New York: Perigee, 1999.

Bradbury, John. *Travels in the Interior of America, in the Years 1809, 1810, and 1811; Including a Description of Upper Louisiana, Together with the States of Ohio, Kentucky, Indiana, and Tennessee, with the Illinois and Western Territories, and Containing Remarks and Observations Useful to Persons Emigrating to Those Countries.* Liverpool: Sherwood, Neely, 1817.

Bradley, Bruce, and Dennis Stanford. "The North Atlantic Ice-Edge Corridor: A Possible Palaeolithic Route to the New World." *World Archaeology* 36, no. 4, Debates in World Archaeology (Dec. 2004): 459–78.

Brandão, J. A., and William A. Starna. "The Treaties of 1701: A Triumph of Iroquois Diplomacy." *Ethnohistory* 43, no. 2 (Spring 1996): 209–44.

Brands, H. W. *The Man Who Saved the Union: Ulysses Grant in War and Peace.* New York: Doubleday, 2012.

———. *Andrew Jackson: His Life and Times.* New York: Anchor, 2006.

Braudaway, Douglas Lee. "A Texan Records the Civil War Siege of Vicksburg, Mississippi: The Journal of Maj. Maurice Kavanaugh Simons, 1863." *Southwestern Historical Quarterly* 105, no. 1 (July 2001): 92–131.

Bremer, Richard G. "Henry Rowe Schoolcraft: Explorer in the Mississippi Valley, 1818–1832." *Wisconsin Magazine of History* 66, no. 1 (Autumn 1982): 40–59.

Bridges, Roger D. "John Mason Peck on Illinois Slavery." *Journal of the Illinois State Historical Society* (1908–1984), 75, no. 3 (Autumn 1982): 179–217.

Brown, James A. "The Archaeology of Ancient Religion in the Eastern Woodlands." *Annual Review of Anthropology* 26 (1997): 465–85.

Brown, Sarah. "The Arkansas Traveller: Southwest Humor on Canvas." *Arkansas Historical Quarterly* 46, no. 4 (Winter 1987): 348–75.

Brown, William Wells. *Narrative of William W. Brown: A Fugitive Slave*. Boston: The Anti-Slavery Office, 1848.

Buchanan, Thomas C. *Black Life on the Mississippi: Slaves, Free Blacks, and the Western Steamboat World*. Chapel Hill: University of North Carolina Press, 2004.

Caldwell, Norman W. "Fort Massac: The American Frontier Post: 1778–1895." *Journal of the Illinois State Historical Society* (1908–1984), 43, no. 4 (Winter 1950): 265–81.

———. "Shawneetown: A Chapter in the Indian History of Illinois." *Journal of the Illinois State Historical Society* (1908–1984), 32, no. 2 (June 1939): 193–205.

Capers, Gerald M., Jr. "Confederates and Yankees in Occupied New Orleans, 1862–1865." *Journal of Southern History* 30, no. 4 (Nov. 1964): 405–26.

Carter, Hodding. *Lower Mississippi*. New York: Farrar & Rinehart, 1942.

Catlin, George. *Letters and Notes on the Manners, Customs and Condition of the North American Indians*. 2 volumes. Philadelphia: Willis P. Hazard, 1857.

Clayton, Lawrence, et al., eds. *The De Soto Chronicles: The Expedition of Hernando de Soto to North America in 1539–1543*. 2 volumes. Tuscaloosa: University of Alabama Press, 1993.

"Cloudburst Drowns 15 in New Mexico." *New York Times*, August 29, 1908.

Coates, Robert M. *The Outlaw Years: The History of the Land Pirates of the Natchez Trace*. New York: Macaulay, 1930.

Coker, William S. "Research in the Spanish Borderlands: Mississippi, 1779–1798." *Latin American Research Review* 7, no. 2 (Summer 1972): 40–54.

Collyer, Robert. *Clear Grit: A Collection of Lectures, Addresses and Poems*. Boston: Beacon Press, 1913.

Congdon, Charles E. *Allegany Oxbow: A History of Allegany State Park and the Allegany Reserve of the Seneca Nation*. Salamanca, N.Y.: Salamanca Area Museum Association, 1997.

Corr, Paul Benjamin. "George Rogers Clark: Conquest of the Northwest—Fort Gage Sesqui-Centennial Observance." *Journal of the Illinois State Historical Society* (1908–1984), 21, no. 2 (July 1928): 260–67.

Coues, Elliott. *The Expeditions of Zebulon Montgomery Pike*, vols. 1–3. New York: Francis P. Harper, 1895.

Cox, Isaac Joslin, ed. *The Journeys of Rene Robert Cavelier, Sieur de La Salle*. New York: Allerton Book Co., 1905. Online facsimile edition at texashistory.unt.edu.

Cramer, Zadok. *The Navigator, Containing Directions for Navigating the Monongahela, Allegheny, Ohio and Mississippi Rivers; with an Ample Account of These Much Admired Waters, from the Head of the Former to the Mouth of the Latter.* Pittsburgh: Cramer, Spear and Eichbaum, 1817. University of Missouri digital facsimile at http://digital.library.umsystem.edu/cgi/t/text/pageviewer-idx?c=umlib;cc=umlib;sid=b186c1e184bc10a98bc32dce94684f2d;rgn=full%20text;idno=umlc000008;view=image;seq=20.

Crist, George Heinrich. "Account of the New Madrid Earthquake." *Virtual Times*, http://hsv.com/genlintr/newmadrd/accnt3.htm.

Crites, Gary D. "Domesticated Sunflower in Fifth Millennium BP Temporal Context: New Evidence from Middle Tennessee." *American Antiquity* 58, no. 1 (Jan. 1993): 146–48.

Croghan, George, and Nicholas B. Wainwright. "George Croghan's Journal. April 3, 1759 to April 30, 1763." *Pennsylvania Magazine of History and Biography* 71, no. 4 (Oct. 1947): 313–444.

"Curiosities Brought Here from Mexico." *New York Times*, August 24, 1902.

Curtis, Byron. *Bluffs to Bayous: A Solo Kayak Expedition down the Mississippi and Atchafalaya Rivers*. Prescott, Wis.: Great Rivers, 2003.

Cushing, G. F. "The Bear in Ob-Ugrian Folklore." *Folklore* 88, no. 2 (1977): 146–59.

De Voto, Bernard. *Across the Wide Missouri*. Boston: Houghton Mifflin, 1947.

———, ed. *The Journals of Lewis and Clark*. Boston: Houghton Mifflin, 1953.

Dictionary of Canadian Biography online: www.biographi.ca. University of Toronto.

Deale, Valentine B. "The History of the Potawatomis before 1722." *Ethnohistory* 5, no. 4 (Autumn 1958): 305–60.

"Deny Nebraska Skull Is of Pre-Human Race." *New York Times*, November 25, 1934.

Department of the Army Office, Assistant Secretary of the Army (Civil Works). *Fiscal Year 2013 Civil Works Budget for the U.S. Army Corps of Engineers.* February 2012. http://www.usace.army.mil/Portals/2/docs/civilworks/press_book/budget2013.pdf.

Devol, George H. *Forty Years a Gambler on the Mississippi.* Cincinnati, Ohio: Devol and Haines, 1887.

Dexter, Ralph W. "Contributions of Frederic Ward Putnam to Ohio Archaeology." *Ohio Journal of Science* 65, no. 3 (May 1965): 110–17.

Dickens, Charles. *The Pilgrim Edition of the Letters of Charles Dickens. Volume 3: 1842–43.*

Din, Gilbert C. "Carondelet, the Cabildo, and Slaves: Louisiana in 1795." *Louisiana History: The Journal of the Louisiana Historical Association* 38, no. 1 (Winter 1997): 5–28.

———. "The Spanish Fort on the Arkansas, 1763–1803." *Arkansas Historical Quarterly* 42, no. 3 (Autumn 1983): 271–93.

Dixon, James E. "Human Colonization of the Americas: Timing, Technology and Process." *Quarternary Science Reviews* 20 (2001): 277–99.

Dow, Lorenzo, and Peggy Dow. *History of Cosmoplite, Or the Four Volumes of Lorenzo Dow's Journal Concentrated in One.* Wheeling, Va.: Joshua Martin, 1848.

Drago, Harry Sinclair. *The Steamboaters: From the Early Side-Wheelers to the Big Packets.* New York: Bramhall House, 1967.

Dufour, Charles L. "The Night the War Was Lost. The Fall of New Orleans: Causes, Consequences, Culpability." *Journal of the Louisiana Historical Association* 2, no. 2 (Spring 1961): 157–74.

Edmunds, R. David. "Tecumseh, the Shawnee Prophet, and American History: A Reassessment." *Western Historical Quarterly* 14, no. 3 (July 1983): 261–76.

Eiseley, Loren C. "Indian Mythology and Extinct Fossil Vertebrates." *American Anthropologist,* New Series, 47, no. 2 (Apr.–June 1945): 318–20.

Ekberg, Carl J. *French Roots in the Illinois Country: The Mississippi Frontier in Colonial Times.* Chicago: University of Illinois Press, 2000.

Ellis, Linda Abess. *Frances Trollope's America: Four Novels.* New York: Peter Lang, 1993.

Ellison, Mary. "African-American Music and Muskets in Civil War New Orleans." *Louisiana History: The Journal of the Louisiana Historical Association* 35, no. 3 (Summer 1994): 285–319.

Emerson, Ralph Waldo. *Emerson's Essays*. New York: Thomas Y. Crowell, 1926.

Emerson, Thomas E. "Materializing Cahokia Shamans." *Southeastern Archaeology* 22, no. 2 (Winter 2003): 135–54.

Engle, Stephen D. "Franz Sigel at Pea Ridge." *Arkansas Historical Quarterly* 50, no. 3 (Autumn 1991): 249–70.

Erdoes, Richard, and Alfonso Ortiz, eds. *American Indian Myths and Legends*. New York: Pantheon, 1984.

Erickson, Edgar L. "With Grant at Vicksburg: From the Civil War Diary of Captain Charles E. Wilcox." *Journal of the Illinois State Historical Society* (1908–1984), 30, no. 4 (Jan. 1938): 441–503.

Evans, G. E. "Prior Lake Effigy Mound Salvage 21 SC-16." *Minnesota Archaeological Newsletter* (University of Minnesota, Department of Anthropology), no. 2 (Spring 1962).

Ewald, Erich L. "A Letter from the Front: Vicksburg, 1863." *Indiana Magazine of History* 91, no. 3 (Sept. 1995): 321–25.

Ewers, John C. "The Bear Cult among the Assinboin and Their Neighbors of the Northern Plains." *Southwestern Journal of Anthropology* 11, no. 1 (Spring 1955): 1–14.

Fairbank, Calvin. *Rev. Calvin Fairbank during Slavery Times*. Chicago: Patriotic Publishing, 1890.

Fandrich, Ina J. "Yorùbá Influences on Haitian Vodou and New Orleans Voodoo." *Journal of Black Studies* 37, no. 5 (May 2007): 775–91.

Faye, Stanley. "Illinois Indians on the Lower Mississippi, 1771–1782." *Journal of the Illinois State Historical Society* (1908–1984), 35, no. 1 (Mar. 1942): 57–72.

Filson, John. "The Discovery, Settlement and Present State of Kentucke (1784): An Online Electronic Text Edition." Edited by Paul Royster. *Electronic Texts in American Studies,* Paper 3. digitalcommons.unl.edu/etas/3.

"Finds Hope in Boston for 'American Race.'" *New York Times*, April 9, 1937.

"Finds Neanderthal Link." *New York Times*, August 22, 1935.

Firestone, R. B., et al. "Evidence for an Extraterrestrial Impact 12,900 Years Ago That Contributed to the Megafaunal Extinctions and the Younger Dryas Cooling." *Proceedings of the Academy of Sciences of the United States of America* 104, no. 41 (Oct. 9, 2007): 16016–20.

Fiske, John. *The Discovery of America*. Boston: Houghton Mifflin, 1898.

Fleming, Thomas. *The Louisiana Purchase*. Hoboken, N.J.: John Wiley and Sons, 2003.

Flenniken, J. Jeffrey. "Reevaluation of the Lindenmeier Folsom: A Replication Experiment in Lithic Technology." *American Antiquity* 43, no. 3 (July 1978): 473–80.

Flexner, James Thomas. *Lord of the Mohawks.* Boston: Houghton Mifflin, 1959.

Flint, Timothy. *Recollections of the Last Ten Years, Passed in Occasional Residences and Journeyings in the Valley of the Mississippi, from Pittsburgh and the Missouri to the Gulf of Mexico, and from Florida to the Spanish Frontier: In a Series of Letters to the Rev. James Flint, of Salem, Massachusetts.* Boston: Cummings, Hilliard, 1826. Online facsimile at archive .org.

"Foreheads and Minds." *New York Times*, June 30, 1935.

Fox, John W., Calvin B. Smith, and Kenneth T. Wilkins, eds. *Proboscidean and Paleoindian Interactions.* Waco, Tex.: Markham Fund of Baylor University Press, 1992.

Franklin, W. Neil. "Pennsylvania-Virginia Rivalry for the Indian Trade of the Ohio Valley." *Mississippi Valley Historical Review* 20, no. 4 (Mar. 1934): 463–80.

Frazier, Ian. *Great Plains.* New York: Penguin, 1989.

Fremling, Calvin R. *Immortal River: The Upper Mississippi in Ancient and Modern Times.* Madison: University of Wisconsin Press, 2005.

Frison, George C. "Experimental Use of Clovis Weaponry and Tools on African Elephants." *American Antiquity* 54, no. 4 (Oct. 1989): 766–84.

Frison, George C., and George M. Zeimens. "Bone Projectile Points: An Addition to the Folsom Cultural Complex." *American Antiquity* 45, no. 2 (Apr. 1980): 231–37.

Fritz, Gayle J. "Multiple Pathways to Farming in Precontact Eastern North America." *Journal of World Prehistory* 4, no. 4 (Dec. 1990): 387–435.

"The Future of the Negro." *New York Times*, December 28, 1898.

Garvey, Dennis W., webmaster. "Heritage Plowed Under: Minnesota's Lost Effigy Mounds," http://freepages.genealogy.rootsweb.ancestry.com /~dgarvey/Mounds/MN_Effigy_Mounds.html.

George III. *The Royal Proclamation, October 7, 1763.* Digital text at solon.org, http://www.solon.org/Constitutions/Canada/English/PreConfederation /rp_1763.html.

Gernon, Blaine Brooks. "Chicago and Abraham Lincoln." *Journal of the Illinois State Historical Society (1908–1984)*, 27, no. 3 (Oct. 1934): 243–84.

"Giants of Other Days." *New York Times*, March 5, 1894.

Gibbon, Guy, ed. *Archaeology of Prehistoric Native America: An Encyclopedia.* New York: Garland Publishing, 1998.

Gibson, Jon L. "Formed from the Earth at That Place: The Material Side of Community at Poverty Point." *American Antiquity* 72, no. 3 (July 2007): 509–23.

———. "Navels of the Earth: Sedentism in Early Mound-Building Cultures in the Lower Mississippi Valley." *World Archaeology* 38, no. 2, Sedentism in Non-Agricultural Societies (June 2006): 311–29.

Ginder, Henry, and L. Moody Simms Jr. "A Louisiana Engineer at the Siege of Vicksburg: Letters of Henry Ginder." *Louisiana History: The Journal of the Louisiana Historical Association* 8, no. 4 (Autumn 1967): 371–78.

Gomez, Gay M. "Describing Louisiana: The Contribution of William Darby." *Louisiana History: The Journal of the Louisiana Historical Association* 34, no. 1 (Winter 1993): 87–105.

Gordon, Harry. "Extracts from the Journal of Captain Harry Gordon, Chief Engineer in the Western Department in North America Who Was Sent from Fort Pitt on the River Ohio, down the Said River &c. to Illinois, in 1766: Reprinted from Pownall's 'Topographical Description of North America' Published, London, 1776." *Journal of the Illinois State Historical Society* (1908–1984), 2, no. 2 (July 1909): 55–64.

Graham, Russell W., C. Vance Haynes, Donald Lee Johnson, and Marvin Kay. "Kimmswick: A Clovis-Mastodon Association in Eastern Missouri." *Science*, New Series, 213, no. 4512 (Sept. 4, 1981): 1115–17.

Grant, Ulysses. "Letter of Grant to His Father, on the Capture of Vicksburg, 1863." *American Historical Review* 12, no. 1 (Oct. 1906): 109.

———. *Personal Memoirs.* New York: Modern Library, 1999.

Greengo, Robert E. "Issaquena: An Archaeological Phase in the Yazoo Basin of the Lower Mississippi Valley." *Memoirs of the Society for American Archaeology*, no. 18 (1964): 1–128.

Gremillion, Kristen J. "Early Agricultural Diet in Eastern North America: Evidence from Two Kentucky Rockshelters." *American Antiquity* 61, no. 3 (July 1996): 520–36.

Griffin, James B. "Adena Pottery." *American Antiquity* 7, no. 4 (Apr. 1942): 344–58.

Gurvich, I. S. "An Ethnographic Study of Cultural Parallels among the Aboriginal Populations of Northern Asia and Northern North America." *Arctic Anthropology* 16, no. 1 (1979): 32–38.

Gushee, Lawrence. "The Nineteenth-Century Origins of Jazz." *Black Music Research Journal* 22, Supplement: Best of BMRJ (2002): 151–74.

Haffner, Gerald O. "Major Arthur Loftus' Journal of the Proceedings of His Majesty's Twenty-Second Regiment Up the River Mississippi in 1764." *Louisiana History: The Journal of the Louisiana Historical Association* 20, no. 3 (Summer 1979): 325–34.

Hall, Robert. "Red Banks, Onto, and the Winnebago: Views from a Distant Rock." *Wisconsin Archeologist* 74, nos. 1–4 (1993): 5–32.

Hallowell, A. Irving. "Bear Ceremonialism in the Northern Hemisphere." *American Anthropologist*, New Series, 28, no. 1 (Jan.–Mar. 1926): 1–175.

Halsell, Willie D. "The Sixteenth Indiana Regiment in the Last Vicksburg Campaign." *Indiana Magazine of History* 43, no. 1 (Mar. 1947): 67–82.

Hanson, Kathleen S. "Down to Vicksburg: The Nurses' Experience." *Journal of the Illinois State Historical Society* (1998–), 97, no. 4 (Winter 2004/2005): 286–309.

Harris, Eddy L. *Mississippi Solo: A Memoir.* New York: Henry Holt, 1988.

Hart, Irving Harlow. "Steamboating on Mississippi Headwaters." *Minnesota History* 33, no. 1 (Spring 1952): 7–19.

Haury, Emil W., et al. "Artifacts with Mammoth Remains, Naco, Arizona." *American Antiquity* 19, no. 1 (July 1953): 1–24.

Hay, Jerry M. *Ohio River Guidebook: Charts and Details from Beginning to End.* Floyds Knobs, Ind.: Inland Waterways, 2011.

Hay, Thomas Robson. "Confederate Leadership at Vicksburg." *Mississippi Valley Historical Review* 11, no. 4 (Mar. 1925): 543–60.

Haydon, F. Stansbury. "Grant's Wooden Mortars and Some Incidents of the Siege of Vicksburg." *Journal of the American Military Institute* 4, no. 1 (Spring 1940): 30–38.

Haynes, Gary. "The Catastrophic Extinction of North American Mammoths and Mastodonts." *World Archaeology* 33, no. 3, Ancient Ecodisasters (Feb. 2002): 391–416.

Hechenberger, Daniel. "The Jesuits: History and Impact: From Their Origins Prior to the Baroque Crisis to Their Role in the Illinois Country." *Journal of the Illinois State Historical Society* (1998–), 100, no. 2 (Summer 2007): 85–109.

Hedeen, Stanley. *Big Bone Lick: The Cradle of American Paleontology.* Lexington: University of Kentucky Press, 2008.

Herzberg, Stephen J. "The Menominee Indians: From Treaty to Termination." *Wisconsin Magazine of History* 60, no. 4 (Summer 1977): 266–329.

Hewitt, Lawrence L. "'There Is No Use in Trying to Dodge God Almighty': Farragut Runs the Port Hudson Batteries." *Louisiana History: The Journal of the Louisiana Historical Association* 26, no. 1 (Winter 1985): 23–40.

Hill, Matthew E. "A Moveable Feast: Variation in Faunal Resource Use among Central and Western North American Paleoindian Sites." *American Antiquity* 72, no. 3 (July 2007): 417–38.

Holland, Robert A. *The Mississippi River in Maps and Views: From Lake Itasca to the Gulf of Mexico.* New York: Rizzoli, 2008.

Hollon, W. Eugene. "Zebulon Montgomery Pike and the Wilkinson-Burr Conspiracy." *Proceedings of the American Philosophical Society* 91, no. 5 (Dec. 3, 1947): 447–56.

———. "Zebulon Montgomery Pike's Lost Papers." *Mississippi Valley Historical Review* 34, no. 2 (Sept. 1947): 265–73.

———. "Zebulon Montgomery Pike's Mississippi Voyage, 1805–1806." *Wisconsin Magazine of History* 32, no. 4 (June 1949): 445–55.

Holmes, W. H. "Fossil Human Remains Found Near Lansing, Kansas." *American Anthropologist*, New Series, 4, no. 4 (Oct.–Dec. 1902): 743–52.

———. "A Sketch of the Great Serpent Mound." *Science* 8, no. 204 (Dec. 31, 1886): 624–28.

Horgan, Paul. *Great River: The Rio Grande in North American History.* Middletown, Conn.: Wesleyan University Press, 1984.

Horowitz, Tony. *Midnight Rising: John Brown and the Raid That Sparked the Civil War.* New York: Henry Holt, 2011.

Howe, Henry F. *Prologue to New England.* New York: Farrar & Rinehart, 1943.

Hrdlička, Aleš. *Recent Discoveries Attributed to Early Man in America.* Washington, D.C.: US Government Printing Office, 1918.

Hudson, Charles. *Knights of Spain, Warriors of the Sun: Hernando de Soto and the South's Ancient Chiefdoms.* Athens: University of Georgia Press, 1997.

Hudson, Charles, and Carmen Chaves Tesser, eds. *The Forgotten Centuries: Indians and Europeans in the American South 1521–1704.* Athens: University of Georgia Press, 1994.

Huffman, Alan. *Sultana: Surviving the Civil War, Prison, and the Worst Maritime Disaster in American History.* New York: HarperCollins, 2009.

Hulbert, Archer Butler. *The Ohio River: A Course of Empire.* New York: G. P. Putnam's Sons, 1906.

Hunter, Louis C. *Steamboats on the Western Rivers: An Economic and Techno-logical History.* New York: Dover Publications, 1949.

Hutchins, Thomas. "Western Pennsylvania in 1760. A Journal of a March from Fort Pitt to Venango, and from Thence to Presqu' Isle. From the Papers of Capt. Thomas Hutchins, Geographer General of the United States." *Pennsylvania Magazine of History and Biography* 2, no. 2 (1878): 149–53.

Institute for Minnesota Archaeology. "From Site to Story: The Upper Mississippi's Buried Past." http://www.fromsitetostory.org/sources/papers/mnhistory/mnhistory.asp.

Irving, Washington. *Astoria: Or, Anecdotes of an Enterprise beyond the Rocky Mountains.* New York: Belford, 1884.

Jackson, Andrew, and Sam B. Smith, eds. *The Papers of Andrew Jackson: 1770–1803.* Nashville: University of Tennessee Press, 1980.

Jaenen, Cornelius J. "French Colonial Attitudes and the Exploration of Joliet and Marquette." *Wisconsin Magazine of History* 56, no. 4 (Summer 1973): 300–310.

Jameson, J. Franklin. *Narratives of New Netherland, 1609–1664.* New York: Charles Scribner's Sons, 1909.

Jameson, J. Franklin, and W. L. Grant, eds. *Voyages of Samuel de Champlain, 1604–1618.* New York: Charles Scribner's Sons, 1907.

Jefferson, Thomas. "Letter to John Holmes, April 22, 1820." Online at Library of Congress. http://www.loc.gov/exhibits/jefferson/159.html.

———. *Notes on the State of Virginia.* Electronic Text Center, University of Virginia. http://etext.virginia.edu/etcbin/toccer-new2?id=JefVirg.sgm&images=images/modeng&data=/texts/english/modeng/parsed&tag=public&part=all.

Jennings, John. "Journal at Fort Chartres, and Trip to New Orleans, 1768." *Pennsylvania Magazine of History and Biography* 31, no. 3 (1907): 304–10.

———. "Journal from Fort Pitt to Fort Chartres in the Illinois Country, March–April, 1766." *Pennsylvania Magazine of History and Biography* 31, no. 2 (1907): 145–56.

Johnson, Jerah. "New Orleans's Congo Square: An Urban Setting for Early Afro-American Culture Formation." *Louisiana History: The Journal of the Louisiana Historical Association* 32, no. 2 (Spring 1991): 117–57.

Jones, Mary Harris. *Autobiography of Mother Jones.* New York: Dover, 2004.

Joslyn Art Museum. *Karl Boomer's America.* Lincoln: University of Nebraska Press, 1984.

Jurkowski, G., J. Ni, and L. Brown. "Modern Uparching of the Gulf Coastal Plain." *Journal of Geophysical Research* 89 (1984): 6247–55.

Kane, Harnett T. *Natchez on the Mississippi.* New York: Crown, 1947.

Kay, Marvin, and George Sabo III. "Mortuary Ritual and Winter Solstice Imagery of the Harlan-Style Charnel House." *Southeastern Archaeology* 25, no. 1 (Summer 2006): 29–47.

"Keeping the Boats Moving Along a Mississippi Dwindled by Drought." *New York Times*, January 17, 2013.

Kellogg, Louise Phelps. *Early Narratives of the Northwest, 1634–1699.* New York: Charles Scribner's Sons, 1917.

———. "The Story of Wisconsin, 1634–1848." *Wisconsin Magazine of History* 2, no. 4 (June 1919): 413–30.

Keplinger, John G. "Who Were the Mound Builders?" *Journal of the Illinois State Historical Society* (1908–1984), 12, no. 1 (Apr. 1919): 45–52.

Kidder, Tristram R. "Climate Change and the Archaic to Woodland Transition (3000–2500 Cal B.P.) in the Mississippi River Basin." *American Antiquity* 71, no. 2 (Apr. 2006): 195–231.

Kinnaird, Lawrence, and Lucia B. Kinnaird. "The Red River Valley in 1796." *Louisiana History: The Journal of the Louisiana Historical Association* 24, no. 2 (Spring 1983): 184–94.

Kirkland, Edwin C. "A Check List of the Titles of Tennessee Folksongs." *Journal of American Folklore* 59, no. 234 (Oct.–Dec. 1946): 423–76.

Koch, Albert C. *Description of Missourium, or Missouri Leviathan: Together with Its Supposed Habits and Indian Traditions Concerning the Location from Whence It Was Exhumed; Also, Comparisons of the Whale, Crocodile and Missourium with the Leviathan, as Described in 41st Chapter of the Book of Job.* Louisville, Ky.: Prentice and Weissinger, 1841.

———. *Journey through a Part of the United States of North America in the Years 1844–1846.* Translated and edited by Ernst A. Stadler. Foreword by John Francis McDermott. Carbondale: Southern Illinois University Press, 1972.

Koegel, John. "Spanish and French Mission Music in Colonial North America." *Journal of the Royal Musical Association* 126, no. 1 (2001): 1–53.

Kouwenhoven, John A. "The Designing of the Eads Bridge." *Technology and Culture* 23, no. 4 (Oct. 1982): 535–68.

Krech, Shepard. *The Ecological Indian: Myth and History.* New York: W. W. Norton, 1999.

Kurtz, Royce. "Timber and Treaties: The Sauk and Mesquakie Decision to Sell Iowa Territory." *Forest and Conservation History* 35, no. 2 (Apr. 1991): 56–64.

La Salle, Robert. "Letter from La Salle to ? (one of his partners)." Sieur de La Salle, Robert Cavelier, Margry, microfilm, vol. 2, 26–94. Also online at http://gbl.indiana.edu/ethnohistory/archives/miamis/M69-79_11b.html.

———. "Memoir of La Salle to Frontenac, Nov. 9, 1680." *Historical Magazine, and Notes and Queries Concerning the Antiquities, History, and Biography of America*, vol. 5, 196–98. New York: Charles B. Richardson, 1861. Digital version available at gbl.indiana.edu/ethnohistory/archives/miamis2/M80-81_1a.html.

———. *Relation of the Discoveries and Voyages of Cavelier de La Salle from 1679 to 1681: The Official Narrative.* Translated by Melville B. Anderson. Chicago: The Caxton Club, 1901.

Lang, James O. "Gloom Envelops New Orleans: April 24 to May 2, 1862." *Louisiana History: The Journal of the Louisiana Historical Association* 1, no. 4 (Autumn 1960): 281–99.

Larson, Lewis H., Jr. "Functional Considerations of Warfare in the Southeast during the Mississippi Period." *American Antiquity* 37, no. 3 (July 1972): 383–92.

Larson, Ron. *Upper Mississippi River History: Fact-Fiction-Legend.* Winona, Minn.: Steamboat Press, 1988.

"The Late Terrible Explosion. Further Particulars of the Explosion of the Steamboat Sultana, and the Fearful Loss of Life." *New York Times*, April 28, 1865.

Latrobe, Benjamin Henry Boneval. *Impressions Respecting New Orleans: Diary & Sketches, 1818–1820.* Edited by Samuel Wilson Jr. New York: Columbia University Press, 1951.

Le Page du Pratz, Antoine Simone. *The History of Louisiana, or of the Western Parts of Virginia and Carolina [microform]: Containing a Description of the Countries That Lye on Both Sides of the River Mississippi: With an Account of the Settlements, Inhabitants, Soil, Climate and Products.* London: T. Becket, 1763. Digital facsimile at http://archive.org/stream/cihm_18173#page/n9/mode/2up.

Leckie, Robert. *George Washington's War: The Saga of the American Revolution.* New York: HarperCollins, 1993.

Leighton, Morris M. "The Peorian Loess and the Classification of the Glacial Drift Sheets of the Mississippi Valley." *Journal of Geology* 39, no. 1 (Jan.–Feb. 1931): 45–53.

Leighton, Morris M., and H. B. Willman. "Loess Formations of the Mississippi Valley." *Journal of Geology* 58, no. 6 (Nov. 1950): 599–623.

Leverett, Frank. "The Preglacial Valleys of the Mississippi and Its Tributaries." *Journal of Geology* 3, no. 7 (Oct.–Nov. 1895): 740–63.

Levin, David. "Giants in the Earth: Science and the Occult in Cotton Mather's Letters to the Royal Society." *William and Mary Quarterly*, Third Series, 45, no. 4 (Oct. 1988): 751–70.

Lewis, Charles L. *David Glasgow Farragut: Our First Admiral*. Annapolis, Md.: United States Naval Institute Press, 1943.

Lewis, T. H. "A New Departure in Effigy Mounds." *Science* 13, no. 318 (Mar. 8, 1889): 187–88.

———. "Notice of Some Recently Discovered Effigy Mounds." *Science* 5, no. 106 (Feb. 13, 1885): 131–32.

Limerick, Patricia Nelson. *Something in the Soil: Legacies and Reckonings in the New West*. New York: W. W. Norton, 2001.

Lindauer, Owen, and John H. Blitz. "Higher Ground: The Archaeology of North American Platform Mounds." *Journal of Archaeological Research* 5, no. 2 (June 1997): 169–207.

Lindell, Josh, Piper Lindell, and Tataboline Brant. *Allegheny River Paddling Guide*. Erie, Pa.: Printing Concepts, 2007.

Linklater, Andro. *An Artist in Treason: The Extraordinary Double Life of General James Wilkinson, Commander in Chief of the U.S. Army and Agent 13 in the Spanish Secret Service*. New York: Walker Publishing Company, 2009.

Lipscomb, Andrew A., and Albert E. Bergh, eds. *The Writings of Thomas Jefferson*. 20 volumes. Washington, D.C.: Thomas Jefferson Memorial Association of the United States, 1903–04.

Long, E. B., with Barbara Long. *The Civil War Day by Day: An Almanac 1861–1865*. New York: Doubleday, 1971.

Loughborough, Mary Ann Webster. *My Cave in Vicksburg*. New York: Appleton, 1864.

Lucasi, Stephen. "William Wells Brown's Narrative and Traveling Subjectivity." *African American Review* 41, no. 3 (Fall 2007): 521–39.

MacClintock, Paul. "The Pleistocene History of the Lower Wisconsin River." *Journal of Geology* 30, no. 8 (Nov.–Dec. 1922): 673–89.

Maclean, John. "Blackfoot Mythology." *Journal of American Folklore* 6, no. 22 (July–Sept. 1893): 165–72.

Maclean, Malcolm. "The Short Cruise of the C.S.S. *Atlanta.*" *Georgia Historical Quarterly* 40, no. 2 (June 1956): 130–43.

Magris, Claudio. *Danube.* London: Harvill Press, 1986.

Marcoux, Jon Bernard. "On Reconsidering Display Goods Production and Circulation in the Moundville Chiefdom." *Southeastern Archaeology* 26, no. 2 (Winter 2007): 232–45.

Mark, Joan. *A Stranger in Her Native Land: Alice Fletcher and the American Indians.* Lincoln: University of Nebraska Press, 1988.

Martin, Ronald D. "Confrontation at the Monongahela: Climax of the French Drive into the Upper Ohio Region." *Pennsylvania History* 37, no. 2 (Apr. 1970): 133–50.

Mathews, Lois Kimball. *The Expansion of New England: The Spread of New England Settlement and Institutions to the Mississippi River, 1620–1865.* New York: Russel & Russel, 1962.

Mazrim, Robert, and Duane Esarey. "Rethinking the Dawn of History: The Schedule, Signature, and Agency of European Goods in Protohistoric Illinois." *Midcontinental Journal of Archaeology* 32, no. 2 (Fall 2007): 145–200.

McConnell, Michael N. *A Country Between: The Upper Ohio Valley and Its Peoples, 1724–1774.* Lincoln: University of Nebraska Press, 1992.

McMullen, Glenn L. "A Massachusetts Soldier at the Siege of Port Hudson, 1863." *Louisiana History: The Journal of the Louisiana Historical Association* 26, no. 3 (Summer 1985): 313–26.

McPhee, John. *Annals of the Former World.* New York: Farrar, Straus and Giroux, 1998.

———. *The Control of Nature.* New York: Farrar, Straus, Giroux, 1989.

Meade, R. H., and J. A. Moody. "Causes for the Decline of Suspended-Sediment Discharge in the Mississippi River System, 1940–2007." *Hydrology Processes* 24 (1984): 35–49.

Mellinger, E. Henry. "Still More Ballads and Folk-Songs from the Southern Highlands." *Journal of American Folklore* 45, no. 175 (Jan.–Mar. 1932): 1–176.

Meltzer, David J. *First Peoples in a New World: Colonizing Ice Age America.* Berkeley: University of California Press, 2009.

———. "The Seventy-Year Itch: Controversies over Human Antiquity and Their Resolution." *Journal of Anthropological Research* 61, no. 4 (Winter 2005): 433–68.

Meltzer, David J., Lawrence C. Todd, and Vance T. Holliday. "The Folsom (Paleo-indian) Type Site: Past Investigations, Current Studies." *American Antiquity* 67, no. 1 (Jan. 2002): 5–36.

Melville, Herman. *The Confidence Man: His Masquerade.* New York: Dix, Edwards, 1857.

Meriot, Christian. "The Saami Peoples from the Time of the Voyage of Ottar to Thomas von Westen." *Arctic* 37, no. 4, Unveiling the Arctic (Dec. 1984): 373–84.

Merrick, George Byron. *Old Times on the Upper Mississippi: Recollections of a Steamboat Pilot from 1854 to 1863.* Minneapolis: University of Minnesota Press, 2001.

Merrill, James M. "Cairo, Illinois: Strategic Civil War River." *Journal of the Illinois State Historical Society* (1908–1984), 76, no. 4 (Winter 1983): 242–56.

Milliman, John D., and Robert H. Meade. "World-Wide Delivery of River Sediment to the Oceans." *Journal of Geology* 91, no. 1 (Jan. 1983): 1–21.

Milner, George R. *The Moundbuilders: Ancient Peoples of Eastern North America.* London: Thames and Hudson, 2004.

Moneyhon, Carl H., and Virginia Davis. "Gray Life in Confederate Arkansas: The Diary of Virginia Davis Gray, 1863–1866." *Arkansas Historical Quarterly* 42, no. 2 (Summer 1983): 134–69.

Montagu, M. F. Ashley. "An Indian Tradition Relating to the Mastodon." *American Anthropologist*, New Series, 46, no. 4 (Oct.–Dec. 1944): 568–71.

Montagu, M. F. Ashley, and C. Bernard Peterson. "The Earliest Account of the Association of Human Artifacts with Fossil Mammals in North America." *Proceedings of the American Philosophical Society* 87, no. 5, Papers on Archaeology, Ecology, Ethnology, History, Paleontology, Physics, and Physiology (May 5, 1944): 407–19.

Moorehead, Warren K. "Dr. Topinard and the Serpent Mound." *Science* 22, no. 567 (Dec. 15, 1893): 331.

Morgan, Lewis Henry. *League of the Iroquois.* New York: Citadel Press, 1993.

Morison, Samuel Eliot. *The European Discovery of America.* New York: Oxford University Press, 1971.

Morrow, Juliet E., and Toby A. Morrow. "Geographic Variation in Fluted Projectile Points: A Hemispheric Perspective." *American Antiquity* 64, no. 2 (Apr. 1999): 215–30.

Moyers, William Nelson. "A Story of Southern Illinois, the Soldiers' Reservation, Including the Indians, French Traders, and Some Early Americans." *Journal of the Illinois State Historical Society* (1908–1984), 24, no. 1 (Apr. 1931): 26–104.

Mundkur, Balaji, et al. "The Cult of the Serpent in the Americas: Its Asian Background." *Current Anthropology* 17, no. 3 (Sept. 1976): 429–55.

Munger, Paul, and Robert McCormick Adams. "Fabric Impressions of Pottery from the Elizabeth Herrell Site, Missouri." *American Antiquity* 7, no. 2 (Oct. 1941): 166–71.

Neider, Charles, ed. *The Autobiography of Mark Twain.* New York: HarperCollins, 1959.

"New Evidence on Man in America." *New York Times*, September 30, 1928.

"The New-Orleans Plague: Sketches of the Yellow Fever." *New York Times*, March 3, 1854.

"The News in Washington." *New York Times*, April 28, 1862.

Norton, Thomas Elliot. *The Fur Trade in Colonial New York.* Madison: University of Wisconsin Press, 1974.

Nothstein, Ira Oliver. "Rock Island and the Rock Island Arsenal." *Journal of the Illinois State Historical Society* (1908–1984), 33, no. 3 (Sept. 1940): 304–40.

Oakleaf, J. B. "Abraham Lincoln and Rock Island County." *Journal of the Illinois State Historical Society* (1908–1984), 5, no. 2 (July 1912): 202–6.

"On the Trail of an Epidemic." *Social Education* 72, no. 1 (2008): S16.

Oneal, Sherrard. "New Orleans Scenes." *Louisiana History: The Journal of the Louisiana Historical Association* 6, no. 2 (Spring 1965): 189–209.

Ontario Historical Society. *Papers and Records.* 4 vols. Toronto, Ont.: Author, 1899. Digital facsimile edition at books.google.com.

"Our Ancient Peoples." *Cleveland Plain Dealer*, October 26, 1887.

"Our Ancient Peoples." *New York Times*, November 1, 1887.

Parkman, Francis. *The Conspiracy of Pontiac and the Indian War after the Conquest of Canada.* Vol. 2. Omaha: University of Nebraska Press, 1994.

———. *A Half-Century of Conflict.* 3 vols. Boston: Little, Brown, 1892.

———. *Montcalm and Wolfe.* 3 vols. Boston: Little, Brown, 1907.

———. *The Oregon Trail.* Garden City, N.Y.: Doubleday, 1946.

Parmenter, Jon William. "Pontiac's War: Forging New Links in the Anglo-Iroquois Covenant Chain, 1758–1766." *Ethnohistory* 44, no. 4 (Autumn 1997): 617–54.

Pauketat, Timothy R. *Ancient Cahokia and the Mississippians*. Cambridge: Cambridge University Press, 2004.

Pease, Theodore C. "The Ordinance of 1787." *Mississippi Valley Historical Review* 25, no. 2 (Sept. 1938): 167–80.

Peniek, James L., Jr. *The Great Western Land Pirate: John A. Murrell in Legend and History*. Columbia and London: University of Missouri Press, 1981.

Petersen, William J. "The Log of the Henry M. Shreve to Fort Benton in 1869." *Mississippi Valley Historical Review* 31, no. 4 (Mar. 1945): 537–78.

Peterson, Charles E. "Notes on Old Cahokia: Part Three: American Domination (1778–1790)." *Journal of the Illinois State Historical Society* (1908–1984), 42, no. 3 (Sept. 1949): 313–43.

Pfeiffer, David A. "Bridging the Mississippi: The Railroads and Steamboats Clash at the Rock Island Bridge." http://www.archives.gov/publications/prologue/2004/summer/bridge.html.

Pitcaithley, Dwight. "Settlement of the Arkansas Ozarks: The Buffalo River Valley." *Arkansas Historical Quarterly* 37, no. 3 (Autumn 1978): 203–22.

Powell, Gina S. "Charred, Non-Maize Seed Concentrations in the American Bottom Area: Examples from the Westpark Site (11-MO-96), Monroe County, Illinois." *Midcontinental Journal of Archaeology* 25, no. 1 (Spring 2000): 27–48.

Powers, Ron. *Mark Twain: A Life*. New York: Free Press, 2005.

Pratt, Harry E. " 'Judge' Abraham Lincoln." *Journal of the Illinois State Historical Society* (1908–1984), 48, no. 1 (Spring 1955): 28–39.

Prentice, Guy. "An Analysis of the Symbolism Expressed by the Birger Figurine." *American Antiquity* 51, no. 2 (Apr. 1986): 239–66.

Proceedings of the New England Anti-Slavery Convention. Boston: Garrison & Knapp, 1834.

Quaife, M. M. "James Wilkinson's Narrative of the Fallen Timbers Campaign." *Mississippi Valley Historical Review* 16, no. 1 (June 1929): 81–90.

Raban, Jonathan. *Old Glory: A Voyage Down the Mississippi*. New York: Vintage, 1998.

Randolph, Vance. "The Names of Ozark Fiddle Tunes." *Midwest Folklore* 4, no. 2 (Summer 1954): 81–86.

Rash, Nancy. "George Caleb Bingham's 'Lighter Relieving a Steamboat Aground.'" *Smithsonian Studies in American Art* 2, no. 2 (Spring 1988): 16–31.

Rawick, George P., ed. *The American Slave: A Composite Autobiography*. Vol. 5. Westport, Conn.: Greenwood Press, 1977.

Reagan, Albert B. "Some Myths of the Hoh and Quillayute Indians." *Transactions of the Kansas Academy of Science* (1903–), 38 (Mar. 28–30, 1935): 43–85.

Reed, Verner Z. "The Ute Bear Dance." *American Anthropologist* 9, no. 7 (July 1896): 237–44.

Rennick, Percival Graham. "The Peoria and Galena Trail and Coach Road and the Peoria Neighborhood." *Journal of the Illinois State Historical Society* (1908–1984), 27, no. 4 (Jan. 1935): 351–431.

Reymann, Joseph A. "An Ecological-Historical Survey of the Mississippi River." *American Biology Teacher* 37, no. 2, Interdisciplinary Environmental Education (Feb. 1975): 94–96.

Risjord, Norman K. "Jean Nicolet's Search for the South Sea." *Wisconsin Magazine of History* 84, no. 3 (Spring 2001): 34–43.

Ritchie, William A. "Another Probable Case of Prehistoric Bear Ceremonialism in New York." *American Antiquity* 15, no. 3 (Jan. 1950): 247–49.

Robinson, Willard B. "Maritime Frontier Engineering: The Defense of New Orleans." *Louisiana History: The Journal of the Louisiana Historical Association* 18, no. 1 (Winter 1977): 5–62.

Rogers, R. A., and L. D. Martin. "A Clovis Projectile Point from the Kansas River." *Transactions of the Kansas Academy of Science* (1903–), 85, no. 2 (1982): 78–81.

Rothert, Otto A. *The Outlaws of Cave-in-Rock: Historical Accounts of the Famous Highwaymen and River Pirates Who Operated in Pioneer Days upon the Ohio and Mississippi Rivers and over the Old Natchez Trace.* Cleveland Ohio: Arthur H. Clark, 1924.

"Rout of Beauregard's Army." *New York Times*, June 5, 1862.

Rugeley, Terry. "Savage and Statesman: Changing Historical Interpretations of Tecumseh." *Indiana Magazine of History* 85, no. 4 (Dec. 1989): 289–311.

Sabin, Edwin L. "Vicksburg, and After: Being the Experience of a Southern Merchant and Non-Combatant during the Sixties." *Sewanee Review* 15, no. 4 (Oct. 1907): 485–96.

Sacks, Howard L. "From the Barn to the Bowery and Back Again: Musical Routes in Rural Ohio, 1800–1929." *Journal of American Folklore* 116, no. 461 (Summer 2003): 314–38.

Sandlin, Lee. *Wicked River: The Mississippi When It Last Ran Wild.* New York: Pantheon, 2010.

Sassaman, Kenneth E. "Poverty Point as Structure, Event, Process." *Journal of Archaeological Method and Theory* 12, no. 4, Agency: Methodologies for Interpreting Social Reproduction, Part 2 (Dec. 2005): 335–64.

Sauer, Carl O. "A Geographic Sketch of Early Man in America." *Geographical Review* 34, no. 4 (Oct. 1944): 529–73.

Saunders, Joe W., et al. "Watson Brake, a Middle Archaic Mound Complex in Northeast Louisiana." *American Antiquity* 70, no. 4 (Oct. 2005): 631–68.

"Says Negroid Group Discovered America." *New York Times*, December 30, 1922.

Scharf, John Thomas. *History of Saint Louis City and County: From the Earliest Periods to the Present Day*. Philadelphia: L. H. Everts, 1883.

Schneider, Paul. *The Adirondacks: A History of America's First Wilderness*. New York: Henry Holt, 1997.

———. *Brutal Journey: Cabeza de Vaca and the Epic First Crossing of North America*. New York: Henry Holt, 2006.

Schneider, Peter. *Line Fence*. Amherst, Mass.: Amherst Writers and Artists Press, 2006.

Schultz, Christian. *Travels on an Inland Voyage through the States of New York, Pennsylvania, Virginia, Ohio, Kentucky and Tennessee, and through the Territories of Indiana, Louisiana, Mississippi and New Orleans Performed in the Years 1807 and 1808; Including a Tour of Nearly Six Thousand Miles with Maps and Plates*. New York: Isaac Riley, 1810.

"Science Skeptical of 'Minnesota Man.'" *New York Times*, January 16, 1938.

"Sciences Progress Brought Up to Date." *New York Times*, November 13, 1921.

"The Scientists Assemble." *New York Times*, August 11, 1887.

"Sees American Man Superior of Woman: Eugenist Says Native Stock of at Least Three Generations Produces Better Males." *New York Times*, September 28, 1921.

Semonin, Paul. *American Monster: How the Nation's First Prehistoric Creature Became a Symbol of National Identity*. New York: New York University Press, 2000.

"The Serpent Mound." *New York Times*, June 12, 1887.

Severin, Timothy. *Explorers of the Mississippi: A History of the Conquistadors, Voyageurs, and Charlatans Who Discovered, Opened Up, and Exploited the Father of Waters*. New York: Alfred A. Knopf, 1968.

Shaw, John Robert. *John Robert Shaw: An Autobiography of Thirty Years, 1777–1807*. Edited by Oressa M. Teagarden and Jeanne L. Crabtree. Athens: Ohio University Press, 1992.

Shea, William L., and Terrence J. Winschel. *Vicksburg Is the Key: The Struggle for the Mississippi River*. Lincoln: University of Nebraska Press, 2003.

Shepard, Paul, and Barry Sanders. "Celebrations of the Bear." *North American Review* 270, no. 3 (Sept. 1985): 17–25.

Shipman, Pat, Daniel C. Fisher, and Jennie J. Rose. "Microscopic Evidence of Carcass Processing and Bone Tool Use." *Paleobiology* 10, no. 3 (Summer 1984): 358–65.

Simcoe, Mrs. John Graves. *The Diary of Mrs. John Graves Simcoe*. Toronto, Ont.: William Briggs, 1911.

Sivertsen, Barbara J. "A Site Activity Model for Kill and Butchering Activities at Hunter-Gatherer Sites." *Journal of Field Archaeology* 7, no. 4 (Winter 1980): 423–41.

Smal-Stocki, Roman. "Taboos on Animal Names in Ukrainian." *Language* 26, no. 4 (Oct.–Dec. 1950): 489–93.

Smelser, Marshall. "Tecumseh, Harrison, and the War of 1812." *Indiana Magazine of History* 65, no. 1 (Mar. 1968): 25–44.

Smith, Bruce D. "Eastern North America as an Independent Center of Plant Domestication." *Proceedings of the Academy of Sciences of the United States of America* 103, no. 33 (Aug. 15, 2006): 12223–28.

———. "Origins of Agriculture in Eastern North America." *Science*, New Series, 246, no. 4937 (Dec. 22, 1989): 1566–71.

Smith, John David. "Vicksburg: Southern City Under Siege." *Louisiana History* 24, no. 1 (Winter 1983): 105–106.

Smith, Lucy Harth. "Negro Musicians and Their Music." *Journal of Negro History* 20, no. 4 (Oct. 1935): 428–32.

Smith, Thomas Ruys. "Independence Day, 1835: The John A. Murrell Conspiracy and the Lynching of the Vicksburg Gamblers in Literature." *Mississippi Quarterly* 59, nos. 1–2 (2005): 129.

———. *River of Dreams: Imagining the Mississippi before Mark Twain*. Baton Rouge: Louisiana State University Press, 2007.

Smith, Vernon L. "The Primitive Hunter Culture, Pleistocene Extinction, and the Rise of Agriculture." *Journal of Political Economy* 83, no. 4 (Aug. 1975): 727–56.

Snyder, J. F. "Fort Kaskaskia." *Journal of the Illinois State Historical Society (1908–1984)*, 6, no. 1 (Apr. 1913): 58–71.

———. "The Kaskaskia Indians: A Tentative Hypothesis." *Journal of the Illinois State Historical Society (1908–1984)*, 5, no. 2 (July 1912): 231–45.

———. "The Old French Towns of Illinois in 1839: A Reminiscence." *Journal of the Illinois State Historical Society* (1908–1984), 36, no. 4 (Dec. 1943): 345–67.

———. "Prehistoric Illinois: Certain Indian Mounds Technically Considered." *Journal of the Illinois State Historical Society* (1908–1984), 1, no. 4 (Jan. 1909): 31–40.

Squier, Ephraim G., and Edwin H. Davis. *Ancient Monuments of the Mississippi Valley.* Washington, D.C.: Smithsonian Books, 1988.

Standing Bear, Luther. *My Indian Boyhood.* Lincoln: University of Nebraska Press, 1988.

Stevens, Paul L. "'One of the Most Beautiful Regions of the World': Paul Des Ruisseaux's Mémoire of the Wabash-Illinois Country in 1777." *Indiana Magazine of History* 83, no. 4 (Dec. 1987): 360–79.

———. "'To Keep the Indians of the Wabache in His Majesty's Interest': The Indian Diplomacy of Edward Abbott, British Lieutenant Governor of Vincennes, 1776–1778." *Indiana Magazine of History* 83, no. 2 (June 1987): 141–72.

Stites, Sara Henry. "Economics of the Iroquois." *Bulletin of the American Geographical Society* 39, no. 11 (1907): 702.

Stokes, George A. "The Lost Panoramas of the Mississippi by John Francis McDermott." *Journal of the Louisiana Historical Association* 1, no. 3 (Summer 1960): 271–72.

Sutcliffe, Andrea. *Steam: The Untold Story of America's First Great Invention.* New York: Palgrave Macmillan, 2004.

Swanton, John R. *Final Report of the United States De Soto Commission.* Washington, D.C.: Smithsonian Institution Press, 1985.

———. *The Indians of the Southeastern United States.* Washington, D.C.: Smithsonian Institution Press, 1979.

Tankersley, Kenneth B. "Variation in the Early Paleoindian Economies of Late Pleistocene Eastern North America." *American Antiquity* 63, no. 1 (Jan. 1998): 7–20.

Taylor, Yuval, ed. *I Was Born a Slave: An Anthology of Classic Slave Narratives, 1770–1849.* Vol. 1. Chicago: Lawrence Hill, 1999.

"Texas Robbers in a Corner." *New York Times,* July 29, 1899.

Thompson, Robert Means, and Richard Wainwright, eds. "Porter to Fox, May 24, 1862." In *Confidential Correspondence of Gustavus Vasa Fox, Assistant Secretary of the Navy.* New York: Naval History Society, 1920.

Thoreau, Henry David. *The Journal, 1837–1864.* New York: New York Review of Books, 2009.

——. *Walden.* New York: Harper and Brothers, 1950.

——. "Walking." In *The Writings of Henry David Thoreau,* vol. 5, *Excursions and Poems.* Boston: Houghton Mifflin, 1906.

Thwaites, Reuben Gold. *Early Western Travels,* vol. 1. Cleveland, Ohio: Arthur H. Clark, 1904.

——, ed. *The Jesuit Relations and Allied Documents.* Cleveland, Ohio: The Burrows Brothers, 1896–1901. Online facsimile edition hosted by Creighton University in Omaha, Nebraska. http://puffin.creighton.edu/jesuit/relations/.

"Train Robber Reprieved." *New York Times,* April 25, 1901.

"Train Robbery in New Mexico." *New York Times,* July 13, 1899.

Trask, Kerry A. *Black Hawk: The Battle for the Heart of America.* New York: Henry Holt, 2007.

"The Treaty of Logg's Town, 1752." *Virginia Magazine of History and Biography* 13 (1906): 154–74. Online facsimile: http://earlytreaties.unl.edu/treaty.00004.html.

Treaty of Paris. Online at http://avalon.law.yale.edu/18th_century/paris763.asp.

Trimble, David B. "Christopher Gist and Settlement on the Monongahela, 1752–1754." *Virginia Magazine of History and Biography* 63, no. 1 (Jan. 1955): 15–27.

Trollope, Frances M. *Domestic Manners of the Americans.* New York: Alfred A. Knopf, 1904.

Trudel, Marcel, and Donald H. Kent. "The Jumonville Affair." *Pennsylvania History* 21, no. 4 (Oct. 1954): 351–81.

Turner, Frederick Jackson. *Rise of the New West, 1819–1829.* New York: Harper, 1907.

Twain, Mark. *The Adventures of Huckleberry Finn.* New York: Bantam, 1981.

——. *Life on the Mississippi.* New York: Penguin Books, 1984.

United States Environmental Protection Agency. "Injurious Wildlife Species; Silver Carp (*Hypophthalmichthys molitrix*) and Largescale Silver Carp (*Hypophthalmichthys harmandi*)." http://www.epa.gov/EPA-IMPACT/2007/July/Day-10/i13371.htm.

US Army Corps of Engineers. *Upper Mississippi River Navigation Charts.* St. Louis: USACE, 2002.

Utley, Robert M. *Sitting Bull: The Life and Times of an American Patriot.* New York: Henry Holt, 1993.

Utley, Robert M., and Wilcomb E. Washburn. *Indian Wars*. Boston: Houghton Mifflin, 1977.

Van Alstyne, Richard W. "The Significance of the Mississippi Valley in American Diplomatic History, 1686–1890." *Mississippi Valley Historical Review* 36, no. 2 (Sept. 1949): 215–38.

"The Vicksburgh Failure; A Full History of the Last Attempt to Capture the Rebel Stronghold. The Glorious Heroism of Our Troops." *New York Times*, January 19, 1863.

Volwiler, A. T. "George Croghan and the Westward Movement, 1741–1782." *Pennsylvania Magazine of History and Biography* 46, no. 4 (1922): 273–311.

Vought, Lelah Ridgway. *Ridgway-Ridgeway Family History*. Privately published, 1973.

Wagner, Margaret, E., Gary W. Gallagher, and Paul Finkelman, eds. *The Library of Congress Civil War Desk Reference*. New York: Simon and Schuster, 2002.

Waguespack, Nicole M., and Todd A. Surovell. "Clovis Hunting Strategies, or How to Make Out on Plentiful Resources." *American Antiquity* 68, no. 2 (Apr. 2003): 333–52.

Wainright, Nicholas B. *George Croghan: Wilderness Diplomat*. Williamsburg: University of North Carolina Press, 1959.

Wallace, Paul A. W. "George Washington's Route from Venango to Fort Le Boeuf 1753." *Pennsylvania History* 28, no. 4 (Oct. 1961): 325–34.

Washington, George. *The Journal of Major George Washington Sent by the Hon. Robert Dinwiddie, Esq; His Majesty's Lieutenant-Governor, and Commander in Chief of Virginia to the Commandant of the French Forces on Ohio to Which Are Added, the Governor's Letter and a Translation of the French Officer's Answer*. Williamsburg, Va.: Printed by William Hunter, 1754. Digital facsimile: George Washington and Paul Royster, eds., "The Journal of Major George Washington (1754)." Electronic Texts in American Studies. Paper 33, 1754. http://digitalcommons.unl.edu/etas/33.

Way, Frederick, Jr. *Rivers of America: The Allegheny*. New York: Farrar & Rinehart, 1942.

Webb, Clarence H. "The Belcher Mound: A Stratified Caddoan Site in Caddo Parish, Louisiana." *Memoirs of the Society for American Archaeology*, no. 16 (1959): iii–xiii, 1–212.

Westwood, Howard C. "The Vicksburg/Port Hudson Gap—The Pincers Never Pinched." *Military Affairs* 46, no. 3 (Oct. 1982): 113–19. Published by the Society for Military History.

Whicker, J. Wesley. "Tecumseh and Pushmataha." *Indiana Magazine of History* 18, no. 4 (Dec. 1922): 318–31.

White, Richard. *The Middle Ground: Indians, Empires, and Republics in the Great Lakes Region 1650–1815*. Cambridge: Cambridge University Press, 1991.

Widmer, Ted. "The Invention of a Memory: Congo Square and African Music in Nineteenth-Century New Orleans." *Revue française d'études américaines*, no. 98 (2003): 69–78.

Wilford, John Noble. "Tools Suggest Earlier Arrival in America." *New York Times,* March 24, 2011.

Wilkinson, Brenda. "George McJunkin: A Chapter in New Mexico History." US Department of the Interior Bureau of Land Management Web site. http://www.blm.gov/nm/st/en/prog/more/cultural_resources/george_mcjunkin_feature/george_mcjunkin_feature.html.

Willoughby, Charles C. "The Serpent Mound of Adams County, Ohio." *American Anthropologist*, New Series, 21, no. 2 (Apr.–June 1919): 153–63.

Wilson, Clifford P. "Where Did Nicolet Go?" *Minnesota History* 27, no. 3 (Sept. 1946): 216–20.

Winschel, Terrence. *Vicksburg: Fall of the Confederate Gibraltar*. Abilene, Tex.: McWhiney Foundation Press, 1999.

Woodward, Susan L., and Jerry N. McDonald. *Indian Mounds of the Middle Ohio Valley*. Blacksburg, Va.: McDonald and Woodward, 2002.

Worthington, Chauncey Ford, ed. *A Cycle of Adams Letters, 1861–1865,* vol. 1. Boston and New York: Houghton Mifflin, 1920, 143–46.

Wright, John Aaron. *The Ville, St. Louis*. Chicago: Arcadia Publishing, 2001.

Wunn, I. "Cave Bear Worship in the Palaeolithic." *Cadernos Lab. Xeolóxico de Laxe* 26 (2001): 457–63.

Ziporyn, Terra. *Disease in the Popular American Press: The Case of Diphtheria, Typhoid Fever, and Syphilis, 1870–1920*. New York: Greenwood Press, 1988.

Zolotarev, Alexander M. "The Bear Festival of the Olcha." *American Anthropologist*, New Series, 39, no. 1 (Jan.–Mar. 1937): 113–30.

INDEX

Page numbers in *italics* refer to illustrations.

ABOUT THE AUTHOR

PAUL SCHNEIDER is the author of the critically acclaimed *Brutal Journey*; the highly praised and successful *The Adirondacks*, a *New York Times Book Review* Notable Book; *The Enduring Shore*; and *Bonnie and Clyde*. He lives in Massachusetts. Find out more at schneiderbooks.com.